The Food Lover's Guide to Paris

THIRD EDITION

The Food Lover's Guide to Paris

PATRICIA WELLS

Photographs by PETER TURNLEY
Front Cover Food Photograph by ROBERT FRESON

Workman Publishing, New York

To Walter, with gratitude
for his unwavering love,
trust, and support.

Copyright 1984, 1988, 1993 by Patricia Wells
Photographs copyright 1984, 1988, 1993 By Peter Turnley
Front cover food photograph copyright 1983, 1993 by Robert Freson
Front cover bistro photograph copyright 1991 by Scully/Daly

Library of Congress Cataloging-in Publication Data.

Wells, Patricia.
The food lover's guide to Paris/ by Patricia Wells. — 3rd ed.
p. cm.
Includes index.
ISBN 1-56305-326-8 (pbk.)
1. Restaurants, lunch rooms, etc.—France—Paris—Guidebooks.
2. Grocery trade—France—Paris—Guidebooks. 3. Cookery, French.
4. Hotels, taverns, etc.—France—Paris—Guidebooks. 5. Paris
(France)—Guidebooks. I. Title.
TX907.5.F72P3778   1993
647.9544—dc20   92-50290
                                                              CIP

Workman books are available at special discounts when purchased in bulk for
premiums and sales promotions as well as for fund-raising or educational use.
Special editions or book excerpts can also be created to specification. For
details, contact the Special Sales Director at the address below.

Workman Publishing Company, Inc.
708 Broadway
New York, NY 10003

Manufactured in the United States of America
Third edition first printing, May 1993
10 9 8 7 6 5 4 3 2 1

Acknowledgments

Thanks to the generosity, enthusiasm, and encouragement of so many fine people over the years, much of the work on this book was transformed into sheer pleasure. I am deeply grateful to Sarah Greenberg, Susan Herrmann Loomis, and Jane Sigal, who have assisted me with the three editions.

I was touched by the generosity of the French chefs, bakers, restaurateurs, and shopkeepers who gave so freely of their time and expertise, and shared their recipes. Special thanks to Jean-Claude Vrinat of Taillevent, Joël Robuchon of Jamin, and bakers Bernard Ganachaud, Lionel and Max Poilâne, and Jean-Luc Poujauran.

None of this would have been possible without the remarkable confidence of Peter Workman and the expert attention of my editor, Suzanne Rafer, who believed in both me and the book when others remained doubtful. Thanks also goes to Deborah Kops for carefully checking the information, and to Paul Hanson and Susan Aronson Stirling for the beautiful design of the book.

Throughout my career, dozens of friends and colleagues have advised, assisted, steered me in the proper direction, and I am delighted to acknowledge them here. Special thanks to all those at the *New York Times,* particularly Craig Claiborne, Arthur Gelb, Annette Grant, and Mike Leahy, who allowed me to combine my love for journalism with my passion for food; to Sam Abt and Vicky Elliott at the *International Herald Tribune,* for the careful and diligent editing of my restaurant reviews; to Berna Huebner and Vivian Cruise, for their companionship and healthy appetites.

I want to offer special thanks to our dearest friends, Rita and Yale Kramer and Lydie and Wayne Marshall, with whom we have shared so many fine feasts on both sides of the ocean, for their encouragement and special friendship. Finally, I thank my parents, Vera and Joseph Kleiber, who instilled in me without fuss or fanfare a natural love and respect for the world's gastronomic bounties.

Introduction to the Third Edition

Walking the streets of Paris, block by block, neighborhood by neighborhood, season after season, has been a personal passion since I moved to this gastronomic capital in 1980. This, the third edition of *The Food Lover's Guide* since 1984, represents the harvest of those adventures, as I charted the city, maps and notes and shared addresses in hand, in search of the new and the unexpected. Each of these journeys elicited emotions of joy, discovery, doubt, and disappointment, but inevitably each excursion unearthed at least one address worthy of sharing with my readers.

I wish I could say that I—along with my assistant Sarah Greenberg—left no stone unturned. But part of the charm and seduction of Paris is the fact that no one, not even the most thoroughgoing among us, can ever know it fully.

On the best of those days—mornings filled with blue skies and filtered northern light—I would cover a good ten miles in a few fruitful hours, scouring markets, taking a close look at a café, wine bar, or restaurant from my list, discovering a cheese shop I'd missed the last time around, sampling a crusty *baguette* or an almond-rich *financier* at a *boulangerie* that lured me indoors with the warm, fresh, and familiar scent of yeast, sugar, nuts, and spices.

There were days, of course, that I would return home tired and disappointed, finding that a famous old food specialty shop had been transformed into a shoe store, a romantic café into a fast food eatery, that the morning *café* and *croissant* simply did not deliver the satisfaction I had been promised.

On those days I would ask myself the questions I am most often asked by others: Is Paris still the capital of gastronomy? Don't all those modern influences—fast food, an increasing industrialization of food preparation, microwaves, and vacuum packing—unavoidably tear away at the rich fabric of France's culture?

The answer is yes—and no. It is not easy to combat mediocrity, and on those evenings when a restaurant dissatisfies because the chef has lowered his standards (or never had them to begin with) I am sad not only to waste an evening, but also to know that Paris, too, can disappoint.

But inevitably, the next restaurant meal, the next visit to the cheese shop, or the next market tour will cheer me once more, as I visit with a chef or a merchant who has dedicated his or her life to maintaining the very best product and service possible.

I am also encouraged by the enduring reality that, within a five-minute walk from my door, I can secure some of the best and the freshest food the world can offer, from sparkling fresh fish and shellfish, to top-quality meat and poultry, to magnificent cheese, expertly roasted coffees, handmade chocolates, organically grown fruits and vegetables.

Paris has changed, France has changed. The culture—once totally traditional, rigid and formal—has become much more open, more flexible. Gastronomically, this means the trend is toward restaurants that are more casual, as the bistro expands its already starring role as a place to find decent, reasonably priced foods and wines. The changes in this book reflect that trend, as many restaurants once considered gastronomic temples have been deleted, making room for those that offer better value for your time and money.

Paris has always been a great town for snacking, and the growing number of sandwich boutiques, bakeries, and pastry shops promising a quick bite attests to the increasing desire for food that's quick, cheap and cheerful. The inclusion of a list of spots, by *Métro* stop, should help you discover the best of them.

These modern trends also mean that shops that once closed at lunch time, weekends, and evenings, have expanded their hours, making Paris more accessible than ever. Likewise, an ever-growing French appetite for other cuisines means you'll find more than just French fare in Paris.

The French, who have accepted me as both an advocate and a critic of their culture, have called me an ecologist for French gastronomy. It is a title I accept with honor, as long as it can be shared with those responsible for each shop, restaurant, market, cooking school, wine bar, café, tea salon, bakery, or pastry shop celebrated in this book. The sure way to stamp out gastronomic mediocrity is to highlight and to encourage excellence, and that's what *The Food Lover's Guide to Paris* is all about.

Paris, 1993

A Taste for Paris

From the moment I set foot in France one chilly, gray January morning in 1973, I knew that Paris was a city I would love the rest of my life. Almost twenty years later, after spending thirteen of those years in this gentle city, each day I am moved by Paris's elegance and beauty, its coquettish appeal. The quality of life here is better than in any other place I know, and eating well has much to do with it.

This is the book I came to Paris to write. Equal only to my passion for food is my love for reporting. I have always thought that one of the most enjoyable aspects of journalism is that you get to know people on their own turf, and you get to poke around, asking the questions that any curious person wants answers to. In researching this book, I—along with various companions—walked just about every street in Paris in search of the gastronomic best the city has to offer, talking, chatting, interviewing, meeting with the city's men and women who are responsible for all things great and edible. We set out to find the crispest *baguette*, the thickest cup of steaming hot chocolate; to spot the most romantic site for a warm morning *croissant* or a sun-kissed summer lunch; to track down the trustiest cheese or chocolate shop; to uncover the happiest place to sip wine on a brisk winter's day. We quickly gave up counting the number of times we got lost or rained out as we checked off addresses and discovered back streets and sleepy neighborhoods. We toured the markets and tea salons, sparred with butchers, laughed with the owners of a favorite bistro, and shared the incomparable aroma of a great loaf of bread as it came crackling from the oven. We rose eagerly at dawn to catch a pastry chef as he pulled the first batch of steaming *croissants* from his wood-fired oven; climbed down rickety ladders into warm and cozy baking cellars to discuss the state of the French *baguette* with a skilled baker; shivered as we toured aromatic, humid, spotless rooms stacked with aging Brie and Camembert, Vacherin and Roquefort. Each day we lunched and dined, sometimes at modest neighborhood bistros, sometimes in fine restaurants. We gathered recipes from pastry chefs, cooks, bakers, and tea shop owners, and tested, tested, tested until my apartment took on the same irresistible mixture of aromas as the food streets and shops of Paris. Throughout, it was an exhilarating labor of love, one from which I hope you will profit, the joy of which I hope you will share.

This is a personal guide, and whenever I had to decide whether to include or delete a shop, a restaurant, a market, I asked myself one question: Would I want to go back there again? If the answer was no, the address was tossed into the ever-growing reject file.

In choosing restaurants, I have tried to be comprehensive but selective. I have tried as best I know how to tell you exactly what I think you will want to know about a restaurant: why you should go, where it is, how to get there, what you'll find when you arrive, and what it will cost. I intentionally did not rate restaurants, for I find personal restaurant ratings clumsy, arbitrary, and generally unreliable. Besides, they make a burdensome science out of what should, essentially, be joyful discovery.

No doubt, some places you will love less than I. Some you will love more. I hope this book will stimulate every reader to explore, look around, and ask questions, and will help everyone to understand just a bit more clearly the history, daily customs, and rich texture of Paris, the great gastronomic capital of the world.

How to Use This Book

Alphabetizing

Within each chapter (with the exception of the chapter on markets), establishments are grouped by the neighborhoods in which they are located, then listed in alphabetical order. Following French style, any articles such as *au, la,* or *le* and words such as *bistro, brasserie, café,* or *chez* that appear before the proper name of the establishment are ignored in the alphabetizing. For example, Chez Pauline, Le Petit Marguery, and Au Pied de Cochon are all listed under the letter *P*. Likewise, when the name of a restaurant is also the full name of a person, such as Guy Savoy, the last name (Savoy) is used for purposes of alphabetizing.

What's an arrondissement?

While many major cities are divided into variously named quarters for easy identification and organization, Paris is divided into twenty *arrondissements*. The *arrondissements* are arranged numerically in a spiral, beginning in the center of the city on the Right Bank (with the 1st *arrondissement* at the Louvre and Les Halles) and moving clockwise, making two complete spirals until reaching the central eastern edge of the city (at the 20th *arrondissement*, at Père Lachaise cemetery).

In organizing the book, we have listed establishments by *arrondissement*, also noting the popular quarters—the Madeleine, Montmartre, Invalides—in which they are located. Because of the spiral arrangement, *arrondissements* that adjoin one another —such as the 3rd, 4th, and 11th at the Marais and the Bastille—are generally listed together, since they overlap within a specific neighborhood, even though *arrondissement* numbers are not consecutive. For convenience, *arrondissements* may be grouped together differently from one chapter to another.

Listings

Each listing presented in *The Food Lover's Guide to Paris* includes the following information: the name of the establishment; its address; its phone number; the closest Métro stop; when it is open and closed.

If applicable, any or all of the following information is also included: whether the establishment is air-conditioned; whether it has a terrace, outdoor dining, or private dining facilities; what the specialties include; and what you can expect to spend.

Abbreviations

The following abbreviations are used for credit cards in the listings:

AE: American Express
DC: Diners Club
MC: Eurocard or MasterCard
V: Visa or Carte Bleue

The following abbreviations are used in the recipes to indicate weights and measures:

cm: centimeter   ml: milliliter
g: gram   kg: kilogram
cl: centiliter

Contents

Cafés

CAFES *135*

Salons de Thé

TEA SALONS *161*

Bistros à Vin

WINE BARS   *175*

Marchés

MARKETS   *194*

Pâtisseries

PASTRY SHOPS   *212*

Boulangeries

BAKERIES　*233*

Fromageries

CHEESE SHOPS   266

Charcuteries

PREPARED FOODS TO GO   286

Chocolatiers

CHOCOLATE SHOP   299

Spécialités Gastronomiques

SPECIALTY SHOPS 310

Vins et Alcools

WINE AND LIQUOR SHOPS 328

Librairies Spécialisées: Gastronomie
FOOD AND WINE BOOKSHOPS   336

Pour la Maison
KITCHEN AND TABLEWARE SHOPS   344

Recipe Contents

Boulangeries

BAKERIES

Fromageries

CHEESE SHOPS

Chocolatiers

CHOCOLATE SHOPS

Spécialités Gastronomiques

SPECIALTY SHOPS

The Food Lover's Guide to Paris

Restaurants
RESTAURANTS

Studying the menu in elegant restaurant surroundings.

I am constantly being asked to name my favorite Paris restaurant. For me, that is akin to trying to name my best friend, favorite piece of music, film, or classic novel. The answer depends on the hour, the season, my mood, the company. This is a personal guide representing a cross section of Paris restaurants, including only those I enjoy returning to, those I recommend to others. I hope they will serve simply as a starting point, enabling you to begin exploring and sorting out until you discover the kinds of restaurants you like. You should not have a bad meal at any listed here. But this doesn't mean you can't.

I dine out in Paris four or five times each week. I always make a reservation and always arrive hungry, for that's one of the best compliments one can pay a chef. I dine anonymously and so am known at few of these restaurants. What do I look for? Final judgment rests on the quality of ingredients, the chef's creativity, and overall service. In menus, I look for a healthy balance of dishes. In wine lists, value and variety are essential. A good restaurant is like good theater: One leaves in a good frame of mind, with a feeling that the time and the money have been well spent.

Likewise, your restaurants and meals should be chosen according to your own mood and appetite, the time of year, and of course, the time of day.

WHERE AM I, ANYWAY?

An American traveler once related this story: She was stopped on a street in Paris by another American visitor, who asked, in a state of sheer frustration, "What I don't understand here is with all these restaurants, how do you tell which ones are French? You know, the ones that serve soufflés." Slightly less complicated, but equally frustrating for visitors, are the distinctions among bistro, brasserie, and restaurant. Although the lines between bistro and restaurant are often blurred, here are a few definitions that should clear the matter.

Bistro

A traditional bistro is a rather small restaurant, traditionally a mom-and-pop establishment with mom at the cash register and pop at the stove. Bistro menus are usually hand-written or mimeographed, and dishes are limited to a small selection of traditional, home-style dishes. Wine is generally offered by the carafe, while wines available by the bottle are listed on the single-page menu. Bistro decor is usually simple, not fancy (though Paris's Belle Epoque bistros have some of the city's most beautiful interiors), often with a long zinc bar, tile floors, paper tablecloths, and sturdy, serviceable tableware. At some of the most modest establishments, diners may share long tables.

Today, the definition of bistro has been widely expanded, due to an increasing appetite for restaurants that are casual and less expensive, offering contemporary decor and updated, traditional fare. So within the new crop of updated bistros, one might find modern art on the walls, waiters dressed in designer uniforms, and such non-traditional fare as grilled tuna, platters of Japanese-inspired raw fish (sushi), and daily specials influenced only by the chef's inspiration of the morning.

Brasserie

Brasserie is French for brewery, and almost all of Paris's large and lively brasseries have an Alsatian connection: That means lots of beer, Alsatian white wines such as Riesling and Gewürztraminer, and usually *choucroute*, that hearty blend of sauerkraut and assorted sausages. Brasseries tend to be brightly lit and full of the sounds of good times, fine places for going with a large group. Generally, snacks or full meals are available whenever the restaurant is open. Brasseries tend to keep late hours, and while a reservation is recommended, one can often get a table without one.

Restaurants

Beyond bistros and brasseries, Paris offers numerous sorts of full-fledged restaurants, some offering elegant and classic cuisine, some specializing in creative, inventive, modern cooking. As well, there are restaurants that specialize in fish or grilled meats, in the cooking of specific regions of France. Classifications for all restaurants listed in the guide appear on page 388.

Reservations

Almost without exception, reservations are necessary. For the grand restaurants, such as Taillevent, Jamin, and L'Ambroisie, reserve weeks to months in advance. For others, reservations can be made several days ahead for popular weekend dinners, though for a weekday lunch, reserving the same day is often sufficient. If you are unable to keep a reservation, call to cancel. Many restaurants now require that advance reservations be confirmed by telephone the day you plan to dine there. Another good reason for reserving: Restaurants freely, and without warning, change opening and closing times and vacation plans, particularly during summer months and holiday periods. So it is always safest to call to make sure the restaurant will be open when you plan to visit.

Dining Hours

Set aside plenty of time for a Paris restaurant meal. In general, expect to spend anywhere from one and a half to three hours at table for a substantial lunch or dinner. If you want to be in and out within thirty minutes to an hour, visit a café, tea salon, wine bar, or brasserie, but don't attempt to rush through a meal at a serious restaurant. Currently, most Parisians begin lunch at 12:30 or 1 P.M. (although one can begin at noon), and most dine starting at 8:30 or 9 P.M. (although some restaurants will accept reservations as early as 7 P.M.). Despite the later hours, most kitchens close early, so a 2 P.M. lunch or 10 P.M. dinner reservation would be stretching it. On the other hand, the majority of cafés and brasseries serve at almost any hour. A few restaurants continue taking orders until 11 P.M. or later, and a list of those can be found in the Ready Reference beginning on page 388.

Prices

The price range of restaurants listed here goes from low to high. I have made no attempt to include restaurants serving mediocre food simply because they are inexpensive. Bargains are few and far between, but there are always ways to cut costs, even in the most expensive restaurants. Forego the before-dinner drink, after-dinner Cognac or cigar, and if you smoke, buy cigarettes at a neighborhood *tabac*, where they will be cheaper than in the restaurant. Share dishes, if you like. You are not obliged to order either cheese or dessert, and if they do not suit your budget or appetite, forget them. You can often cut costs by ordering from a fixed-price menu (though it is not always cheaper than ordering *à la carte*), or by opting for a carafe of wine or an inexpensive house wine. More and more restaurants are offering wine by the glass, generally cheaper than a bottle or half-bottle.

In all cases, the price noted with each restaurant listing represents an average meal for one person, including a first course, main course, cheese or dessert, as well as the service charge. Generally, a good inexpensive meal can be had for 200 francs, a good moderately priced meal for 300 francs, while a luxury meal, in a higher class of restaurant with more expensive wines, will range from 800 to 1,000 francs. Almost without exception, prices are the same for lunch and dinner.

Advice on Paying the Bill and Tipping

No subject is more confusing to visitors than French restaurant bills. You need remember only one fact: You are never required to pay more than the final "net" total on the bill. Service, which ranges from twelve to fifteen percent, depending upon the class of the restaurant, must be included in the price of individual dishes, and is part of the final bill. Etiquette does not require you to pay more than the total. If you have particularly enjoyed the meal, if you feel the *maître d'hôtel* or *sommelier* has offered exceptional service, if you are in a particularly generous mood, then you might leave anywhere from a few francs to five percent of the total bill as an additional tip, preferably in cash.

Credit Cards

The majority of Paris restaurants accept credit cards, and almost all will accept traveler's checks in French francs. Although every attempt has been made to ensure the accuracy of credit card information in this guide, policies change rapidly. When reserving, it is a good idea to confirm credit card information. If you are sharing the bill with another person or couple and you both wish to pay by credit card, most restaurants will oblige by dividing the bill between the two or more credit cards. Out of kindness to the waiters and *sommelier*, any tips (beyond the obligatory twelve to fifteen percent service charge) should be left in cash.

A Private Room

Many restaurants, including such establishments as Taillevent, Jamin, and Le Grand Véfour, offer private dining rooms for anywhere from eight to several hundred people. Some rooms, such as those at Taillevent, are particularly elegant and well appointed. Others may be drab, uncomfortable, and less appealing than the restaurant's main dining room, so see the room before making plans.

There are advantages and disadvantages in reserving a private room. One advantage is that it is easier to organize a special feast. The main disadvantage is that you must plan several weeks ahead and in most cases will need a French-speaking person to make arrangements. Also keep in mind that since your group will be set apart from the main dining room, you will miss much of the "theater" and ambience that goes with the dining experience. There is no extra charge for the private rooms, and in many cases the total bill will be less expensive than if the group chose from the regular menu. Where private rooms are available, such facilities are noted with each restaurant description, and a separate listing can be found in the Ready Reference beginning on page 388.

What to Expect at the Table

Suggestions on Ordering

There are four simple things to keep in mind when ordering in a Paris restaurant. First, think about what foods are likely to be fresh and in season. Thank goodness the French are still fanatical about freshness, and about eating only what is naturally in season. When dining out in Paris, I often go on seasonal "binges," eating asparagus, melon, scallops, oysters, or game day after day when they are at their peak. If you see melon on the menu in January, or scallops during July, beware.

Second, take the time to learn about the restaurant's specialties. Every restaurant has at least one or two dishes of which it is particularly proud, and the majority of restaurants either offer a *plat du jour* or underline or boldface their specialties. These dishes, assuming they are to your liking, will usually be a good buy, and generally fresh. Note that the fish is usually freshest on Fridays (when the demand is greatest) and least fresh on Mondays, when the wholesale market is closed.

Third, stick to your guns and order the kind of food you really like to eat. This is a caveat to those diners who will blindly accept a critic's or a waiter's suggestion, then all too late realize that they hate tripe, or duck, or whatever it was that was recommended.

Finally, today many restaurants offer a tasting menu, or *menu dégustation*, which allows diners to sample small portions of from four to eight different dishes. I am generally opposed to such menus, for in the end they are rarely good buys and inevitably provide more food than it is humanly (and healthily) possible to eat. Because a tasting menu offers so many different dishes, it is difficult, if not impossible, to take with you a memorable impression of the meal or the restaurant. While the *menu dégustation* is often easier on the kitchen, you just may get the feeling that the dishes you are eating came off of an assembly line.

Butter

Most, but not all, restaurants offer butter at the table. If you don't see butter, just ask for it. Only at the smallest cafés will a supplement be charged. Since the French do not always butter their bread, restaurants do not systematically offer it, unless you order a dish that generally calls for buttered bread—*charcuterie*, oysters served with rye bread, sardines, or radishes, or the cheese course. Almost all French butter is unsalted.

Coffee

The French have very specific coffee-drinking habits. Many Frenchmen begin their day with a *café au lait*—usually lots of hot milk with a little bit of coffee. During the rest of the day they drink either black coffee or *café crème* (coffee with steamed milk). But in restaurants, the coffee taken after meals is always black coffee, never coffee with added milk. Some restaurants will provide cream or milk if requested, some will not. In France coffee is always taken at the very end of the meal (never with the meal), almost served as a course of its own. In finer restaurants, chocolates and/or *petits fours* might also be served.

Fish, Meat, and Poultry

Almost all fish, meat, and poultry taste better when cooked on the bone. If you have problems boning fish, ask if the dish you are ordering is boned (*sans arêtes*), and if not, ask the waiter to debone it before serving (*enlevez les arêtes*). The French prefer their meat and some poultry (particularly duck) cooked quite rare or *rose*. But if rare meat or poultry really bothers you, be insistent, and ask for it *bien cuit* (well done). Be prepared for the waiter to wince. (For rare meat, order it *saignant*; for medium, *à point*.)

Salt and Pepper

Some chefs are insulted if diners alter their creations with additional seasonings, and so do not offer salt and pepper at the table. If you don't see any, just ask for them. But do be sure to taste the food before reaching for the mill or shaker.

Water

I am always shocked when, in this day and age, people ask "Is it safe to drink the water in Paris?"

Of course it is. Perhaps visitors assume that because the French are so passionate about bottled water—a table of eight diners might include four different preferred brands of mineral water—that tap water is unsafe. Either tap water (ask for *une carafe d'eau*) or mineral water (*plat* is flat bottled water, *gazeuse* is bubbly mineral water) may be ordered with all meals. If ordering Perrier brand mineral water, don't be surprised if only small bottles are available. The French consider Perrier too gaseous to drink with meals, so most restaurants stock only small bottles, for drinking as an *apéritif* or with mixed drinks.

Wines and Liquor

This is one area where I firmly advise you to follow the rule "When in Paris, do as the Parisians do." Most Frenchmen do not drink hard liquor before meals and few restaurants are equipped with a full bar. If you are accustomed to drinking hard liquor before meals, try to change your habits during a Paris visit. The liquor will numb your palate for the pleasures to follow, and requests for a martini or whiskey before a meal will not put you in good stead with the waiter or the management. Almost all restaurants offer a house cocktail—most often a Kir, a blend of either white wine or Champagne with *crème de Cassis* (black currant liqueur). I personally dislike most of these concoctions (which can be expensive and run up the bill) and always ask for the wine list when requesting the menu. Then, I usually order as an *apéritif* a white wine that will be drunk with the meal, or at least with the first course.

Selecting Wines

I have learned almost all I know about wines by tasting, tasting, tasting in restaurants: I study wine lists, keep track of average prices and favorite food and wine combinations, and am always eager to sample a wine that's new or unfamiliar to me.

Although I have found some *sommeliers*, or wine stewards, to be outrageously sexist (I was once refused even a simple glance at a wine list, and a few *sommeliers* still bristle when I insist on ordering the wine), generally I haven't found them to be unfair or unwilling to help when I sought information or assistance. If you don't know a lot about wine, ask the *sommelier's* advice. Give him a rough idea of your tastes and the price you would like to pay. This assumes, of course, that you share a common language. If you do not, ask simply whether there is a *vin de la maison* (house wine).

If you are knowledgeable about wine, you will want to study the wine list. Don't allow yourself to be pressured or bullied into making a quick decision (this isn't always easy), and if pressed, simply explain that you are fascinated by the restaurant's wonderful selection and would like a few minutes to examine and fully appreciate the list of offerings.

Prices for the same wines vary drastically from restaurant to restaurant: some have large, long-standing wine cellars, others are just getting started. I love wine, consider it an essential part of any good meal, and probably tend to spend slightly more than the average diner on a good bottle. When dining in a bistro or brasserie, I often order the house wine, either by the carafe or by the bottle.

The staff of Julien (see entry, page 89).

PALAIS-ROYAL, LES HALLES, MADELEINE, OPERA, BOURSE

1st and 2nd arrondissements

BRISSEMORET
5 Rue Saint Marc, Paris 2.
Tel: 42.36.91.72.
Métro: Bourse.
Reservations, noon to 2 P.M.
    and 8 to 11:30 P.M.
Closed Saturday and
    Sunday.
Credit card: V.
A la carte, 200 to 270
    francs.

SPECIALTIES:
Bistro: fonds d'artichauts frais
(fresh artichoke bottoms),
champignons frais à la crème
(fresh mushrooms in cream),
magret de canard (pan-fried
breast of fattened duck), crème
caramel (custard with caramel).

Parisian friends are always slipping me pieces of paper scribbled with addresses of their dining finds. One of these finds is Brissemoret, a pocket-handkerchief-size bistro near the Place des Victoires. I like to think of Brissemoret as a sort of affordable L'Ami Louis (see page 33). It has nine tables in a cramped space that can accommodate about 25 diners at a time, and chef-owner Claude Brissemoret never has any trouble filling those chairs. The bistro's lack of pretension, its traditional and unfussy fare, and a touch of nostalgia all keep diners coming back.

From the age of ten, chef Brissemoret dreamed of owning a small restaurant. He worked with chef Charles Barrier in Tours, then as a private cook for a bourgeois Parisian family, until he stumbled upon this run-down 1930s bistro. Now in his forties, Monsieur Brissemoret works out of a tiny kitchen, turning out classic bistro fare: thick slabs of *foie gras,* a chicken-liver *terrine* that would make any French housewife beam with pride, simple green salads topped with freshly cooked artichokes, and a stunningly good *fricassée* of duck, served with sweet and succulent *clémentines.* At lunchtime the clientele comes from the nearby stock exchange; later in the day a mixed international crowd fills the candle-lit tables. Reservations are essential. You can book as late as 10 P.M., and join the hungry local after-theater crowd.

Paris bistro conviviality.

CARRE DES FEUILLANTS
(Alain Dutournier)
14 Rue de Castiglione,
   Paris 1.
Tel: 42.86.82.82.
Fax: 42.86.07.71.
Métro: Tuileries.
Reservations, 12:15 to 2:30
   P.M. and 7:30 to 10:30 P.M.
Closed Saturday lunch,
   Sunday, and August.
Credit cards: AE, DC, V.
Private dining room for 8
   to 30.
Air-conditioned.
250-franc lunch menu, 550-
   franc menu dégustation
   (700 francs, with wine).
   A la carte, 380 to 500
   francs.

SPECIALTIES:
Seasonal: Emincé de St. Jacques
au céleri truffé (sliced scallops
with truffled celery), rouget rôti,
pommes de terre à la moelle
(roasted red mullet with potatoes
and marrow), lièvre à la royale
(wild hare stew).

Maturity is a lovely state, a time when one can begin to reap the benefits of past labors, when dreams and ambitions fall into place and life takes on a wholesome, natural rhythm. To catch a chef at his peak of maturity is a joyful moment, for everything about his restaurant takes on a relaxed, professional air. There is an aura of accomplishment all about; one senses that the chef is right with himself, and we can all sit down and have a good time. Alain Dutournier seems to be at that moment in his professional development. Dutournier, who generously transmits his love and respect for the best ingredients of France's southwest— tiny violet-tipped artichokes, fresh golden *girolles*, farm-raised chicken from the Chalosse and beef from Bazas—simply bursts with enthusiasm for his own creative, full-flavored style of cooking. His incredible *barigoule de poivrades et de petits gris*, a superbly fragrant dish full of happy flavors, earthy aromas, and a soothing aftertaste, blends artichokes, snails, and a hit of basil. His duck, roasted to perfection and served with barely a teardrop of fat, is accompanied by a perfect marriage of golden turnips and bright green, briny olives. As ever, the dining experience becomes a true gastronomic event with the presence of the well-informed staff. Bring with you a sense of adventure, let them select your wine, and you're sure to leave with a satisfied soul.

**AU COCHON D'OR DES
   HALLES**
(Chez Beñat)
31 Rue du Jour, Paris 1.
Tel: 42.36.38.31.
Métro: Les Halles.
Reservations, noon to 2:15
   P.M. and 7:30 to 10:15 P.M.
Closed Saturday lunch and
   Sunday.
Credit card: V.
A la carte, 240 to 260
   francs.

Beñat Errandonéa, originally from the Basque country in France's southwest, took over this traditional Les Halles bistro at the end of 1989. Since then he's been offering up the best and heartiest fare of his native region, all the while perpetuating the long tradition of the tiny, popular restaurant. He's maintained the ever-popular first-course dishes of curly endive and bacon (*frisée aux lardons*); of rich bone marrow (*moelle*) poached in broth and served with a sprinkling of coarse sea salt; as well as the main-course dishes, pan-fried steaks of veal and beef. But Monsieur Errandonéa has added sturdy platters of *piperade* (scrambled eggs and peppers topped with ham from Bayonne), *confit* (preserved goose), and *foie gras* (breast of fat-

SPECIALTIES:
Basque bistro: plats du jour (changing daily specials), moelle pochée à la croque au sel (poached bone marrow served with coarse sea salt), blanquette de veau à l'ancienne (veal stew with egg and cream-enriched sauce).

tened duck), and such changing daily specials as sautéed rabbit. The wine list is brief, but offers the *patron's* favorite Bordeaux, Château Labégorce-Zédé, a rich and perfumed Margaux well worth a try.

AUX CRUS DE BOURGOGNE
3 Rue Bachaumont, Paris 2.
Tel: 42.33.48.24.
Fax: 40.26.66.41
Métro: Sentier.
Reservations, noon to 2 P.M. and 7:45 to 10:30 P.M.
Closed Saturday, Sunday, holidays, and August.
Credit card: V.
Sidewalk terrace.
Private dining room for 12 to 20.
A la carte, 230 francs.

SPECIALTIES:
Bistro: langouste fraîche mayonnaise (poached spiny lobster with mayonnaise), foie gras d'oie frais (terrine of fattened goose liver), boeuf gros sel (boiled beef and root vegetables), confit de canard, pommes sautés (preserved duck with sauteed potatoes), clafoutis aux fruits de saison (seasonal fruit flan).

Back in 1932, when Pauline Larcier opened Aux Crus de Bourgogne in the neighborhood of the wholesale fruit and vegetable market of Les Halles, she decided she'd offer non-bistro fare at bistro prices. She charged so little for such luxury products as fresh *foie gras* and *langouste* that no other restaurant could compete, and her tables were full day and night.

"She was the Darty of her day," jokes her grandson, Francis, referring to the competitively priced French appliance store. He took over the ever-lively bistro when she died a decade ago, and about the only things that have changed are the phone number's prefix (once GUtenberg, now 42 33), and the prices of the *foie gras* and *langouste.*

Today, at 80 francs each, the two luxury items are nevertheless relative bargains: Francis continues to prepare the *foie gras* (fattened goose liver) according to his grandmother's recipe, and the family still ships seven to eight tons of *langouste* (plump spiny lobster) from the Breton port of Roscoff to Paris each year.

When you walk in the door at Aux Crus de Bourgogne, you feel as though you've wandered into a 1930's film, where everything's in black and white and everyone's speaking rapid-fire French in high-pitched, Parisian voices. The walls have that familiar, blackish-brown tone, the lights are bright, and your eyes are almost blinded by the sea of red and white checkered tablecloths and stacks of napkins perched atop the old radiators. In short, it's a classic and a haven for bistro nostalgia buffs. Not surprisingly, the clientele is very up-to-date: mostly young professionals out for a quick and easy bite on the way home from work. The food is fine, without fanfare: authentic *coq au vin,* prepared with a fine, mature chicken. Gargantuan portions of *boeuf gros sel,* with deliciously moist and chewy cuts of meat, plenty of vegetables, cornichons and mustard. Desserts—a lemon meringue pie and clafoutis—are better forgotten. The wine list offers a standard choice, with a very drinkable Morgon, *cru* Beaujolais.

GAYA
17 Rue Duphot, Paris 1.
Tel: 42.60.43.03.
Fax: 42.60.04.54.
Métro: Concorde or
    Madeleine.
Reservations, noon to 2:30
    P.M. and 7 to 10:30 P.M.
Closed Sunday and Monday.
Credit cards: AE, V.
Private dining room for 10
    to 60.
Air-conditioned.
A la carte, 200 to 250
    francs.

SPECIALTIES:
Fish and shellfish: salade de crevettes (shrimp salad), tartare de poisson (raw sea bass and salmon), petite lotte rôtie (roasted baby monkfish).

Gaya is the "baby" bistro of the grand fish restaurant, Goumard-Prunier, and the prices, service, and ambience here all make it a great stop for fish lovers. Gaya offers noble fish at less noble prices, without sacrificing quality: Try a deliciously fresh tartare of sea bass and salmon; a platter of tiny *lotte* (monkfish) merely roasted; or strips of sole *(goujonnettes)* simply sautéed in oil. Their apple tart is a rare delight, and the bright yellow tiled decor makes for a happy, wholesome ambience.

CHEZ GEORGES
1 Rue du Mail, Paris 2.
Tel: 42.60.07.11.
Métro: Bourse.
Reservations, noon to 2 P.M.
    and 7 to 9:30 P.M.
Closed Sunday and
    holidays.
Credit cards: AE, V.
Air-conditioned.
A la carte, 300 francs.

SPECIALTIES:
Bistro: salade de frisée au lard oeuf poché (curly endive salad with bacon and a poached egg), escalope de saumon à l'oseille (salmon with sorrel), coeur de filet grillé sauce Béarnaise (grilled steak with Béarnaise sauce), steak de canard aux cèpes (pan-fried duck breast with wild boletus mushrooms).

There are days when ambience alone counts for fifty percent of one's pleasure in dining. Walk in from the cold, face a room of happy people chatting, eating, relaxing, you're already halfway there. That's the way I felt on my last visit, arriving late and hungry at this classic 1930s bistro. Every centimeter of the long, narrow dining room was filled with an energetic crowd in the mood for some old-fashioned bistro feasting.

Chez Georges does not disappoint. On a recent visit, I began with the *salade de frisée au lard oeuf poché,* neither the best nor the freshest I've ever tasted, but it satisfied. (Sometimes it's just the idea of the huge, generous white porcelain bowl of salad that pleases, even more than the resulting flavors.) It helps when everything is served, as it is at Chez Georges, by scurrying, ever-smiling waitresses dressed primly in black with white frilly aprons. There are no long faces here. Next I feasted on the *coeur de filet sauce Béarnaise,* grilled beef served almost blood rare and perfectly charred on the outside. The meat had real flavor, real juices and color, and the tarragon-flavored Béarnaise, served on the side, added just the right punch of flavor.

As good as ever is the *steak de canard aux cèpes*—one of their classics and worth going out of your way for if you love wild boletus mushrooms and rosy duck breast. The house Chinon fit the mood and the moment. Who can ask for more?

GOUMARD-PRUNIER
9 Rue Duphot, Paris 1.
Tel: 42.60.36.07.
Fax: 42.60.04.54.
Métro: Concorde or
   Madeleine.
Reservations, noon to 2:30
   P.M. and 7 to 10:30 P.M.
Closed Sunday, Monday,
   and the week of
   August 15.
Credit cards: AE, DC, V.
Private dining room for 4
   to 30.
Air-conditioned.
A la carte, 350 to 500
   francs.

SPECIALTIES:
Fish and shellfish: homard breton grillé ou poché (grilled or poached Brittany lobster), petits rougets poêlés entier (whole, pan-fried red mullet), turbot de ligne grillé (grilled, line-caught turbot), huîtres, oursins, clams, praires (raw oysters, sea urchins, clams in season).

In 1872, Alfred and Catherine Prunier opened a modest little restaurant at 9 Rue Duphot, offering raw oysters, grilled fish and meats, and *"vins judicieusement choisis."* The Pruniers were the first in Paris to offer oysters raw—on the half shell—for up until this time the shellfish was necessarily cooked. The establishment grew and grew, as did the rage for sparkling fresh oysters. By 1897, Parisians were hooked, and soon Prunier began a door-to-door service to the city's best *bourgeois* homes, complete with specially outfitted *écailler* or oyster openers who traveled through the city in long white aprons and wooden shoes, transporting woven baskets of the shellfish on their heads. Soon the Pruniers acquired their own oyster parks and fishing boats in Brittany, began importing caviar from Russia, and developed a sturgeon fishing business in France's Gironde river, spawning a business in true French caviar. By 1930, Prunier employed 600 men to deliver fish and shellfish throughout the city. By 1960, the Prunier galaxy included more than 2,000 employees, selling more than 500,000 kilos of fish and shellfish each year.

The Parisian appetite for fish never waned, but by 1980 Restaurant Prunier was sold, survived several proprietors, fell out of favor, and finally closed. The famed Prunier restaurant (now Goumard-Prunier) has reopened under the ownership of Jean-Claude Goumard, whose elegant fish restaurant Gaya at 17 Rue Duphot had managed to gain a solid Michelin star. Goumard—a Breton who won his first fishing competition at the age of six, in fact worked as an apprentice at the original Prunier. If price was not in question, I'd lunch or dine at Prunier every other day, feasting on the fish and shellfish they insist is never more than 36 hours from the water, and that has never touched the ice that would "burn" the fish, and dilute its delicate flavors. The place shines with a sense of true quality, a quality that can only be achieved by rigorous standards and consistent attention to detail. On a recent visit, I realized I had almost forgotten what sheer luxury great fish can be, specifically when it is so pure and fresh that you want to weep, and when it is treated with utmost respect. Such was a tiny appetizer of sparkling fresh crabmeat, tossed in an almost invisible vinaigrette, with just a touch of chives. Or *tartare de bar,* tiny cubes of firm and fresh sea bass veiled with fruity, top-quality olive oil. But best of all was the *turbot de ligne* (fresh turbot caught by line, not in a net) accompanied by a mix of wild mushrooms and sauced with a balsamic vinegar sauce, which married perfectly with the firm, alabaster-toned fish. The restaurant has been totally refurbished, with a sparkling first floor kitchen open to view, a fine collection of Lalique lighting, and sunny, golden yellow tiles. They've thankfully saved the fabulous 1930 toilettes designed by Majorelle. (The same quality, with lower prices, can be found at Goumard's nearby annex, Gaya. See page 14).

LE GRAND VEFOUR
17 Rue de Beaujolais, Paris 1.
Tel: 42.96.56.27.
Fax: 42.86.80.71.
Métro: Bourse or Palais-
   Royal–Musée du Louvre.
Reservations, 12:30 to 2
   P.M. and 7:30 to 10:15
   P.M.
Closed Saturday, Sunday,
   and August.
Credit cards: AE, DC, MC, V.
Private dining room for 8
   to 20.
Air-conditioned.
305-franc lunch menu. A la
   carte, 600 to 700 francs.

Owners may change, chefs may come and go (too often for my taste), yet Le Grand Véfour remains one of a handful of truly historic Parisian dining spots. Napoleon is said to have dined with Josephine in this elegant, red, white and black restaurant that began as a café in the 1760s. Later guests included writers Victor Hugo and Colette, and artist Jean Cocteau, whose drawing still graces the menu cover of one the city's most beautiful restaurants. (Among the sixteen tables, there are several with brass plaques commemorating many of the famous who have dined here, and these tables can be requested when making reservations.) Go when there's an occasion to celebrate—dress fit to kill, and hope someone else is paying. Le Grand

*The dining room at
Le Grand Véfour.*

SPECIALTIES:
*Seasonal: ravioles de foie gras à
la crème truffée (foie gras raviolis
in truffle cream), saumon mi-cuit
en terrine (lightly cooked salmon
in terrine), pigeon de bresse rôti
(roast pigeon from Bresse).*

Véfour is a romantic spot for lunch on a sunny summer afternoon, when you can dine looking out on the garden and playgrounds of the Palais-Royal. That said, recent visits have been gastronomically disappointing: Chef Guy Martin has fine credentials, but he seems to be trying just a bit too hard. Many dishes—such as a lovely roast wild duck, or *col vert*—were overly fussy, and I found myself wishing he would simply roast, or sauté, or grill, and not cut everything up into bite-size pieces for me. Service is terribly well-meaning, but can be overbearing. So look for simplicity, hope to find a few bargains on the extensive (but expensive) wine list, and go with the thought that you're part of history.

ISSE
56 Rue Sainte-Anne, Paris 2.
Tel: 42.96.67.76.
Métro: Pyramides.
Reservations, noon to 2 P.M.
and 7 to 10 P.M.
Closed Saturday lunch,
Sunday, Monday lunch,
two weeks in August,
and two weeks at
Christmas.
No credit cards.
A la carte, 250 to 300
francs.

Issé—a favorite among the city's Japanese restaurants—offers some of the best sushi, sashimi, and tempura in town. This small, casual, two-story restaurant not far from the Paris Opéra, has a lovely spark, a certain electricity, even though the brown decor is hopelessly plain. The place bustles at lunch and dinner, as Japanese businessmen fill the upstairs dining room, downing chilled bottles of dry Kirin beer, along with their sushi, sashimi, and bowls of cloud-like tofu. Downstairs is more casual, with a sushi bar and a few tables for a quick sushi snack. The atmosphere is not unlike a typical

SPECIALTIES:
Japanese: poissons cru (raw fish),
sushi bar, grillades (grilled
meats).

Parisian bistro, with waiters weaving past carrying trays full of steaming tofu, giant boats of fresh, multi-toned sushi, and tiny bamboo trays stacked with crisy tempura. Go with at least two other diners, and order the giant sushi platter, an impressive selection of neat little rounds and rectangles of raw fish fillets in vinegared rice. The assortment includes chunks of silvery-skinned mackerel, mounds of bright red caviar, and little slabs of chewy, snow-white squid. There is also bright red fatty tuna, perfect pink crabmeat, remarkably fresh salmon, as well as giant scallops and shrimp, all set on little beds of rice, and served with a dab of the fiery green horseradish, known as wasabi. The chef, Mitsuro Sudo, is also known for his excellent appetizers, such as a feather-light portion of grilled eggplant, soft, moist, warm, and full-flavored. Equally wonderful are the stuffed zucchini blossoms filled with crabmeat. As a close to a Japanese feast, try the delicate passion fruit sorbet.

LESCURE
7 Rue de Mondovi, Paris 1.
Tel: 42.60.18.91.
Métro: Concorde.
Service, noon to 2:15 P.M.
  and 7 to 10:15 P.M. No
  reservations.
Closed Saturday evening,
  Sunday, last two weeks
  of August, and one week
  at Christmas.
Credit card: V.
Sidewalk tables.
Air-conditioned.
100-franc menu. A la carte,
  140 to 180 francs.

SPECIALTIES:
Bistro: terrine de foies de volaille
(chicken liver terrine),
maquereaux au vin blanc
(mackerel in white wine), raie au
beurre noisette (skate in hazelnut
butter), poulet aux riz en sauce
basquaise (chicken with rice in
tomato sauce), gibier (game, in
season), confit de canard
(preserved duck).

A great address to know when you're visiting the Louvre or shopping along Rue Saint-Honoré and in the mood for a quick, inexpensive meal. In good weather, tables tumble out onto the sidewalk (it would be an exaggeration to call it a terrace), while inside, diners sit elbow to elbow beneath rafters dangling with strings of garlic and country sausage. This is very simple, basic, French home cooking, nothing fancy but generally satisfying. I've enjoyed the poule au pot, and the travers de porc demi-sel (meaty salt-cured spareribs on a bed of cabbage). Many ingredients could be fresher here, and some dishes taste as though they've been reheated one time too many. But the service is swift, the price is right, and it all comes with a welcoming smile.

LOUIS XIV
1 bis Place des Victoires,
    Paris 1.
Tel: 40.26.20.81.
Métro: Bourse.
Reservations, noon to 2:30
    P.M. and 7:30 to 10:30 P.M.
Closed Saturday, Sunday,
    and August.
Credit cards: AE, V.
Terrace.
Private dining room for 10.
175-franc menu. A la carte,
    250 francs.

SPECIALTIES:
*Lyonnais bistro: filets de hareng
pommes à l'huile (salade of
marinated herring and potatoes
bathed in oil), pissenlits au lard
(salad of dandelion greens and
bacon), la mâche betterave (salad
of lamb's lettuce and beets), lapin
à la moutarde (rabbit with
mustard sauce), canard rôti aux
olives (roast duck with olives),
entrecôte grillé à la moelle (grilled
beef steak with bone marrow),
Beaujolais by the carafe.*

This popular neighborhood bistro is the site of one of my most romantic Parisian dining experiences. Rain poured that holiday evening in May, and we sat alone on the terrace, sheltered by the blue and white awnings. No traffic, no glaring neon, just gentle street lights, the sound of rain, the architectural splendor of the lovely Place des Victoires. Although inside the dining room bustled, it seemed as though the waiter was there only for us. The food here is basic and simple, just a step above average. Try the *salade frisée,* topped by a warm soft-cooked egg and tossed in a dressing that's nicely acidic. Duck lovers should order the *aiguillettes de canard*—thin strips of duck breast cooked evenly rosy but not overly rare—and the *lapin à la moutarde* can be thoroughly satisfying. I loved the seasonal dessert, a *sablée aux fraises,* very thick shortbread pastry topped with mounds of fresh strawberries.

AUX LYONNAIS
32 Rue Saint-Marc, Paris 2.
Tel: 42.96.65.04.
Fax: 42.97.42.95.
Métro: Bourse.
Reservations, 11:30 A.M.
    to 3 P.M. and 6:30 to
    11:30 P.M.
Closed Saturday lunch,
    Sunday, and mid-July
    through mid-August.
Credit cards: AE, DC, V.
Private dining room for 12
    to 30.
87-franc menu. A la carte,
    150 to 200 francs.

SPECIALTIES:
*Lyonnais bistro: poule gros sel
avec ses légumes (chicken poached
with vegetables), lapin aux
échalotes (rabbit with shallots),
tarte Tatin (upside-down apple
tart).*

Aux Lyonnais—a long-time old-fashioned stand-by just steps from the French stock exchange—is the sort of bistro that greets you with open arms, and gives you a feeling that time has somehow stood still on the Rue Saint-Marc. The bright, blood red exterior and French-style doors that open out onto the street welcome you into this intimate and charming spot. Aux Lyonnais is best at lunch time, when the office workers pour in and the noise level reaches a fine, musical high.

The interior is properly frayed—with creamy white walls, crispy green and pink enamel tiles, and gigantic mirrors (covered, unfortunately, by modern paintings that jolt you back into the present). The lean, young waitresses in skimpy black skirts and frilly white half-aprons are right out of a 1950's film, and seem almost amused by their role in it all.

The food is basic, and without surprises. For starters, I always opt for the giant salads served out of thick, white, footed bowls. A favorite is the *salade frisée aux lardons,* made up of thick slices of poached pork sausage, chunks of bacon, curly endive and a soothing, warm poached egg. Another worthy option is a huge green salad tossed with sautéed chicken livers. About half the dining room wisely orders up their special *petits pâtés chaudes* (tiny, well-seasoned sausage patties wrapped in caul fat), and there is always a daily special (on my last visit it was a hearty serving of sautéed kidneys, or *rognons*). Other good bets include the chicken in a creamy tarragon sauce or rabbit sautéed with an avalanche of shallots. The *baguettes* are state-of-the-art, the *tarte Tatin* won't win any awards but is quite good enough, and Pierre Ferraud's winning selection of Beaujolais is not likely to disappoint.

CHEZ PAULINE

5 Rue Villedo, Paris 1.
Tel: 42.96.20.70.
Fax: 49.27.99.89.
Métro: Pyramides.
Reservations, 12:15 to 2:30 P.M. and 7 to 10:30 P.M.
Closed Saturday dinner, Sunday, Christmas week, two weeks in August, and Saturday lunch from September through May.
Credit cards: AE, V.
Private dining room for 16.
Air-conditioned.
220-franc lunch menu. A la carte, 350 to 500 francs.

SPECIALTIES:
Updated luxury bistro: salade tiède de tête de veau et de pommes de terre (warm salad of headcheese and potatoes), jambon persillé comme en Bourgogne (Burgundian parsleyed ham), poularde de Bresse rôtie, pour deux (roast Bresse chicken, for two), soupe de cerises au vin rouge (warm soup of cherries in red wine).

Steady and solid, this timeless, upscale bistro is a favorite haunt of Parisian professionals, who make it a heavy-duty spot for the proverbial business lunch. In the evenings, the crowd varies, but always includes a healthy dose of traveling gastronomes speaking a myriad of languages.

The menu here—which changes regularly and seasonally—offers something for everyone, and includes plenty of no-nonsense fare: roasted Bresse chicken, pigeon in a salt crust; elementary platters of white springtime asparagus, thick slabs of pan-fried salmon.

On my last visit, I opted for a pair of daily specials, including a copious and memorable portion of tiny wild *mousseron* mushrooms cooked with white summer truffles, and a less worthy *brochette* of vegetables and lamb shoulder, marred by the bland-flavored lamb.

Service here is super swift and rather impersonal, but the staff manages to get the job done. Chef/owner André Genin follows a steady course, wisely mixing the tried and true bistro classics—such as parsleyed ham, or a salad of head cheese and potatoes—with inspirations of the moment.

The wine list always offers a revelation or two, and I adore their assortment of fresh and dried herb teas brought to the table so diners can blend their own private mix.

POMMES PONT-NEUF

At the end of the 19th century, merchants with deep-fat fryers on rolling carts lined the Pont-Neuf bridge. They cut potatoes into slender sticks, fried them, and bundled them into paper cones. The French food writer Curnonsky exclaimed: "Fried potatoes are one of the most spiritual creations of the Parisian genius." But potatoes were not always so well loved: In 1787 Antoine Parmentier introduced the potato to France, with great hopes that this curious tuber would become so popular they would call it a *parmentier.* To promote the potato, he offered a dinner for 100 at the Hôtel des Invalides. The menu included potato soup, potato salad, potato fritters, a brioche made with potato flour, and to end the meal, potato liqueur.

PHARAMOND
24 Rue de la Grande-
  Truanderie, Paris 1.
Tel: 42.33.06.72.
Fax: 40.28.01.81.
Métro: Les Halles.
Reservations, noon to 2:30
  P.M. and 7:30 to 10 P.M.
Closed Sunday and Monday
  lunch.
Credit cards: AE, DC, V.
Sidewalk terrace.
Private dining room for 4
  to 18.
A la carte, 300 to 350
  francs.

SPECIALTIES:
Normand: carte du marché (daily specials), tripes à la mode de Caen (beef tripe and vegetables cooked in cider and apple brandy), coquilles Saint-Jacques au cidre (scallops in apple cider sauce), canette au citron (duck with lemon), crème brûlée.

Pharamond is one of the those old-time, tried and true, beautiful Parisian restaurants that seem to age with remarkable grace. Traditional and spotless, this place is almost an anachronism in a neighborhood overrun with fast-food eateries and trendy boutiques. Pharamond's belle époque interior is among the most beautiful in Paris, with stunning pastel tiles, grand mirrors, cozy banquettes, and crisp, white damask linens. Even the waitresses seem to have walked out of the past—professionals who know how to keep their distance, yet manage to dish out a healthy dose of personal service and charm at the same time. The food here has remained first-rate. Although I must confess that *tripes à la mode de Caen* (tripe cooked in apple cider and served in old-fashioned brass braziers) is not one of my favorite dishes, this is the place to sample it if you are so inclined. My tastes lean towards other specialties, including fresh oysters on the half shell, or warm oysters bathed in butter sauce and set on a bed of cooked leeks, roast saddle of lamb, scallops in apple cider sauce, or duck with lemon. There is also an entire range of specialties grilled over a wood fire, including lamb kidneys, veal, and beef. Dessert offerings include their apple *tourte* with Calvados and *crème brûlée.*

AU PIED DE COCHON

6 Rue Coquillière, Paris 1.
Tel: 42.36.11.75.
Fax: 45.08.48.90.
Métro: Les Halles–Châtelet.
Open 24 hours.
   Reservations accepted.
Open daily.
Credit cards: AE, DC, V.
Terrace.
Private dining room for
   20 to 40.
Air-conditioned.
A la carte, 200 to 250
   francs.

SPECIALTIES:
Brasserie: banc d'huîtres et de fruits de mer toute l'année (fresh oysters and shellfish, year-round), soupe à l'oignon (onion soup), viandes grillées (grilled meats), choix de beaujolais (choice of Beaujolais wines).

Au Pied de Cochon may appear to be hokey and touristy, but many a late evening I've wandered in with a group of friends for an enjoyable meal of onion soup, fresh fish and shellfish, and uncomplicated good times. The restaurant draws a varied crowd of Parisians, Frenchmen in from the provinces, as well as foreign tourists. There's a filling and adequately fresh seafood platter, which often features wonderfully nutty, almond-like raw clams; a famed and delicious *andouillette* (chitterling sausage); and the entire assortment of Georges Duboeuf Beaujolais (including the oddball white) to lighten up the evening. The decor is properly glitzy, gay, and bright—there is such an overkill of murals, chandeliers, and marble that somehow more becomes less, and it's quite all right. The onion soup may not be the best in the world, but it's good enough to satisfy a craving and cure nostalgic longings for a Paris of days past. Do not feel slighted if you are sent to dining rooms on the upper levels: service here is remarkably democratic.

PIERRE AU PALAIS-ROYAL

10 Rue de Richelieu, Paris 1.
Tel: 42.96.09.17.
Métro: Palais-Royal–Musée du Louvre.
Reservations, noon to 2 P.M. and 7 to 10 P.M.
Closed Saturday, Sunday and August.
Credit cards: DC, V.
260-franc menu. A la carte, 350 to 400 francs.

SPECIALTIES:
Jambon persillé (parsleyed ham), maquereaux frais au cidre (mackerel in cider), saucisson lyonnais poché au beaujolais (pork sausage poached in Beaujolais), filet de bar grillé au beurre blanc (grilled sea bass with white butter sauce), lotte en papillote à la tomate fraîche (steamed monkfish with fresh tomatoes), tarte Tatin (upside-down apple tart).

A classic neighborhood spot, situated right behind the Comédie Française. This welcoming little restaurant is filled with regulars day and night, Frenchmen who often come by themselves with their newspapers, or with large groups to enjoy the hearty, varied fare. Best bets are the first-course *maquereaux au cidre,* silvery little mackerel cooked in cider and cider vinegar and garnished with apples, warm sausages poached in Beaujolais, and their famed *estofinade* (salt cod cooked with potatoes, herbs and cream).

PILE OU FACE
52 bis Rue Notre-Dame-
    des-Victoires, Paris 2.
Tel: 42.33.64.33.
Fax: 42.36.61.09.
Métro: Bourse.
Reservations, noon to 2 P.M.
    and 8 to 10 P.M.
Closed Saturday, Sunday,
    and August.
Credit card: V.
Private dining room for 8
    to 20.
Air-conditioned.
235-franc lunch menu. A la
    carte, 300 to 460 francs.

SPECIALTIES:
Seasonal: ravioles d'escargots aux herbes (snail ravioli with herbs), pigeonneau rôti a l'huile de truffes (roast pigeon with truffle oil), cartes de produits de la ferme (special menu of farm poultry and egg specialties), marmelade de lapin au romarin (rabbit with rosemary), pintade farcie avec de cerfeuil (guinea hen with chervil stuffing), chocolat de Marianne (warm, roasted chocolate mousse), pain maison (homemade bread), chocolats maison (homemade chocolates and candies).

Au Pied de Cochon (see entry, facing page).

Even in the best of worlds, magical meals are few and far between—meals that surprise you with new flavor combinations, that tease you with seemingly offbeat marriages, make you take a second look at ingredients you've all but forgotten.

But in a decade of visits to the small, cozy restaurant Pile ou Face, I've rarely found anything but magic. In some ways, it's no surprise, for the trio of restaurateurs—Alain Dumergue, Claude Udron, and Philippe Marquent—are the sort of people who never, ever stop growing, learning, stretching themselves to advance and improve.

It wasn't enough, a few years back, when chef Claude decided to make his own crusty rolls and perfect a complex assortment of handmade sweets and chocolates. They also bought a country house in Normandy, soon planted a full-scale vegetable and herb garden, redeemed dozens of fruit trees from years of neglect, and set about—with intense naiveté—raising their own chickens and rabbits. Now on weekends, in addition to tending the garden and the barnyard, the trio races around the region in search of young farmers who might additionally supply fresh, unusual, exceptional products for the restaurant.

Their latest love is country pigeons that taste like no other bird you're likely to find today. After plenty of trial and error, chef Claude decided the best bet was to debone the birds, tenderize them in cream, then use a combination of pan-frying and roasting to make for moist, ultra-tender, full-flavored poultry. The pigeon is served with "home-style" servings of mashed potatoes smoothed out with olive oil, and a well of fragrant, black truffle-laced gravy set in the center.

Equally satisfying are his marriages of *pain d'épices,* or French gingerbread, and *foie gras;* his guinea hen served with a full-flavored fresh chervil stuffing; *coquilles Saint-Jacques* that are cooked ever so simply in a non-stick pan, then dusted with curry powder and sprinkled with sweet butter; or normally banal *colin* (hake) that's elevated to new heights by cutting it into thick steaks, like salmon, and serving it on a bed of wild *girolles* mushrooms. For dessert, the unexpected becomes expected, like a *feuilleté de framboises* with layers of fruit and little homemade cat's tongue cookies, instead of puff pastry; or an incomparable warm chocolate mousse, enough to send you swooning all the way home. The homemade rolls and chocolates are worth a detour all on their own.

Marmelade de Lapin au Romarin Pile ou Face
PILE OU FACE'S RABBIT WITH ROSEMARY

Four and a half cups of rosemary? Yes. This is a remarkably delicious and simple dish to prepare, and a favorite of diners at Pile ou Face (see entry, page 23). I sampled it the first time I lunched at Pile ou Face (French for "heads or tails"), and now it's become a favorite at home, made with either rabbit or chicken and served with rice or fresh homemade pasta. The dish can easily be prepared ahead of time, then reheated.

1 fresh rabbit or chicken, 2½ to 3 pounds (1.25 to 1.5 kg), cut into serving pieces
1 cup (250 ml) dry white wine
1 quart (1 liter) water
1 onion, halved
2 carrots, sliced into rounds
2 bay leaves
1 teaspoon dried thyme
Salt and freshly ground black pepper to taste
4½ cups (100 g) fresh rosemary on the stem
1 cup (250 ml) *crème fraîche* (see recipe, page 279) or heavy cream, preferably not ultrapasteurized
½ teaspoon whole black peppercorns

1. In a large skillet combine the rabbit (or chicken), wine, water, onions, carrots, bay leaves, thyme, salt and pepper, and 4 cups (90g) of fresh rosemary. If you are using dried rosemary, add the entire amount. Cover and simmer for 45 minutes.

2. Remove the rabbit pieces and set them aside to cool. Strain the liquid into a medium-size saucepan, discarding the vegetables and herbs, and, over high heat, reduce to 2 cups (500 ml).

3. Meanwhile, remove the rabbit meat from the bones, cutting the meat into bite-size chunks. (The dish may be prepared several hours ahead to this stage.)

4. Stem the remaining ½ cup of rosemary.

5. In a large skillet combine the reduced stock with the *crème fraîche* or heavy cream and peppercorns and heat through. Add the stemmed rosemary and the rabbit pieces.

6. Cook over medium heat until the flavors have blended and the meat is thoroughly heated. Adjust seasoning, if necessary. Serve hot, with rice or fresh pasta.

Yield: 4 servings

GRATIN DE POMMES DE TERRE ET TOPINAMBOURS
PILE OU FACE
PILE OU FACE'S POTATO AND JERUSALEM ARTICHOKE GRATIN

I crave crusty, golden gratins, and this one is a winner. Rich with the nutty flavor of Jerusalem artichokes, it offers a change of pace from the traditional potato gratin. Jerusalem artichokes are back in fashion in France, having fallen out of favor after World War II when they were considered "ordinary" fare. Today they're loved because they are easy to grow (they put down roots wherever they're planted) and because of their delightfully nutty flavor. This recipe come from Claude Udron, the chef at Paris's Pile ou Face, who offered it to me along with a sack of freshly picked Jerusalem artichokes from his garden in Normandy.

1 pound (500 g) baking potatoes, well scrubbed
1 pound (500 g) Jerusalem artichokes, well scrubbed
1 tablespoon freshly squeezed lemon juice
Sea salt and freshly ground white pepper to taste
Freshly grated nutmeg
2 to 3 cups (50 to 75 cl) heavy (whipping) cream

1. Preheat the oven to 375°F (190°C).

2. Peel and thinly slice the potatoes. Rinse the potatoes to rid them of starch. Dry thoroughly with a thick towel. Set aside.

3. Fill a large bowl with water and add the lemon juice. Peel and thinly slice the Jerusalem artichokes and drop the slices into the bowl of acidulated water as they are prepared. Rinse and dry thoroughly in a thick towel before continuing.

4. Alternate layers of potatoes and artichokes in an oval baking dish (about 9 × 13 inches; 23 × 33 cm) and season generously with the salt, pepper, and nutmeg to taste. Cover just to the top with cream. Place in the center of the oven and bake until the vegetables are soft and the top is golden, about 1 hour. Serve immediately.

Yield: 4 to 6 servings

LA TOUR DE MONTLHERY
(Chez Denise)
5 Rue des Prouvaires, Paris 1.
Tel: 42.36.21.82.
Métro: Louvre-Rivoli.
Continuous service, 7 A.M. Monday to 7 A.M. Saturday. Reservations accepted.
Closed Saturday, Sunday, and mid-July through mid-August.
Credit cards: MC, V.
A la carte, 180 to 200 francs.

If I had not been in the city for a long, long time and wanted an instant hit of old Paris, I'd go straight from the airport to La Tour de Montlhéry, a modest, bustling, elbow-to-elbow bistro in the heart of old Les Halles. With walls chockablock full of artwork, hams and sausages dangling from the beams, and waiters who gently tease every female in sight, this long, narrow bistro is right out of an old-time French film. Lots of hugging and hand-shaking go on here, for most of the crowd is made up of regulars, but that doesn't mean that strangers are met with cold, dark stares. Much of the food is remarkably good and fresh, particularly the state-of-the-art curly endive salad (tossed with Poilâne country bread scrubbed gener-

SPECIALTIES:
Bistro: salade frisée aux croutons
ailés (curly endive salad with
garlic croutons), saumon cru
mariné au citron (fresh raw
marinated salmon), saumon
braisé à la moutarde de meaux
(salmon braised with coarse-
grain mustard), haricot de
mouton (mutton and white
beans), pied de porc pané (breaded
pig's foot), profiteroles (choux
pastry with ice cream and
chocolate sauce).

ously with garlic), and the soul-satisfying mutton with white beans, served in gigantic portions out of huge white porcelain gratin dishes. The house Brouilly goes down very well, and waiters serve up endless baskets of fresh Poilâne bread. If I were a cartoonist, I'd come here just to sketch the clientele—mostly beefy, happy, hearty men who've lived a fine gastronomic life, indeed.

VAUDEVILLE
29 Rue Vivienne, Paris 2.
Tel: 40.20.04.62.
Fax: 49.27.08.78.
Métro: Bourse.
Reservations, noon to 3 P.M.
and 7 P.M. to 2 A.M.
Open daily.
Credit cards: AE, DC, V.
Sidewalk terrace.
159-franc lunch menu. 108-
franc menu, after 11 P.M.
only. A la carte, 200 to
250 francs.

SPECIALTIES:
Brasserie: banc d'huîtres et de
fruits de mer toute l'année (fresh
oysters and shellfish, year-
round), foie gras frais, gelée au
Riesling (fresh fattened duck
liver in a Riesling wine gelatin),
poisson du marché (fresh seasonal
fish), grillades (grilled meats).

A lively and dependable 1925 brasserie filled with mirrors, marble, and the sounds of good times. Go with a large group, order up carafes of the house Riesling, and feast on oysters, scallops, mussels, or sole. Meatier specialties, such as pork knuckle with lentils, calf's liver, and a duck and white bean cassoulet, are also part of the huge brasserie menu that changes from day to day. In good weather, reserve a table on the sidewalk terrace, facing the imposing Bourse, or stock exchange. Note the well-priced late night menu, a good feature for night owls watching their centimes.

CHEZ LA VIEILLE
37 Rue de l'Arbre Sec,
Paris 1.
Tel: 42.60.15.78.
Métro: Pont-Neuf.
Open for lunch only.
Reservations, noon to
1:45 P.M. Closed
Saturday, Sunday, and
August.
No credit cards.
A la carte, 300 to 350
francs.

A s everyday cooks, we tend to forget a single but important rule: Try not to complicate that which is first of all a very simple cuisine, a cuisine of common sense. Each weekday morning Adrienne Biasin not only tries to remember that rule, but to put it into practice. And that's how it's been since 1945, when Adrienne began working in Paris bistros at the age of twenty-four. Back then, she was the youngest worker in the all-night Les Halles restaurant, so everyone called her the old lady, la vieille. Now she's seen her seventieth birth-

SPECIALTIES:
Bistro: terrine de foies de volaille (chicken liver terrine), harengs pommes à l'huile (salad of marinated herring and potatoes bathed in oil), navarin d'agneau (lamb stew with spring vegetables), boeuf aux carottes (beef with carrots), pot-au-feu (beef simmered with root vegetables), boeuf en daube (beef stew), veau de lait (milk-fed veal).

day, and mumbles about retirement, but in a not very convincing way. Paris without Adrienne Biasin would be a lesser place, for her homey little restaurant—Chez la Vieille—is truly one of the finest bastions of authentic French home cooking, genuine *cuisine ménagère.* It's bistro fare, but typically Parisian, not Lyonnaise, a repertoire based on large cuts of meat, the most elementary vegetables, dishes that not only take to reheating or second-day service, but actually improve as they age.

Adrienne's food is comforting as well as comfortable, surprising in its simplicity and lack of complication. She works alone, cooking out of a kitchen no bigger than a closet, with standard housewife's equipment. Her sister, Madeleine, and a single waitress, Martine, handle service. And she is open only for lunch. Dressed in white canvas tennis shoes, white anklets, and a huge white apron, she looks almost helpless and pixie-like. Yet tired eyes, and a slowing gait unmask her age. As ever, Adrienne is a bit temperamental; her restaurant is a world of its own. The china is mismatched, there is no sense of luxury, the bar dates from the late fifties, when Adrienne took over an already flourishing bistro. She has her fans, regulars who have come every day for twenty-five years. Men dine alone on salad, steak, and a few glasses of Margaux, and if they're on a diet she won't feed them kidneys or calves' liver. Even if they beg. At Chez la Vieille, there's no menu, and the food Adrienne prepares follows the rhythm of the seasons and her mood. Beef with carrots, spring lamb stew, boiled beef and vegetables are her stock in trade, but there's always plenty of *tomates farcies, ratatouille,* a quintessential *céleri remoulade,* and letter-perfect renditions of herring marinated in oil, onions stuffed with well-seasoned meat, and rabbit with mustard. You won't be offered soup ("Soup is for dinner time"), and desserts tend to be more copious than memorable. But Adrienne offers a beef with carrots so pure, so heavenly, so bursting with flavor, you can't understand why other cooks dare to make such a dish taste banal. Perfect, too, is pan-fried breast of fatted duck, or *magret,* thick and rich but not at all greasy, served with crunchy

COTE DE BOEUF EN CROUTE DE SEL CHEZ ADRIENNE
CHEZ ADRIENNE'S RIB STEAK WITH SALT AND PEPPER

Pan-broiling is a quick and delicious way to prepare thick cuts of meat, such at the popular côte de boeuf, or beef rib. This version, from Adrienne Biasin's homey bistro Chez la Vieille (better known as Chez Adrienne—see entry, page 26), is coated with crushed black peppercorns and coarse sea salt, and served with a marvelous shallot sauce. The beef is just as tasty the next day, cubed and tossed in a salad. Likewise, any leftover shallot sauce is great spread on toasted homemade bread.

Shallot sauce:

3 tablespoons (1½ ounces; 45 g) unsalted butter

7 ounces (200 g) shallots, minced

Salt and freshly ground white pepper to taste

¾ cup (18.5 cl) dry white wine

¾ cup (18.5 cl) beef or chicken stock

2 teaspoons black peppercorns

4 tablespoons coarse sea salt

1 beef rib steak, bone in, cut 1½ inches (4 cm) thick, about 2 pounds (1 kg), at room temperature

3 tablespoons (1½ ounces; 45 g) unsalted butter

3 tablespoons peanut oil

1. Prepare the shallot sauce: In a medium-size saucepan, heat the butter over medium heat. When the butter begins to foam, add the shallots and cook until softened but not colored, about 5 minutes. Season lightly with salt and pepper. Add the wine and the stock, and cook until most of the liquid is reduced and the sauce is thick and almost jam-like, 30 to 40 minutes. (The sauce may be prepared up to 30 minutes ahead. Keep warm, covered, in the top of a double boiler over simmering water. Just before serving, taste for seasoning.)

2. Meanwhile, on a work surface, crush the peppercorns with a heavy mallet or with the bottom of a heavy skillet. Alternatively, crush the peppercorns in a mortar with a pestle. In a small bowl, combine the crushed peppercorns and sea salt. Press the mixture onto both sides of the meat. Set aside for about 30 minutes at room temperature.

3. Heat a very large cast-iron or heavy-bottomed skillet over high heat for 5 minutes. Add the 3 tablespoons butter and the oil. When the butter has melted, add the steak and sear for 2 minutes on each side, turning with a two-pronged fork inserted into the side of the meat so that the coating is not disturbed. Reduce the heat to medium and cook, without turning, until the meat is done to taste, about 8 minutes more for rare, 10 minutes more for medium-rare, and 12 minutes more for medium. Transfer the beef to a cutting board, cover loosely with foil, and let rest for at least 10 minutes, and up to 25 minutes.

4. To serve, carve the beef into ½-inch (1 cm) thick slices and arrange them on warmed serving plates. Spoon the shallot sauce alongside.

Yield: 4 servings

golden sautéed cubed potatoes. No one touches the telephone but Adrienne, even if she's just slipped the pineapple tart into the little wall oven and the *pot-au-feu* needs tending. She'll screen the calls and if she doesn't like the sound of your voice, or the tables are already filling up, you won't get a table. Don't give up, keep trying. And when you go, don't ask for a green salad and an omelet. She'll toss you out on your ear.

REPUBLIQUE, BASTILLE, LES HALLES, ILE SAINT-LOUIS

3rd, 4th, and 11th arrondissements

AMBASSADE D'AUVERGNE
22 Rue du Grenier Saint-Lazare, Paris 3.
Tel: 42.72.31.22.
Fax: 42.78.85.47.
Métro: Rambuteau.
Reservations, noon to 2 P.M. and 7:30 to 10:30.P.M.
Open daily. Closed two weeks in summer.
Credit card: AE, MC, V.
Private dining rooms for 10 to 35.
Air-conditioned.
A la carte, 180 to 240 francs.

SPECIALTIES:
Auvergnat, including daily specialties: Monday, pot-au-feu (beef with vegetables); Tuesday, daube de canard aux pâtes fraîches (duck stew with fresh pasta); Wednesday, gigot brayaude (seven-hour leg of lamb); Thursday, poule Rouergate (roast chicken stuffed with rice and Cantal cheese); Friday, estofinado (casserole of salted codfish); Saturday, mille-feuille de chou farci à l'ancienne (stuffed cabbage).

I would be hard-pressed to name a Parisian restaurant with more regional soul than Ambassade d'Auvergne, a veritable temple devoted to such robust delights as the Auvergne's sturdy pork sausage, beef from Salers, seven-hour leg of lamb, and potatoes and cabbage in many wondrous forms. (for their *chou farci,* or stuffed cabbage recipe, see page 31.)

For a decade now, this large yet quietly familial and casual restaurant just steps from the Beaubourg has been a personal favorite, a place I love to go when I crave the simple, the rustic, the robust, all at prices that won't break the bank.

On my last visit—a dark wintry eve—I came prepared for portions of hearty, homey fare. So we ordered up the old favorites, along with a bottle of berry-like red Chanturgue, from the vineyards surrounding the town of Clermont-Ferrand.

We weren't disappointed, but left feeling as though something was missing. Every dish, from the vinegary-pungent salad of cabbage showered with warm bacon (*émincé de choux verts aux lardons chauds—for recipe, see page 30*) to the pleasing *saucisses d'auvergne* served with generous portions of rich *aligot* were as we'd remembered, but everything had just a slightly tired edge. For instance, the *aligot*— that smooth and unctuous mix of potato purée infused with garlic and gentle *tomme fraîche* (fresh curds used in preparing Cantal cheese)—could have used a touch more garlic, a touch more seasoning.

The coarse sausages were a bit too dry, the beef from Salers, ordered rare, spent just a few too many moments on the heat. It's the difference between food that nourishes and food that astonishes. In short, it's all about that final touch, the 10 or even 20 percent that transforms a familiar dish into a memorable one.

It's not easy, with the same repertoire night after night, and this of course is the risk one takes with such thoroughly traditional cuisine. The owners—Nicole Areny and Françoise Mouiler—are well aware of that, and they're hardly asleep at the wheel. At each table, they've placed a small questionnaire, asking diners to grade them on decor, service, food quality, and price. My advice, in a word, is to leave the menu just as it is, but to pay greater attention to details, to season with greater care, to give a freshly modern edge to an already marvelous and rustic cuisine.

EMINCE DE CHOUX VERTS AUX LARDONS CHAUDS
HOT CABBAGE AND BACON SALAD

This is such a simple and delicious dish, I'm surprised more Paris restaurants don't offer it. The salad is generally on the menu at Ambassade d'Auvergne, a solid restaurant with hearty fare (see entry, page 29). There it's served as a first course, but at home I make the salad often as part of a light meal that might also include a cheese tray, fresh homemade bread, and a favorite wine from Provence. Do use the best-quality slab bacon or side pork and red wine vinegar you can find. I like to add lots and lots of coarsely ground black pepper.

½ medium cabbage
Salt and freshly ground
    black pepper to taste
6 ounces (185 g) slab
    bacon or side pork,
    rind removed, cut
    into bite-size cubes
½ cup (125 ml) best-
    quality red wine
    vinegar

1. Cut the cabbage by hand into thin (⅛-inch; 4-mm) slivers. Do not use a food processor or the cabbage is likely to be too fine and will release too much liquid. Place in a large salad bowl and sprinkle lightly with salt and pepper.

2. In a large skillet, cook the bacon over medium-high heat, stirring frequently. Cook until very crisp. Leaving the bacon and the rendered fat in the pan, deglaze it with the red wine vinegar, stirring constantly. There will be a lot of smoke, but don't be concerned.

3. Add the cabbage, stir, then reduce the heat to low. Cover the pan to allow the cabbage to sweat a bit, and to allow the flavors to blend. Let sit for about 5 minutes, stir, then taste for seasoning. The cabbage should be just slightly wilted, but still crisp. Serve immediately.

Yield: 4 to 6 servings

CHOU FARCI AMBASSADE D'AUVERGNE
AMBASSADE D'AUVERGNE'S STUFFED CABBAGE

This is a "Sunday-night supper" dish; it's easy to make and popular with those who love hearty one-dish meals. I also find it fun to make. The Ambassade d'Auvergne (see entry, page 29) features the cuisine of the Auvergne region in central France, where cabbage, sausage, and smoked bacon are daily fare. The restaurant's version is stuffed with well-seasoned pork sausage, prunes, and Swiss chard, the popular green and white ribbed vegetable known in France as Blette. Chopped fresh spinach can be substituted, but when I could find neither Swiss chard nor spinach in the market, I made the dish anyway, and it was a big hit. Be sure to cook the bacon just before serving, so it offers a crispy contrast in color and texture. Bring the whole cabbage to the table on a platter, and slice it in front of the family or guests, for it forms a pretty mosaic pattern.

Stuffing:
6 ounces (185 g) fresh
    Swiss chard or
    spinach, rinsed,
    dried, and coarsely
    chopped
1 large bunch parsley,
    minced
1 large onion, minced
1 clove garlic, minced
10 ounces (310 g) pork
    sausage meat
1 egg
1 slice white bread,
    soaked in 2
    tablespoons milk
Salt and freshly ground
    black pepper

1 cabbage
Salt and freshly ground
    black pepper to taste
6 ounces (185 g) prunes,
    pitted
1 cup (250 ml) dry
    white wine
1 quart (1 liter) meat or
    poultry stock
6 ounces (185 g) slab
    bacon, rind removed,
    cut into bite-size
    pieces

1. Preheat the oven to 475°F (245°C).

2. In a large bowl, combine the stuffing ingredients and mix until well blended. Season to taste.

3. Bring a large pot of water to boil. Separate the leaves of the cabbage and blanch them in the boiling water for 5 minutes. Rinse under cold water until cool, then drain.

4. Lay a dampened 24 × 24-inch (60 × 60-cm) piece of cheesecloth on a work surface. "Reconstruct" the cabbage, beginning with the largest leaves, arranging the leaves so the outer side, where the rib is most prominent, is on the inside. Season each layer with salt and pepper. Continue until all the leaves have been used.

5. Form the stuffing into a ball, pushing 4 pitted prunes into the center. Place the ball of stuffing in the center of the cabbage and bring the leaves up to envelop the stuffing. Bring the cheesecloth up around the rounded cabbage and tie securely. Place the cabbage in a deep baking dish. Add the remaining prunes and the wine, season to taste, and cover with the stock.

6. Bake for 1½ to 2 hours. Just before serving, sauté the slab bacon in a small skillet until very crisp. Unwrap the cabbage and place on a serving platter. Garnish with the prunes and grilled bacon. Cut into wedge-shaped pieces and serve immediately.

Yield: 4 to 6 servings

L'AMBROISIE

9 Place des Vosges, Paris 4.
Tel: 42.78.51.45.
Métro: Saint-Paul or
    Chemin-Vert.
Reservations, noon to 2:15
    P.M. and 8 to 10:15 P.M.
Closed Sunday, Monday,
    three weeks in August,
    and the first two weeks
    of February.
Credit card: V.
Air-conditioned.
A la carte, 1,000 francs.

SPECIALTIES:
Seasonal: feuilleté de truffes
(truffles in puff pastry, mid-
December to mid-March),
cromesquis d'huîtres, sauce tartare
(fried oysters with creamy tartar
sauce), croustillant d'agneau de
Pauillac au beurre de romarin
(crispy roast lamb with rosemary
butter), tarte sablée au chocolat
(chocolate tart in shortbread
pastry).

It has taken some years, since the demise of *nouvelle cuisine*, for an authentically new and distinct style of French cooking to take hold. Today one calls it *cuisine moderne* and at its best, it pairs all the best qualities of the classics with a wise understanding of the way we really want to eat today. The emphasis is on flavor, on health, on quality ingredients. Today, simplicity wins out over an excessively decorated style.

The modern chef also realizes that if you want to offer true quality, you must keep the dining room small. A fine example of this modern movement is Bernard Pacaud, whose almost austere style of cooking has made him one of the best chefs working in Paris today.

His L'Ambroisie is one of the prettiest, most welcoming, most romantic dining rooms in the city: fabulous antique tapestries, ancient stone floors, impeccable lighting, ebullient sprays of flowers. And room for no more than thirty-eight diners.

Pacaud is a quiet individualist, and his brief menu reflects that sort of independence. In the two small dining rooms in his restaurant on the historic Place des Vosges, in the Marais, Pacaud offers a cuisine that is short on pretension and long on flavor: Try the soothing braised oxtail, or the delicately smoked salmon topped with a whimsical shower of perfect matchstick potatoes.

Today, Pacaud the perfectionist has reached a point of maturity, all the while continuing to simplify and honor ingredients to the summit. It's as though Pacaud has taken all the weight out of food, leaving behind just the purest of flavors.

His food appeals because his combinations sort of sneak up on you and surprise you with their power. Take his *feuillantine de langoustines aux grains de sésame*, a dish with great play of textures, and vibrant, yet subtle, flavors. On a bed of wilted spinach he builds a *langoustines* "sandwich," with plump, almost cloud-like crustaceans layered between two round, paper-thin, sesame-studded sheets of pastry, all sauced with a delicate curry sauce.

Pacaud has created a whole medley of smooth, almost mousse-like preparations, including his now-classic red pepper mousse; a soothing *dariole,* or little mold of *foie gras;* and a ravishing dessert, a bitter chocolate tart so light it all but lifts off the plate itself. Add to that an extensive (and expensive) wine list, and the quiet charms of Pacaud's wife, Danièle, and the maître d', Pierre Le Moullac, and you're in a win-win situation.

L'AMI LOUIS
32 Rue du Vertbois,
    Paris 3.
Tel: 48.87.77.48.
Métro: Temple.
Reservations, noon to 2 P.M.
    and 8 to 11 P.M.
Closed Monday, Tuesday,
    and July 14 through
    August 26.
Credit cards: AE, V.
A la carte, 700 to 750
    francs.

S P E C I A L T I E S :

Bistro: foie gras (fattened duck liver), poulet rôti entier (whole roast chicken), grenouilles à la provençale (frog's legs sautéed with garlic and tomatoes), côte de boeuf (grilled rib of beef), gigot d'agneau (leg of lamb, spring only), coquilles Saint-Jacques à la provençale (scallops sautéed with garlic and tomatoes, from October to April only), gibier (game, from October to February).

The air is fragrant with a mix of sizzling garlic, simmering oil, bubbling butter. The single portion of *foie gras* would easily feed three hearty trenchermen. Louis, the round and jovial maître d'hôtel, parades down the narrow aisles of the twelve-table restaurant, a platter of giant sizzling snails firmly in hand.

This must be L'Ami Louis, the most authentic, the most expensive, the most dilapidated bistro in the world. Even the telephone number that hangs behind the cash register—Turbigo 77 48—lets you know from the start that this is a haven for the nostalgic. It's the land of wood-fired stoves and red-checkered tablecloths, a land that can't exist in the present, but only the past.

Antoine Magnin, who from 1930 until his death in 1987 worked his gentle magic with *foie gras,* chicken, and game, is still there in spirit, a framed portrait hanging from the flaking, cordovan-colored walls.

He loved the stars and the stars loved him (he kept a photograph of actress Romy Schneider taped to his kitchen wall). For him nostalgia meant the pre-war era, when he claimed to have served more wild, baby birds, such as *ortolans* and *bécasse,* than any restaurant in Paris, and when 100 lobsters a day passed from his stoves.

I've been a faithful client for well over a decade and must admit that nothing, but nothing has changed over the years. Some nights the fries are fragrant and crisp. On others they're limp and soggy. The whole roast chicken, carved at the table, is always bathed in goose fat, then finished off with a few healthy clumps of butter, for good measure. The mutton chops are always fatty, the tender milk-fed leg of lamb is delicately perfumed, expertly roasted in a wood-fired oven.

The clientele, no matter the day, is always classy. One evening a friend counted twelve sable coats, which Louis casually tossed onto the metal coat racks above our heads.

We go, and will continue to go, not because you can't find roast chicken, fries, or *foie gras* elsewhere, but because it is there.

L'Ami Louis.

ASTIER
44 Rue Jean-Pierre
  Timbaud, Paris 11.
Tel: 43.57.16.35.
Métro: Parmentier or
  République.
Reservations, noon to 2 P.M.
  and 8 to 10.30 P.M.
Closed Saturday, Sunday,
  first two weeks of May,
  August, and holidays.
Credit card: V.
Universal 130-franc menu.

SPECIALTIES:
Bistro: terrine de foies de volaille
(chicken liver terrine), filets de
harengs pommes à l'huile (salad
of marinated herring and potatoes
bathed in oil), lapin à la
moutarde (rabbit with mustard
sauce).

Much of the pleasure of dining, of true gastronomy, is the joy of surrounding yourself with like-minded people. The most luscious *foie gras,* the richest chocolate cake, the most exquisite sip of a well-aged Bordeaux, will give you little pleasure if those around you do not share in the enjoyment. What's worse is to approach pleasurable foods while those around you chatter about their waistlines, their cholesterol levels, the evils of fat, of chocolate, of wine. So it is always a pleasure to dine at the little elbow-to-elbow Parisian bistro, Astier, where everyone seems to come with honest hunger, and a yearning for thick slabs of rustic *pâté de foies de volailles,* hearty portions of mahogany-hued *civet de biche,* soothing *lapin à la moutarde,* and gigantic platters of cheese that are passed from table to table at the appointed moment.

Here, gluttony is a pardonable sin, and no one will make a face or point their finger if you happen to cut into seconds of the creamy Coulommiers cheese, or ask for another bottle of Chave's remarkable red Hermitage.

Astier, situated near the Place de la République, is part of that breed—now rarer and rarer—of authentic Paris bistros. It's democratic, generous, and you can almost always be assured of a good meal and good times. Yes, it's boisterous and too brightly lit, and service can be a bit slapdash, but that's also part of the charm. If you are looking for a quiet romantic evening for two, this isn't the spot.

I applaud the single good-value menu, which changes regularly, and allows a first course, main course, cheese and dessert for all. On my last visit, I particularly loved the well-seasoned chicken liver terrine, the generous *salade de mâche et betteraves* (lamb's lettuce and beets), and the rustic rabbit with mustard sauce, or *lapin à la moutarde.* One visit, however, the fatted duck breast, or *magret de canard,* was a bit on the tough side, and the bread didn't seem as crusty and wonderful as I remembered.

BARACANE-BISTROT DE L'OULETTE
38 Rue des Tournelles, Paris 4.
Tel: 42.71.43.33.
Métro: Bastille.
Reservations, noon to 2:30 P.M. and 7 to 11 P.M.
Closed Saturday lunch and Sunday.
Credit cards: AE, MC, V.
75-franc lunch menu; 115-franc dinner menu. A la carte, 140 to 220 francs.

S P E C I A L T I E S :
Southwestern: salade Quercynoise aux gésiers confits (green salad with preserved duck gizzards), terrine de poireaux, vinaigrette de xérès (leek terrine with sherry vinegar vinaigrette), confit de canard aux pommes de terre persillées (preserved duck with parsleyed potatoes), le cabécous de Rocamadour (goat's milk cheese from Rocamadour), clafoutis aux poires (pear flan).

Baracane-Bistrot de l'Oulette, just a few steps from the Place de Vosges in the Marais, offers the best bargain, and certainly some of the finest food of the crop of modern Paris bistros. Owner Marcel Baudis—who originally opened L'Oulette on this spot several years ago—has moved on to new quarters in the Bercy neighborhood near the Gare de Lyon.

One of Baudis' assistants—Frédéric Dupont—now tends the kitchen at Baracane, while the amiable Thierry Obiegly tends to the small, narrow dining room, unchanged from its L'Oulette days. Chef Baudis, a native of Montauban in France's southwest, offers a signature of solid country fare that's unfussy, ultra-fresh, and intelligently seasoned. With its 75-franc menu at lunch, 115-franc menu at dinner, and a wine list with all selections priced at under 100 francs, Baracane offers what the French call *"qualité-prix",* or good value for the money. Some of the best selections here include a gargantuan salad of finely julienned Belgian endive and Bleu des Causses—the cow's milk blue cheese from central France that's aged in natural caves for three to six months; an ethereally light terrine of *pintade,* or guinea hen; and an earthy *daube de joue de boeuf,* or stew of tender beef cheeks, cooked in a well-aged Cahors, the inky red wine from the southwest. Not to mention the wonderful bread from a favorite Paris baker, Jean-Luc Poujauran.

BENOIT
20 Rue Saint-Martin,
    Paris 4.
Tel: 42.72.25.76.
Métro: Châtelet or Hôtel
    de Ville.
Reservations, noon to 2 P.M.
    and 7:30 to 10 P.M.
Closed Saturday, Sunday,
    and August.
No credit cards.
Private dining room for
    12 to 18.
Air-conditioned.
A la carte, 420 to 570
    francs.

SPECIALTIES:
Bistro: filet de saumon fumé
mariné (smoked salmon
marinated in oil and vegetables),
salade de boeuf à la parisienne
(beef and vegetables in aspic),
poulet fermier sauté au vinaigre
(chicken sautéed in vinegar,
tomatoes, and tarragon), boeuf à
la ficelle (boiled filet of beef on a
string).

At Benoit, owner Michel Petit continues to run one of the city's best high-class bistros, always making an effort to please and satisfy. Over the years, Benoit has remained one of my standbys, the place I go for superb *salade de boeuf;* an imaginative mussel soup flavored with smoked bacon, and great roast game or poultry with wild mushrooms, when in season.

With its sparkling fresh, nostalgic, turn-of-the-century decor, Benoit is a bright, plant-filled spot that's equally appealing at lunch and dinner. The boyish and bespectacled Monsieur Petit is the grandson of the original owner, Benoit Matray, who founded the restaurant in 1912. He took over the restaurant in 1959, and today serves as the chic bistro's *"chef d'orchestre,"* playing the role of lamb as well as lion.

Monsieur Petit makes sure the menu offers a mix of old and new, and he is always updating (and trying to lighten) the classics, so diners leave hungering to return. Some highlights of recent visits include a hearty *jarret de veau,* or veal knuckle, served with a mix of tomatoes and green olives; a soothing chicken in tarragon vinegar and tomato sauce; smoked salmon marinated in oil and vegetables (see recipe, facing page); and a stunning *charlotte aux fruits rouges,* a refreshing dessert of lady fingers filled with raspberries and wild strawberries.

Perhaps it is a pot-au-feu they are enjoying.

SAUMON FUME MARINES AUX AROMATES BENOIT
BENOIT'S MARINATED SMOKED SALMON WITH HERBS

Bistro goes modern in this updated version of marinated smoked salmon. At one of my favorite bistros, Benoit, they marinate house-smoked salmon as one would smoked herring— that is, smothered in onions, carrots, herbs, and oil. The dish is served as a first course, out of large white terrines, and is accompanied by a vinaigrette-dressed potato salad. It's a wonderful dish to have on hand to serve with a tossed green salad or with sliced potatoes. Any good-quality smoked fish can be used here, including trout, salmon trout, sturgeon, or salmon.

12 ounces (375 g) smoked fish (such as filets or thin slices of salmon, salmon trout, trout, or sturgeon)
2 shallots, sliced in thin rounds
2 onions, sliced into thin rounds
2 carrots, sliced into thin rounds
2 bay leaves
2 teaspoons fresh thyme leaves
12 whole black peppercorns
2 to 3 cups (50 to 75 cl) peanut oil

1. In a 1-quart (1-liter) oval or rectangular terrine, layer half of each of the ingredients, except for the oil, in this order: smoked fish, shallots, onions, carrots, bay leaves, thyme, peppercorns. Add a second layer in the same order. Add enough oil to cover. Cover securely and refrigerate for at least 2 days and up to 2 weeks.

2. Remove the terrine from the refrigerator 1 hour before serving. To serve: With a large fork, carefully remove a portion of fish, drain it thoroughly, and place on a small salad plate. Garnish with a few rounds of carrots and onions. Serve with bread, warm potato salad, or a tossed green salad.

Yield: 8 servings

CARTET
62 Rue de Malte, Paris 11.
Tel: 48.05.17.65.
Métro: République.
Reservations, noon to 1:30 P.M. and 7:30 to 9:30 P.M.
Closed Saturday, Sunday, and August.
No credit cards.
A la carte, 250 to 320 francs.

When the weather turns cool (which can be much of the year in Paris) my thoughts turn to Lyonnaise-style vinegar-rich salads showered with fragrant *lardons,* steaming platters of *gratin de pommes de terre,* and hefty portions of meat, the kind that "sticks to the bones." And this is not to mention a seemingly endless parade of desserts—all you can eat of chocolate cake, lemon tart, fruit, you name it.

It's days like this that lead me back to Cartet, a minuscule restaurant on a hard-to-find block off the Place de la République, where simple, hearty, traditional fare has been served up since 1932. That's when Madame Cartet began holding court, urging on the handful of diners that squeezed into her six-table restaurant. She pushed, coaxed,

SPECIALTIES:
Lyonnais bistro: choix de charcuteries maison (choice of homemade charcuterie, including parsleyed ham, headcheese, and chicken liver terrine), soufflé de tourteaux (crabmeat soufflé), boeuf à la ficelle (boiled filet of beef on a string), saucisson chaud de Lyon (warm pork sausage from Lyons), tarte au citron (lemon tart).

insisted even, until you left the restaurant bursting with a sense of well-being.

For the past few years, Cartet has been the sanctum of Marie-Thérèse and Raymond Nouaille, who have changed little—very little—during their reign. This is simple fare, without adornment, satisfying by its uncomplicated, unfussy nature. The dishes I most recommend include the *salade au lard* (see recipe, facing page), a classic that's getting harder and harder to find. Served up in a big glass bowl, the salad is a blend of crispy *frisée*, nicely trimmed rectangles of bacon, and a perfectly pungent vinegar-rich dressing. Next I'd go for the *gigot d'agneau aux herbes de Provence* (leg of lamb), a dish that's fragrant, meaty, homey and oh so satisfying. These are served up with all the *gratin de pommes de terre* you can eat (here it's a flavorful layered blend of potatoes, garlic, cream, and freshly grated Gruyère cheese). The best desserts include the rich chocolate mousse and the super-tart *tarte au citron,* filled with lemon juice, cream, eggs and sugar.

Don't bother with Cartet if you're looking for the fashionable, the chic, the trendy. Go with a big appetite; it's sure to be satisfied.

A good meal always deserves a bit of concentration.

CHARDENOUX
1 Rue Jules-Vallès, Paris 11.
Tel: 43.71.49.52.
Métro: Charonne.
Reservations, noon to 2 P.M. and 8 to 10 P.M.
Closed Saturday, Sunday, and August.
Credit cards: AE, V.
A la carte, 200 to 250 francs.

If you're looking for an off-the-beaten-path bistro with a true neighborhood feel and untouched, turn-of-the-century decor, then Chardenoux is it. It's been a personal favorite for years, through several owners, and the current patron—Bernard Passavant—seems to be keeping it all together. The restaurant alone could serve as a stage set, with its bentwood chairs, zinc bar, etched-glass windows, and colorful floor tiles. The food here is honest, wholesome, well-seasoned, and without

SPECIALTIES:
Bistro: oeufs en meurette (eggs
poached in red wine), salade de
roquefort, noix, et endives (salad
of roquefort, walnuts, and
Belgian endive), pot au feu (beef
with simmered vegetables), côte de
veau fermier aux morilles (farm-
raised veal chop with wild morel
mushrooms), cerises à la
savoyarde (warm cherries with
vanilla ice cream).

frills—what more can one ask? Best bets include the copious salad of Belgian endive, roquefort, and walnuts; a delicious and super-thick veal chop as good as any I've sampled just about anywhere, served with tender morel mushrooms and a generous serving of steamed, fresh spinach; and a superb *pot-au-feu*, served from a giant white bowl, and accompanied by a little jute sack of Brittany sea salt. Recently I sampled Guy Jullien's Côtes-du-Rhône, Beaumes-de-Venise, and it helped make the evening all that much better. And if it's on the menu, do try the cerises à la savoyarde, deliciously warm, pitted cherries, with vanilla ice cream.

SALADE AU LARD CARTET
CARTET'S SALAD OF BACON, GREENS, SHALLOTS, AND PARSLEY

This is the quintessential Parisian bistro salad: bitter winter greens tossed with plenty of hot bacon in a vinegary dressing. This is the version served in copious, all-you-can-eat portions at the tiny historic bistro, Cartet, not far from the Place de la République. The basic problem with most salads of this sort is that the hot bacon fat is tossed with chilled greens, thus creating a coating that has an unpleasant mouth feel. In this recipe, the bowl itself is warmed, along with the shallots and vinegar, a process that not only brings everything to the same temperature but also slightly cooks the shallots, making them more digestible. The parsley and chives add a touch of springtime. Chef Raymond Nouaille serves this with an all-purpose red wine, such as a Beaujolais or a Côtes-du-Rhône.

2 large shallots, minced
2 tablespoons best-
    quality red wine
    vinegar
2 ounces (60 g) slab
    bacon, rind removed,
    cut into matchstick-
    size pieces
2 tablespoons peanut oil
4 cups (1 liter)
    dandelion greens,
    curly endive, or other
    firm greens, rinsed,
    dried, and torn into
    bite-size pieces
Small handful fresh flat-
    leaf parsley leaves
Small bunch fresh
    chives, minced

1. Preheat the oven to 350°F (175°C).

2. Combine the shallots and vinegar in a large, shallow ovenproof bowl. Place in the center of the oven and cook just until the mixture is warmed through, about 5 minutes. Remove from the oven, cover with a large plate or lid, and set aside to keep warm.

3. Meanwhile, in a medium-size nonstick skillet, heat the oil over medium-high heat. Add the bacon and cook, stirring frequently, until the bacon is browned and just slightly crisp, 4 to 5 minutes.

4. Place the greens in the warmed bowl with the shallots and vinegar. Pour the bacon and fat over the greens, add the parsley and chives, and toss until thoroughly and evenly coated. Serve immediately.

Yield: 4 servings

CROUTES AUX MORILLES MADAME CARTET
MADAME CARTET'S MORELS AND COMTE CHEESE
ON GRILLED TOAST

When I first moved to Paris, friends took me to Madame Cartet's minuscule restaurant near the Place de la République (see entry, page 37), where I first learned to love the cooking of her native Bourg-en-Bresse, northeast of Lyons. There, wild morel mushrooms were once abundant, and families would serve up hearty portions of fresh mushrooms cooked in cream, then grilled on fresh country bread. I've embellished Madame Cartet's recipe a bit, combining fresh and dried mushrooms and adding a touch of rich cow's-milk cheese from the Jura, an authentic, well-aged Comté. This recipe can serve as a main-course luncheon dish, or as an introduction to a wintertime dinner. Serve it with a fruity red wine.

1 ounce (30 g) dried
    morels
3 ounces (90 g) fresh
    mushrooms, washed
    and thinly sliced
½ cup (125 ml) *crème*
    fraîche (see page 279)
    or sour cream
8 slices whole-wheat
    bread
4 ounces (125 g) Comté
    or Gruyère cheese,
    finely grated
Salt and freshly ground
    black pepper to taste
Small handful of fresh
    chives, minced

1. Combine the morels with 2 cups (500 ml) of water in a medium-size saucepan. Bring to a boil over high heat, then allow to cook away vigorously, uncovered, until the liquid is reduced by half. This should take about 20 minutes. Strain the liquid through dampened cheesecloth. Rinse the morels, return them to the strained liquid, and reserve.

2. Preheat the broiler.

3. Combine the morels and their liquid, the fresh mushrooms, and the *crème fraîche* in a medium-size saucepan, and cook over medium heat until about half the liquid has been absorbed. The mixture should be fairly thick and creamy, and not too dry.

4. Toast the bread on both sides under the broiler.

5. Add the cheese to the mushroom mixture and cook, stirring constantly, just until the cheese has melted and is incorporated into the mixture. Season with salt and pepper.

6. Spread a generous portion of the mushroom and cheese mixture onto each piece of toast, sprinkle liberally with chives, and broil just until hot and bubbling. Serve immediately.

Yield: 8 servings

LE GRIZZLI

7 Rue Saint-Martin, Paris 4.
Tel: 48.87.77.56.
Métro: Châtelet or Hôtel-
de-Ville.
Reservations, noon to 2:30
P.M. and 7:30 to 10 P.M.
Closed all day Sunday,
Monday lunch, and
Christmas week.
Credit card: V.
Terrace.
Private dining room for 30.
Menus at 120 francs (lunch
only) and 145 francs. A
la carte, 150 to 200
francs.

SPECIALTIES:
Bistro: ratatouille froide à l'oeuf
poché (cold ratatouille with warm
poached egg), pièce de boeuf cuite
sur l'ardoise (beef cooked on a
slate stone), fricot de veau aux
queues de cèpes séchées (veal
shoulder braised in white wine
with vegetables and dried wild
mushrooms).

White lace curtains, green leatherette ban-quettes, *blanquette d'agneau* and Beaujolais. Need one even pronounce the word "bistro?" The very thought makes hearts leap with hopes that we'll find an honest grilled steak, some bona fide home cooking, a wine that's more than just "drinkable."

Despite the restaurant's name, they don't serve bear steak at Le Grizzli, but owner Bernard Arney (formerly director of the nearby Ambassade d'Auvergne) has managed to create a fine Parisian bistro atmosphere in this spruced up—but not "renovated"—turn-of-the-century restaurant.

The food is solid, without pretense, and the menu, thank goodness, remains both imaginative and authentic (though I admit to missing the pres-ence of at least a green salad). I loved their gener-ous serving of cold ratatouille topped with a warm poached egg. It's a first course that, at lunch at least, could make a meal. One could easily become a regular here, returning each time to sample the homey *fricot de veau,* veal stew that's reminiscent of Arney's Auvergnat childhood, and one that's just as welcome in 1990s Paris. Lean and meaty chunks of veal shoulder are cooked for hours in a blend of herbs and white wine, and the dish arrives bright and lively, garnished with strips of carrot, soothing slices of turnip, and meaty wild mushrooms. (My serving, alas, arrived hot on the top, cold on the bottom, perhaps a result of a kitchen in a rush.)

Meats here are cooked *"sur d'ardoise,"* over pieces of slate set directly on the flame, the way it's still done in the Auvergne in central France. Our steak was rare and tender, as ordered, with a copi-ous garnish of sautéed potatoes, potato chips, green beans, tomatoes, and endive.

Le Grizzli offers an extraordinary farm-made and farm-aged Saint-Nectaire cheese (even the best cheese shops in Paris can't compete with this one), earthy rye bread, and a rich and fruity Loire Valley red, Saumur-Champigny, from Vacher-Sauzay.

BRASSERIE DE L'ISLE
   SAINT-LOUIS
55 Quai de Bourbon,
   Paris 4.
Tel: 43.54.02.59.
Métro: Pont-Marie.
Continuous service, noon to
   1 A.M. No reservations.
Closed Wednesday, Thurs-
   day lunch, February
   school vacation, and
   August.
No credit cards.
Sidewalk terrace.
A la carte, about 150 to 200
   francs.

SPECIALTIES:
*Alsatian brasserie: choucroute
garnie (sauerkraut, pork, and
sausages), jarret de porc aux
lentilles (pork knuckle with
lentils), omelettes (omelets), munster
au cumin (Alsatian cow's milk
cheese with cumin), tarte à l'oignon
(onion and cream tart).*

They don't come more tried and true than this. Always bustling, noisy and crowded, this Ile Saint-Louis institution hits the spot when your mood is jovial and social. The price is right, the beer is chilled, and the selections are authentically Alsatian. I love to go for Sunday lunch with a crowd, and order up sauerkraut and sausages, a mug of beer, and a slice of Alsatian Munster, served with a sprinkling of cumin alongside.

L'IMPASSE
4 Impasse Guéménée,
   Paris 4.
Tel: 42.72.08.45.
Métro: Saint-Paul or
   Bastille.
Reservations, noon to 2 P.M.
   and 7:30 to 9:30 P.M.
Closed Saturday and
   Sunday lunch, Monday,
   and August.
Sidewalk terrace.
Credit card: V.
A la carte, 150 to 200
   francs.

SPECIALTIES:
*Bistro: Gâteau de foies de
volaille (chicken liver terrine),
foie de veau (calf's liver),
blanquette de veau aux riz (veal
stew with rice), tarte Tatin
(upside-down apple tart).*

A small, family restaurant with plenty of village charm, L'Impasse is right out of a picture book. Neighborhood locals wander past the tiny two-room restaurant that spills out onto the sidewalk with a wave and a hello, while inside there's that gentle, even murmur of laughter and good times. The cuisine is stalwart and traditional, with plenty of *blanquette, lapin,* calf's liver, and *sole meunière.* But the menu makes just the right number of forays into the present, with a satisfying, chilled gazpacho for the warmer months, or a basic platter of poached codfish served with a simple tomato sauce. This place—with its romantic white candles on every table, beamed ceilings and exposed stone walls—is about as unfussy, as tried and true as they come. Do bring along a dose of patience, for service is a bit pokey. My single critique of the food is that it lacks basic seasoning. But that doesn't stop me from coming back, or wishing for a personalized napkin ring to store in the back room. The wine list is reliable, with a good Brouilly and Saumur-Champigny, and prices for wine and food are amazingly reasonable.

CHEZ JANOU
2 Rue Roger-Verlomme,
Paris 3.
Tel: 42.72.28.41.
Métro: Bastille or Saint-
Paul.
Reservations, noon to 2 P.M.
and 7 to 11 P.M.
Closed Saturday, Sunday,
and holidays.
Credit card: V.
Terrace.
A la carte, 200 to 260
francs.

SPECIALTIES:
*Bistro: Concombres à la crème
(cucumbers in cream), fromage
blanc aux herbes (creamy cottage
cheese with herbs), jarret de veau
aux trois légumes (veal shank
with three vegetables), profit-
erolles au miel et chocolat amer
(cream puffs with honey and
bittersweet chocolate).*

Wih its overgrown spider plants, huge central wooden bar, and sweet lily-of-the-valley
wall tiles, it's impossible to imagine that Chez
Janou is only steps from the ultra-trendy, citified
Place des Vosges. The bistro, built as a neighborhood café in 1912, is now a lot like a friendly front
porch, with Janou Chavvelot and her smiling
daughter Marie-Odile as welcoming neighbors.
The cuisine here is straight from the traditional
French homemaker's kitchen, and includes sorrel
soup, meaty braised veal shanks, and rhubarb tart.
The Chavvelots have a garden outside of Paris
which supplies the restaurant with such delights
as nutty Jerusalem artichokes—*tompinambours*—
served warm and tossed with richly flavored hazelnut oil. The food often just misses the target in
execution and technique, but the surroundings
and pleasant outdoor terrace manage to make up
for any lapses, meaning that once you've dined at
Chez Janou, you'll be eager to return.

CHEZ JENNY
39 Boulevard du Temple,
Paris 3.
Tel: 42.74.75.75.
Fax: 42.74.38.69.
Métro: République.
Reservations, continuous
service, 11:30 A.M.
to 1 A.M.
Open daily.
Credit cards: AE, DC, V.
Sidewalk terrace.
Private dining room for
10 to 150.
160-franc menu. Children's
menu: 80 francs. A la
carte, 120 to 180 francs.

SPECIALTIES:
*Alsatian brasserie: plateaux de
fruits de mer toute l'année
(platters of fish and shellfish
year-round), choucroute garnie
(sauerkraut, pork, and sausages),
presskoph (Alsatian head cheese),
leberwurst (pork liver sausage),
grillades au feu de bois (wood-
fire grilled meats).*

Big, bright, bustling and folkloric, Chez Jenny
is one of my favorite spots for sampling copious platters of Alsatian *choucroute,* that cool-
weather feast of sausages, meats, and sauerkraut.
But this gigantic, family-style restaurant offers
more than that: One finds specialties such as
Alsatian headcheese, pork liver sausage, meats
grilled over a wood fire, a selection of fish, as well
as platters of raw fish and shellfish. This is the sort
of place you can go for onion soup late at night,
or a snack of *quiche* and salad at lunchtime. The
Alsatian wine selection is enticing and includes
regional wines from such names as Trimbach and
Schlumberger.

CHOUCROUTE CHEZ JENNY
CHEZ JENNY'S SAUERKRAUT, SAUSAGES, AND BACON

I've yet to find better choucroute *in Paris than the variation served at Chez Jenny, a giant Alsatian brasserie (see entry, page 43). Here the hearty platters of sauerkraut, sausages, bacon, and potatoes arrive in perfect order: The sauerkraut is ultimately digestible (not too bland, acidic, fatty, or greasy), and it is neither dried out from overcooking nor swimming in watery juices, as is too often the case. The sausages are first-rate, and fresh, and the crisply grilled slab bacon is a wonderful touch. You know the platter is at its best when it complements, as well as compliments, chilled Alsatian Riesling. Here is a home version of Chez Jenny's house specialty.*

3 pounds (1 kg, 500 g) sauerkraut, preferably fresh bulk sauerkraut, not canned

3 tablespoons lard or goose or chicken fat

2 onions, coarsely chopped

2 cups (500 ml) Riesling wine

1 cup (250 ml) fresh chicken stock or water

2 pounds (1 kg) pork chops

Freshly ground black pepper to taste

2 cloves

6 juniper berries

2 bay leaves

2 cloves garlic

6 knackwurst

6 fresh German frankfurters

1 pound (500 g) smoked pork sausage, such as Polish kielbasa

2 pounds (1 kg) new potatoes

1 pound (500 g) slab bacon, cut into large chunks

1. Preheat the oven to 350°F (175°C).

2. Rinse the sauerkraut in a colander under cold running water. If it is very acidic or very salty, repeat several times. Drain well.

3. In a large casserole over low heat, melt the fat and add the onions. Sauté until the onions are wilted, then add the wine and stock or water.

4. Add the pork chops. Cover with the sauerkraut. Add the pepper, cloves, juniper berries, bay leaves, and garlic. Cover, and bake in the oven for 1 to 1½ hours.

5. In separate saucepans cook each variety of sausage in gently simmering water for about 20 minutes. Do not allow the water to boil or the sausages will burst. Drain all the sausages, slice the kielbasa, and keep all warm until serving time.

6. Meanwhile, steam or boil the potatoes. Allow them to cool just enough to handle, then peel. Keep warm.

7. Just before serving, grill the slab bacon until very crisp.

8. To serve, drain the sauerkraut (removing the herbs and spices) and mound it in the center of a large heated platter. Surround the sauerkraut with the pork chops, the sausages, including the sliced kielbasa, the potatoes, and the grilled bacon. Serve with several kinds of mustard and plenty of chilled white Riesling wine.

Yield: 8 to 10 servings

MIRAVILE
72 Quai de l'Hôtel de Ville,
Paris 4.
Tel: 42.74.72.22.
Fax: 42.74.67.55.
Métro: Pont-Marie.
Reservations, noon to 2 P.M.
and 8 to 10:30 P.M.
Closed Saturday lunch and
Sunday.
Credit cards: AE, V.
Small terrace.
Private dining room for 50.
Air-conditioned.
Menu at 200 francs (lunch
only). A la carte, 450 to
600 francs.

SPECIALTIES:
Contemporary: fraîcheur d'huîtres
spéciales et cresson, salé au caviar
(oysters in a sauce of cream and
caviar), farcies à l'escabeche de
moules (tomatoes stuffed with
seasoned mussels), saumon mariné
(salmon marinated in oil and
herbs), pain maison (homemade
bread).

Several years ago, while Muriel and Gilles Epié were comfortably installed in their tiny and popular Left Bank restaurant, Miravile, along the Quai de la Tournelle, they were coaxed to look at an available space across the river. And, *voilà!* it was love at first sight. They rebuilt from scratch what was formerly Au Quai des Ormes, and now they are happily installed in quarters that, by Paris standards at least, are spacious, bright and accessible.

The couple has created a restaurant that's at once modern and bright, with flattering lighting and tones of ochre, blue, and green that offer a sense of quiet elegance. I walked in one chilly evening, welcomed by the fragrance of bread fresh from the oven, a sure sign that this wasn't going to be yet another cold, impersonal restaurant.

Gilles Epié, one of the young stars of modern Paris, continues to offer a cuisine that's inventive, varied, and instantly appealing. Unfortunately, he retains one bad habit—a heavy hand with the salt shaker—that can mar otherwise fine fare. And while his food sometimes suffers from a lack of classically applied techniques, he manages to recover with a spirit and a style of cuisine that can only make you smile.

I love his *fraîcheur d'huîtres spéciales et cresson, salé au caviar,* a dish that arrives like a fresh sea breeze, with copious portions of fresh oysters, a soothing sauce of cream and caviar, and a little bundle of salad for added refreshment. Marry that with a sip of Didier Dagueneau's Pouilly Fumé and a slice of Epié's bread, warm from the oven, and you're in heaven. I like the idea of the *agneau persillé aux cocos doucement pimentés* better than the execution: The crusty portions of double-thick lamb chops were lovely, but the tiny beans were oversalted, and I don't go along with the modern concept of scattering seasonings—in this case mildly hot pepper—helter-skelter all over the plate, even onto the edges.

It's obvious from the desserts that Epié is using, to best advantage, his new pastry kitchen. Two desserts worth a second try include his *chaudcolat mousse* (soft on the inside, crusty on the outside) and his *tarte café fort,* a must for coffee-lovers.

OYSTERS

He was, indeed, a brave man who first ate an oyster. But from the moment that intrepid gentleman slid it down his throat, this pale, glistening, meaty shellfish was destined for stardom, and one can be certain that Frenchmen eagerly shouldered their gastronomic responsibilities.

Up until the 1850s oysters were so plentiful in Paris they were considered poor man's food, even though the journey from the Brittany shores to Paris was never a simple one. Oysters traveled in wooden carts laden with ice, and as it melted it was regularly replenished at ice houses set along the route.

During the eighteenth century, oyster criers filled the streets of Paris, carrying wicker hampers on their backs filled with their inexpensive fare. Although the colorful hawkers are gone, today France remains a major oyster producer—cultivating some 1,400 tons of precious shallow, round, flat-shelled Belon-style *plates* oysters and more than 81,000 tons of deep, elongated, crinkle-shelled *creuses* oysters. From Cherbourg in the north to Toulon along the Mediterranean, French fishermen in high rubber boots and thick jerseys carry out their battle with nature. Each oyster is nursed from infancy to maturity, a labor of three to four years.

Baby oyster larvae begin life floating in the sea with plankton, searching about for something to grip onto. Their survival rate is low: Out of a batch of 100,000 larvae, only a dozen survive.

Six to seven months later the larvae have grown to spats—now about the size of a fingernail—and are detached and moved along to another *parc* (oyster bed) where they remain from 1 to 2½ years.

Then, the flat-shelled *plates* are often dispatched to river estuaries, where the shallow, warmish blend of salt and fresh water helps them develop their distinctly sweet, creamy flavor.

The more common, crinkle-shelled *creuses*—which grow twice as fast as the *plates*—might be transferred several times before they swing into their final stage of development. They spend the last few months of their lives in swampy, shallow, slightly alkaline fattening beds known as *claires,* where they pick up their unusual green tinge by feasting on certain flourishing microscopic blue algae. The longer the oysters remain in the fattening beds, the greener, more richly flavored, and more valuable they become.

Just before oysters are ready for the market, they spend a few days being purified in reservoirs. There they are dipped in and out of water so they learn to keep their shells shut. As long as the oyster remains chilled and the shell stays closed during transport, the oyster can survive on its own store of saline solution. Once out of the water, it will easily stay alive for eight days in winter, two days in warmer summer months.

Oysters are generally available in a number of sizes. The larger are more expensive, though not necessarily better. They are best eaten raw, on the half shell from a bed of crushed ice, without lemon or vinegar. They need no further embellishment than a glass of Muscadet or Sancerre and a slice of buttered rye bread.

Plates: The two most popular types of flat French oyster are the prized *Belon,* a small, elegant oyster that is slightly salty, faintly oily, with a hint of hazelnut; and the fringy, green-tinged *Marennes.* *Plates* are calibrated according to their weight; the smallest, and least expensive, no. 5, offers about 1 ounce (30 grams) of meat, while the largest, and most expensive, no. 0000, called the *pied de cheval,* or horse's hoof, about 3 ounces (100 grams).

Creuses: France's most common oyster—deep, elongated and crinkle-shelled. The *creuse* is sometimes called the *Portugaise,* even though this variety of oyster was essentially replaced by the *Japonaise* after the Portuguese oyster was struck by a gill disease in 1967.

The three common subcategories of *creuse* relate to the method of final aging, or fattening. The smallest are the *huîtres de parc;* the medium-size is known as *fines de claires,* oysters that have spent about two months aging in the fattening beds or *claires,* with forty to fifty oysters to the square meter; and the *spéciales,* the largest, aged in fattening beds for up to six months, just three to five oysters to the square meter.

Creuses are calibrated according to weight, from the smallest, and least expensive, *petite,* which weighs a bit over 1 ounce (50 grams), to the largest, and most expensive *très grosse,* about 3 ounces (100 grams).

CHEZ PAUL
13 Rue de Charonne,
   Paris 11.
Tel: 47.00.34.57.
Métro: Bastille or Ledru-
   Rollin.
Open daily.
Reservations, noon to 2 P.M.
   and 8 to 12:30 A.M.
Credit cards: AE, V.
A la carte, 100 to 150 francs.

SPECIALTIES:
Bistro: plats du jour (changing
daily specials), salade de pissenlit
aux lardons (bitter greens with
cubed bacon), steak tartare
(seasoned raw beef), tarte Tatin
(upside-down apple tart).

When you're in the mood for authentic, old-fashioned, popular everyday bistro fare, this well-worn restaurant not far from the Bastille will hit the spot. The faded ochre walls, the mismatched black and white tile floors, the abandoned telephone booth in the corner, and the sweet waitresses (one of them could pass as Simone Signoret's daughter) serve as a fine stage set for unfussy platters of crudités (mixed raw vegetable salads), daily specials such as *choux farci* (stuffed cabbage), and a marvelously modern platter of rabbit stuffed with goat cheese and mint, served with world-class sautéed potatoes. The Côtes-du-Rhône from Domaine Chante-Bise is not bad, and the bill is light enough to allow you to bounce out the door.

CHEZ PHILIPPE
(Auberge Pyrénées-
   Cévennes)
106 Rue de la Folie-
   Méricourt, Paris 11.
Tel: 43.57.33.78.
Métro: République.
Reservations, noon to 2:30
   P.M. and 7 to 10:30 P.M.
Closed Saturday, Sunday,
   August, and holidays.
Air-conditioned.
Credit cards: AE, V.
A la carte, 300 to 400
   francs.

SPECIALTIES:
Regional: les cochonnailles de
pays (platter of sausages and
cured meats), les crudités
(assorted raw vegetables), la
pipérade Basquaise (scrambled
eggs with tomatoes, peppers, ham
and chorizo sausage), paella
(paella: including rice, squid,
mussels, chicken, and chorizo
sausage), coq au vin bourguignon
(mature male chicken cooked in
red Burgundy wine), foie gras,
cassoulet (casserole of beans and
meats), poissons du jour (daily
fish special).

Year after year, very little changes at the folkloric little Chez Philippe, and that's all for the better. Returning here is almost like being an adult who goes back to a childhood home to find that Mother didn't discard favorite novels, and that the old beat-up furniture is right where it had always been.

Like the best bistros, Chez Philippe takes on the personality of its owner—Philippe Serbource—a solid, serious, earnest man who for years has pleased diners with a cuisine that's partially Burgundian (snails, frog's legs, and *jambon persillé*) and partially Basque (with such Spanish-border dishes as paella and *pipérade).*

When I go, I always follow the advice of Monsieur Serbource, and I do not go wrong, and neither will you. It has lead me to hearty servings of capon stuffed with a meaty, well-seasoned pork mixture, accompanied by generous servings of fresh wild *girolles* mushrooms and quarters of golden sautéed potatoes. The same delicious garnish arrived with his famous goose *confit,* which was tender, meaty, and not overly salty. And, too, the highly seasoned paella was superb, served steaming hot from a gleaming copper saucepan, layered with mussels, fiery chorizo, squid, chicken, and of course golden Spanish rice.

The wine list is brief but carefully selected. Again, follow the *patron's* selection—such as the

Aligoté or the Gevrey-Chambertin—and you'll part well-fed and satisfied.

A SOUSCEYRAC
35 Rue Faidherbe, Paris 11.
Tel: 43.71.65.30.
Fax: 40.09.79.75.
Métro: Faidherbe-Chaligny.
Reservations, noon to 2 P.M.
    and 7:30 to 10 P.M.
Closed Saturday lunch,
    Sunday, and August.
Credit cards: AE, V.
Private dining room for 20.
Air-conditioned.
175-franc lunch menu.
    A la carte, 300 francs.

SPECIALTIES:
Bistro: foie gras, gibier (game), lièvre à la royale (wild hare stew, served Fridays only, mid-October to mid-December).

If you ever began to question whether France is still France and whether you can still find a traditional, authentic family restaurant in Paris proper, then reserve at A Sousceyrac. Don't expect a red carpet, a chic clientele, a buddy-buddy welcome. Anticipate instead, food that is carefully cooked, roasted, stewed—old-fashioned fare that's full of flavor and character. You'll find a duck stew, or *civet,* where the meat has been cooked to its limits, meaning it's soulful and delicious. You'll find imaginative dishes, such as the thin wafers of celeriac topped by summer truffles, all sprinkled with lemon juice. The mousse of wild grouse was deliciously rich and aromatic. Even starters such as artichoke bottoms topped with mayonnaise and lobster—most often dull and unimaginative—help one understand how classics remain classics. Desserts—warm cherries in cherry sauce, *profiteroles,* chestnut ice cream, and a pear tart—are all delightfully behind-the-times, delicious. What more can one say?

LE TRUMILOU
84 Quai de l'Hôtel de Ville,
    Paris 4.
Tel: 42.77.63.98.
Métro: Hôtel de Ville or
    Pont-Marie.
Reservations, noon to 3 P.M.
    and 7 to 11 P.M.
Closed Monday.
Credit card: V.
Terrace dining.
Menus at 65 and 80 francs.
    A la carte, 100 to 150
    francs.

SPECIALTIES:
Bistro: plat du jour (changing daily specials), salade frisée aux lardons (curly endive salad with bacon), omelette aux fines herbes (herb omelet), salade niçoise (green salad with tuna, capers, olives, and hard-cooked eggs).

Yes, I know, the food is not the most spectacular in the world. But where else along the Seine can you find a window table with a view of the river as well as Notre Dame? You'll also find hearty omelets, generous salads, mounds of mussels, and enough beef or lamb to feed an army. Go with a group when you're counting your *centimes,* order up a bottle of Saumur-Champigny, and simply enjoy.

LE VIEUX BISTRO
14 Rue du Cloître-Notre-
Dame, Paris 4.
Tel: 43.54.18.95.
Fax: 45.08.10.70.
Métro: Cité or Maubert-
Mutualité.
Reservations, noon to
2 P.M. and 7:30 P.M. to
10:45 P.M.
Open daily. Closed
Christmas eve and day.
Credit card: V.
Private dining room for 30.
A la carte, 250 to 300
francs.

SPECIALTIES:
Lyonnais bistro: poireaux
vinaigrette (leeks in vinaigrette),
frisée au lard (curly endive salad
with bacon), saucisson chaud,
pommes à l'huile (warm poached
pork sausage with potato salad),
boeuf bourguignon (beef stew in
red wine), civet de canard (duck
stew), rognons de veau sauce
moutarde à l'ancienne (veal
kidneys with whole-grain
mustard), poires "belle Hélène"
(poached pears with chocolate
sauce).

Who would ever dream of finding a solid, substantial, reliable, and old-fashioned bistro directly across the street from Notre Dame? No, this is not a tourist trap, but a bona fide restaurant that's filled with local businessmen by day, and neighborhood Parisians by night. Owner Fernand Fleury runs a tight ship, where the waiters are perfectly correct and the food looks and tastes as if it wandered off the pages of Larousse Gastronomique. The *salade frisée* is a model of its kind, served with sizzling cubes of bacon and topped with a warm, soft-cooked egg. The same goes for the *boeuf bourguignon,* served as tender chunks of beef married to soft, tiny white onions in a rich sauce. Desserts could not be more classic, and include a fine, homemade *crème caramel;* lovely bowls of *fromage blanc* served with fresh cream; and a hefty *tarte Tatin,* or upside-down apple tart.

LE VILLARET
13 Rue Ternaux, Paris 11.
Tel: 43.57.89.76.
Métro: Oberkampf or
Parmentier.
Open for dinner only.
Reservations 7:30 P.M. to
1 A.M. Closed Sunday
and August.
Credit card: V.
A la carte, 175 to 200
francs.

SPECIALTIES:
Bistro: terrine de foies de canard
(homemade duck liver terrine),
canard sauvage aux figues (wild
duck with figs), crème brûlée à la
vanille (rich vanilla custard
with caramelized sugar top).

Imagine a tidy and recently updated bar on a Parisian street unknown even to all-knowing taxi drivers. The food here is robust, copious, and hearty, the atmosphere is devil-may-care, happy-go-lucky, distinctly "working" class. Neither the diners nor the *patron* ever heard of France's no-smoking regulations, and you have the feeling this is an authentic—albeit recent—neighborhood hangout. The narrow 12-table restaurant—lacking even a sign at the entrance—is called Le Villaret. The owner is Michel Picquart, whose popular and *populaire* bistro, Astier, has been a favorite for years. He's left Astier in the hands of his former employees, and now holds court here.

Le Villaret is as no-nonsense as his old bistro, with such traditional fare as huge *terrines* of smoked herring filets marinated in oil with onions and carrots and served with warm sliced potatoes; glistening green salads topped with mounds of preserved duck gizzards or *gésiers;* warm plates of sliced, pan-fried *boudin noir,* or pork blood sausage, served with warm pears. Main courses are generous and sure to satisfy: Try the huge, tender, meaty veal chop, or *côtes de veau,* served with an excellent potato gratin and a flavorful zucchini gratin; or the *faux filet,* good quality pan-fried beef. Prices are reasonable, with first courses at around 30 francs and main courses under 80 francs. There's a small selection of wine, including an excellent Chinon, Domaine de La Roche.

LATIN QUARTER, LUXEMBOURG, SEVRES-BABYLONE

5th and 6th arrondissements

LE CAMELEON
6 Rue de Chevreuse, Paris 6.
Tel: 43.20.63.43.
Métro: Vavin.
Reservations, noon to 2 P.M. and 8 to 10:30 P.M.
Closed Sunday, Monday, and August.
No credit cards.
A la carte, 200 to 250 francs.

SPECIALTIES:
Bistro: courgettes marinés au citron (lemon-marinated zucchini), tendrons de veau aux pâtes fraîches (veal stew with fresh pasta), morue à la provençale (salt cod in herbed tomato sauce, with potatoes and garlic mayonnaise), saucisse de campagne maison (homemade country pork sausage), fondant aux poires (golden pear cake).

There are restaurants that I go to with a single, special dish in mind, and it doesn't even seem to matter if the rest of the meal pales in the shadow of that one favorite dish. At Le Caméléon, an old Montparnasse neighborhood bistro on the Rue de Chevreuse, I have two favorite dishes, and always have an impossible time choosing between the *morue à la provençale* and the *tendrons de veau aux pâtes fraîches.* (I've solved it by always visiting Le Caméléon with a friend who orders nothing but the cod, which is served with boiled potatoes and a rich *aïoli.* This way, I always get to sample it, no matter what I order!).

The *tendrons de veau* are rich, gelatinous, and chewy, the perfect sort of bistro fare that demands long, slow, patient cooking. Here they're cooked in a mixture of white wine, onions, carrots, tomatoes and herbs, then served with a mound of fresh pasta, making for a classic presentation.

Raymond and Jacqueline Faucher's Le Caméléon is a most democratic place, where you'll find elderly matrons sipping *apéritifs* at noon, as well as large groups of young Parisians digging into their *bavette du boucher* (grilled beefsteak) in the evenings. You don't come here for the decor (the black floral wallpaper could give you a headache), but in the end, the haphazard furnishings seem to simply add to the charm.

On my last visit, I opted for one of the daily specials—hearty portions of *lyonnais* sausages sliced and cooked in a huge bowl of lentils—and was not at all disappointed. Their *frisée aux lardons*—served with a warm egg atop the greens—is okay, but nothing out of the ordinary. For dessert, be sure to try the excellent *fondant aux poires* (see recipe, facing page) a sort of half cake, half tart, filled with delicate pear flavors.

Jacqueline is a pert and businesslike *patronne*, although when the restaurant fills up, service can lag. But that will just give you time to study the short but remarkably varied wine list. The *patron* offers wines from every region of France, including the rich and full-bodied Saint Péray, a white northern Rhône wine from winemaker Jean-François Chaboud; Yves and Stéphane Mureau's prize-winning Chinon; and Corrine Couturier's deep, syrah-rich Cairrane, Domaine Rabasse-Charavin.

CAMPAGNE ET PROVENCE
25 Quai de la Tournelle, Paris 6.
Tel: 43.54.05.17.
Métro: Maubert-Mutualité.
Reservations, 12:30 to 2 P.M. and 8 to 11 P.M., Friday and Saturday until 1 A.M.
Closed Saturday lunch and all day Sunday.
Credit card: V.
A la carte, 180 to 200 francs.

SPECIALTIES:
Provençale: Mesclun aux olives (salad of mixed Provençal greens and herbs with black olives), pâtes au pistou (pasta with basil sauce), tapenade de lapin (roasted rabbit with a black olive purée).

If you can't make a trip to the south of France, Campagne et Provence will at least put you in a Provençal frame of mind, with its *salade niçoise*, pasta with *pistou,* and stew of duck with olives.

This Quai de la Tournelle bistro is housed in the quarters of Gilles Epié's old Miravile (now located across the Seine on the Quai de l'Hôtel de Ville). While the decor is modern and rather impersonal, the location is great, the price is right, and food above average. I most enjoyed the garlic-rich *salade de mesclun*, a tumble of mixed greens and herbs, tossed with black olives, and the *tapenade de lapin,* roasted rabbit coated with a black olive purée. The duck stew tasted as though it had been reheated one time too many, and service is amateurish and slightly distracted. Wines are well priced: Best bets include Guigal's Côtes-du-Rhône and both red and white Graves, Château Archambau.

FONDANT AUX POIRES LE CAMELEON
LE CAMELEON'S GOLDEN PEAR CAKE

Each time I dine at the bustling little Montparnasse bistro Le Caméléon (see entry, page 51), I order this simple, satisfying dessert. Pear desserts are wonderful, for pears that are slightly cooked give off a distinctly "pear" flavor, one that's soothing, gentle, and reassuring. This unusual "double batter" method of constructing the cake makes for a soft and moist dessert that's truly fondant, *or meltingly tender. It's really half cake, half tart and goes well with a sweet chilled Beaumes-de-Venise from Provence, or a sip of Poire Williams, a clear pear brandy.*

3 large ripe pears (about 1½ pounds; 750 g), peeled, cored and quartered, with each quarter cut into 4 slices
5 large eggs
6 tablespoons (10 cl) peanut oil
1 tablespoon rum
6 tablespoons (55 g) unbleached all-purpose flour
1¼ cups (250 g) sugar
5 tablespoons (2½ ounces; 75 g) butter, softened
1 to 2 tablespoons sugar, for garnish

1. Preheat the oven to 425°F (220°C). Butter a 9-inch (23-cm) round cake pan.

2. Lay the pear slices in the prepared cake pan in circles, starting at the outside and working toward the center.

3. Prepare the first batter: In a medium-size bowl, whisk together 3 of the eggs, the oil, and the rum. In the bowl of a mixer, combine the flour and ½ cup (100 g) of the sugar. Add the liquid ingredients to the dry ingredients and mix until thoroughly blended. Set aside.

4. Prepare the second batter: Slowly cream the softened butter with the remaining ¾ cup (150 g) sugar until well blended. Add the remaining 2 eggs, one at a time, beating well after each addition, until the batter is thick and smooth.

5. Pour the first batter over the pears. Place in the center of the oven and bake just until the cake has begun to set and is bubbly, about 10 minutes. Remove from the oven and pour the second batter on top. Reduce the oven temperature to 350°F (175°C). Return the cake to the center of the oven and continue baking until firm and golden, about 20 minutes more. Remove to a rack to cool, dusting the top lightly with a few tablespoons of sugar. Serve at room temperature. Cut into pie-shaped wedges, using a spatula to transfer the wedges to dessert plates.

Yield: 8 servings

AUX CHARPENTIERS

10 Rue Mabillon, Paris 6.
Tel: 43.26.30.05.
Fax: 46.33.07.98.
Métro: Mabillon.
Reservations, noon to 2 P.M.
  and 7 to 10:30 P.M.
Closed Sunday, holidays,
  and Christmas week.
Credit cards: AE, DC, V.
Terrace in summer.
A la carte, 180 to 260
  francs.

S P E C I A L T I E S :
*Cuisine bourgeoise: plats du jour
(changing daily specials), boeuf à
la ficelle (boiled beef and vegetables), caneton rôtie sauces olives
et porto (roast duck with olives
and port), selle d'agneau rôtie
(roasted saddle of lamb),
lapereau rôti (roasted young
rabbit).*

Take a trip to old Paris, where Monday it's *sauté de veau*, Tuesday it's *boeuf mode*, Wednesday, Thursday, and so on, it's all the rest. Aux Charpentiers is a fine Left Bank refuge, where the food is far from outstanding but perhaps never was. Go with a group, and you'll all be sure to find something to your taste on the long, varied menu. I always love the idea of ordering separate vegetables, or sampling many orders of their varied hors d'oeuvres. Nothing here ever truly disappoints, and I always leave glad that places such as this still exist.

LES DELICES
D'APHRODITE

4 Rue de Candolle, Paris 5.
Tel: 43.31.40.39.
Métro: Censier-Daubenton.
Reservations, noon to 2 P.M.
  and 7 to 11:30 P.M.
Closed Monday.
Sidewalk terrace.
Air-conditioned.
Credit card: V.
A la carte, 130 to 190 francs.

S P E C I A L T I E S :
*Greek: spanakopetes (spinach-
cheese phyllo triangles), moussaka
(layered casserole of eggplant and
meat), dolmas (herb and meat-
stuffed grape leaves), yaourt de
brebis au miel et aux noix
(sheep's milk yogurt with honey
and walnuts).*

When you've had your fill of *blanquette de veau* and *steak-frites*, this is the spot to go for a little Mediterranean-style cuisine and ambience. It's not quite a trip to Greece, but you'll be sure to leave in a cheery mood: The Mavrommatis family operates a lively, youthful, and busy little restaurant right across from the Saint-Médard church. Decorated in sky blue and white, this casual restaurant offers good value for the money. Diners often share platters, or simply order a single course. The food is delicately spiced (seasoning could be a bit more authoritative), clean, and refreshing. I've eaten my way through much of the menu, and recommend the lovely spinach and cheese phyllo triangles, the moussaka, the nice warm herb and meat-stuffed grape leaves, and the fabulous sheep's milk yogurt, served with honey and walnuts. Unless you're a big fan of Greek wine, stay with the French. A Saumur-Champigny is always a good bet.

DODIN BOUFFANT
25 Rue Frédéric-Sauton,
Paris 5.
Tel: 43.25.25.14.
Fax: 43.29.52.61.
Métro: Maubert-Mutualité.
Reservations, 12:30 to 2
P.M. and 8 to 11 P.M.
Closed Sunday, August, and
two weeks at Christmas.
Credit cards: AE, DC, V.
195-franc lunch menu. A la
carte, 350 to 400 francs.

SPECIALTIES:
*Seasonal, fish: fruits de mer
(fresh seafood platter), saumon
fumé (house smoked salmon),
gibiers en saison (game, in
season), fricassée de morue à la
provençale (salt cod, onions,
tomatoes, zucchini, and potatoes
with fresh basil and parsley).*

Whether we're considering a restaurant, a treasured piece of literature, or the work of a much-admired artist, one always returns to "old favorites" with a certain sense of trepidation. Will it be as good as I remembered?

Recently, I returned with good friends to a restaurant we all loved for a weeknight dinner to catch up on news, put our elbows on the table, and have a happy, good-natured time. The restaurant was Dodin Bouffant, a rather solid standby that comes to mind when I'm in the mood for fresh fish and shellfish, and where I've always loved the bustle, the din, mixed with a quiet touch of grown-up, thoroughly Parisian, sophistication.

I've returned time and again for their brilliant *fricassée de morue à la provençale*, a bright and full-flavored blend of salt cod, tomatoes, peppers, onions, zucchini and a healthy hit of fresh herbs (see recipe, page 56); the varied pasta creations; and superb house-smoked herring.

But on my recent visit, it seemed that only the old standbys—the *morue* and the delightful fresh, smoked herring served with a warm potato salad—had any life left in them. The dining room seemed more like a factory than a trendy, Left Bank bank restaurant, and the remaining dishes all had a worn-out, almost exhausted pallor. "No taste," pronounced the friend as she toyed with the pale blend of pasta, mussels and *coquillettes*. My daily special, a simple platter of grilled shrimp, lacked that fresh punch and flavor. (Why bother with daily specials if they're not the least bit special?)

The game (on this evening, *col vert aux figues*—wild duck with figs) was so tame the flavor was almost nonexistent, and the famed *soufflé aux fruits* was beautiful but thoroughly lacked personality. It seemed like so much "food as fuel." Only the rich and golden 1988 Châteauneuf-du-Pape *blanc* from Beaucastel delivered what we had come for: a sense of freshness, of grown-up sophistication, of celebration.

FRICASSEE DE MORUE A LA PROVENÇALE DODIN BOUFFANT
DODIN BOUFFANT'S FRICASSEE OF SALT COD, TOMATOES,
POTATOES AND ONIONS

This is a vibrant, summer sort of dish from Dodin Bouffant (see entry, page 55) that virtually delivers the sun and the sea to the table. I love the abundance of fresh vegetables, the play of lively flavors, the crunch of the zucchini, and the soft, soothing quality of the salt cod. Be sure to prepare this in a large quick-reacting skillet that will maintain high heat and let things really sauté, not get soggy. I like to use an old-fashioned thin black metal frying pan. With this dish, try a chilled rosé de Provence.

1 pound (500 g) salt cod
2 tablespoons extra-virgin olive oil
½ pound (250 g) onions, peeled and cut lengthwise into thin strips
½ pound (about 2 medium; 250 g) potatoes, peeled and thinly sliced
½ teaspoon fresh thyme, or ¼ teaspoon dried
½ pound (250 g) zucchini, cut into thin rounds
½ pound (about 3 medium; 250 g) tomatoes, cored, peeled, seeded, and coarsely chopped
1 tablespoon best-quality sherry wine vinegar
Small bunch fresh parsley leaves, minced

1. One day before preparing the *fricassée*, soak the salt cod in plenty of cold water, changing the water at least three or four times during the soaking period.

2. Cook the cod: Drain the cod and cover it with fresh water. Bring just to a simmer and immediately remove the pan from the heat. Cover, and let stand for 15 minutes. Drain, scrape off the fatty skin, and remove any bones. Cut or tear into bite-size pieces and set aside. The cod is now ready to use.

3. Heat the oil in a large skillet over medium-high heat. Add the onions and cook, stirring constantly, until soft, just 3 to 4 minutes. Add the potatoes and thyme and continue to sauté, keeping the vegetables in constant motion. Cook just until the potatoes begin to soften but are still crunchy. Add the zucchini and toss for about 2 more minutes, then the salt cod, tomatoes, and vinegar, and cook for an additional 2 minutes.

4. Serve immediately, showered with parsley. The dish is also delicious cold, and can be refrigerated for up to one day.

Yield: 4 to 6 servings

L'ECAILLE DE P.C.B.
5 Rue Mabillon, Paris 6.
Tel: 43.26.12.84.
Métro: Mabillon.
Reservations, noon to 2 P.M.
and 7:30 to 10 P.M.
Closed Saturday lunch and
Sunday.
Credit cards: AE, MC, V.
Private dining room for 12.
Air conditioned.
Menus at 125 francs (lunch
only) and 210 francs.
A la carte, 300 to 500
francs.

SPECIALTIES:
Fish and shellfish: La soupe de
poissons maison (homemade fish
soup), tartare de poissons aux
herbes (raw, chopped fish seasoned
with herbs), dorade rôtie au
romarin frais (whole roast porgy
with fresh rosemary), homard
grillé entier (whole grilled
lobster).

This popular hangout of the Left Bank's publishing crowd has undergone some much needed facelifting, transforming a cozily outdated Basque bistro into a slick, chic, elegantly pretty fish restaurant decorated to resemble a ship's interior. The shiny wooden walls, white curtains, blue tiles, and simple lighting now make a perfect backdrop for a seaworthy meal. Run by Pierre and Colette Bardeche, Ecaille is not without its critics, and I have been among them. Complaints range from slow and inefficient service, to fish that's not properly cooked, to prices that are just too high. But over time I've had more good times than bad, with each meal better than the last. Recently I have swooned over a *tartare* of *daurade*, prepared *à la minute*—perfectly fresh porgy chopped by hand, tossed with herbs, oil, and seasoning, and served with deliciously fresh toasted rye bread rubbed ever so lightly with garlic. Chef Bardeche's real love is roasting, and his roasted sea bass, or *bar*, was cooked to the millisecond of perfection, with a faint whiff of Pernod and branches of wild fennel.

LES FONTAINES
9 Rue Soufflot, Paris 5.
Tel: 43.26.42.80.
Métro: Luxembourg.
Reservations, noon to 3 P.M.
and 7:30 to 10 P.M.
Closed Sunday and August.
Credit card: V.
A la carte, 150 to 180
francs.

SPECIALTIES:
Bistro: céleri rémoulade (celeriac
in creamy dressing), salade des
endives au bleu (Belgian endive
salad with blue cheese), coquilles
Saint-Jacques à la provençale
(sautéed scallops with tomatoes
and garlic), raie aux câpres
(skate with capers in butter
sauce), poulet à la crème (sautéed
chicken with cream), gibier
(game; in fall and winter), tarte
Tatin tiède (warm upside-down
apple tart).

If one ever doubted that there was still good food to be had in simple Paris neighborhood cafés, then one hasn't tried Les Fontaines, really a café on the outside but a restaurant on the inside.

Nothing about its decor would make you suspect Les Fontaines is anything more than a spot to play pinball or grab a glass of wine and a *croque monsieur* in the middle of the day. But don't let the paper tablecloths confuse you. Owner Roger Lacipière, a native of France's rugged Auvergne, is a specialist in meat and game, and if you're in the mood for hearty salads of endive and blue cheese, giant and beautifully aged steaks, and fruity Chinon, then this is the spot. The clientele is very Left Bank intellectual: everyone looks studious or professorish, and you'll often see men and women dining alone, with their obligatory newspaper, *Le Monde*, to keep them company.

LE BISTROT D'HENRI

16 Rue Princesse, Paris 6.
Tel: 46.33.51.12.
Métro: Mabillon.
Reservations, noon to 2:30
  P.M. and 7 to 10:30 P.M.
Closed Sunday and Monday
  at lunch.
No credit cards.
Universal 160-franc menu.

SPECIALTIES:
Bistro: salade de haricots verts
frais (fresh green bean salad),
poivrons grillés (grilled red
peppers), mozzarella tomates
(mozzarella and tomatoes), poulet
fermier au vinaigre (chicken in
vinegar sauce), gigot rôti au four
(roast leg of lamb), gratin
dauphinois (creamy potato
gratin).

The popular and well-populated Left Bank is not known for restaurants offering great *"qualité-prix,"* and Le Bistrot d'Henri is a welcome exception. This is a tried and true spot, where the welcome is warm, the quality unchanging, the price always right. With its bare wooden tables, black and white checkered floors, and French doors that open onto the Rue Princesse, Le Bistrot d'Henri has a rather modern, no-frills air. Yet the quality of the food is way above average, with refreshingly simple salads of green beans or grilled red peppers, rare-cooked top-quality beef, meltingly tender and fragrant slices of leg of lamb, and healthy portions of potato gratin offered with each and every main course. Desserts are traditional—*crème caramel* and chocolate mousse—and the wine list offers some respectable choices, including Pierre Ferrand's energizing Chinon, Château Le Ligré.

BRASSERIE LIPP

151 Boulevard Saint-
  Germain, Paris 6.
Tel: 45.48.53.91.
Fax: 45.44.33.20.
Métro: Saint-Germain-des-
  Prés.
Open daily, 8 to 2 A.M.
  Continuous restaurant
  service noon to 1 A.M.
  Reservations accepted.
Credit cards: AE, DC, V.
Enclosed terrace for light
  snacks.
Air-conditioned.
A la carte, 270 to 320
  francs.

SPECIALTIES:
Brasserie: plats du jour
(changing daily specials),
choucroute garnie (sausages, pork,
and sauerkraut), cassoulet maison
(casserole of meat, sausage and
white beans), blanquette de veau
(veal stew with vegetables), gigot
d'agneau (roast leg of lamb).

The menu tells you in English, big and bold, NO SALAD AS A MEAL. That should tip you off to the fact that many a diner has come here, appetite-less, looking for a touch of history and a dose of nostalgia. Lipp has been a Parisian institution since 1900, and today its bright lights, colorful tiles, and big-city bustle make it as appealing as ever. So, do go, bring your hunger with you, and unless you're a Parisian star or are a bonafide regular, expect to be sent to the upstairs dining room (the main floor is the choice "see and be seen" spot). But upstairs is not such a bad place after all, for the waiters are jovial and thoroughly professional (they've seen everything, I'm sure), the food varies from mediocre to hit-the-spot delicious, and if you're counting *centimes* you can have a decent meal for not too much money. My most recent dinner included a rather overcooked and underseasoned serving of fresh artichoke bottoms, perfectly rosy portions of cold leg of lamb (*gigot rôti froid*) served with a tossed green salad in a huge white bowl, and a state-of-the-art *crème caramel*. The wine list is brief, but offers some wise choices, including a deliciously tannic Bordeaux, Ramage La Batisse. A good spot to know on days when everything else in Paris is closed.

LAPIN A LA MOUTARDE
RABBIT WITH MUSTARD

Rabbit with mustard sauce is a classic bistro dish, and a year-round favorite. Traditionally, lapin à la moutarde *is served with rice, but I love it with fresh homemade pasta, which absorbs the wonderfully delicious sauce. Do use top-quality French whole-grain mustard; fresh, not frozen, rabbit; and a solid, full-bodied white wine. An Alsatian Riesling is an excellent wine for this dish, but I've also prepared it with Gewürztraminer, as well as with a white Hermitage. You can also experiment by adding various herbs to the sauce just before serving: Fresh rosemary, summer savory, or thyme would be lovely. If you can't find fresh rabbit, chicken makes an excellent substitute.*

⅓ cup (80 ml) peanut oil

1 tablespoon (½ oz; 15 g) unsalted butter

1 fresh rabbit (or chicken), 2½ to 3 pounds (1.25 to 1.5 kg), cut into serving pieces

½ cup (125 ml) whole-grain mustard

3 cups (750 ml) dry white wine

1 cup (250 ml) *crème fraîche* (see recipe, page 279) or sour cream

Salt to taste

1 small handful minced fresh parsley

1. Preheat the oven to 350°F (175°C).

2. In a Dutch oven or large ovenproof skillet, heat the oil and butter over medium-high heat. When hot, quickly brown the rabbit. Do not crowd the pan, and turn the pieces, making sure that each is thoroughly browned. Discard the excess oil.

3. Brush the rabbit pieces evenly with mustard, reserving 3 tablespoons for the sauce. Place the rabbit in the oven, covered, and bake for 20 minutes. Pour the wine over the rabbit, making sure all pieces are moistened, and continue cooking, covered, another 25 minutes.

4. Remove from the oven, and reserving the cooking liquid, place the rabbit pieces on an ovenproof dish. Lower the oven heat to 200°F (90°C). Cover the rabbit with foil and keep warm in the very low oven.

5. Prepare the sauce: Over high heat reduce the reserved cooking liquid by half. This should take 8 to 10 minutes. Whisk in the *crème fraîche* or sour cream, the reserved mustard, and salt. Reduce the heat and continue cooking for 3 to 4 minutes.

6. To serve, arrange the rabbit pieces on a platter, and cover with the sauce. (Or fill a platter with fresh cooked pasta, toss with the sauce, and arrange the rabbit pieces on top of the pasta.) Sprinkle with the minced parsley.

Yield: 4 to 6 servings

LE MACHON D'HENRI

8 Rue Guisarde, Paris 6.
Tel: 43.29.08.70.
Métro: Mabillon.
Reservations, noon to 2:30
P.M. and 7 to 11:30 P.M.
Closed Sunday dinner.
No credit cards.
A la carte, 150 francs.

SPECIALTIES:
Bistro: salade de haricots verts
frais (fresh green bean salad),
mozzarella tomates (mozzarella
and tomatoes), confit de lapin
aux gratin dauphinois (preserved
rabbit with creamy potato
gratin), tarte au citron (lemon
tart), gâteau au chocolat
(chocolate cake).

No bigger than a postage stamp, this crowded, lively, Left Bank bistro is a sea of gastronomic happiness amid rows of stale tourist traps. It's hard not to have a good time here, where young waiters animate the dining room, flirting with the ladies, joking with the men, single-handedly keeping diners joyful and well fed. The fare is quintessential bistro, and you shouldn't go wrong with the fresh green bean salad, daily specials of lamb or beef, a great chocolate cake, memorable chocolate mousse, and a decent lemon tart.

CHEZ MAITRE PAUL

12 Rue Monsieur-le-Prince,
Paris 6.
Tel: 43.54.74.79.
Métro: Odéon or
Luxembourg.
Reservations, 12:15 to 2:30
P.M. and 7 to 10:30 P.M.
Closed Saturday lunch and
Sunday.
Credit cards: AE, DC, V.
Private dining room for 20.
180-franc menu, including
wine. A la carte, 180 to
200 francs.

SPECIALTIES:
Cuisine of the Jura and Franche-
Comté: saucisse de Montbéliard
chaude, pommes à l'huile (warm,
cumin-flecked sausage and
potatoes bathed in vinegar and
oil), poulet au vin jaune (chicken
in sherry-like white wine), foie de
veau au vin de paille (calf's liver
in sweet white wine), poulette à
la crème gratinée (grilled,
gratinéed chicken).

"*Changement de Propriétaire*," a sign that gives pause. I winced when I heard that Chez Maître Paul's longtime owners, Monsieur et Madame Gaugain, were giving up their tiny, cottage-like restaurant on Rue Monsieur-le-Prince. For years, it had been a totally reliable place to go when hunger struck and you were in the mood for cumin-flecked *saucisse de Montbéliard chaude*, a soothing *poulette à la gratinée*, a glass of light yet solid and fruity red *vin d'Arbois*.

Well, despite the "*changement*" and a totally new decor, Chez Maître Paul remains faithful to its Franc-Comtoises origins. The new *patron*, Jean-François Debert, seems to be making an effort to change little else.

He's enlarged and modernized what was once a minuscule, old-fashioned dining room, but has retained the charming upstairs salon for private affairs. He's also added a list of daily specials that might include a traditional (but pleasing) salad of *mâche* and *betteraves* (beets), or another of escarole, cheese, and walnuts. He's also retained the kitchen as well as dining room staff.

The best dish here is still the *poulette à la crème gratinée* (see recipe, page 64), chicken that's roasted, then gratinéed with a touch of cream and Comté, so the skin is embellished with a thick, rich, golden crust. The *poulet au vin jaune* (with cream and the Jura's local sweet wine) and *poulet au vin blanc d'Arbois* remain as modest examples of simple home cooking. (My only complaint here is that the food has a tendency to come off as bland, from a simple lack of basic seasoning. To succeed in the kitchen, salt and pepper are as essential as top-quality ingredients.)

Aside from the regional specialties, one can always be assured of fresh, briny oysters, and simple but satisfying *filet de turbot, sauce mousseline*. The wine list is limited, but offers diners a chance to try the unjustly little-known wines of the Jura.

MOISSONNIER
28 Rue des Fossés-Saint-
    Bernard, Paris 5.
Tel: 43.29.87.65.
Métro: Jussieu or Cardinal-
    Lemoine.
Reservations, noon to
    2 P.M. and 7 to 10 P.M.
Closed Sunday dinner,
    Monday, and August.
Credit card: V.
A la carte, 220 to 280
    francs.

S P E C I A L T I E S :
Cuisine lyonnaise and Franc-
Comtoise: les saladiers lyonnais
(varied assortment of meat and
vegetable salads), boudin
campagnard aux pommes fruits
(blood sausage with apples), carré
d'agneau rôti persillé, pour deux
personnes (roast rack of lamb,
for two).

Who doesn't love abundance? Especially when the abundance has to do with food with a Lyonnais flavor. I'm speaking, in short, about the tradition known as *"les saladiers lyonnais,"* the procession of huge terra cotta bowls that all but march to your table, bowls filled with wonderfully gelatinous *pieds de veau* (calf's foot), crunchy *grattons* (cracklings), soothing *filets de hareng* (herring filets), or hearty chunks of *cervelas* pork sausage. Then maybe some tart red cabbage, a spoonful of soft red beans, a serving of well-seasoned lentils, or thin slices of *museau de boeuf* (beef muzzle) in vinaigrette. If that's not enough, head for the potatoes bathed in oil, or a green salad tossed with beef. And don't forget to save room for a sparkling, fresh salad of escarole, julienned strips of ham, and slices of apples, (see recipe, page 63) or a simple duet of escarole and beef.

You'll find all this and more at Moissonnier, now well into its thirtieth year as one of Paris' more generous, family restaurants. A no-frills, two-story affair, this is the sort of place I love to go with a large group of friends for a joyous evening of good food and good times.

Monsieur and Madame Louis Moissonnier came north to Paris from the Lyons area some decades ago, when wine merchants still inhabited the edge of the 5th arrondissment along the Rue des Fossés-Saint-Bernard. The Moissonnier menu, with a dual accent of the Jura and the Lyonnais, has changed imperceptibly over the years. There are always salads of crunchy escarole tossed with slivers of nutty Comté from the Jura (see recipe, below), mackerel marinated in white wine, the standard *frisée aux lardons*, and *breuzi*, the air-dried beef of the Franche-Comté.

Main courses are equally pantagruelian, with one of the best versions of *petit salé aux lentilles* I've sampled in years, with huge chunks of well-trimmed pork, meaning you're getting plenty of meat and not all gristle. On a most recent visit, the *carré d'agneau* (for two) was slightly fatty but still won me over with its moistness and flavor, and the good variety of daily specials—such as the *civet de lapin aux pâtes fraîches*—means that you can visit often without being bored by an unchanging menu.

SALADE VERTE AU COMTE MOISSONNIER
MOISSONNIER'S TOSSED GREEN SALAD WITH GRUYERE

This is one of those make it or break it recipes: If you can secure the freshest and crispiest escarole and top-quality, well-aged Gruyère cheese from France or from Switzerland, you've got it made. It's a thoroughly satisfying Saturday afternoon salad, a winter pick-me-up. This is one of the many salads served at the fine, old-fashioned Restaurant Moissonnier: Chef-owner Louis Moissonnier prepares it with a fine Comté cheese from the Jura, and serves it with a slightly chilled Beaujolais, preferably a light Regnié.

2 tablespoons best-quality red wine vinegar
Salt
½ cup (12.5 cl) peanut oil
Freshly ground black pepper
1 head escarole, rinsed, dried, and torn into bite-size pieces
7 ounces (200 g) imported Comté or Gruyère cheese
Small handful of fresh flat-leaf parsley leaves
Small handful of fresh chives, minced

In a large salad bowl, whisk together the vinegar and salt. Whisk in the oil, then season to taste with the pepper. Add the escarole. Remove the rind from the cheese and cut into matchstick-size pieces. Sprinkle the cheese, parsley, and chives on top of the greens. Toss to coat thoroughly and evenly with the vinaigrette. Season with additional salt and pepper, if desired. Serve.

Yield: 4 servings

SCAROLE A LA JULIENNE DE JAMBON ET AUX POMMES
ESCAROLE SALAD WITH HAM AND APPLES

The first time I saw this salad at the homey Left Bank restaurant, Moissonnier (see entry, page 61), I assumed it was a typical—and ever-pleasing—salade mixte, or greens tossed with strips of ham and cheese. My eyes were fooled, for my palate told me otherwise—what I assumed was cheese turned out to be apples. I like the combination because the slight acidity of the apples cuts the fattiness of the ham, making for a fine and filling first-course salad. Use the best-quality ham you can find, preferably a thick slice from a freshly cooked, unsmoked country ham. Serve with an equally acidic wine, such as a Beaujolais.

2 tablespoons best-quality red wine vinegar
Salt
½ cup (12.5 cl) peanut oil
Freshly ground black pepper to taste
1 head escarole, rinsed, dried, and torn into bite-size pieces
¼ pound (250 g) thickly sliced unsmoked cooked ham, cut into matchstick-size pieces
2 Golden Delicious apples, peeled, cored, and cut into matchstick-size pieces
Small handful of fresh chives, minced

In a large salad bowl, whisk together the vinegar and salt. Add the oil and season to taste with pepper. Add the escarole. Sprinkle the ham, apples, and chives on top of the greens. Toss to coat thoroughly and evenly with the vinaigrette. Season with additional salt and pepper, if desired. Serve.

Yield: 4 servings

Reciting the day's specials.

POULETTE A LA CREME GRATINEE CHEZ MAITRE PAUL
CHEZ MAITRE PAUL'S BROILED GRATINEED CHICKEN

This is the dish I order whenever I dine at Chez Maître Paul (see entry, page 60), a small, newly refurbished Left Bank restaurant that specializes in the foods of the Jura. This dish combines many of the region's specialities, including free-range chicken, fresh cream, and the nutty cow's milk cheese known as Comté. Serve this with plenty of boiled rice and a fruity red wine.

1 free-range roasting
  chicken, (about 3
  pounds; 1.25 kg),
  well-rinsed and
  patted dry
½ cup freshly squeezed
  lemon juice
3 tablespoons peanut oil
2 pounds (1 kg) mush-
  rooms, rinsed,
  trimmed, and
  patted dry
Salt
2 tablespoons (1 ounce;
  30 g) unsalted butter,
  at room temperature
2 tablespoons superfine
  flour, such as
  Wondra
2 cups (50 cl) hot
  chicken stock
1 cup (25 cl) *crème fraîche*
  (see Recipe Index
  page 279) or heavy
  (whipping) cream
Freshly ground black
  pepper to taste
freshly grated nutmeg to
  taste
2 cups (about 5 ounces;
  160 g) freshly grated
  imported Comté or
  Gruyère cheese

1. Prepare the chicken: Place the chicken on a work surface, breast side down. With poultry shears or a sharp knife, split the bird lengthwise along one side of the backbone. Open it flat and press it down with the heel of your hand to flatten completely. With a sharp knife, make slits in the skin near the tail and tuck the wing tips in to secure. The bird should be as flat as possible to ensure even cooking.

2. Place the chicken in a roasting pan and add 5 table-spoons of the lemon juice and the oil. Marinate at room temperature for 10 minutes, turning the chicken once or twice.

3. Meanwhile, thinly slice the mushrooms. In a large saucepan, combine the mushrooms, the remaining 3 tablespoons lemon juice, a pinch of salt, and water to cover. Cover and cook over medium heat until the mushrooms are tender and most of the liquid has been absorbed, about 25 minutes. Set aside and keep warm.

4. In a medium-size, non-aluminum saucepan, melt the butter over low heat. Add the flour and cook gen-tly, whisking constantly, until the mixture separates slightly and takes on a granular look, 2 to 3 minutes. Do not let the mixture brown. Whisking constantly, add the chicken stock all at once, whisking to blend the mixture smoothly. Increase the heat to medium and, whisking steadily, bring the mixture to a boil. When the sauce boils, reduce the heat to low and sim-mer gently, whisking occasionally, until the stock reduces to a scant cup, about 40 minutes. Remove from the heat and let cool slightly. Stir in the *crème fraîche*. Season with salt, pepper, and nutmeg to taste. (The sauce may be prepared up to 1 hour in advance. Keep warm in the top of a covered double boiler, over simmering water.)

5. Preheat the broiler for 15 minutes.

6. Remove the chicken from the marinade and season generously with salt and pepper. Broil the chicken 5 inches (13 cm) from the heat, breast side up for about 10 minutes. Baste occasionally with the marinade so

the skin gets browned. Using tongs so you do not pierce the meat, turn the chicken over and broil, basting occasionally, about 15 minutes more. The chicken is done when the juices run clear when the thighs are pierced with a skewer. Season again with salt and pepper. Quarter the chicken and set aside.

7. Reheat the oven heat to 475°F (245°C).

8. In a shallow baking dish just slightly larger than the chicken, spread the mushrooms and their liquid in an even layer. Place the quartered chicken on top of the mushrooms and pour the cream sauce over all. Sprinkle with the grated cheese. Place in the center of the oven and bake until the cheese has melted and is lightly browned, about 15 minutes. Serve immediately, from the baking dish, with white or brown rice alongside.

Yield: 4 to 6 servings

**MOULIN A VENT,
CHEZ HENRY**
20 Rue des Fossés Saint-
   Bernard, Paris 5.
Tel: 43.54.99.37.
Métro: Jussieu.
Reservations, 12:30 to 2 P.M.
   and 7:30 to 10:15 P.M.
Closed Sunday, Monday,
   holidays, and August.
Credit card: V.
Sidewalk terrace.
A la carte, 200 to 280
   francs.

S P E C I A L T I E S :
*Bistro: Les cochonnailles au poids
(varied sausages, sold by weight),
boeuf à la ficelle (boiled fillet of
beef on a string), le riz au lait
(rice pudding).*

Loud, busy, old-fashioned, and purely Parisian, this decades-old bistro is the place to go with a crowd when you're in the mood for red meat and Beaujolais. Chez Henry is pure bistro, with a barely legible menu in purple ink, a jovial *patron*, sausages hanging from the ceiling. This is one spot that offers authentic *boeuf à la ficelle*, top quality fillet of beef that's tied tightly with a string, then cooked quickly in boiling water. The boiling technique seals the outside of the meat, making for a beef that's perfectly rare and without a trace of fat. (Don't be turned off by the unappetizing gray appearance of the meat—the inside will be gloriously red and delicious.) Other dishes worth trying—if they're on the menu that day—include a refreshing salad of mushrooms and green beans, another of perfectly cooked and thinly sliced artichoke bottoms, and a classic *sole meunière*. The *magret de canard*, or breast of fattened duck, was dreadfully dry and tough. Stay away on a hot day: The ventilation is almost nonexistent.

THAT PARISIAN PALLOR

"City dwellers of long standing and newly arrived rustics were widely different in appearance and manners. The former were large and plump, pink and white, their complexion unspoilt by work in the fields, and their physical ideal was the round-bellied bulk of the self-made bourgeois, accustomed to good food and unwearied by manual labor. The *patronnes* of inns and brothels were always fresh and pale, real Parisians who neither knew nor liked the sun, which scarcely penetrated the narrow streets of the old *quartiers.*"

The People of Paris, An Essay in Popular Culture in the 18th Century, by Daniel Roche

PERRAUDIN
157 Rue Saint-Jacques,
Paris 5.
Tel: 46.33.15.75.
Métro: Luxembourg.
Reservations, noon to 2:30
P.M. and 7:30 to 10:30 P.M.
Closed Saturday and
Monday lunch, Sunday,
and last two weeks of
August. First two weeks
in August, open for
dinner only.
No credit cards.
Courtyard dining.
59-franc lunch menu. A la
carte, about 150 francs.

SPECIALTIES:
Country bistro: oeufs cocotte à la
crème et au bacon (eggs with
cream and bacon), gigot d'agneau
au gratin dauphinois (roast leg of
lamb with potato gratin), tarte
Tatin (upside-down apple tart),
vin au verre (wine by the glass).

One of the best-buy bistros of the Latin Quarter, this traditional student hangout—with red and white checkered cloths, worn Art Deco tile floors, and motherly waitresses—is the place to come for hearty, no-frills fare. The soup here is honest, the *plats du jour* homey, and I doubt that anyone ever left hungry. I love the *estouffade de boeuf* (a well-seasoned beef stew, marinated in wine and topped with a few complimentary olives), the fine potato gratin served with thick slices of lamb, and the filling lentils with salt pork. The *tarte Tatin* is just okay (with that decayed sort of crust you find in so many cheap bistros). But, this is one of the last spots you'll find the old-fashioned fil-tered coffee, served in tiny individual metal filters set atop your coffee cup.

A staff luncheon at Chez Maître
Paul (see entry, page 60).

CHEZ RENE
14 Boulevard Saint-
    Germain, 75005 Paris 5.
Tel: 43.54.30.23.
Métro: Maubert-Mutualité.
Reservations, 12:15 to
    2:30 P.M. and 7:45 to
    10:30 P.M.
Closed Saturday, Sunday,
    August, and two weeks
    at Christmas.
Credit card: V.
A la carte, 200 francs.

SPECIALTIES:

*Bistro: plats du jour (changing
daily specials), saucisson chaud
(warm poached pork sausage),
salade de boeuf (cold beef salad
tossed with tomatoes, potatoes,
and cornichons), andouillette au
pouilly (tripe sausage poached in
white wine) coq au vin (chicken
in red wine), poulet rôti (roast
chicken), boeuf bourguignon (beef
stewed in red wine, onions,
mushrooms, and bacon), plateau
de fromages (varied cheese
platter).*

Split-second impressions are so important. The last time I walked into Chez René—a quintessentially Parisian Left Bank bistro—my eyes instantly focused on a trio of diners devouring selections from the restaurant's triple platter of cheeses. So, it was decided. At least I knew from the beginning how my dinner would end.

On the right day, in the right mood, Chez René can be a cheery breath of Beaujolais country air right at the end of the Boulevard Saint-Germain. It's the sort of place where the food is plain but not banal, and though the menu may be familiar, it still holds the ability to surprise. Don't come here for garnishes of chervil or *sel fin de Guèrande*, fussy presentations, or the wine of the century. Go with an eye toward tradition, and you're sure to have a good time.

It was Tuesday, so I chose the *plat du jour* that's been a specialty here for more than 35 years, *haricot de mouton*, mutton with white beans (see recipe, page 68). The seasoning might have been a touch more assertive, but portions were copious, the hearty chunks of meat were properly falling off the bone, and the platter of white beans assuaged a certain hunger for something substantial.

To begin, try perhaps a platter of plump white asparagus, or the satisfying *gratin de blettes*, or Swiss chard gratin, a frankly old-fashioned dish that still has modern appeal. A good warm-weather main course is the *salade de boeuf*, a mixture of tomatoes, potatoes, *cornichons*, and big chunks of beef tossed with a mustardy vinaigrette.

The house Beaujolais is more than drinkable, and I highly recommend the cheese tray, particularly the vast selection of goat cheeses from the Beaujolais, offered in multiple stages of *affinage*, from the fresh, white and moist, to the firm, blue-gray and tangy.

HARICOT DE MOUTON CHEZ RENE
CHEZ RENE'S MUTTON WITH WHITE BEANS

This is a regular plat du jour—daily special—at the popular Left Bank bistro, Chez René (see entry, page 67). Haricot de mouton is a classic bistro dish, and one that French women prepare often at home, usually with either lamb or mutton shoulder. I prefer it with big, hearty chunks of lamb and lots and lots of white beans. If you have fresh herbs around, all the better.

Lamb or mutton:

3 tablespons (1 ½ oz; 45 g) unsalted butter

3 tablespoons olive oil

3½ pounds (approximately 1.75 kg) lamb or mutton shoulder, cut into 2-inch (5-cm) chunks (a butcher can do this for you)

⅓ cup (45 g) unbleached all-purpose flour

1 cup (250 ml) dry white wine

3 cups (750 ml) water

2 fresh tomatoes, cubed

4 carrots, peeled and cut into 1-inch (2.5 cm) rounds

2 medium onions, halved

2 teaspoons fresh thyme, or 1 teaspoon dried

3 bay leaves

3 tablespoons chopped fresh parsley

4 whole cloves

Salt and freshly ground black pepper to taste

Beans:

1 pound (500 g) dried white beans

2 bay leaves

6 whole cloves

2 teaspoons dried thyme

Salt

1. In a deep 12-inch skillet, heat the butter and oil over medium-high heat. When hot, begin browning the lamb. You may want to do this in batches. Do not crowd the pan, and be sure that each piece is thoroughly browned before turning.

2. When all the lamb is browned, sprinkle with the flour and mix well. Leaving the lamb in the skillet, add the white wine, then the 3 cups of water, and deglaze the pan, scraping up any browned bits. Add the tomatoes, vegetables, herbs, and spices, and cook, covered, over medium heat for about 1 hour and 15 minutes. Season to taste with salt and pepper.

3. While the lamb is cooking, prepare the beans. Rinse them well, put them in a large saucepan, and cover with cold water. Over high heat, bring to a boil. Once boiling, remove the pan from the heat, leave covered, and let rest for 40 minutes.

4. Drain the beans, discarding the cooking liquid (to help make the beans more digestible). Rinse the beans and cover again with cold water. Add the bay leaves, cloves, and thyme, and bring to a boil over medium heat. Cook, covered, over medium heat for about 40 minutes. The beans should be cooked through but still firm. Add salt to taste.

5. To serve, check the lamb and beans for seasoning, then arrange meat on a platter, surrounded by the white beans.

Yield: 6 servings

LA ROTISSERIE D'EN FACE
2 Rue Christine, Paris 6.
Tel: 43.26.40.98.
Métro: Saint-Michel or
Odéon.
Reservations, 12:30 to
2 P.M. and 7 to 10 P.M.
Closed Saturday lunch and
all day Sunday.
Credit card: V.
Universal 175-franc menu.

SPECIALTIES:
*Bistro: viandes grillées et rôties
(grilled and spit-roasted meats
and poultry), tarte alsacienne
tiède aux pommes (warm
Alsatian apple tart), pain
maison (homemade bread).*

With his Rôtisserie d'en Face, Jacques Cagna has attracted a youthful Paris-Paris Left Bank crowd with his single, 175-franc *prix-fixe* menu at lunch and dinner. Everything from roast chicken to saddle of lamb can be ordered from the grill, while starters change daily, ranging from smoked salmon to cubed, parsleyed ham, or *jambon persillé.* The cooking here has been rather inconsistent (astonishingly good one day, underwhelming the next), and Cagna has yet to establish a personality or signature dish. Some best bets include the grilled chicken with crispy potatoes fried in their skins, his terrific multi-grain bread (homemade), and Jean-Marsanne's red Saint-Joseph.

LA TABLE DE FES
5 Rue Saint-Beuve, Paris 6.
Tel: 45.48.07.22.
Métro: Notre-Dame-des-
Champs.
Open for dinner only.
Reservations 8 P.M. to
midnight.
Closed Sunday and the last
three weeks in August.
Credit card: V.
Private dining room for 30.
A la carte, 200 to 250
francs.

SPECIALTIES:
*Moroccan: couscous, pastilla des
fès (savory pigeon pastry), tajine
de mouton aux pruneaux (mutton
stew with prunes), poulet citron
(chicken with preserved lemon),
desserts maison (homemade
desserts).*

Couscous—which is both the tiny grain of semolina and the national dish of Morocco, prepared in numerous variations—has become an almost integral element in modern French cooking: You'll find couscous salads in the *charcuteries*, in supermarkets, and on the menu at many a corner café.

When I'm in a casual mood and hungry for couscous, I reserve a table at La Tables des Fès, the brightly lit and lively Moroccan dining room near Montparnasse. I like to go with a group, so we can sample a wide variety of highly flavored dishes. The *merguez* is super-spicy, and the *tajines* are moist and filling. Try either the chicken with pickled lemons, or chicken with plump, moist prunes. And it's impossible not to take "seconds" of the fine, delicate, hand-rolled couscous, which is served in traditional fashion, mounded on a large, round, clay platter. With the couscous comes the delicious broth, which contains chickpeas and raisins, and with it, as much fiery *harissa,* red pepper sauce, as your palate will endure. Formerly known as Aissa Fils, this popular restaurant—which really doesn't get going until about 10:30 at night—is lively, crowded, and noisy, with everyone getting just a bit more vocal on the heady Moroccan red wine.

LET THEM EAT PEAS

"Eat peas with the rich and cherries with the poor" is an old French saying. The rich were able to afford the best crop of peas, the very earliest. The finest cherries of the season, however, are the last: They are usually the ripest and most flavorful, also the cheapest and most plentiful. During the seventeenth century, the French became impassioned over the fashionable pea: At court, women would dine with the king, feasting on peas, then return home to eat more before going to bed, even if it meant indigestion. "It is a fashion, a furor," wrote one court chronicler.

LA TIMONERIE
35 Quai de la Tournelle,
    Paris 5.
Tel: 43.25.44.42.
Métro: Maubert-Mutualité.
Reservations, noon to 2 P.M.
    and 7:30 to 10:15 P.M.
Closed Sunday and Monday.
Credit cards: MC, V.
Air-conditioned.
195-franc menu. A la carte,
    350 to 450 francs.

S P E C I A L T I E S :

Modern: petatou poitevin servie avec une crème de ciboulette (fresh goat cheese and potato tart), foie gras chaud sur pommes de terre séchée au four, vinaigrettes et échalotes (warm fatted duck liver on a bed of potatoes, with vinaigrette and shallots), épaule d'agneau au lait et son rôti de pain à l'ail confit (milk-fed lamb shoulder with garlic bread), tarte aux pommes chaudes (warm apple tart), tarte fine au chocolat (chocolate tart).

Parmentier. Pipérade. Tian. Words that by their very existence can cause us to salivate. All on their own, they warm our gastronomic hearts. It's funny how those code words, when they appear on a menu, put us in a hungry, receptive mood. That's the way I feel when dining at La Timonerie, a thoroughly charming little restaurant on the Quai de la Tournelle.

Chef Philippe de Givenchy gives us the rustic and the modern all on one plate, satisfying our desire for succulent strips of braised veal breast, golden gratins of macaroni, stuffed cabbage, and oxtail. But he does it all with a very modern accent, with a *parmentier* of crab, a *pipérade* of *mussels*, a *tian* of *codfish.* The delicious strips of veal breast arrive off the bone, arranged almost like a haystack, accompanied by a deliciously gratined macaroni. The gratin had been tossed with a blend of tomatoes and olives, lightening and heightening what can be a bland and heavy dish.

Equally inventive are his little bundles of green asparagus. Tied at the bottom with thin strips of chicken skin, they were pan-fried just until crisp-tender, and served with the delicious pan juices. It's the kind of dish that makes you say, "Of course, why didn't I think of that."

I loved as well his *petatou Poitevin*, a tartlet of fresh goat cheese and thinly sliced potatoes, served with a refreshing salad of *pourpier* (purslane) and fresh chervil. In short, it's food that's clean, crisp, and distinctly modern.

For dessert, sample the light and refreshing *soupe d'oranges*, sprinkled with bits of basil, or the fine duo of tarts—one chocolate, one vanilla.

I do have a few complaints about La Timonerie: Most food lacks even the most basic seasoning (how about just a touch of salt, a spray of herbs?); warm dishes are served on cold plates; and the pastries are not properly prebaked and thus come off pale and undercooked. But in the end, de Givenchy's decor is as sweetly seductive and as calming as his food. With waxed terra-cotta tiles on the floors, rough wooden boards on the walls, a bright spray of pastel flowers, the effect is almost English country. It's a decor obviously done on a budget and in truth, it's a relief from the onslaught of self-consciously "decorator decorated" restaurants now à la mode.

An every day affair.

VIVARIO
6 Rue Cochin, Paris 5.
Tel: 43.25.08.19.
Métro: Maubert-Mutualité.
Reservations, noon to 2 P.M. and 7 to 10 P.M.
Closed Saturday and Monday lunch, Sunday, and mid-August to mid-September.
Credit cards: AE, V.
Private dining room for 12 to 40.
A la carte, 200 to 220 francs.

Like a breath of refreshing Mediterranean air, Vivario is a small, bustling, relaxed Corsican bistro-trattoria specializing in the simple, rustic cuisine of Corsica and Sicily. Everything I've sampled here comes across with a real sense of authenticity: That is, flavors are dense and fully developed, and the kitchen seems to let ingredients speak for themselves. For starters, try the *aubergines à la sicilienne*, slices of fried eggplant layered with a bit of rich tomato sauce and a touch of cheese; or the *moules à la sicilienne*, huge bowls of steamed mussels topped with that same rich tomato sauce.

There are always one or two pasta dishes on the menu (the rigatoni sauced with pancetta, tomatoes and cheese is good), and main courses include a fine leg of lamb served with white beans; poached sausages and white beans; and cabri rôti, or roasted goat. For dessert, order the refreshing *orange vénitienne*, whole peeled oranges poached in a light syrup and topped with orange zest. The Corsican house red is heady, the good *baguettes* come from Boulangerie Beauvallet down the street, the fat gray cat's name is Ravioli, and in the summertime, one can't go wrong by reserving a table on the small sidewalk terrace of the quiet residential street.

GRATIN DE MACARONI PROVENÇAL LA TIMONERIE
LA TIMONERIE'S PROVENÇAL MACARONI GRATIN

I could make a meal of this warming macaroni gratin laced with tomatoes, black olives, and herbs, and topped with Parmesan. The recipe comes from Philippe de Givenchy, chef at the small Left Bank restaurant, La Timonerie. There, the gratin is served as an accompaniment to a tender veal stew, but it could also serve as a side dish to roast chicken, baked fish, or as a main luncheon dish with a tossed salad. For this dish, use a good-quality imported pasta, such as ziti, penne, or rigatoni.

10 ounces (300 g) short
   imported tubular
   pasta
Sea salt
1½ cups (175 g) brine-
   cured imported black
   olives, such as
   Niçoise, pitted and
   chopped
5 medium tomatoes,
   cored, peeled, seeded
   and chopped
2 teaspoons fresh thyme
   leaves
¼ cup (6 cl) extra-virgin
   olive oil
½ cup (about 2 ounces;
   50 g) freshly grated
   imported Parmesan
   cheese

1. Preheat the oven to 400°F (200°C).

2. Bring 3 quarts (3 liters) of water to a rolling boil. Salt the water, add the macaroni, and cook just until tender, about 10 minutes. Drain well and transfer to a large bowl. Toss with the olives, tomato, thyme, and olive oil. Transfer to a baking dish (about 9 × 13 × 2-inches; 23 × 33 × 5-cm). Sprinkle with the Parmesan cheese. Bake until warmed through and browned on top, about 10 minutes. Serve immediately.

Yield: 4 to 6 servings

TENDRONS DE VEAU AU MACARONI PROVENÇAL LA TIMONERIE

LA TIMONERIE'S BRAISED VEAL WITH PROVENÇAL MACARONI

An updated version of an old bistro classic, this is La Timonerie (see entry page 70) chef Philippe de Givenchy's recipe for braised veal, which he serves with a lively, Provençal gratin of macaroni. It's the sort of dish I love to prepare on a cool day, making the house fragrant and warm. In France, the dish is prepared with tendrons, *the cartilaginous rib-like portion of the breast of veal. But one could use any good cut of stewing veal, including the breast, short ribs, veal shoulder and shoulder chops, and the heel of round or shank. Serve this with the Provençal Macaroni on the facing page.*

2 tablespoons (1 ounce; 30 g) unsalted butter

2 tablespoons extra-virgin olive oil

2 pounds (1 kg) breast of veal, bone in (ask your butcher to cut across the lower breast portion to make several strips of equal width)

Sea salt and freshly ground black pepper to taste

2 onions, coarsely chopped

1 imported bay leaf

1 large sprig of fresh thyme, or 2 teaspoons dried

4 medium tomatoes, coarsely chopped

2 tablespoons (1 ounce; 30 g) unsalted butter, cut in pieces and chilled

1. In a large, deep-sided 12-inch (30-cm) skillet, heat the butter and oil over medium-high heat. When hot, brown the veal in batches, about 5 minutes per side. Be patient when browning: To retain all of its flavor, the veal should be thoroughly browned. Carefully regulate the heat to avoid scorching the meat. As each batch is browned, remove the veal to a platter and season generously with salt and pepper.

2. When all of the veal is browned, discard the fat in the skillet. Return all of the meat, and any cooking juices that have collected on the platter, to the pan and add 1 quart (1 liter) water, along with the onions, bay leaf, thyme, and tomatoes. Cover and simmer over low heat until the meat is very tender, about 1 hour. Keep an eye on the pan, making sure the liquid remains at a quiet, gentle simmer.

3. When the veal is cooked, transfer to a warmed platter and season generously with salt and pepper. Cover with foil and keep warm. Strain the cooking liquid through a fine-mesh sieve, discarding the vegetables. Return the sauce to the skillet and reduce over high heat to 1½ cups (37.5 cl) about 5 minutes. Off the heat, whisk in the chilled butter, in pieces, whisking just to blend. Taste for seasoning. Moisten the veal with a ladle full of sauce, transferring the rest to a warm sauce boat. Serve, with the macaroni gratin on the side.

Yield: 4 servings

FAUBOURG SAINT-GERMAIN, INVALIDES, ECOLE MILITAIRE

7th arrondissement

ARPEGE
84 Rue de Varenne, Paris 7.
Tel: 45.51.47.33.
Fax: 44.18.98.39.
Métro: Varenne.
Reservations, noon to 2 P.M.
and 7:30 to 10 P.M.
Closed Saturday and
Sunday lunch.
Credit cards: AE, DC, V.
Private dining room for 12.
Air-conditioned.
Menus at 290 francs (lunch
only), 690 and 790
francs. A la carte, 800 to
1200 francs.

SPECIALTIES:
Contemporary: homard et navet à
la vinaigrette aigre douce (lobster
and turnips in sweet and sour
vinaigrette), langoustines rôties
aux senteurs de Provence (giant
shrimp roasted with fresh herbs),
gibier (game in season),
feuilletage au chocolat (chocolate
puff pastry), pain maison
(homemade bread).

One key to either what is new, popular, or the coming trend in Paris dining can be found at Alain Passard's renovated Arpège. The modern look—in tones of peach set off by pale pearwood walls—is a welcome change from the dark brown and red decor inherited from his predecessor, Alain Senderens, who moved on to the historic Lucas Carton on the Place de la Madeleine. Chef Passard—lean, boyish, and effervescent—continues to set trends with his almost revolutionary return to tableside service. He and his friendly, unpretentious staff manage to involve the public in the act of cooking as they dine: Instead of simply waiting for someone to deliver a perfectly arranged dinner plate, diners engage in lively interchange with the bevy of waiters as they carve, fillet, sauté, garnish, and place the finishing touches on Passard's greatly varied cuisine.

In truth, most diners don't spend all that much time in their kitchens anymore, and even the most learned gourmande is relatively removed from the everyday process of seasoning, carving, and the mysteries of the transformation of simple cooking juices into a smooth, sublime sauce.

Best bets here include simple roasts—duck, pigeon, lamb or game in season—his always popular roasted *langoustines* (similar to sweet, giant shrimp) and my personal favorite, *Saint-Pierre*, the sweet-fleshed fish known as John Dory, roasted with fresh, fragrant bay leaves slipped under the skin. Passard's style of cooking remains whimsical, and on the surface at least, seems almost haphazard. But look deeper and you'll find someone who is always experimenting and pushing creativity to its limits. As ever, his crusty sourdough breads, admirably unpretentious service, and the presence of one of the city's more remarkably priced wine cellars all help make Arpège a memorable, pleasurable, dining experience.

LA CIGALE
(Chez Pierre et Micheline)
11 bis Rue Chomel, Paris 7.
Tel: 45.48.87.87.
Métro: Sèvres-Babylone.
Reservations, 12:30 to 2
P.M. and 7:30 to 10 P.M.
Closed Saturday, Sunday,
and August.
Credit card: V.
Sidewalk terrace.
155-franc menu. A la carte,
200 francs.

SPECIALTIES:
*Bistro: assiette de crudités (mixed
raw vegetable salads), terrine
landaise de canard (duck
terrine), salade aux filets d'oie
fumé (smoked goose breast salad),
côtelettes d'agneau, flageolets (lamb
chops with white beans), pavé de
boeuf grillé, frites (grilled
beefsteak with French fries), tarte
ou pâtisserie maison (daily
homemade tart or pastry).*

*An enclosed terrace allows plenty
of natural lighting.*

When you find yourself in the neighborhood of Le Bon Marché department store and you're about to collapse from hunger, Pierre and Micheline Grocat are sure to cure what ails you. It's hard to believe one can still find a "mom and pop" bistro in the trendy Sèvres-Babylone quartier, but La Cigale is it. A handful of tables (a few stretched out onto the sidewalk along with their giant black Labrador), a hyper-traditional menu of thick grilled beefsteaks (try the *pavé grillé*), truly fresh and golden fries, and homemade desserts to warm the heart—the food's not great, but satisfies. Service is sweet, if a bit pokey. If the fruity, concentrated, Saumur-Champigny, Domaine Filliatreau, is still on the wine list, go for it.

LA FONTAINE DE MARS
129 Rue Saint-Dominique,
Paris 7.
Tel: 47.05.46.44.
Métro: Ecole-Militaire.
Reservations, 12:30 to 2
P.M. and 7:30 to 10 P.M.
Closed Sunday.
Credit cards: MC, V.
Terrace.
85-franc lunch menu. A la
carte, 180 to 200 francs.

SPECIALTIES:
*Southwestern bistro: Panaché de
crudités (mixed raw salads),
boudin aux pommes fruits (blood
sausage with apples), confit de
canard pommes sarladaises
(preserved duck with pan-fried
potatoes), clafoutis aux fruits de
saison (custard-based fruit tart).*

La Fontaine de Mars has almost everything going for it—location, decor, nostalgia, cleanliness, friendliness. If only the food were better! Not far from the Eiffel Tower and in a super-chic, well-bred neighborhood, this sparkling and newly refurbished gem could serve as a bistro stage set, with its red and white checkered linens, cute red and white curtains, tiny zinc bar, and shelves filled with kitchen antiques. The staff is efficient and friendly, when seated on the shaded terrace you feel as though you're in the center of the world, and the classic bistro menu makes your mouth water. Unfortunately—from the platter of *crudités* (raw vegetables), to the pan-fried *dorade* (porgy) with a *chiffonnade* of cooked fennel, and on to the pear *clafoutis* (custard-based tart)—the food is unrelievedly ordinary. The house Saumur—a red from the Loire—is fine, but steer clear of the carafe wines.

LE MACONNAIS
10 Rue du Bac, Paris 7.
Tel: 42.61.21.89.
Métro: Rue du Bac.
Reservations, noon to 2 P.M.
    and 8 to 10 P.M.
Closed Saturday lunch,
    Sunday, August, and
    Christmas week.
Credit card: V.
A la carte, 125 to 175
    francs.

SPECIALTIES:
Lyonnais bistro: jambon persillé
(parsleyed ham), steak au poivre
(pan-fried steak with coarse black
peppercorns), poulet à la crème
(sautéed chicken with cream
sauce), fromage fort (spreadable,
seasoned fresh cheese).

A nice, quiet, village-like bistro in a chic neighborhood not known for good, bargain-priced restaurants. Le Mâconnais has been on the Rue du Bac since the turn of the century, and although the decor and the mood are slightly tired, this totally serviceable restaurant should assure a pleasant dining experience. The food is straight from Lyon, including sausages (dried and cooked varieties) from the famed Bobosse in Beaujolais; decent pan-fried steaks; a delicious *poulet à la crème*; and a piquant *fromage fort*, a Lyonnais specialty of spreadable, fresh cheese seasoned with garlic. So order up a bottle of Saint-Amour, Domaine du Paradis (how can one go wrong with that name?), and have a swell time.

L'OEILLADE
10 Rue de Saint-Simon,
    Paris 7.
Tel: 42.22.01.60.
Métro: Rue du Bac or
    Solférino.
Reservations, 12:15 to 2
    P.M. and 8 to 11 P.M.
Closed Saturday lunch,
    Sunday, and the last two
    weeks in August.
Credit cards: MC, V.
Air-conditioned.
145-franc menu. A la carte,
    230 to 300 francs.

SPECIALTIES:
Bistro: ragout d'artichaut aux
cives (ragout of artichokes with
spring onions), tournedos de thon
au poivre vert (tuna steaks with
green peppercorns), coq au vin de
poitou (mature male chicken
stewed in red wine of the Poitou),
noisettes d'agneau au gratin
dauphinois (boneless lamb chops
with potato gratin), cuisse de
canard sauce à la vigneronne
(duck leg stewed in red-wine
sauce), pomme au four caramelisée
à la crème anglaise (baked
caramelized apple with vanilla
custard sauce).

The conversation stopped abruptly as I scooped up a soothing spoonful of potato purée, and along with it the warm, rich, full-flavored cooking juices from the *poulet rôti* and announced: "This dish was made with love."

And so it goes at L'Oeillade, a cramped, noisy, Left Bank bistro that's bursting at the seams with youthful energy and appreciative customers. L'Oeillade also offers some of the best "qualité-prix" to be found in a Paris bistro today. Chef Jean-Louis Huclin and his partner, Pascal Molto, took over L'Oeillade in 1991, and their 145-franc menu—with a changing daily choice of about ten first and second courses as well as dessert—has played to a packed audience ever since. They both spent years working with Colette Dejean at Paris' Chez Toutoune, where the simple but satisfying formula was popularized.

The bargain prices and the copiousness would, of course, have no gastronomic significance if the food were banal. Which it's not. You can tell from the first bite, from looking around at the mouth-watering dishes of your neighbors, from the selection of menu items themselves, that this is food prepared with care, attention, feeling, and generosity. Chef Huclin's meaty terrine—passed from table to table—is well-seasoned, moist, fresh, and fragrant. The bread is crusty and fresh. With the *brandade de morue* (salt cod purée), he's succeeded where so many others have failed, creating a satisfying dish that's light and not overly rich. The *brandade* is slipped under the *salamander* ever so briefly, offering your palate a rich contrast of textures, both creamy-smooth and crunchy.

From start to finish—a simple *salade de mesclun* topped with fresh, baby green asparagus, to the subtle and simple *poulet rôti*—L'Oeillade offers the sort of food most of us only dream of eating at lunch and dinner: *salade Parisienne à la queue de boeuf* (oxtail salad), *rouget grillé* (grilled red mullet), *coq au vin du beaujolais* (chicken cooked in Beaujolais), *mousse au chocolat*.

My only complaint with the food is that it lacks attentive seasoning: A light touch of salt and pepper at just the right moment can perform miracles. Otherwise, go and enjoy.

TAN DINH
60 Rue de Verneuil, Paris 7.
Tel: 45.44.04.84.
Fax: 45.44.36.93.
Métro: Rue du Bac or
Solférino.
Reservations, noon to 2 P.M.
and 7:30 to 11 P.M.
Closed Sunday and August.
No credit cards.
Private dining room for 30.
A la carte, 250 francs.

SPECIALTIES:
Vietnamese: raviolis vietnamiens à l'oie fumée (raviolis filled with smoked goose), rouleaux de crevettes asam (fried spring rolls filled with fresh shrimp), pâtes fraîches aux crevettes piquant, (pasta with spicy shrimp sauce), émincée de filet de boeuf tan dinh (thin strips of marinated beef).

If I had time for a single French colonial meal on Paris' Left Bank, I would head straight for Tan Dinh, where the warm welcome of the Vifian family, their refreshingly original Vietnamese cuisine, and the extraordinary wine list is sure to offer a unique experience. Freddy Vifian and his brother Robert (who learned English in Vietnam, playing in a rock band that entertained American soldiers) trade off in the kitchen, allowing one or the other time to indulge in their favorite pastime—wine tasting and collecting. Their father, Robert, plays the role of family host.

The menu is limited, but that doesn't mean one is likely to go away hungry. Their most famous dishes—all of them conceived by the Vifians, who have created a sort of Vietnamese "nouvelle cuisine"—include fragrant raviolis filled with smoked filet of goose (*raviolis vietnamiens à l'oie fumée*), lovely deep-fried springrolls filled with fresh shrimp (*rouleau de crevettes asam*), superb fresh pasta with spicy shrimp sauce (*pâtes fraîches aux crevettes piquant*), and the *émincée de filet de boeuf tan dinh*, the thin strips of marinated beef that are ideal with one of the many fine Bordeaux and Côtes-du-Rhône from their immense wine cellar.

JULES VERNE

Parc de Champ de Mars
(second floor, Eiffel
Tower), Paris 7.
Tel: 45.55.61.44.
Fax: 47.05.94.40.
Métro: Bir-Hakeim-
Grenelle or Champ de
Mars.
Reservations, noon to 3 P.M.
and 7:15 to 10:30 P.M.
Open daily.
Credit cards: AE, DC, V.
Air-conditioned.
290-franc menu (weekday
lunch only). A la carte,
650 to 800 francs.

SPECIALTIES:
Traditional: lasagne de
coquillages, beurre aux truffes
(shellfish lasagne with truffle
butter), blanc de turbot à la
vapeur, crème d'algues (steamed
filet of turbot with algae cream),
coeur de filet de boeuf rôti au vin
de chinon et sel de Guérande
(roast filet of beef in red wine
from Chinon and sea salt from
Brittany).

On March 31, 1889, Gustave Eiffel and his band of workers raced up the stairs of his newly constructed tower to plant the tricolor on the top, unofficially celebrating the completion of what writers of the day called "that useless and monstrous architectural caprice." For its hundredth birthday, the tower was totally restored, and its "grand" restaurant, the Jules Verne (open since 1984), offers one of the finest views of the city. Diners enter from their own "foot" of the tower, where top-coated gentlemen greet expected guests and usher them into the glass-enclosed elevator to ascend the 123 meters to the second level. Despite the view, I recommend the Jules Verne only during daytime hours, for the harsh and unflattering table lighting makes this one of the most unattractive places to dine in the evening. The food here ranges from decent to less than satisfying, but order simply and you should have a good time. The outgoing and very professional director—Guy Courtois, formerly of Le Grand Véfour—will take excellent care of you.

Freshly-opened briny oysters.

MADELEINE, SAINT-LAZARE, CHAMPS-ELYSEES, PLACE DE TERNES

8th arrondissement

ANDROUET
41 Rue d'Amsterdam,
Paris 8.
Tel: 48.74.26.93.
Métro: Liège or Saint-
Lazare.
Reservations, noon to 2:30
P.M. and 7:30 to 10:30 P.M.
Closed Sunday and
holidays.
Credit cards: AE, DC, V.
Private dining room for 25.
Air-conditioned.
Menus at 175 francs (lunch
only), 230 and 250
francs. A la carte, 250
francs. Cheese *dégustation,*
200 francs.

S P E C I A L T I E S :
Cheese: homard au roquefort
(lobster with Roquefort cheese),
trio de canard au chambertin
(duck in red wine), croquette
de camembert Marie Harel
(Camembert croquettes named for
the bicentennial of the inventor of
Camembert in 1991).

Androuët is not the homey, cozy, wonderful cheese heaven it was in the past, yet it remains the only spot in Paris where you can truly seek your fill of cheese, waltzing through the entire litany of famous French and Swiss raw-milk cheeses, aged in the cellars beneath the shop. The modern, butter-yellow decor is not to my taste, and on the last several visits the cheese, unfortunately, had not been allowed to age. As a result too many varieties were bland, chalky, and anemic— just the opposite of the ideal cheese, which is earthy and oozing with character. But this is still the spot to begin—and proceed with—your cheese education, as you march on through the multi-course *dégustation.* As ever, the tasting begins with the high-fat, triple-cream cheeses (Lucullus, Grand Vatel, La Butte), moves on to pressed varieties (the Swiss Tête de Moine, Reblochon, Tomme de Savoie), then to the soft cheeses like Brie and Camembert. Next come the spiced cheeses and those aged in ash (try the refined Soumaintrain or rustic Feuille de Dreux); a healthy assortment of goat cheeses, or *chèvres*; the *fromages forts* (such as the powerful Pont l'Evèque and Livarot); and finally the blue varieties, including Roquefort and Fourme d'Ambert. And if you're still hungry on the way out, you can stop and select from the hundred or so offerings in the main-floor cheese boutique. (See also *Fromageries.*)

An informal formality—attentive
tableside service.

LE BOEUF SUR LE TOIT
34 Rue du Colisée, Paris 8.
Tel: 43.59.83.80.
Fax: 45.63.45.40.
Métro: Saint-Philippe-du-
Roule.
Continuous service, noon
to 2 A.M.
Open daily.
Credit cards: AE, DC, V.
Private dining room for
30 to 40.
Air-conditioned.
159-franc lunch menu, 108-
franc menu, after 11 P.M.
A la carte, 250 francs.

SPECIALTIES:
Brasserie: banc d'huîtres et fruits
de mer, toute l'année (fresh oysters
and shellfish, year-round),
grillades (grilled fish and meat),
poissons du marché (seasonal
fish).

Le Boeuf sur le Toit—huge, bustling, ever-packed and generally reliable—is one of Jean-Paul Bucher's group of highly successful brasseries that include Brasserie Flo, Vaudeville, Julien, La Coupole and Terminus Nord. The remodeled "Boeuf" is solid 1920s, pure Art Deco, with towering mirrored walls, posters, spectacular period chandeliers, cozy banquettes and soaring ferns. The original 1920s brasserie of the same name, which settled at this location in the 1940s, was frequented by Pablo Picasso, Coco Chanel, and Maurice Chevalier. Today, film stars, artists, models, and Parisian businessmen and women fill the expansive dining room. From the moment you enter—passing mountains of shellfish, glistening oysters, sea urchins, mussels, and clams—you know you're in for a good time. Excellent Riesling by the carafe, and traditional brasserie fare, including platters of shellfish, daily fish specials, *cassoulet*, and *steak tartare*.

A cheerful presentation of
l'addition.

CAVIAR KASPIA
17 Place de la Madeleine,
Paris 8.
Tel: 42.65.33.32.
Fax: 42.66.60.11.
Métro: Madeleine.
Continuous service noon to
12:30 A.M. Reservations
accepted.
Closed Sunday.
Credit cards: AE, DC, V.
Air-conditioned.
A la carte, 450 francs.

SPECIALTIES:
Caviar, smoked salmon, and
smoked fish.

Both elegant and informal, this tiny restaurant just above the Caviar Kaspia boutique—a shop devoted to food fantasies—is the perfect spot for a quick lunch in the Madeleine-Opéra neighborhood. Try for one of the window tables overlooking the church, and settle into the luxurious world of caviar, salmon, and icy vodka. You can make a fine meal out of the fresh, plump blinis served with a few thin slices of tender smoked salmon. Or, if the budget allows, sample thirty grams (about an ounce) of caviar, either Beluga, Sevruga, Osetra, or the less-expensive but no less delicious pressed caviar (*caviar pressé*), just enough to tease the palate and fill you full of fine food memories for the day.

CHIBERTA
3 Rue Arsène-Houssaye,
Paris 8.
Tel: 45.63.77.90 and
45.63.72.44.
Fax: 45.62.85.08.
Métro: Charles-de-Gaulle–
Etoile.
Reservations, noon to 2:30
P.M. and 7:30 to 10:30 P.M.
Closed Saturday, Sunday,
August, and one week at
Christmas.
Credit cards: AE, DC, MC, V.
Private dining room for
20 to 35.
Air-conditioned.
A la carte, 500 to 600
francs.

SPECIALTIES:
Seasonal contemporary: filets
de rouget à la crème d'olive et
marjolaine (red mullet filets with
marjoram-seasoned cream of
olives), bar au four, purée de
pommes de terre et poireaux
(baked sea bass with purée of
potatoes and leeks).

In any profession, adaptiveness is a major key to success. And in today's rocky restaurant world, it's those establishments that have kept pace with the times that manage to keep their tables full and their clientele more than content. Chiberta—with a modern decor that's stood the test of time— tends to prove the point. All button-down, hushed, and business-like, Chiberta offers top- quality ingredients, prepared with remarkable sim- plicity and great attention to detail. In the early 1980s, when *nouvelle cuisine* was still the rage, Chiberta topped the charts with its *bavarois* of smoked salmon with fresh tomato *coulis*, salads of spiny lobster with peaches, crayfish *consommé* topped with caviar. We all thought it was great— then—when we seemed to crave food you didn't have to bite into or chew. Well, Chiberta has shifted with the times. And while chefs have come and gone, director Louis-Noël Richard remains in control, creating an atmosphere that is welcoming, smart, and modern, without a touch of snobbery. On my last visit, the menu offered succulent roasted leg and shoulder of milk-fed lamb from the Pyrénées, not to mention whole joints of beef, of duck, and of rabbit. No more boneless chicken breasts, rabbit chopped up into mystery meat, or nursery-style food. Today's Chiberta offers an array of brilliant, wholesome salads, including one that combines crunchy-smooth purslane (*pourpier*) with the freshest of red mullet (*rouget*); and another that brings together tender, green asparagus tips, moist and flavorful guinea hen, and an avalanche of greens. But the real star of the evening was the perfectly roasted lamb shoulder, spring-fresh and tender, served with pan juices touched with just a hint of cream. With it, don't pass up Simon Bize's soothing 1985 Savigny-les-Beaune.

**FERMETTE MARBEUF
1900**
5 Rue Marbeuf, Paris 8.
Tel: 47.20.63.53.
Fax: 40.70.02.11.
Métro: Franklin-D.-
   Roosevelt.
Reservations, noon to 3 P.M.
   and 7:30 to 11 P.M.
Open daily. Closed May 1.
Terrace.
Credit cards: AE, DC, V.
Menus at 160 francs
   (weekday dinners and
   Sunday lunch only), and
   250 francs. A la carte,
   250 francs.

SPECIALTIES:
*Traditional: agneau de lait rôti
(roasted milk-fed lamb), pintade
aux lentilles (roasted guinea hen
with green lentils), tagliatelles
aux truffes (fresh pasta with
black truffles), terrines
d'aubergines au cumin (eggplant
terrine with cumin).*

A cook is only as good as his ingredients. And if all those ingredients happen to be among the best France has to offer—products that have the government seal of approval—the battle is already half won. Fermette Marbeuf 1900, the large and rambling turn-of-the-century historic monument off the Champs-Elysées, offers just that, with its menu made up of products that have been awarded the top-quality AOC (*Appelation d'Origine Contrôlée*). Those include the prized black truffles from Tricastin in Provence; delicious black olives from Nyons and guineau hen, or *pintade*, both from the Drôme; tiny green lentils from Le Puy in the Auvergne; raw-milk Camembert from Normandy; and a special honey from the Lorraine. All of these are nicely woven into the Fermette's 250-franc AOC menu. For such a large and rambling place, service is especially personal, and the frilly Art Nouveau decor puts you in a festive mood, indeed. If the classic, full-flavored Chinon—Domaine des Galluches —is still on the wine list, go for it. A great *tous les jours* place to remember on days when everything else is closed.

**LES GOURMETS DES
TERNES**
87 Boulevard de Courcelles,
   Paris 8.
Tel: 42.27.43.04.
Métro: Ternes.
Reservations, noon to 2 P.M.
   and 7:30 to 10 P.M.
Closed Saturday, Sunday,
   August, and two weeks
   at Christmas.
Credit card: V.
Air-conditioned
Sidewalk terrace.
A la carte, 165 francs.

SPECIALTIES:
*Bistro: viandes grillées et frites
(grilled meats and French fries),
radis beurre (radishes and
butter), filet de harengs à l'huile
(herring filets marinated in oil),
escargots (snails), betteraves
rouges en salade (beet salad).*

A nyone looking for a superb grilled steak in totally unpretentious surroundings should reserve a table at Les Gourmets des Ternes, a modest bistro near the Place des Ternes. The *complet* sign appears in the window at around eleven each morning, meaning that all the tables are already reserved. The neighborhood businessmen know a good deal when they find it. This is a well-worn spot, improved with a new coat of paint a few years back. Although none of the chairs or light fixtures match and the waitresses lost interest a long time ago, the regulars keep returning, enjoying the chic and lively crowd, the solid, simple fare. In the summertime, you can enjoy a meal on the small sidewalk terrace.

LA MAISON DU VALAIS
20 Rue Royale, Paris 8.
Tel: 42.60.23.75 and
42.60.22.72.
Métro: Concorde or
Madeleine.
Reservations, noon to 3 P.M.
and 7:15 to 10:30 P.M.
Closed Sunday and three
weeks in August.
Credit cards: AE, DC, MC, V.
Terrace.
Private dining room for 15
to 26.
Air-conditioned.
Menus at 90 francs
(raclette) and 200 francs,
wine included. A la
carte, 230 francs.

SPECIALTIES:
Swiss: raclette (melted Swiss
cheese with potatoes and
condiments), fondue maraichère
(cheese fondue with steamed
vegetables), grillades au feu de
bois (meats and chicken grilled
over wood fire), poisson du jour
(daily fish specials), omble
chevalier sauvage (salmon trout
from Lake Geneva), coquelet rôti
à la graine de moutarde (roast
baby chicken with whole-grain
mustard).

On those cold, gray, rainy Paris days—of which there are more than most of us care to endure—nothing lifts the spirits and fills the soul like a generous serving of *raclette*: firm, golden cheese that's sliced, then melted to a fragrant and creamy pool, and served with steaming fresh potatoes cooked in their skins. La Maison du Valais, with its cozy first-floor dining room overlooking the glitter of Rue Royale is my favorite spot in Paris for sampling this Swiss-style specialty. Here the *raclette* is served *à volonté*, which means that refills keep on coming until you put on the brakes. I'd love to know the record number of helpings, and have to admit that when I go, I lose count. The potatoes are served out of a lovely, cone-shaped copper steamer, so they stay nice and warm. Service is so swift that it's sometimes hard to keep up with platter after platter of sizzling cheese. With the meal they serve a wonderful condiment of onions and mustard, a perfect foil for the rich, warm cheese. If you're particularly hungry that day, begin the meal with an *assiette valaisanne*, a generous platter of thinly sliced country ham (*jambon cru de montagne*) and *viande de Grison*, the popular Swiss-style air-dried beef, sliced parchment-thin and served with tiny tart *cornichon* pickles. The wine list features some very pleasant Swiss wines, including the light, white Swiss Fendant from the region of the Valais.

MARQUISE AU CHOCOLAT TAILLEVENT
TAILLEVENT'S CHOCOLATE CAKE

This is the dessert I order almost every time I dine at Taillevent (see entry, page 87), the finest restaurant in Paris. The cake is rich and classic, rather like a ripened chocolate mousse. A marquise *is easy to make and requires no baking. Taillevent adds its signature by serving it with a rich pistachio sauce, actually a* crème anglaise *flavored with ground pistachio nuts. The sauce is a bit time-consuming, but not difficult. The cake may, of course, be served without a sauce, or with a plain* crème anglaise. *Both the cake and the sauce should be made twenty-four hours before serving.*

9 ounces (280 g) bittersweet chocolate (preferably Lindt or Tobler brand), broken into pieces
¾ cup (100 g) confectioners' sugar
¾ cup (6 ounces; 185 g) unsalted butter, at room temperature
5 eggs, separated
Pinch of salt
Pistachio sauce, optional (recipe follows)

1. Make the chocolate batter: Place the chocolate in the top of a double boiler, and melt over simmering water. Add these ingredients in the following order, mixing well after each addition: ½ cup (70 g) confectioners' sugar, all the butter, and the egg yolks.

2. In a small mixing bowl, beat the egg whites with a pinch of salt until stiff, then add the remaining sugar and beat another 20 seconds, or until glossy.

3. Remove the chocolate batter from the heat, and add one third of the egg white mixture, folding it in gently but thoroughly. Then gently fold in the remaining whites. Don't overmix, but be sure that the mixture is well blended.

4. Rinse an 8½-inch (22-cm) springform pan with water. Leave the pan wet and fill it with the mixture. Refrigerate for 24 hours. Remove from the refrigerator about 30 minutes before serving. To serve, pour several tablespoons of the pistachio sauce onto a dessert plate. Place a thin slice of the *marquise* in the center of the plate, and serve.

Yield: One 8½-inch (22-cm) cake; 8 to 10 servings

SAUCE A LA PISTACHE
PISTACHIO SAUCE

⅓ cup (100 g) pistachio
paste (see recipe
below)
1 quart (1 liter) milk
8 egg yolks
1¼ cups (250 g) sugar

1. Prepare the pistachio paste.

2. In a medium-size saucepan combine the pistachio paste with the milk and bring the mixture to a boil over medium heat. Remove from the heat, cover, and allow it to steep for 5 minutes, then strain through cheesecloth or a fine-mesh sieve into another medium-size saucepan. Set aside.

3. In a medium-size mixing bowl combine the egg yolks and sugar, and beat until thick and light. Whisk in half the warm, strained milk, then whisk the mixture back into the remaining milk.

4. Warm the sauce gently over medium heat, stirring constantly, until it thickens. Do not allow the sauce to boil or it will curdle. You can prepare this 24 hours in advance and refrigerate, removing it from the refrigerator 1 hour before using.

Yield: 1 quart (1 liter)

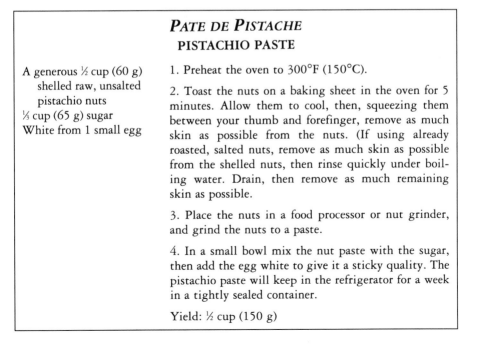

PATE DE PISTACHE
PISTACHIO PASTE

A generous ½ cup (60 g)
shelled raw, unsalted
pistachio nuts
⅓ cup (65 g) sugar
White from 1 small egg

1. Preheat the oven to 300°F (150°C).

2. Toast the nuts on a baking sheet in the oven for 5 minutes. Allow them to cool, then, squeezing them between your thumb and forefinger, remove as much skin as possible from the nuts. (If using already roasted, salted nuts, remove as much skin as possible from the shelled nuts, then rinse quickly under boiling water. Drain, then remove as much remaining skin as possible.

3. Place the nuts in a food processor or nut grinder, and grind the nuts to a paste.

4. In a small bowl mix the nut paste with the sugar, then add the egg white to give it a sticky quality. The pistachio paste will keep in the refrigerator for a week in a tightly sealed container.

Yield: ½ cup (150 g)

LE BISTROT DE MARIUS
6 Avenue George V,
  Paris 8.
Tel: 40.70.11.76.
Métro: George V or Alma-
  Marceau.
Open daily, lunch and
  dinner. No reservations.
Terrace.
Air-conditioned.
Credit cards: AE, V.
A la carte, 200 to 230
  francs.

SPECIALTIES:
Fish and shellfish: salade de
coques aux épinards (baby clams
on a bed of spinach), sardines
crus marinés (sardine filets
marinated in oil and lemon
juice), daurade grillé (grilled
whole sea bream), plateau de
fruits de mer (raw and cooked
fish and shellfish).

Although modern dietary advice tells us all to "eat more fish," most of our budgets can't concur. The prices of fresh fish and shellfish continue to soar, especially at restaurants devoted solely to fruits of the sea. Restaurateurs aren't blind to the growing public appetite for fish. Le Bistrot de Marius is a newer addition to the group of Pont d'Alma area restaurants that includes the nearby Marius et Janette and Chez Francis. And to my mind, it's the best and most authentic of the trio.

In this day and age, it's almost too much to hope for: An authentic bistro, bustling, noisy, fun, even bright and attractive, with the freshest of fish and shellfish. For the moment, this Provençal-inspired bistro with its charming red, white and blue Pays Basque china and linens, could hardly offer more.

The walls are filled with posters (albeit poor copies), the menu sings of the sea, and the food has a fresh and lively air. The *salade de coque aux épinards*—baby clams on a bed of young, fresh spinach—makes a fine, light starter, as do the super-fresh *sardines crus marinés*, firm and silvery filets of sardines with the flavors of the sea. To the sardines, add a touch of the coarse sea salt served from little bowls at each table, and you've a veritable feast.

Equally good here are the light and fresh strips of whiting (*aiguillettes de merlan*), lightly pan-fried and served with fresh asparagus; and the *dorade grillé*, two whole healthy-sized sea bream, served with the classic garnish of boiled potatoes, parsley and lemon.

ROYAL MADELEINE
11 Rue Richepanse, Paris 8.
Tel: 42.60.14.36.
Métro: Madeleine or
  Concorde.
Reservations, noon to 3 P.M.
  and 6:30 to 10 P.M.
Closed Sunday.
Credit cards: AE, DC, V.
Sidewalk terrace.
145-franc menu. A la carte,
  170 to 250 francs.

Even in traditional Paris, it's hard to find a restaurant as orthodox as this one. Since 1943, when the grandparents of the current owner, Denis Eche, took over an already thriving establishment, this active neighborhood restaurant has served as a favorite haunt for businessmen and office workers in the Place de la Madeleine *quartier*. Monsieur Eche's grandmother decorated the dining room, which has a charmingly old-fashioned air: Walls are plastered with framed copies of old newspapers, collec-

SPECIALTIES:
Bistro: oysters (from October through April), potage aux légumes (vegetable soup), filets de harengs pommes à l'huile (marinated herring with potato salad), brochette de coquilles Saint-Jacques (grilled scallop brochettes), entrecôte grillé (grilled beefsteak), tarte aux pommes chaudes (warm apple tart).

TAILLEVENT
15 Rue Lamennais, Paris 8.
Tel: 45.63.96.01 and
    45.61.12.90.
Fax: 42.25.95.18.
Métro: Charles-de-Gaulle–
    Etoile or George V.
Reservations, 12:30 to 2
    P.M. and 7:30 to 10 P.M.
Closed Saturday, Sunday,
    and August.
Credit card: V.
Private dining room for
    6 to 32.
Air-conditioned.
A la carte, 800 francs.

tions of pewter spoons and old scales, and numerous brass candlesticks and candlestick lamps.

This is a lunchtime spot (reservations are essential), and the single 75-seat dining room is packed, with ladies in floppy red hats, young couples in blue jeans, businessmen diving into their *potage aux légumes* and grilled *entrecôte* and *pommes frites.*

From October through April, oysters are their specialty, platters of top-quality from Oleron, on the Atlantic Coast. I'm a particular fan of their *papillons*, the tiny delicate "butterfly" oysters, served with plenty of butter and slices of fresh rye bread.

There's always a very homey *plat du jour*— such as a meaty Provençal beef stew, or *daube*, or a tasty salt cod and garlic purée known as *brandade*—along with a litany of very traditional French fare. The wine list is brief, but offers good value, including the well-priced Saumur-Champigny, a fresh-flavored red from the Loire valley.

These are difficult days when what one looks for in a restaurant is security and assurance: Assurance that the surroundings will be perfect, there will be no surprises in either service or cuisine. You may enter the dining room exhausted, filled with worries, tense, but you'll leave feeling carefree, satisfied, and happy. That's just part of the magic of Taillevent, perhaps France's most flawless restaurant, directed by the incomparable Jean-Claude Vrinat. Vrinat is unique in the world, and knows more about running a dining room than any ten *maîtres d'hôtel*. He knows more about selecting, storing, and serving wine than any 120 sommeliers.

And so it's not a surprise that, after all these decades, Taillevent remains in a class of its own, still at the very top. It has become fashionable to criticize Tallevent as a "has been" restaurant serving a classic cuisine in need of renovation. I disagree. Who can complain about a perfectly roasted *pintade de Challons façon-demi-deuil*, deliciously moist guinea hen that's studded with black truffles beneath the crispy skin and painstakingly carved before your very eyes? Or who could find fault with the *suprême de bar au gros sel*, perfectly roasted

sea bass that's totally simple and totally satisfying.
When you have the freshest ingredients, it's best
not to fuss, but let the quality speak for itself. And
do not say that Taillevent does not innovate: Try
the soothing, surprising, *crème de lentilles aux truffes*,
a warming soup tossed with a dollop of whipped
cream dotted with black truffles, and you'll see
what I mean. Desserts remain wedded to a fine
classicism, including the light and lovely *soufflé
chaude* (a blanket of crêpes filled with sweet lime-
flavored pillows), as well as the ever delicious *marquise au chocolat à la pistache* (see recipe, page 84).
The decor—rich with wood, deep tones of blue and
red, and the sumptuousness of the Napoleon III
hôtel particulier—is designed to make you feel as
though you're among the fortunate pampered. One
could dwell for pages on the wine list, a work of
art all on its own. Just put yourself in Monsieur
Vrinat's hands: You won't be disappointed.

GRANDS BOULEVARDS, PLACE DE CLICHY, GARE DU NORD

9th and 10th arrondissements

BRASSERIE FLO
7 Cour des Petites-Ecuries,
    Paris 10.
Tel: 47.70.13.59.
Fax: 42.47.00.80.
Métro: Château-d'Eau.
Reservations, noon to 3 P.M.
    and 7 P.M. to 1 A.M.
Open daily.
Credit cards: AE, DC, MC, V.
Air-conditioned.
99-franc menu (lunch only),
    108-franc menu (after
    11 P.M.).
A la carte, 250 francs.

An authentic 1900s Alsatian brasserie (reopened the first day of the May 1968 riots)
with a faithful and flashy clientele. Flo is frequently too crowded, too noisy, too hectic, and
always a lot of fun. Go with a group, and order up
platters of *choucroute*, fish or shellfish. There are
always drinkable Alsatian wines available by the
pitcher.

AU GIGOT FIN
56 Rue de Lancry, Paris 10.
Tel: 42.08.38.81.
Métro: Jacques-Bonsergent.
Reservations, noon to 2 P.M.
and 6 to 10 P.M.
Closed Saturday lunch and
Sunday.
Credit cards: AE, MC, V.
Private dining room for 20
to 25.
Menus at 55 francs (lunch
only), 85, 110, and 175
francs. A la carte, 200
francs.

SPECIALTIES:
*Bistro: gigot au four (roasted leg
of lamb), épaule d'agneau au four
(roast shoulder of lamb), tartes
maison (homemade fruit tarts).*

Take a trip back to the 1930s, the world of bistros with etched-glass windows, lace curtains, hurried waitresses with their hair dyed red-orange, and a bar laid out with the day's dessert specials: tarts layered with apricots, cherries, or plump purple plums. Those in search of a cheap and cheerful spot for a weekday lunch need look no further: Au Gigot Fin's 55-franc lunch is one of the city's better bargains. On my last visit, I feasted on a simple salad of ripe tomatoes topped with vinaigrette; thick slices of perfectly cooked leg of lamb (*gigot*, of course, is the house specialty) served with fresh green beans; excellent *baguettes*; and a very much homemade plum tart. This is not grand cuisine, but it's good enough, considering the price. There are three small dining rooms, and just a pair of waitresses, but service is swift, if impersonal. Other specials include such *plats ménagères* as sauté of rabbit, *sole meunière*, and lamb in every guise. Afterwards, take a long walk along the Quai de Valmay and the pleasant canal.

JULIEN
16 Rue du Faubourg Saint-
Denis, Paris 10.
Tel: 47.70.12.06.
Fax: 42.47.00.65
Métro: Strasbourg Saint-
Denis.
Reservations, noon to 3 P.M.
and 7 P.M. to 1:30 A.M.
Open daily.
Credit cards: AE, DC, MC, V.
Air-conditioned.
99-franc menu (weekday
lunch only); 143-franc
menu (weekends and
holidays, lunch only);
108-franc menu (after
11 P.M.). A la carte, 250
francs.

SPECIALTIES:
*Brasserie: plats du jour (changing
daily specials), cassoulet d'oie
(casserole of goose and white
beans), foie gras (fatted duck
liver), poissons du marché
(variety of fresh fish), grillades
(grilled meats and fish), homard
à la nage (poached lobster).*

Despite its rather seedy location, Julien remains one of the city's most chic, and most popular nighttime addresses. One look inside this stunning 1890s dining hall and you understand: Who could not love the mahogany bar, the Art Nouveau mirrors and murals, the noisy brasserie charm? Service can be a bit rushed, depending upon the waiter and the time of day. But the menu offers enough variety to please even the most finicky in the crowd. Try the *foie gras, cassoulet d'oie,* (casserole of goose and white beans), and the fabulous *profiterole au chocolat,* little rounds of *chou* pastry filled with ice cream and served with a steaming hot pitcher of chocolate sauce.

SAUMON EN RILLETTES JULIEN
JULIEN'S SALMON PATE

Julien is one of Paris's prettiest restaurants (see entry, page 89), and this is one of Julien's most pleasant first courses. The recipe combines smoked and fresh salmon, butter, and Cognac, and it's melt-in-your-mouth delicious, especially served on wedges of toasted homemade rye bread, with a glass of Champagne before a festive meal.

4 ounces (125 g)
   skinned fresh salmon
   fillet
½ cup (125 ml) dry
   white wine
1 tablespoon olive oil
2 tablespoons Cognac
Salt and freshly ground
   black pepper to taste
4 ounces (125 g) smoked
   salmon
6 tablespoons (3 ounces;
   90 g) unsalted butter
Thin slices of warm
   toast

1. Cut the fresh salmon into bite-size pieces. In a small saucepan combine the salmon and wine, and bring slowly to a boil over medium heat. Remove from the heat and drain the salmon, discarding the wine.

2. In a small saucepan heat the olive oil and add the salmon. Cook gently over medium heat for about 5 minutes. Do not let it brown. Add the Cognac, salt, and pepper. Remove from the heat and set aside.

3. Cut the smoked salmon into bite-size pieces. In a small saucepan over medium heat, sauté the smoked salmon in half the butter until it is heated through, 3 to 5 minutes. Remove from the heat, cool the salmon and the butter, then blend in a food processor, adding the remaining butter.

4. Working by hand, combine the fresh salmon and smoked salmon mixtures with a fork in a small bowl until well blended. Check for seasoning. Transfer the rillettes to a serving dish or bowl, and carefully smooth the top. Refrigerate at least 12 hours before serving.

5. To serve, remove from the refrigerator about 30 minutes beforehand. Serve with thin slices of warm toast.

Yield: 4 to 6 servings

LE ROI DU POT-AU-FEU
34 Rue Vignon, Paris 9.
Tel: 47.42.37.10.
Métro: Madeleine.
Continuous service, noon
to 9:30 P.M. No
reservations.
Closed Sunday.
Credit card: V.
Sidewalk terrace.
A la carte, 150 to 170
francs.

SPECIALTIES:
Pot-au-feu (beef simmered with fresh vegetables).

This funky little bistro off the Place de la Madeleine is great on a chilly fall or winter afternoon, when a nourishing dish of boiled beef, marrow, and vegetables is what's needed to warm the soul. The decor here is a bit kitschy, but humorous just the same—cartoons paper the walls, an old piano stands beside the zinc bar, and the chatty staff makes a *fête* of even the simplest lunch. Here the *pot-au-feu* begins with the traditional bouillon, steaming beef broth ladled from the stockpot in which the meat and vegetables have simmered. Next comes the enormous platter of beef, vegetables, and fresh, fragrant marrow, served with puckery *cornichons*, mustard, and coarse salt. The bistro serves a young Gamay d'Anjou, from the caves of Lucien Legrand, still one of the city's better wine shops.

TERMINUS NORD
23 Rue de Dunkerque,
Paris 10.
Tel: 42.85.05.15.
Métro: Gare du Nord.
Continuous service, 11 A.M.
to 1:30 A.M. Reservations
accepted.
Open daily except
Christmas eve.
Credit card: AE, DC, V.
Sidewalk terrace.
Private dining room for 10.
159-franc lunch menu; 109-franc menu, after 11 P.M.
only.
A la carte, 180 to 250
francs.

SPECIALTIES:
Brasserie: plats du jour (changing daily specials), choucroute garnie (sauerkraut, pork, and sausages), foie gras (fatted duck liver), plateau de fruits de mer (platter of fish and shellfish), poissons et viandes grillés (grilled fish and meats).

Terminus Nord is a rambling, authentic 1925 brasserie right near the Gare du Nord, making it a perfect place to stop before or after a trip north. But you don't have to wait for a trip to bring you to this end of town: The year-round *banc* of fresh oysters and shellfish is enough to lure most diners, along with excellent grilled Mediterranean *rouget* (red mullet), grilled, sliced leg of lamb, and inexpensive wines that go down easily amid the old-time atmosphere.

POT-AU-FEU
BEEF SIMMERED WITH VEGETABLES

"Eating pot-au-feu *is an act that gives significance to life," wrote one French critic. A bit precious, to be sure, but few peasant dishes are as healthfully nourishing, fragrant, or satisfying as a superb* pot-au-feu. *In its most classic form, the dish begins with a shallow, steaming bowl of bouillon, ladled from the pot in which the meat, marrow, and vegetables have been slowly simmering. To the bowl one might add garlic-touched croutons, freshly grated Parmesan or Gruyère cheese, a few grains of coarsely ground black pepper. The second course is made up of the meat, vegetables, and accompaniments, a procession of condiments that might include fiery horseradish, three or four varieties of mustard, coarse salt, puckery* cornichons, *and tiny white pickled onions. This recipe is based on the one shared with us by Le Roi du Pot-au-Feu (see entry, page 91).*

2 pounds (1 kg) short
    ribs of beef
2 pounds (1 kg) boned
    beef shank
2 pounds (1 kg) oxtail,
    cut into 2-inch
    (5-cm) lengths
Coarse (kosher) salt and
    freshly ground black
    pepper to taste
6 small onions, each
    peeled and studded
    with a clove
4 leeks, cleaned of sand
1 fennel bulb, trimmed,
    washed, and
    quartered
6 whole carrots, peeled
4 cloves garlic, unpeeled
Bouquet garni: 2 bay
    leaves, 2 sprigs fresh
    parsley, and 1 tea-
    spoon dried thyme,
    tied in a piece of
    cheesecloth
1 whole apple, washed
Approximately 1½
    pounds (750 g) beef
    marrow bones, cut
    into 2-inch (5-cm)
    lengths, and each
    length wrapped in
    green portion of leek
    (to seal in the marrow)

1. Using household string, tie in two separate bundles the ribs of beef and the boned shank, so they retain their shape and fit compactly into a large stockpot. Place the oxtail on top of the other meat. Cover the meat completely with cold water and cook, uncovered, over medium-high heat. The water should barely simmer, never boil.

2. After about 20 minutes, carefully skim all traces of foam (which is impurities) and grease from the surface of the stock. Careful skimming is necessary to producing a fine *pot-au-feu.*

3. Move the pot halfway off the heat so that the foam rises on one side of the stock only, making it easier to skim. Continue cooking for another 20 minutes.

4. Season the liquid lightly with coarse salt (about 1 tablespoon should finely season this dish) and pepper. Add the vegetables, using only the white portions of the leeks; the garlic; the bouquet garni; and the apple, which will help absorb some of the fat. Skim again and cook another 40 minutes. Skim frequently, and after about 30 minutes, test the vegetables to see if they are cooked.

5. Once the vegetables have cooked, transfer them to a heatproof dish and moisten with bouillon. Cover with aluminum foil and keep warm, in a low oven.

6. Continue cooking the meat, skimming if necessary, for 1 hour more. About 15 minutes before serving, add the marrow bones, submerging them in the bouillon.

7. To serve the first course, place a slice of toast rubbed with garlic in a warmed soup bowl, cover with bouillon, and sprinkle with freshly grated Parmesan cheese.

Garnishes and
   condiments:
Toast rubbed with garlic
Freshly grated Parmesan
   cheese
Horseradish
Several mustards
Cornichons

8. To serve the second course, remove the twine from the meat and cut it into chunks. Place it on a warmed platter, surrounded by the marrow bones and the vegetables, discarding the bouquet garni and the apple. Serve with the horseradish, a variety of mustards, *cornichons*, coarse salt, and pepper. The dish can easily be reheated.

Yield: 4 to 6 servings

GARE DE LYON, DAUMESNIL, GOBELINS

5th, 12th, and 13th arrondissements

AUBERGE ETCHEGORRY
41 Rue Croulebarbe,
   Paris 13.
Tel: 43.31.63.05.
Métro: Gobelins or
   Corvisart.
Reservations, noon to
   2:30 P.M. and 7:30 to
   10:30 P.M.
Closed Sunday.
Credit cards: AE, DC, V.
Terrace.
Private dining room for 20.
Air-conditioned
Menus at 145 and 195
   francs. A la carte,
   220 to 300 francs.

S P E C I A L T I E S :
Basque and southwestern: foie gras de canard (fatted duck liver), confit (preserved duck), pipérade (scrambled eggs with tomatoes, peppers, ham, and chorizo sausage), paella pour deux (paella for two: including rice, squid, clams, mussels, chicken, and chorizo sausage), gâteau basque (cake filled with almond paste).

When in the mood for a homey, no-frills meal, you'll find what you're searching for in the frankly old-fashioned Auberge Etchégorry, a traditional Basque restaurant not far from the Place d'Italie. The decor might serve as a country bistro stage set from the 1950s, with hams, sausages, garlic, and fiery Basque red peppers hanging from the rafters, and dark floral wallpaper that could have been replaced a good decade ago.

But the menu is good, the service sweet and personal, and the prices are right, so who could ask for more? I love the earthy, bright flavors of Basque cuisine, with its hot red pepper *piments de Espelette*, richly scented and flavored spicy chorizo sausage, as well as Pantagruelien paella, a dish borrowed from Spain, just across the border. You'll find all that here, along with such southwestern specialties as duck *confit* with potatoes; *magret*, or fatted duck breast with wild *cèpe* mushrooms; cold *confit* with sorrel; and *cassoulet*.

I always opt for the earthy, flavorful *pipérade*, a casserole of scrambled eggs mixed with a highly seasoned tomato and pepper sauce, all topped with slices of salty ham from Bayonne as well as thin rounds of spicy chorizo. (Too bad the bread for sopping up the delicious sauce is so boring.)

Although the menu notes that you must be two to order the house paella, if you smile nicely, they'll serve a "single" portion that in fact is copious enough for two. On a bed of saffron-colored rice they've baked a cornucopia of ingredients, including rings of squid, moist and meaty portions of chicken, langoustines, tiny clams or *coques*, mussels, and more chorizo. The results are fresh, traditional, filling, and delicious.

We devoured, as well, the soothing duck *confit*, which was moist and not cloyingly salty, served with a golden crisp skin and mounds of sliced sautéed potatoes with a proper touch of garlic.

The small but adequate wine list includes specialties from the Basque country, such as the light and drinkable Yrouleguy, as well as more substantial wines from just to the north, including a dense and delicious Madiran, Cru de Paradis, and a good, ink-black Cahors from Château Triguedina.

Desserts follow suit, with a homey and not-too-sweet *gâteau Basque* (this version filled with *frangipane,* or almond paste, instead of the classic black cherries) and a wonderfully satisfying *tarte* layered with sweet apples and purple prunes.

MARTY
20 Avenue des Gobelins, Paris 5.
Tel: 43.31.39.51.
Fax: 43.37.63.70.
Métro: Gobelins.
Reservations, noon to 2 P.M. and 7 to 10 P.M.
Open daily.
Credit cards: AE, DC, V.
Sidewalk terrace.
Private dining room for 10 to 50.
150-franc menu, wine included. A la carte, 200 to 300 francs.

SPECIALTIES:
Brasserie: plats du jour (changing daily specials), plateau de fruits de mer (platter of fish and shellfish), poissons et viandes grillés (grilled fish and meats).

One of those veritable Parisian institutions—a large, and very elegant brasserie—where you'll rarely see a tourist. The locals manage to fill up the tables all on their own, for this family-owned spot retains a lovely sense of dignity, history, and tradition. It's not the sort of place you're likely to accidentally run into one of your college fraternity brothers. That said, the food could be a bit more spectacular, but you shouldn't go wrong with a *plateau de fruits de mer*, the lobster salad, or a nice dish of salmon served with wild *girolles* mushrooms (when in season). Along with fish and shellfish specialties, the regulars enjoy steak tartare, and a deliciously sweet cherries-jubilee-like dessert of flaming fresh fruit and vanilla ice cream. Service is attentive and very professional.

L'OULETTE
15 Place Lechambeaudie,
Paris 12.
Tel: 40.02.02.12.
Métro: Dugommier or
Bercy.
Reservations, noon to 2:15
P.M. and 8 to 10:15 P.M.
Closed Saturday lunch and
all day Sunday.
Credit cards: AE, V.
Terrace.
Air-conditioned.
Menus at 130 francs (lunch
only) and 160 francs.
A la carte, 240 to 340
francs.

S P E C I A L T I E S :
*Contemporary southwestern: brik
d'escargots a l'artichaut et aux
amandes (phyllo pastry with
snails, artichokes, almonds,
cinnamon and herbs), escabèche de
calamars (squid seared in olive
and spices), faux-filet de "boeuf
de Salers" (pan-fried beefsteak
from the Auvergne).*

Youthful ambition pays off in any profession, and cooking is no exception. Both qualities apply to Marcel and Marie-Noëlle Baudis, who at the end of 1991 moved from their tiny bistro near the Place des Vosges to the "hinterlands" of Paris, the newly active 12th arrondissement, not far from the Gare de Lyon. The new L'Oulette is Art Deco modern, with bare wood floors, halogen spots, purple-toned upholstered chairs, and the simplest of linens, china, and tableware.

In the move, Baudis—a native of Montauban, in France's southwest—has hardly lost his touch. His dishes still taste as though they came from a friendly French farm kitchen: They're warm, homey, and unaffected. With each bite, you can taste the fact that he loves food and cares about good ingredients and—most of all—loves to cook. The new menu offers some of the old favorites, such as the *escabèche de calamars* (tiny squid sizzled in olive oil, deglazed with white wine, then infused with an array of spices) and the *brik d'escargots* (phyllo pastry wrapped around a mix of snails, artichokes, almonds, cinnamon and herbs). One fine new inspiration is his *croustillant de cèpes*—a starter of chunky, fresh, wild boletus mushrooms seared with precision and topped with crunchy, paper-thin potato galettes. It's a warmingly satisfying dish that's perfect accompanied by a slightly chilled Pacherenc, a surprisingly substantial white wine from France's southwest.

From October through May, expect fresh sea scallops, quickly seared, then served with a cool lentil salad topped with transparent slices of various smoked fish. But my favorite new dish of all is his roasted duck, or *caneton de Challans*. Tasting it made me realize how truly special duck can be, given the right chef. His is meaty, without the fat, and crusty, without that dried-out quality. No sauce, no frills, just delicious duck served with an avalanche of delicate *mousseron* mushrooms. Warming desserts include little eat-with-your-fingers wands of French toast made for dipping in a warm cinnamon cream. Try, as well, whole roasted figs paired with a cool raspberry *granité*.

SALADE VERTE AUX ECHALOTES
ET AUX CIBOULETTES L'OULETTE
L'OULETTE'S FIELD SALAD WITH SHALLOTS AND CHIVES

Give me salad, salad, and more salad! This simple variation on a very familiar theme comes from Marcel Baudis, chef at L'Oulette, the restaurant he runs with his wife, Marie-Noëlle (see entry, page 95). One evening I asked if Chef Baudis would prepare us a simple green salad, and this is what he came up with. The combination of shallots and chives is used often in Baudis' native town of Montauban in France's southwest. Marinating the shallots in oil softens their often harsh flavor.

Dressing:
1 shallot, minced
¼ cup (6 cl) extra-virgin
   olive oil
2 teaspoons best-quality
   red wine vinegar
2 teaspoons sherry wine
   vinegar
Sea salt to taste
Salad:
6 cups (1.5 l) loosely
   packed bite-size
   pieces of mixed
   greens, rinsed and
   dried (such as a
   mixture of curly
   endive, radicchio,
   watercress, lamb's
   lettuce, dandelion
   greens, and arugula)
1 shallot, minced
⅓ cup chopped fresh
   chives
Sea salt and freshly
   ground black pepper
   to taste

1. Prepare the dressing: In a small bowl, combine the shallot and oil, and stir to blend. Set aside at room temperature for at least 1 hour and up to 24 hours.

2. In another small bowl combine the vinegars and salt, and stir to blend. Add the shallot and oil mixture, and stir to blend. Taste for seasoning.

3. In a large, shallow salad bowl, combine the salad greens, shallot, and chives, and toss with your hands. Pour the vinaigrette over the salad and toss gently and thoroughly until the greens are evenly coated. Season to taste and serve immediately.

Yield: 4 to 6 servings

LE PETIT MARGUERY
9 Boulevard du Port-Royal,
Paris 13.
Tel: 43.31.58.59.
Métro: Gobelins.
Reservations, noon to
2 P.M. and 7:30 to 10 P.M.
Closed Sunday, Monday,
August and Christmas
week.
Credit cards: AE, DC. V.
Private dining room for 16.
Menus at 160 francs
(lunch only), 320, and
450 francs. A la carte,
350 to 450 francs.

SPECIALTIES:
Seasonal: champignons de
cueillette (wild mushrooms, in
season), gibier (game, in season),
coquilles Saint-Jacques (fresh
scallops, October to May), lièvre à
la royale (wild hare stew, winter
months only).

There are times when we're all in the mood for a boisterous, gay, thoroughly carefree evening, and one spot in Paris that promises that is Le Petit Marguery, the bright and bustling restaurant run by the three brothers named Cousin.

While Michel and Jacques tend to the stoves, jovial and mustachioed young Alain handles the front of the house, bustling about, adding a sense of theater and drama, and, yes, a pleasant coziness. This is a model, turn-of-the-century, family-run bistro, one of the last of a small 1920s "chain" of eighteen Petit Marguerys all over Paris. The decor here has changed little over the years, with old-fashioned chandeliers, beautiful tile floors, mirrored walls, and a barely legible hand written menu that changes from day to day. The brilliant blue and rose walls are a bit offbeat, but they do add a festive air.

The Cousin brothers' fare is both traditional and innovative, and though the menu changes wisely with the seasons, one can always be assured of fresh *coquilles Saint-Jacques* from October to May, game in the winter months (diners come all the way from Belgium just for Cousin game), and fresh wild mushrooms whenever they appear in the market.

The Cousins grew up in the Poitou, so many of their dishes are favorites from their childhood, including an inventive green salad that's showered with thin slices of pork sausage conserved in walnut oil; *pintadeau fermier*, or guinea hen, smothered with wild *cèpes*; and the marvelous *petit salé de canard*, duck that is cured in salt brine for a full week, then poached and served with butter-rich cabbage.

On our most recent visit, we sampled an impeccable assortment of dishes, including a bright *maquereaux frais marinés au poivre vert* (fresh marinated mackerel with green peppercorns), a delightfully seasoned dish, showered with shallots and only a touch of assertive green peppercorns; a sort of *jambon persillé sauvage*, that is, a parsley-flecked *hure de sanglier*, (or wild boar); and a winning portion of *gigot d'agneau de lait des Pyrénées*, milk-fed lamb from the Pyrenees. *Crème brûlée* fans will swoon over the rich *crème à la cassonade*, burnt custard cream served with excellent honey ice cream.

LE TRAIN BLEU
Gare de Lyon
Place Louis Armand,
   Paris 12.
Tel: 43.43.09.06.
Fax: 43.43.97.96.
Métro: Gare de Lyon.
Reservations, noon to
   1:45 P.M. and 7 to 10 P.M.
Open daily.
Credit cards: AE, DC, V.
Private dining room for 30.
195-franc lunch menu;
   280-franc menu. A la
   carte, 300 francs.

SPECIALTIES:
Brasserie: saucisson chaud
Lyonnais aux pommes persillées
(warm lyonnais pork sausages
with parsleyed potatoes), gigot
d'agneau rôti (roast leg of lamb),
dos de saumon grillé Béarnaise
(grilled salmon with tarragon
sauce) côte de veau laitier Foyot
aux pâtes fraîches (breaded veal
chop with fresh pasta).

If you are looking for the quintessential Parisian brasserie, you have it in Le Train Bleu, the grand, glorious, sparkling *belle époque* restaurant decorated in 1900 in honor of the World's Fair. In 1972, it was declared an historic national monument. Le Train Bleu's two giant dining rooms—with their eclectic, "neo-renaissance baroque" decor—are adorned with signed paintings by more than thirty provincial artists, each selected to depict the glories of his region, serving as giant postcards from the sunniest spots in the south of France. The paintings fill the walls, and bleed onto the ceiling of these ballroom-like rooms, and their cheeriness is particularly welcoming on those gray Parisian days.

Train stations are always points of suspension and anticipation—everyone is either coming or going, so this is a perpetual no man's land—making Le Train Bleu a particularly intriguing spot. I love to go simply to people watch, gazing at the pair of chatty Germans seated on the adjacent banquette; wondering who that gentleman is, dining alone in the corner with his *Paris Match* and half-bottle of Bordeaux.

The food here is more than "correct," meaning there's a good chance you'll leave here satisfied, with an appetite to return another day. Try the top-quality poached Lyonnais pork sausage (direct from the Lyonnais *charcuterie*, Sibilia), served with warm, steamed potatoes; a satisfying salad of green beans, lobster, and lamb's lettuce; a totally acceptable salmon steak served with the tarragon-flavored Béarnaise sauce; and a fine *steak tartare*, prepared tableside, and seasoned to your taste. The service is as good as one might anticipate at a place as bustling as this, although it might be a touch more personal and cheery. The dull white bread, on the other hand, desperately needs attention. The wine list offers a fair, and fairly priced assortment of French wines, including a fine red Saint-Joseph from winemaker Philippe Faury. The restaurant offers a 280-franc menu *"très grande vitesse,"* which it promises to deliver in 45 minutes. Le Train Bleu was the legendary train that, from the 1920s until the 1970s, brought passengers from Paris and Calais to the blue skies of the Côte d'Azur.

AU TROU GASCON
40 Rue Taine, Paris 12.
Tel: 43.44.34.26.
Fax: 43.07.80.55.
Métro: Daumesnil.
Reservations, noon to 2 P.M.
and 7:30 to 10 P.M.
Closed Saturday, Sunday,
August, and one week at
Christmas.
Credit cards: AE, DC, V.
Air-conditioned.
Menus at 200 francs (lunch
only) and 450 francs. A
la carte, 380 to 550
francs.

SPECIALTIES:
*Updated southwestern: huîtres à
la bordelaise (oysters on the half
shell, served with warm, spicy
sausages), petit pâté chaude de
cèpes au jus de persil (warm
pastry filled with wild
mushrooms, topped with parsley
sauce), le vieux jambon de
Chalosse "au couteau" (slices of
aged ham from the southwest),
cassoulet maison (casserole of
white beans, homemade sausages,
mutton, pork, duck and tomatoes,
September to February), agneau
de lait des pyrénées rôtie sur l'os,
pour deux (baby lamb from the
Pyrénées, roasted on the bone, for
two), tourtière landaise (layers of
flaky pastry filled with apples).
Exceptional wine list.*

Au Trou Gascon, Alain and Nicole Dutournier's charming southwestern restaurant—always cozy and welcoming with its festive, *fin de siècle* decor—remains one of my favorite Paris dining spots. Yes, it's hidden on the edge of town. And yes, the atmosphere is less charged, a touch less lively than it was in the days before Dutournier left to devote his labors to his other Paris restaurant, Carré des Feuillants. Yet Au Trou Gascon is in good hands with Madame Dutournier, who oversees the restaurant with seasoned attention and care.

Au Trou Gascon has always been known as the spot to sample southwestern cuisine with a lighter, modern touch, where heaviness, but not flavor, has been removed. One can still find all the trustworthy regional specialties—the incredibly fine ham from Chalosse; hearty *cassoulet* served from a beautiful white bowl; giant scallops of pan-seared *foie gras*, served with *reine de reinette* apples and a *confit* of onions.

In warmer weather, I also go to amuse and excite the palate with their fine array of fish dishes. There is always a fresh selection, such as salmon roasted with fresh fava beans and ham, or pan-seared red mullet (*rouget*) with the freshest of young leeks.

From time to time, chef Bernard Broux offers a truly remarkable shoulder of lamb (*épaule d'agneau*) *boulangère*: The youngest of Pyrénées lamb is roasted to perfection, so that the outside is

*The business lunch, a Paris
tradition.*

*I*n 1806 the Restaurant Véry, the "dearest restaurant in Paris," opened near the Palais-Royal and soon became host to the famous. The painter Fragonard died there while eating an ice cream, and Balzac ate Pantagruelian meals there, usually at the expense of his editor. The restaurant enjoyed a huge success, according to reviews of the day: "Impeccable decor, delicious cuisine."

pleasurably crisp, while the delicate, meaty interior is soft, juicy, chewy, and full of earthy flavors. Served in copious portions, the meat is set on a bed of tender potatoes, surrounded by healthy servings of wild mushrooms. (You must be two for this dish, so go with a lamb lover!)

On recent visits, there were certain dishes that lacked that old-time Dutournier pizzazz—the delightful sounding salad of fava beans, asparagus, and mushrooms needed a more vibrant vinaigrette to hold it all together, and the dessert of mixed red fruits (*fruits rouges*) could have been fresher.

Cheese lovers should save room for the *brebis*, sheep's milk cheese from Dutournier's native southwest, along with the *cabecous de Rocamadour*, tiny discs of goat's milk cheese, among the best you will find anywhere in France.

As ever, the wine list is appealing and reasonably priced, with a changing list of *"bouteilles du moment,"* suggested bottles of the day.

LES ZYGOMATES
7 Rue de Capri, Paris 12.
Tel: 40.19.93.04.
Métro: Daumesnil or
    Michel-Bizot.
Reservations, noon to 2 P.M.
    and 7:45 to 10:15 P.M.
Closed Saturday lunch (all
    day June to September),
    all day Sunday, and the
    first three weeks of
    August.
Credit card: V.
65-franc lunch menu; 120-
    franc dinner menu. A la
    carte, 150 to 220 francs.

SPECIALTIES:

Contemporary bistro: compote de lapereau à l'estragon (compote of rabbit with tarragon), rognons à l'aigre doux (kidneys in sweet and sour sauce), volaille à la crème de ciboulette (chicken with cream and chives), fondant au chocolat (chocolate mousse cake).

*O*n the bistro scene, a favorite new spot—in the low-rent 12th arrondissement—is Les Zygomates, a truly charming neighborhood restaurant fashioned out of a turn-of-the-century charcuterie. The expansive mirrors, marble counters, and walls of etched glass are enough to satisfy anyone's nostalgic longings. The cuisine is simple, and a perfect balance of traditional and contemporary bistro fare. Les Zygomates' bargain-priced menus offer plenty of fresh fish (squid, herring, salmon, and cod were on the menu on my last visit), refreshing platters of raw vegetables, and a satisfying *fondant au chocolat*. "Les zygomatiques," by the way, is French for the facial muscles used to smile.

MONTPARNASSE, DENFERT-ROCHEREAU, GRENELLE, PORTE DE VERSAILLES

14th and 15th arrondissements; Issy-les-Moulineaux

L'ASSIETTE
181 Rue du Château,
Paris 14.
Tel: 43.22.64.86.
Métro: Pernéty or Mouton-
Duvernet.
Reservations, noon to 2 P.M.
and 8 to 10:30 P.M.
Closed Monday, Tuesday,
August, and Christmas
week.
Credit cards: AE, V.
A la carte, 400 to 500
francs.

SPECIALTIES:
Seasonal, southwestern: gibier, en saison (game, in season), champignons sauvage, en saison (wild mushrooms, in season), saumon rôti au sel de Guèrande (roast salmon seasoned with Brittany sea salt), petit salé de canard (poached, salt-cured duck with buttery cabbage).

L'Assiette's Chef-owner Lucette Rousseau knows what she's after, has a keen eye for quality and freshness, and has managed to attract a loyal and consistent following. L'Assiette is loud, elbow to elbow, and casual to excess. Yet if you're after top-quality ingredients prepared with remarkable simplicity and great attention to detail, this bistro should fill the bill—assuming you are willing to pay the price. Today's best chefs let great ingredients shine, and that's where Lucette—better known as the beret-wearing Lulu—comes into the picture. L'Assiette's decor is no-frills (bare wooden tables and bare wooden chairs), and many diners are affronted by the incongruity of minimal com-

Lucette Rousseau, organized and passionate.

fort with maximal prices. Well, my response to that is, just go dine elsewhere. For nowhere in Paris are you likely to find more fragrant, more succulent, or fresher wild morel mushrooms, thicker filets of perfectly cooked salmon from France's own Loire, or such delicious platters of baby, spaghetti-like eels known as *piballes*, tossed with fresh parsley and a joyous hit of garlic. In the spring, you'll also find first of the season green asparagus from the Vaucluse, baby lamb from the Pauillac region, and, much of the year, gargantuan lobster salads, moist, glistening, and garden fresh. With all comes good bread from the Moulin de la Vierge. So sample a simple Saumur-Champigny, and make a toast to tradition, as well as staying power. One caveat: Service can be amateurish and lackadaisical, not up to the quality of the food.

LA CAGOUILLE
10-12 Place Brancusi,
  (across from 23 Rue de
  l'Ouest), Paris 14.
Tel: 43.22.09.01.
Fax: 45.38.57.29.
Métro: Gaîté.
Reservations, noon to 2:30
  P.M. and 7:30 to 10 P.M.
Open daily. Closed April
  13, May 1 to 10, June 1,
  the last three weeks in
  August, November 2,
  and Christmas week.
Credit cards: AE, V.
Private dining room for 6
  to 20.
Sidewalk terrace.
150-franc lunch menu. A la
  carte, 250 to 400 francs.

S P E C I A L T I E S :
Fish and shellfish: petites lottes
frites, sauce anchois (tiny fried
monkfish with anchovy sauce),
moules de bouchot "brûles-doigts"
("burn your fingers" mussels),
Saint-Jacques poêlées et
vinaigrette tiède (pan-seared
scallops with warm vinaigrette),
pavé de thon rouge et ratatouille
(tuna steak with ratatouille,
June to September).

Chef Allemandou exhibits a fierce loyalty for his native Cognac country, showing Parisians how fresh fish can be, how simply it can be prepared. When La Cagouille is "on," the grilled sardines will seem to have jumped from the waters of Brittany right onto your plate and the moules *"brules-doigts"* ("burn your fingers mussels") will make one remember how distinguished a mussel can be when it's at the peak of freshness and not overcooked. Likewise, the *saumon à l'unilatéral*— salmon cooked on just the skin side, and ever so quickly—can demonstrate that when it comes to fish, freshness and precision in cooking is all. That said, I've had numerous reader complaints about service and the rather unpleasant, modern decor. And I agree, at times La Cagouille can seem less than serious. But I'm willing to stick with Monsieur Allemandou a bit longer. With his fish and shellfish, sample the well-chosen Saint-Véran, from Léon Saumaize in the village of Vergisson in Burgundy. And if you're willing to go the limit, stick around for a glass of Allemandou's vieux Pineau, certain to be a palate-pleaser, a new taste discovery.

SALADE DE LARDONS DE THON LA CAGOUILLE
LA CAGOUILLE'S SALAD OF TUNA AND CURLY ENDIVE

This wonderfully modern bistro dish is an updated version of the classic frisée aux lardons, or curly endive salad with bacon. I sampled it during one of my frequent visits to the popular fish bistro La Cagouille (see entry, facing page), where the menu seems to change moment by moment, depending upon what bargains chef Gérard Allemandou has found in the wholesale market that morning. It's a fine main-course salad, for serving with a chilled red Chinon or Beaujolais and crusty grilled bread.

1 head curly endive, rinsed and dried
1 large bunch chives
4 small white onions, shallots, or scallions, cut into thin rings
1 thick slice fresh tuna steak (about 1 pound; 500 g, untrimmed)
Salt and freshly ground black pepper to taste
⅓ cup (80 ml) extra-virgin olive oil
⅓ cup (80 ml) best-quality red wine vinegar

1. Tear the leaves of curly endive into bite-size pieces. Combine the endive, chives, and onions in a large, shallow salad bowl, and toss.

2. Cut the tuna into 1-inch (2.5-cm) cubes.

3. Place the tuna in a nonstick frying pan, and, over medium-high heat, quickly brown the cubes. They will cook in just a minute or two and should remain rather rare on the inside. Season generously with salt and plenty of freshly ground black pepper.

4. Add the oil to the tuna in the pan and heat until it sizzles. Then very slowly add the red wine vinegar, stirring to coat the tuna with the oil and vinegar.

5. Quickly spoon the tuna, oil, and vinegar on top of the greens, toss thoroughly, and serve immediately.

Yield: 4 servings

LE CLOS MORILLONS
50 Rue des Morillons, Paris 15.
Tel: 48.28.04.37.
Métro: Convention or Porte-de-Vanves.
Reservations, noon to 2 P.M. and 8 to 10 P.M.
Closed Saturday lunch, Sunday, one week in February, and three weeks in August.
Credit card: V.
Menus at 160 francs (lunch only), 230 francs, and 285 francs. A la carte, 275 to 375 francs.

Chef Philippe Delacourcelle, who spent five years running various French restaurants all over Asia, returned to France with a changed palate, and he shares his culinary adventures in a manner that's fittingly thoughtful and subdued. His food doesn't shout, rather it approaches you with a straightforward hello and a handshake.

I love his *blanc de pintadeau tiède à l'huile vanilée sur lit de mâche*: the tenderest breast of guinea hen is bathed in a sauce just faintly flavored with vanilla, all on a bed of perfect *mâche*. Equally good is his *saumon grillé sur sa peau, riz sauvage aux épices*, a healthy portion of fresh salmon grilled to a crisp, and served with a generous mound of well-seasoned wild rice.

Two successful potato dishes include a feather-light flan sprinkled with chives and fresh-flavored hazlenut oil, as well as a generous serving of small potatoes topped with warm oysters and bathed in an eye-opening red wine sauce.

Beginning dinner with a toast.

SPECIALTIES:
Seasonal contemporary: terrine pressé de pommes de terre et foie gras (terrine of potatoes and fatted duck liver), petites pommes de terre farcies à la matelote d'huîtres (tiny potatoes stuffed with oysters), médaillon de lotte poêlées (pan-fried médaillon of monkfish), canette de Challans rôtie (roast duck from Challans).

Delacourcelle runs the restaurant with his brother, Marc, with whom he shares a passion for the wines of their native Loire. So we have here an impressive, well-priced list that includes the seldom-seen Chinon blanc, from the Château de Ligré; Alphonse Mellot's trustworthy Sancerre; and a large selection of the rare white Jasnières. From other regions, they offer a bold Cairanne, the Côtes-du-Rhône Villages from Rabasse Charavin and Dauvissat's dependable Chablis. Le Clos Morillons is the kind of restaurant that hits the spot at the end of a harried, hassle-filled day.

CONTRE-ALLEE
83 Avenue Denfert-
    Rochereau, Paris 14.
Tel: 43.54.99.86.
Métro: Denfert-Rochereau.
Reservations, noon to 2 P.M.
    and 8 to midnight.
Credit card: V.
Terrace.
Air-conditioned.
A la carte, 250 francs.

SPECIALTIES:
Contemporary light: cabillaud rôti au parmesan (roast cod with Parmesan cheese), tagliatelles maison (homemade pasta), mousse de fromage blanc au coulis de fruits rouges (fresh cheese mousse with red berry sauce).

Travelers eager to take part in a gathering of bonafide French yuppies should reserve a table at Contre-Allée, a bright, casual, modern restaurant that breaks away from the traditional French mold. Yes, one can come here for steak and Beaujolais, but the menu changes regularly, and there is always a varied selection of fresh, homemade pastas, gigantic mixed salads, and vegetarian platters. Contre-Allée is particularly appealing in warm weather, when a series of tables move out onto the terrace and under the shade of the giant trees lining the Avenue Denfert-Rochereau, not far from Montparnasse. Inside, the decorative theme is bull fighting (posters and enlarged color photos line the ochre-toned walls), and the atmosphere is young, club-like, and relaxed.

LA COUPOLE
102 Boulevard du
   Montparnasse, Paris 14.
Tel: 43.20.14.20.
Fax: 43.35.46.14.
Métro: Vavin.
Reservations, noon to 3 P.M.
   and 7 P.M. to 1:30 A.M.
Open daily except
   Christmas eve.
Credit cards: AE, DC, V.
Air-conditioned.
109-franc menu, after 11
   P.M., wine included. A la
   carte, 230 to 280 francs.

SPECIALTIES:
Brasserie: plats du jour
(changing daily specials), plateau
de fruits de mer (platter of fish
and shellfish), poissons et viandes
grillés (grilled fish and meats).

The brasserie magnate Jean-Paul Bucher (whose high-quality "Flo" brasseries continue to multiply) purchased this hundred-year-old Left Bank haunt in 1988, and has done his best to maintain its durable charm. La Coupole—built in 1927 and newly restored to its original state, including mosaics, original plaster, and Art Deco light fixtures—remains a personal favorite, a huge and largely democratic spot seating up to 350 diners. The food here seldom disappoints (nor does it stun you with pleasure), but new Spanish-oriented items, such as their gazpacho and salt cod (*morue*) salad are quite good. And of course one never goes wrong with half a dozen oysters, grilled fish, and a touch of chilled Alsatian white wine.

LE DOME
108, Boulevard du
   Montparnasse, Paris 14.
Tel: 43.35.25.81.
Fax: 42.79.01.19.
Métro: Vavin.
Reservations, noon to 3 P.M.
   and 7 P.M. to midnight.
Closed Monday and August.
Credit cards: AE, DC, V.
Enclosed Terrace.
Private dining room for 10.
Air-conditioned.
A la carte: 350 to 500
   francs.

SPECIALTIES:
Fish and shellfish: plateau de
fruits de mer (platters of fresh
fish and shellfish), soupe de
poissons (fish soup), bouillabaisse
(fish soup), turbot rôti, sauce
Hollandaise (roast turbot with
Hollandaise sauce).

For all cooks, the rule's the same. If you can secure the freshest of fresh ingredients, your job is half done. And when the ingredients are fish and shellfish, one might even say, 75 percent done. Then the cook's job becomes one of a minimalist: The less done the better. At historic, ever popular Le Dôme, they understand fish and shellfish. The price of your meal may not always be to your liking, you may find that some dishes lack a touch of sophistication, and the service may lag at times. But you will not find fault with freshness.

Order a plate full of *bouquets bretons*, the tiny, salmony pink shrimp that taste almost nutty, and of the sea, and you'll see what I mean. These full-flavored, fresh little shrimp have no relationship to 99 percent of the shrimp commonly found in French markets. These arrive still vibrantly alive, whereas the majority may have been cooked days in advance, and perhaps frozen. Sample the Brittany-fresh *crevettes,* or shrimp, with a bit of the Dôme's crusty bread spread with a healthy dose of salty Breton butter, and you're on your way to heaven.

Delicious as well—though designed for those with a touch of patience—is the *friture de céteaux,* tiny sole the size of a child's hand. Gently fried and served whole, the delicate little Atlantic fish are served with deep-fried celery leaves and a fine *sauce tartare*. (No matter that you may have to carefully remove some of the tiny skeletal bones. Whenever fish is cooked whole and on the bone, you're always rewarded with greater flavor.)

On a sunny Saturday afternoon, I love nothing better than to secure a table on the lively Dôme terrace, and order up a dozen briny oysters to enjoy with a glass of Didier Dagueneau's rich and golden Pouilly Fumé or André Bonhomme's almond-like Mâcon-Viré. Another favorite is their grilled fish of the day: The waiter parades to your table with an entire platter of varied bright, firm, and glossy fish. One day you may choose a bright-eyed bar, on another a glistening *Saint-Pierre*. Once cooked, the fish is filleted tableside, and served with nothing more than a sprinkling of fragrant extra-virgin olive oil and a few drops of freshly squeezed lemon juice. Desserts are quite fine, especially the perfect *tarte aux framboises*, and the pleasing array of fresh fruits and sorbets.

BISTROT DU DOME
1 Rue Delambre, Paris 14
Tel: 43.35.32.00.
Métro: Vavin.
Reservations, 12:30 to 2 P.M.
    and 7:30 to 10:30 P.M.
Open daily.
Credit cards: AE, V.
Sidewalk terrace.
Air-conditioned.
A la carte, 190 to 260
    francs.

SPECIALTIES:
Fish and shellfish: fricassée de patagos (tiny steamed clams, bathed in cream, curry, garlic, and parsley), éperlans frits (fried smelt), thon grillé (grilled tuna).

The secrets to creating a successful restaurant are not really so mysterious: Stick to what people love to eat, keep the menu simple, and make everyone feel as though there's good value in the air. This is exactly what to expect at the Bistrot du Dôme, a bright and cheerful offshoot of the well-known brasserie, Le Dôme, in Paris' Montparnasse neighborhood. Fish is the main event here, and the menu—displayed on a blackboard within easy viewing distance—changes from day to day and generally features five to six first courses and an equal number of main courses. Sardines and *rouget* (red mullet) are grilled ever so simply; tuna is sliced into thick meaty steaks and pan fried; while tiny smelts, or *éperlans*, are lightly breaded and deep fried. Often, the daily menu also features *cabillaud* (cod) or *rascasse* (angler fish), merely poached and set upon a bed of dressed greens.

But the biggest success of all is the *fricassée de patagos*, an uncomplicated dish of fresh tiny clams that are steamed and then infused in a garlic and curry-seasoned cream, then sprinkled with finely

Readying the next mouthful.

snipped parsley leaves. The end result is fragrant and rich, yet so light that you long for seconds, even thirds.

The small yellow, blue, and white dining room allows barely enough elbow room between tables, and is generally packed at lunch and dinner, so reservations are advised. The brief wine list is truly inventive in its pricing: all the wines are well priced. Do try the Vouvray *sec* from Gaston Huet, a white that marries perfectly with Bistrot du Dôme's simple fish and shellfish preparations. For dessert, sample a selection of fruit sorbets or a fresh fruit salad.

LE DUC
243 Boulevard Raspail,
Paris 14.
Tel: 43.20.96.30.
Fax: 43.20.46.73.
Métro: Raspail.
Reservations, noon to 2:30
P.M. and 8 to 10:45 P.M.
Closed Saturday, Sunday,
and Monday.
No credit cards.
A la carte, 500 to 850
francs.

S P E C I A L T I E S :
Fish and shellfish: dorade grillé
nature (grilled porgy), loup grillé
nature (grilled sea bass), salade
de crabe frais (fresh crab salad).

Some restaurants are like private clubs that, from time to time, deign to let non-members in for an evening. Le Duc, where the fish is still among the freshest to be found in Paris, is one of those clubs. If you're not a member, just getting a table will be no simple matter. Call and call again and maybe if you're lucky, they'll give you a reservation. Then, of course, once they do condescend to let you in, they'll suggest that you wait at the smoke-filled bar for a table. *"Un bon moment,"* or an hour, should be just about right. Then, as long as you're already seated at the bar, why don't you just eat there, they suggest. Forget it! That's not my idea of dining, and that's not why I came.

Once you're seated in the dining room, things calm down. The waiters (who all seem to have been trained on the Côte d'Azur) begin to warm up, for they know once you take a bite of Paul Minchelli's exquisite fish preparations, you'll be putty in their hands. And they're right.

The Minchelli brothers have a very special way with fish, coming from the "minimalist" school of cooking. Take the *dorade royale*, gorgeous pink-tinged petals of fish, paper thin, embellished only with a few drops of exquisite extra-virgin olive oil, salt, and freshly ground pepper. Equally perfect is the *dorade grillé*, at its peak of freshness, cooked whole with all the flavorful skin and bones, filleted tableside. Bathed in fennel-infused oil, it's a sheer marvel. The fresh crab salad is a crab-lover's delight: a perfectly simple mound of fresh, moist, almost-sweet crabmeat, served with a fresh mayonnaise or a simple drizzle of oil.

I loved a bit less the *lotte à la provençale*. It had perfectly lovely ingredients—fresh *courgettes* and chunks of *lotte*—but everything arrived virtually swimming in oil. The wine list is very brief, and offers a drinkable Chablis. So you decide: If you'd walk a few kilometers for really fresh fish, then go and take your chances.

ERAWAN
76 Rue de la Fédération,
Paris 15.
Tel: 47.83.55.67.
Métro: La Motte-Piquet.
Reservations, noon to 2:30
P.M. and 7 to 10:30 P.M.
Closed Sunday and August.
Credit cards: AE, V.
Air-conditioned.
Menus 132, 158, 164, and
175 francs. A la carte,
200 to 250 francs.

SPECIALTIES:
Thai: yam Hoy men Phou (spicy salad of mussels, basil, and lemon grass), hor Mok Kuon (spicy shrimp steamed in banana leaves), khao phat ruam mit (rice sautéed with shrimp, crab, and Thai sausages).

This lovely, lively, elegant restaurant not far from Unesco and the Eiffel Tower, offers some of Paris's best, and most accessible Thai food. Erawan has two small dining rooms, nicely decorated in pastel colors, and uses lovely blue and white china throughout. You'll leave feeling healthy and not heavy, having feasted on salads, fish simmered in a refreshing coconut milk sauce, fabulous rice cooked with snippets of sausage, shrimp, and crab, and all manner of dishes filled with the flavor and fragrance of basil, lemongrass (*citronelle*), mint, and spices. If you adore spicy-hot food, you'll find it here in the salads of spicy shrimp and lemongrass, the classic Thai beef, spice and lemongrass, and mussels stuffed with herbs and spices. If you want a sampling of Thai food, there are a variety of inexpensive fixed menus. With the meal, sample a chilled Bandol rosé.

SAUMON NATURE SAUCE BASILIC LE DUC
LE DUC'S SALMON WITH BASIL SAUCE

There are many versions of fish cooked on a plate, and this is one of my favorites. It is such a simple, natural, uncomplicated method of steaming fish that I wonder why it isn't more popular. At Le Duc, a Left Bank restaurant devoted to fish (see entry, page 107), this version appears on the menu from time to time. When preparing it, I use two large Pyrex pie plates—so that I can keep track of the salmon steaks as they cook—placed on top of a couscous cooker. At Le Duc, the salmon is served quite rare; it is considered done when the base of the fish turns white. Those who prefer their salmon fully cooked can just continue cooking until the fish is opaque throughout, about 20 minutes.

¼ cup (60 ml) fresh basil leaves, firmly packed
½ cup (125 ml) extra-virgin olive oil
3 medium tomatoes, cored, peeled, seeded, and chopped
Salt and freshly ground black pepper to taste
1 tablespoon (½ ounce; 15 g) unsalted butter
4 salmon steaks, (each weighing about 6 to 8 ounces; 180 to 250 g)

1. Prepare the sauce: Wash and dry the basil leaves and snip into shreds, or a *chiffonnade*, with a scissors. Combine the basil, oil, tomatoes, salt, and pepper in a small bowl. Cover, and set aside to marinate for 1 hour.

2. Place the salmon steaks in a single layer on the bottom of a large buttered pie plate, preferably glass. Invert a second buttered pie plate, also preferably glass, over the first plate. Place the plates on top of a large pot of boiling water and cook to desired doneness. It will take about 10 minutes for rare salmon, 20 minutes for the salmon to be cooked through.

3. To serve, place each steak in the center of a warmed dinner plate, and spoon the basil sauce all over.

Yield: 4 servings

KIM-ANH
15 Rue de l'Eglise, Paris 15.
Tel: 45.79.40.96.
Métro: Saint-Charles.
Reservations, noon to 2:30 P.M. and 7 to 10:30 P.M.
Open daily.
Credit cards: AE, DC, V.
Air-conditioned.
200-franc menu. A la carte, 250 to 330 francs.

SPECIALTIES:
Vietnamese: langoustines caramelisées (caramelized prawns with Thai rice), coquelet farci (chicken stuffed with spices), lamelles de bouef sautées aux vermicelles (strips of beef sautéed with noodles and spices).

For elegant and traditional Vietnamese fare, head over to the 15th arrondissement and the Rue de l'Eglise, where, evenings only, Caroline Kim-Anh and her husband entertain a select twenty or so diners in their tiny dining room, charmingly decorated with bamboo and wicker. Before moving to France, Mr. Kim-Anh sold American cars in Saigon, while his wife perfected her own brand of home cooking. Here you'll find all the best elements of Vietnamese cuisine: The food is light, refreshing, full of fresh herbs, light sauces, and gentle spicing. Try the strips of beef sautéed in a mix of vermicelli, peanuts, and shallots marinated in vinegar; the caramelized *langoustines* served with the aromatic Thai rice; and the delightful crab stuffed with a blend of fragrant herbs.

SOUPE DE PECHES
SUMMER PEACH SOUP

Prepare this delightfully summery dessert when peaches and nectarines are at their height of flavor. It's a simple make-ahead dessert, leaving you free the rest of the day. The recipe comes from David Van Laer, chef at the lively, contemporary bistro, Manufacture (see entry below). Orange-flower water, a popular and pungent flavoring used regularly in the south of France, is optional. Instead, use grated orange zest.

6 ripe peaches
6 ripe nectarines
1 cup (120 g)
  confectioners' sugar
2 cups (50 cl) dry white
  wine, preferably
  Chardonnay
1 tablespoon orange-
  flower water or
  grated zest of 1
  orange
30 fresh mint leaves

Peel and quarter the peaches and nectarines. Sprinkle with sugar (the amount will vary according to taste and the sweetness of the fruit). Add the wine, orange flower water, and mint leaves. Cover and refrigerate for 2 hours. Serve cold, in individual champagne coupes.

Yield: 6 to 8 servings

MANUFACTURE
20 Esplanade de la
  Manufacture (at 30 Rue
  Ernest Renan), 92130
  Issy-les-Moulineaux.
Tel: 40.93.08.98.
Fax: 40.93.57.22.
Métro: Porte de Versailles.
Reservations, noon to 2:30
  P.M. and 8 to 10:30 P.M.
Closed Saturday lunch, all
  day Sunday, and three
  weeks in August.
Credit cards: AE, V.
Garden terrace.
Air-conditioned.
A la carte, 200 to 250
  francs.

Chef Jean-Pierre Vigato, of the restaurant Apicius, has found great success with his Manufacture, a large and loft-like restaurant situated just across the Paris line near the Porte de Versailles. Here, his young assistant, David Van Laer, translates Vigato's cuisine to the letter, offering a welcoming mix of modern and rustic fare. The menu changes regularly, inspired by Van Laer's creative mood of the moment, and one can always anticipate unusual (and usually successful) combinations, often punctuated by garlic, anchovies, capers, mustard, herbs, or olive oil. Those who love organ meats will be delighted with Van Laer's thickly sliced kidneys in a heady mustard sauce, or his famed *cocotte de cochon*, a virile combination of pig's head, ears, cheeks, and tail on a bed of

SPECIALTIES:
Modern bistro: petite salade de
céleri et foie gras cru (salad of
celery and fresh foie gras), terrine
de poireaux (leek terrine), la
dorade rôtie à la crème de
romarin (roast porgy with
rosemary cream), le lapereau
confit ail et persil (confit of
rabbit with garlic and parsley),
le gâteau chocolat tiède et fondant
(warm chocolate cake), poêlée de
cerises (cherries sautéed in butter
and sugar, with vanilla ice
cream).

polenta. On a recent visit, I loved the traditional salad of curly endive tossed with bacon and topped with a pair of perfectly poached eggs, and a thick sauce of red wine. The wine list offers some real bargains, including Château Beaucastel's Vieille Ferme.

ARC DE TRIOMPHE, TROCADERO, PORTE MAILLOT

16th and 17th arrondissements

APICIUS
122 Avenue de Villiers,
Paris 17.
Tel: 43.80.19.66.
Fax: 44.40.09.57.
Métro: Villiers.
Reservations, 12:30 to 2 P.M.
and 7:30 to 9:30 P.M.
Closed Saturday, Sunday,
August, and Christmas
week.
Credit cards: AE, V.
Air-conditioned.
A la carte, 500 to 850
francs.

SPECIALTIES:
Seasonal, contemporary: foie gras
de canard poêlé en aigre doux
(pan-fried duck liver with sweet
and sour sauce), rougets grillés à
la plaque (grilled red mullet),
pieds de porc rôties en crépinette
(pig's feet wrapped in caul fat).

Jean-Pierre Vigato reminds me a bit of a track star who also plays the violin, a man of multiple talents who appreciates both the overtly physical and the aesthetically refined sides of life.

Admittedly, I was slow to warm to the food at Vigato's modern and fashionable restaurant Apicius, located on the trendy side of Paris' 17th arrondissement. At one point I pretty much relegated his food to the sort favored by people more concerned about their waistlines than their palates.

You can find that type of fare still—tiny fresh rouget, or red mullet, bathed in a few drops of olive oil; unadorned fresh langoustines, simply pan-fried; steamed raie, or skate, sprinkled with coarse grains of salt—and it's nothing to sneer at. One could remain forthrightly cheery on a steady diet of his most simplified fare.

But in truth, it's Vigato's daily changing "plat bourgeois" that seems to please him most, and on days one decides to throw caution to the wind, it's a definite reason to book a table. Imagine an earthy, refined, well-seasoned pâté de lièvre (wild hare terrine), sliced into thick fragrant slabs and served with crusty bread from Jean-Luc Poujauran, one of Paris' best bakers. Or a highly perfumed *râble de lièvre,* richly flavored and mahogany-hued, served with a mouth-soothing celery root purée, a dish that makes you want to take a long walk in the woods on a sun-glazed winter's day. Or better yet, go for rustic platters of braised beef cheeks, or *joues de boeuf,* tender and chewy, a dish that cries out for sips of J. L. Grippat's stunning Saint-Joseph, a velvety, cherry-like, lush Rhône red, and one that's usually a good value.

On one visit, Vigato's friends from the Savoie had just arrived with mountainous chunks of aged, farm cheese, and we were fortunate to have rationed the Saint-Joseph, so that we were able to savor it with a golden *dégustation* of buttery mountain Beaufort and tangy *tomme de Savoie au marc.*

Service here varies from friendly and polished to painfully slow and awkward, for Vigato insists on personally taking each order, and that causes inevitable, frustrating delays. But go with a healthy dose of patience and a good appetite, and enjoy!

LA BUTTE CHAILLOT

112 Avenue Kléber,
Paris 16.
Tel: 47.27.88.88.
Fax: 47.04.85.70.
Métro: Trocadero.
Reservations, noon to
2:30 P.M. and 7 to
12:30 A.M.
Open daily.
Credit cards: AE, V.
Sidewalk terrace.
Private dining room for 20.
Air-conditioned.
110-franc lunch menu. A la carte, 230 to 300 francs.

S P E C I A L T I E S :
Bistro: roasted and grilled meats: poitrine de veau au romarin à la broche (rotisserie-roasted veal breast with rosemary), volaille fermière rôtie à la broche, pommes purée (rotisserie-roasted farm chicken with potato puree), ravioles du Royans au persil simple (tiny cheese raviolis tossed with parsley).

Guy Savoy has been an aggressive bistro-maker, with four satellites to his name, and La Butte Chaillot is the trendiest of them all. Located just steps from the Trocadero, La Butte Chaillot attracts a well-heeled, frankly bourgeois clientele. The small, two-story restaurant is starkly modern, with bright aqua leather chairs, lots of glass, and a huge warming fireplace for cool weather days. But the menu is vintage Guy Savoy, meaning there's lots that's familiar (such as rotisserie chicken with a smooth potato purée; roasted breast of veal; Charolais beef with Béarnaise sauce and shoestring potatoes), and plenty of Savoy signature dishes, including a sparkling fresh platter of *huîtres en nage glacé;* soft and fragrant oysters resting on a bed of tangy cream and topped with jellied oyster liquor; and his "rustic-modern" soup of creamy lentils, paired with a touch of luxury-priced *langoustines,* or shrimp-like crustaceans. The wine list is brief, with wines by the glass. For a special treat, try André Ostertag's Alsatian Pinot Noir. La Butte Chaillot also offers a quick-service "plat du jour" at lunchtime. Too bad the bread isn't better.

LA *FRICASSEE DE POULET AUX MORILLES LA COQUILLE*
LA COQUILLE'S FRICASSEE OF CHICKEN WITH MORELS

I must have visited La Coquille (see entry, page 114) a dozen times before sampling this thoroughly satisfying bistro dish. I always seemed to be ordering the game or the boudin (blood sausage) or the beautifully cooked scallops, and just ignored the chicken. Now it is a favorite, and one that is particulary welcoming on a cold wintry evening. This version is lighter than most, though for a richer dish, one could substitute cream for the morel cooking water, reducing it as instructed in the recipe.

1 ounce (30 g) dried
   morels
3 tablespoons extra-
   virgin olive oil
1 tablespoon (½ ounce;
   15 g) unsalted butter
1 chicken (about 3 to 4
   pounds; 1.5 to 2 kg),
   cut into serving
   pieces
Salt and freshly ground
   black pepper to taste
2 shallots, finely minced
¼ teaspoon sweet
   paprika
1 cup (250 ml) *crème
   fraîche* (see page 279)
   or heavy cream
Small handful of parsley
   or chervil, minced,
   for garnish

1. Combine the morels with 2 cups (500 ml) of water in a medium-size saucepan. Bring to a boil over high heat, then allow to cook away vigorously, uncovered, until the liquid is reduced by half. This should take about 20 minutes. Strain the liquid through dampened cheesecloth. Rinse the morels, return them to the strained liquid, and reserve.

2. Melt the oil and butter in a large, deep-sided 12-inch (30-cm) skillet over high heat. (If you do not have a pan large enough to hold all the chicken pieces in a single layer, cook the chicken in several batches.) Season the chicken liberally with salt and pepper, and when the fats are hot but not smoking, brown the chicken on one side until the skin turns an even, golden brown, about 5 minutes. Carefully regulate the heat to avoid scorching the skin. Turn the pieces and brown them on the other side for an additional 5 minutes.

3. Remove the chicken pieces to a large platter. Discard all but 1 tablespoon of the fat remaining in the pan. In the pan, over medium heat, brown the shallots. Then mix in the paprika.

4. Combine the *crème fraîche,* morels, and strained liquid, stir well, and add to the skillet. Return the chicken to the skillet and cook covered, over low heat, until the chicken is cooked to desired doneness, about 20 minutes.

5. Serve with cooked rice or steamed new potatoes, sprinkling each serving with fresh parsley or chervil.

Yield: 4 servings

LA COQUILLE
6 Rue du Débarcadère,
   Paris 17.
Tel: 45.74.25.95.
Métro: Porte Maillot or
   Argentine.
Reservations, noon to to
   2:30 P.M. and 7 to
   10:30 P.M.
Credit card: AE, V.
Closed Sunday, Monday,
   August, and Christmas
   week.
Air-conditioned.
A la carte, 330 to 450
   francs.

SPECIALTIES:
*Elegant bistro: scallops in season
(October to May), fricassée de
poulet aux morilles (chicken with
wild morel mushrooms), foie gras,
soufflé au praslin (hazelnut
soufflé), tarte aux pommes (thin
apple tart). Alsatian wines.*

Sometimes I wonder just how great a role memory plays in the pleasures we derive from eating. Often, when I return to a familiar restaurant in search of previously enjoyed pleasures, it's hard to distinguish the immediate enchantment from past satisfactions.

La Coquille, a dependable Parisian family restaurant situated between the Etoile and Porte Maillot is, for me at least, one of those "memory lane" establishments. I've been a regular here for more than a decade, and though I'm sometimes elated, sometimes less enthused, I keep going back for the menu, the homey surroundings, the specialties that make La Coquille stand out from the others.

Chef and owner Clément Lausecker took over from the Blache family some years ago, and the few minor changes he's made to the dependable menu are for the better. From October through May one can always count on perfectly fresh oven-roasted scallops in their shells, embellished with a touch of butter and gentle seasoning.

La Coquille has long made a specialty of fresh and vibrant first-of-the-season asparagus, served with a simple vinaigrette or a fine sauce *mousseline,* and more recently the Lauseckers have been serving the giant green variety, direct from Provence.

I'm all for the chef's addition of a daily fish special: On my last visit he prepared a thoroughly satisfying grilled *bar,* cooked to perfection and served with a soothing *beurre blanc.* There is always game in season, a homey *fricassée de poulet aux morilles* (see recipe, page 113), hearty grilled *boudin noir aux pommes,* and a wonderfully old-fashioned *pigeon en cocotte,* served rosy rare. As ever, there is the famed *soufflé au praslin de noisettes,* hazelnut soufflé (see recipe, page 118), and chef Lausecker's fine, thin apple tart, *tarte aux pommes.*

LE BISTROT D'A COTE— FLAUBERT

10 Rue Gustave-Flaubert, Paris 17.
Tel: 42.67.05.81.
Fax: 47.63.82.75.
Métro: Courcelles or Ternes.
Reservations, 12:30 to 2:30 P.M. and 7 to 11:30 P.M.
Open daily.
Credit cards: AE, V.
Sidewalk terrace.
Air-conditioned.
175-franc menu (lunch and Sunday). A la carte, 260 to 320 francs.

SPECIALTIES:
Lyonnais: gratin de macaroni au jambon de Vercours (macaroni and ham gratin), le sabodet lyonnais aux ravioles de romans (pork sausage with tiny ravioli), filet de boeuf grillé, gratin dauphinois (grilled beef and potato gratin), petits pots au chocolat (chocolate pots de crème).

As the granddaddy of satellite bistros, Le Bistrot d'à Côté has never lost its appeal, with its Lyonnaise menu of chicken liver *terrine,* pork sausages and lentils, and macaroni gratin with country ham. The decor is bistro-beautiful, with tin ceilings, mirrored walls, and bookshelves lined with Art Deco clocks and radios, and a prized collection of Michelin red guides dating back to the early part of the century. Rostang's formula works, for the restaurant is busy lunch and dinner, and is particularly appealing in good weather, when tables tumble out onto the tiny sidewalk of this upper-middle-class, residential neighborhood. Service can be cold and snippy at times, the quality of the food varies from high to low. Make note of the fine cheese platter—including a Saint-Marcellin, a goat cheese, and a Swiss *tête-de moine*—and the well-priced Saint-Joseph.

Chef Michel Rostang at his Bistro d' à Côte—Flaubert.

BISTRO DE L'ETOILE— LAURISTON

19 Rue Lauriston, Paris 16.
Tel: 40.67.11.16.
Métro: Charles-de-Gaulle— Etoile.
Reservations, noon to 2:30 P.M. and 7:30 to midnight.
Closed Saturday lunch and Sunday.
Credit cards: AE, V.
Air-conditioned.
A la carte, 200 to 260 francs.

Parisian chef Guy Savoy's firmament shines bright, and a favorite star is Le Bistro de l'Etoile on the Rue Lauriston just off the Etoile. With room for about fifty diners, this modern, mirrored bistro is decorated in Savoy's signature color—a clean bottle green—with touches of daffodil yellow. The chef, William Ledeuil, spent several years under Savoy's tutelage, and seems to have a good head on his shoulders. All those common bistro ingredients are here—beets and Bordeaux, *tendrons de veau* and *gratin dauphinois, crème brûlée* and *tarte aux pommes*—except in modern costume.

SPECIALTIES:
Modern bistro: ravioles de
Romans aux champignons et
parmesan (miniature cheese
ravioli with mushrooms and
Parmesan), tendrons de veau de
lait, macaronis au jus de pistous
au jambon fumé (milk-fed lamb
breast of veal with macaroni,
pistou sauce and smoked ham),
tarte tiède aux pommes (warm
apple tart).

Chef Ledeuil will take tiny white asparagus, and rather than pairing it with a traditional (and most times banal) *sauce mousseline* or vinaigrette, he sauces it with a perky *sauce ravigote,* or mustardy vinaigrette spiced with capers, herbs, and shallots. As a starter one evening, he offered an unusual *terrine* of beets with avocado purée: Perfectly cooked beets were sliced oh-so-thin, then stacked in layers, with a smooth avocado filling. The *sauce ravigote* had another chance to shine, serving here as a bright flavor accent, turning the dish into a fine palate teaser. During the course of many visits, I've loved his meltingly moist and copious portions of rabbit in a delicately flavored ginger sauce, properly cooked tuna steaks served on a bed of fennel, and pleasantly lean slices of *tendrons de veau,* served with a *macaronis au jus de pistou au jambon fumé.*

I particularly applaud chef Ledeuil's approach to tuna. So many chefs sear the life out of tuna, leaving the interior raw, making for an often soggy, unpalatable mess. Here the tuna steak is pan-fried like a beefsteak, then set to rest, giving the juices time to flow back into the fish, producing fish that is moist, well-cooked, but never dry.

Desserts can be hit or miss. I don't quite get the point of his soggy *pain perdu au praliné,* with a sauce that tastes like evaporated milk. But he wins my heart with the warm and crackling *tarte aux pommes,* that perfect combination of apples, butter and sugar, and the sort of dish that will have me, for one, coming back for more.

The brief wine list offers some real stars, including the unfiltered Alsatian Pinot Noir from Ostertag, and a meaty Saumur from Château Langlois in the Loire.

CHEZ FRED
190 bis Boulevard Péreire,
  Paris 17.
Tel: 45.74.20.48.
Métro: Péreire.
Reservations, 12 to 2 P.M.
  and 7:30 to 11 P.M.
Closed Sunday and three
  weeks in August.
Credit cards: AE, DC, V.
Sidewalk terrace.
145-franc menu (lunch
  only, including wine).
A la carte, 200 to 220
  francs.

SPECIALTIES:
Lyonnais bistro: plats du jour
(changing daily specials), salade
mixte (tossed salad), côtelettes
d'agneau vert pré (lamb chops
with watercress garnish),
saucisson chaud pommes à l'huile
(warm poached pork sausage with
potatoes bathed in oil), tarte
maison (homemade tart), mousse
cassis et son coulis (black currant
mousse with black currant sauce).

H ere is a good-natured bistro where handsome, chatty waiters serve up a fine and well-priced litany of daily specials, such as *gigot d'agneau, petit salé, tête de veau, pot-au-feu, boeuf à la mode, sauté d'agneau.* The decor here is *grand-mère* 1930, with walls covered with mirrors, old china, and a collection of umbrellas left behind by absent-minded customers. I love the fact that they've maintained traditional daily specials: If *pot-au-feu* is on the menu, it's got to be Thursday!

JAMIN
32 Rue de Longchamp,
  Paris 16.
Tel: 47.27.12.27.
Métro: Trocadéro.
Reservations 12:30 to
  2:15 P.M. and 7:30 to
  10:15 P.M.
Closed Saturday, Sunday,
  and July.
Credit cards: AE, DC, V.
Private dining room for 14.
Air-conditioned.
Menus at 890 and 1,200
  francs. A la carte, 800
  to 900 francs.
Note: The restaurant is
  scheduled to move to
  55 Avenue Raymond-
  Poincaré, Paris 16, at the
  end of 1993.

C ertainly, the only task more difficult than getting to the top of your profession is staying there. Joël Robuchon, unquestionably the finest chef working in France today, has shown us all that staying there is what he intends to do. And it is very much in Robuchon's style that he does it *his* way. He's obsessed with perfection, all the while aware that it is unattainable. A maniac for detail, he insists that everyone around share his devotion to the smallest of tasks. Yet through it all, he is modest to a fault, surprising even himself with the quality of the food he puts before us. Of course, without talent and vision, none of this would add up to what Robuchon's cooking is all about: an intensity of flavors, a distillation of ingredients, so that what we taste is the very essence of a mushroom, a pea, a *langoustine,* a slice of apple.

We're talking modern history, but there is little question that Robuchon's influence on French cuisine will be seen for years in the future. He's taught us to respect every ingredient, no matter how humble: Pig's head, rabbit, even chicory—are all noble prod-

SPECIALTIES:
Seasonal, contemporary: seasonal menus of truffles, shellfish, wild mushrooms; gelée de caviar à la crème de chou-fleur (caviar jelly with cauliflower cream), côte de veau de lait aux morilles et asperges (milk-fed veal chop with wild morel mushrooms and asparagus), suprême de pigeon au chou et foie gras (pigeon breasts with cabbage and foie gras), turban de pommes à la canelle (apple, pineapple, and cinnamon molds).

ucts to enjoy to their fullest. Who else would have made us rethink combinations, such as cauliflower and caviar? Yet he does not forget that we can never have our fill of the classics: *foie gras,* lobster, truffles. This is not spur-of-the-moment cooking, but an intelligent, well-considered expression of the way he knows we want to eat today.

As one who is almost categorically opposed to the modern-day menu *dégustation,* I find that Robuchon is one of the few chefs to studiously construct a menu so that it is like a fine symphony,

SOUFFLE AU PRASLIN DE NOISETTES LA COQUILLE
LA COQUILLE'S HAZELNUT SOUFFLE

La Coquille is a favorite neighborhood bistro (see entry, page 114), and this is its signature dessert. I sampled the soufflé the first time I dined there one cold wintry evening. As my love for La Coquille grew, so did my fondness for this light, hazelnut-filled dessert.

Praline powder:
¾ cup (100 g) hazelnuts
½ cup (100 g) sugar
1 teaspoon unsalted
    butter for buttering a
    cookie sheet
Pastry cream:
1 cup (250 ml) milk
½ vanilla bean
6 eggs, separated
3 tablespoons sugar
¼ cup (30 g) all-purpose
    flour (do not use
    unbleached flour)
Pinch of salt
1 tablespoon (½ ounce;
    15 g) unsalted butter,
    for buttering a 4-cup
    (1-liter) soufflé mold
¼ cup (60 ml) kirsch

1. Preheat the oven to 300°F (150°C).

2. Toast the hazelnuts on a baking sheet in the oven for 5 minutes. While they are still warm, rub them in a dish towel to remove as much skin as possible. Cool, then chop coarsely by hand.

3. In a medium-size saucepan over low heat, melt the sugar until it dissolves and becomes slightly rust-colored. Add the nuts and stir until they are thoroughly coated with sugar. This is now your praline.

4. Turn the praline out onto a cool buttered cookie sheet and allow to harden, about 5 minutes. When hard, place the praline in a food processor and grind to a powder. Set aside. (The praline powder can be made in advance and stored in an airtight container. It can be refrigerated for a week or frozen indefinitely.)

5. Prepare the pastry cream: In a medium-size saucepan over medium heat, bring the milk and vanilla bean to a boil. Remove from the heat, cover, and allow to steep for 5 minutes.

6. In a medium-size mixing bowl combine 4 of the egg yolks with the sugar, then the flour. Remove the vanilla

designed to build to crescendos, taking our palates on condensed, culinary pleasure voyages.

Whether it is a simple roast chicken showered with truffles, a cream of wild mushroom soup that extracts the very essence of wildness from the fabulous fungi, or a very basic apple tart flavored with a healthy dose of cinnamon, he shows us all what heights cuisine can reach. Tables are not easy to come by (lunch is easier than dinner), and the prices don't allow many of us to indulge on a regular basis. But keep the phone number close at hand, and don't give up until they find you a table. You won't regret it.

bean from the milk and whisk the milk into the egg mixture. (You may rinse the vanilla bean and reserve it for another use.) Place the mixture in a medium-size saucepan and cook over medium heat, stirring constantly, until it begins to boil. Continue cooking for 2 minutes, stirring constantly. Remove from heat and add the 2 additional egg yolks, whisking until well blended. (The soufflé can be prepared ahead up to this point.)

7. Preheat the oven to 325°F (165°C).

8. To finish the soufflé, in a large bowl add half the praline powder to the pastry cream and mix until well blended.

9. In another large bowl beat the egg whites with a pinch of salt until stiff but not dry. Add one-third of the egg white mixture to the pastry cream mixture and fold in gently but thoroughly. Then gently fold in the remaining whites. Don't overmix, but be sure that the mixture is well blended.

10. Butter the soufflé mold. Gently pour the soufflé mixture into the mold and sprinkle the remaining praline powder on top of the soufflé. This will form a golden crust when the soufflé is baked. Bake for 12 to 15 minutes.

11. Remove the soufflé from the oven, sprinkle with the kirsch, and serve immediately.

Yield: 4 servings

ROTI D'AGNEAU AUX HERBES EN CROUTE DE SEL JAMIN
JAMIN'S ROASTED LAMB WITH HERBS COOKED IN A SALT CRUST

This remarkably simple and flavorful dish is a popular item at chef Joël Robuchon's Restaurant Jamin (see entry, page 117). The lamb roasts in a thyme-infused salt crust, which actually serves as a hermetic, flavorful roasting shell. The crust is discarded after cooking.

Salt Crust:

½ cup (150 g) table salt

1 cup (240 g) coarse (kosher) salt

1 egg, separated

3¾ cups (525 g) all-purpose unbleached flour

4 tablespoons fresh thyme leaves, or 2 tablespoons dried thyme, mixed with 1¼ cups (310 ml) water

Lamb:

2 pounds (1 kg) boneless roasting lamb (a portion of leg of lamb works very well)

Freshly ground black pepper

1 teaspoon fresh thyme leaves, or ½ teaspoon dried thyme

Pinch of salt

1 teaspoon coarse (kosher) salt

1. Preheat the oven to 400°F (205°C).

2. Prepare the salt crust: In a large bowl, blend together the two salts, the egg white, flour, and thyme and water mixture. Knead until well blended. It is essential that the dough be firm, not too moist or sticky, or the lamb will steam, not roast. If necessary, knead in additional flour for a firm dough. Roll out the dough so it is large enough to wrap the lamb.

3. Season the lamb with the pepper and thyme. Completely wrap the lamb in the salt crust, pressing all the seams together and checking to make sure it is well sealed, and place on a baking sheet.

4. Just before roasting, combine the egg yolk with the pinch of salt and ½ teaspoon water to make a glaze. With a pastry brush, brush the glaze over the surface of the crust. Sprinkle all over with coarse salt.

5. Place the lamb in the oven and roast for 25 to 30 minutes for rare (or until the interior of the lamb is cooked to 112°F, or 45°C, when measured with a meat thermometer). For well-done lamb, cook an additional 5 to 10 minutes. The crust should be a deep golden brown. Let the lamb rest in the crust for 1 hour before serving. (The lamb will remain warm.)

6. To serve, cut open the crust at one end, remove the lamb, and cut the meat on the diagonal into very fine slices. Discard the crust. Serve with buttered fresh pasta or a potato gratin.

Yield: 4 servings

LA NIÇOISE
4 Rue Pierre Demours,
   Paris 17.
Tel: 45.74.42.41.
Métro: Ternes or Porte-
   Maillot.
Reservations, 12:30 to
   2:30 P.M. and 7:30 to
   10:30 P.M.
Closed Saturday and
   Sunday lunch.
Credit cards: AE, DC, V.
Private dining room for
   10 to 60.
Air-conditioned.
220-franc lunch menu.
A la carte, 200 to 280
   francs.

SPECIALTIES:
*Niçoise: fonds d'artichauts à la
barigoule (artichokes braised in
white wine), sauté de lapin au
pistou (sautéed rabbit with garlic
and basil purée), selle d'agneau
aux herbes, ratatouille niçoise
(roast saddle of lamb with
provençal vegetables).*

Parisian television personality and restaurateur Denise Fabre offers Parisians some of the best fare from her native Nice: There's an authentic beef *daube à la provençale;* a beautifully seasoned platter of stuffed sardines; and a perfectly respectable *artichaut à la barigoule,* or artichokes braised in white wine (see recipe, page 126). The *salade niçoise* could have been fresher, and the honey ice cream topped with *marc de Provence* is a big mistake, but the jovial and efficient service should leave you with an appreciative smile.

PORT ALMA
10 Avenue de New York,
   Paris 16.
Tel: 47.23.75.11.
Métro: Alma-Marceau
Reservations, noon to 3 P.M.
   and 7:30 to 10:30 P.M.
Closed Sunday and August.
Credit cards: AE, DC, V.
Private dining room for 15.
Air-conditioned.
200-franc lunch menu. A la
   carte, 400 to 600 francs.

SPECIALTIES:
*Fish and shellfish: friture
d'éperlans (deep-fried whitebait),
tartare de thon (salad of minced
raw tuna), bar cuit dans sa
croûte de sel (sea bass cooked in a
salt crust), côte de boeuf de Salers
poêlée au sel de Guérande (pan-
fried rib of beef from Salers),
crème brûlée aux noix (caramel
cream with nuts).*

Port Alma, the bright and elegant quay-side restaurant overlooking the Eiffel Tower, is un-questionably one of the best fish restaurants in Paris. Several years ago, chef Paul Canal left Le Dôme at Montparnasse to make it on his own, and though there are still some rough edges, Pont Alma is the kind of place where one can joyfully consider becoming a regular.

When it comes to freshness, creativity, and surprises, Canal's got it made. In summertime, he offers tender fried zucchini blossoms, gently filled with a fresh-flavored "salad" of herbs and tiny scallops. Or consider a refreshing crabmeat gazpacho, filled not with meager snippets, but generous mounds of sweet, tender crabmeat.

I applaud any fish restaurant that makes the effort to display platters of fresh, whole fish to help you make a selection (as well as determine fresh-ness for yourself). Port Alma always offers such a choice, and on my last visit we opted for a whole *bar en croûte de sel,* or sea bass cooked in a crust of sea salt, certainly the finest and most miraculous method for cooking whole fish. It's also the trickiest, for once that fish is hidden in a bed of sea salt (a process in which the salt serves as a tightly sealed baking vessel), you simply have to trust your oven and your judgment to know when the fish is properly cooked. Here it's filleted tableside, and served with a rich and creamy fennel gratin.

Other excellent choices include a light salad of mixed greens and baby clams, or *coques;* a warm, beautifully seasoned salad of *langoustines;* and *Saint-Pierre* served on a bed of zesty ratatouille.

The menu changes according to the market, and prices are well within reason, considering the high cost of fresh fish and shellfish. Canal generally offers an assortment of grilled fish of the day, such as *dorade* (porgy) or sole, served with a light *beurre blanc.* There's a modern rendition of *goujonnettes de sole* (here served with a tossed salad and a curry-flecked sauce); giant *coquilles Saint-Jacques,* served on a bed of leeks or braised with a touch of saffron; and a welcoming *friture* of the freshest of anchovies from the port village of Collioure.

The wine list is brief, but offers Didier Dagueneau's excellent Pouilly Fumé, Bernard Gripa's pleasing Saint-Joseph *blanc,* and a fine Mâcon-Viré "Vieilles Vignes" from André Bonhomme. Service, as directed by Canal's outgoing wife, Sonya, is discreet, yet attentive. And tables are well arranged, so you don't feel as though the next table is overhearing your private conversation.

LE RELAIS DU PARC
55 Avenue Raymond-
   Poincaré, Paris 16.
Tel: 44.05.66.10.
Fax: 44.05.66.00.
Métro: Victor-Hugo.
Reservations, noon to 2 P.M.
   and 7:30 to 10 P.M.
Open daily.
Credit cards: AE, V.
Air-conditioned.
A la carte, 250 to 300
   francs.

Leave it to Joël Robuchon—the undisputed master of modern French cooking—to figure out what Parisian diners are looking for today. While waiting to transfer his own restaurant, Jamin, from the Rue du Longchamp to the Avenue Raymond-Poincaré, the modest young chef took over the restaurant next door to where he was moving. That is, the hotel dining room of Le Parc Victor-Hugo. The Relais du Parc is demure, moderately quiet, and about as dignified as you can get while still serving up hearty portions of herring and steamed potatoes, oxtail, and chocolate mousse. It's as if the high toque decided to don corduroys for the weekend.

S P E C I A L T I E S :
*Bistro: Filets de hareng marinés
aux pommes tièdes (marinated
herring with warm potato salad),
soupe crémeuse de potiron (creamy
pumpkin soup), lotte rôtie à l'ail,
petites pâtes au safran (roasted
monkfish with garlic and saffron
pasta), civet de lapin au lard
fumé (rabit stew with smoked
bacon), tarte fine aux pommes
(thin apple tart).*

GUY SAVOY
18 Rue Troyon, Paris 17.
Tel: 43.80.40.61.
Fax: 46.22.43.09.
Métro: Charles-de-
   Gaulle–Etoile.
Reservations, noon to 2 P.M.
   and 7:30 TO 10:30 P.M.
Closed Saturday lunch and
   Sunday.
Credit cards: AE, MC, V.
Private dining room for
   10 to 30.
Air-conditioned.
600-franc menu. A la carte,
   600 to 800 francs.

S P E C I A L T I E S :
*Seasonal, contemporary: huîtres
en nage glacé (oysters on a bed of
cream, topped with jellied oyster
liquor), bar en écailles grillés
aux épices douces (sea bass grilled
with its skin, served with a
sweet, spicy juice of ginger,
vanilla, pepper and cream),
bricelets de grué de cacao et sorbet
chocolat amer (caramelized rind
of cocoa beans layered with
bittersweet chocolate sorbet in a
mocha crème anglaise.)*

In typical Robuchon style, he does not miss a beat, and once you've sampled his state-of-the-art veal stew, his densely-flavored crown of oxtail on a bed of carrots, or his popular apple tart, you'll be certain to have sampled the best that exists of the genre. Service is up to par, with Serge Calvez the outgoing and thoroughly responsible man in charge. The decor at Le Relais du Parc resembles a consummate movie set, a Frenchman's image of a perfect English back porch, glossy white and manicured, with neat flowers and footed white porcelain bowls of bright orange clementines reflected in rectangles of spotless, mirrored French doors. The wine list—with selections from Dagueneau and Madame Raffault in the Loire, Javer and Tollot-Beaut in Burgundy, and Guigal, Gripa and Graillot in the Rhône—should keep drinkers happy for a good, long time.

In today's contemporary cuisine, style is everything. Any chef with a decent budget can secure the best and the freshest of fish, shellfish, meats, fruits, and vegetables. What he does with these ingredients, and how he weaves them into a harmonious whole, distinguishes him from all the others.

Guy Savoy, one of the finest chefs cooking in France today, has that sort of welcome, distinguished style. When you leave his restaurant after a well-orchestrated *menu dégustation,* you're struck by his extraordinary range of flavors. No ingredient is forced, masked, overworked. And he's not afraid to cross cultural lines, adding exotic spices, risotto, and basmati rice when the spirit moves him.

The ever-smiling Savoy loves green—a symbol of freshness, light, and springtime—and rather subtly works the color into his cheery decor, his plates, and the food he serves. And his own personal joy is reflected in his creations. Restaurant Guy Savoy, near Paris' Etoile, is the kind of restaurant I like to reserve for special friends and special evenings.

A longtime favorite is his *huîtres en nages glacées,* soft and fragrant mouthfuls of sea-rich oysters, set upon a bed of tangy sour cream, another longtime signature. Savoy combines such earthy ingredients as lentils with luxury-priced *langoustines,* turning them into a uniquely flavored frothy soup that's typical of his "rustic-modern" fare. He takes an exotic blend of spices and creates a palate-opening sauce for the freshest of *bar,* grilled in its flavorful skin. *Ris de veau* become tender, tiny "*chaussons,*" served with tiny "sandwiches" of layered potatoes and fresh black truffles. And plump, moist, pigeon arrives on a bed of richly flavored risotto.

Dessert lovers will swoon over his *mille-feuilles vanille et coulis de fruits rouges,* a dessert he's made a signature classic, light, feathery, airy, and yet one that's full of character and flavor.

Service is solid, self-assured, and not the least bit pretentious, with a wine list and *sommeliers* who obviously love what they're doing. Take their advice, and that of chef Savoy, and you'll be sure to share their pleasure. (Note also his "satellite" bistros, page 112 and 115.)

LE SCHEFFER

22 Rue Scheffer, Paris 16.
Tel: 47.27.81.11.
Métro: Trocadéro.
Reservations, noon to
    2:30 P.M. and 7:30 to
    10:30 P.M.
Closed Sunday, and two
    weeks at Christmas.
Credit card: MC, V.
A la carte, 150 to 200
    francs.

SPECIALTIES:

Bistro: salade d'épinards frais avec son oeuf poché (fresh spinach salad with warm poached egg), terrine de légumes maison (homemade vegetable terrine), navarin d'agneau printanier (spring lamb stew), escalope de saumon à la vapeur (steamed fresh salmon), côte de boeuf grillé (grilled rib of beef), cerise à l'eau de vie (cherries in brandy), glace au miel avec son coulis de framboise (honey ice cream with fresh raspberry sauce).

With its red and white checkered tablecloths, multicolored collection of posters, efficient female service, and chic clientele, Le Scheffer is worth the vigorous hike up the steps of the Trocadéro when you're in the vicinity. The ambience is friendly and familiar and the cuisine has a refreshing simplicity. On my last visit, I sampled a sparkling, fresh salad of baby spinach topped with a perfectly poached egg, and a serviceable brochette of beef. The salmon, the platter of fresh green beans, and a summery salad of ratatouille were all top rate.

MARINADE DE THON TIEDE ET FENOUIL, VINAIGRETTE AUX AGRUMES
WARM FRESH TUNA WITH FENNEL AND SPICY CITRUS VINAIGRETTE

Chef William Ledeuil of Bistro de l'Etoile—Lauriston (see entry, page 115)—one of Guy Savoy's "satellite" bistros—is one of Paris' most creative chefs. Each time I dine there, which is often, I'm stunned by the clever culinary ideas that spring from his tiny kitchen. This is a recent creation, one that can easily be created at home, to the oohs and aahs of all attending. I love the idea of gently marinating the tuna first, so it is already infused with a piquant vinaigrette. The marinade also begins to "cook" the tuna slightly and assures that the fish does not dry out during its brief time in the oven. Note that the tuna is not really cooked, just warmed. Make sure everything is super fresh, and your palate will be rewarded.

Marinade and Tuna:
2 tablespoons freshly squeezed lemon juice
6 tablespoons extra-virgin olive oil
2 to 3 drops Tabasco sauce
1 thick slice fresh tuna steak (1 pound; 500 g), cut ¾ inch (2 cm) thick

Vinaigrette:
1 lime
1 orange
2 tablespoons balsamic vinegar
1 star anise
⅛ teaspoon curry powder
⅛ teaspoon paprika
⅛ teaspoon ground cardamon
5 tablespoons extra-virgin olive oil

Fennel:
2 pounds (1 kg) fresh fennel, rinsed and trimmed
3 tablespoons extra-virgin olive oil
Sea salt to taste
Several sprigs fresh thyme

1. About 5 hours before preparing the dish, marinate the tuna: In a shallow glass dish combine the lemon juice, oil, and Tabasco. Place the tuna in the dish. Cover with plastic wrap and refrigerate, turning the tuna from time to time. Remove the tuna from the refrigerator 1 hour before cooking. (The tuna can be marinated up to 24 hours, but I prefer a shorter marinade).

2. Prepare the vinaigrette: Zest the lime and orange, then blanch the zest in boiling water for 1 minute. Drain and set aside. Juice the lime and orange and place it in a small saucepan, along with the vinegar, star anise, and spices. Over high heat, reduce to a thick syrup, about 5 minutes. While still warm, add the oil. Taste for seasoning. Set aside.

3. Preheat the broiler.

4. Prepare the fennel: Place the fennel in a large saucepan, cover with water, and add the oil, thyme, and salt to taste. Bring to a simmer over moderate heat, and simmer gently until the fennel is tender, about 20 minutes. Drain. Cut each bulb lengthwise into thin slices. Transfer the fennel—overlapping the slices—to a warmed serving platter. Moisten with some of the warm vinaigrette, cover, and keep warm in a low oven.

5. Remove the tuna from the marinade and place on a broiling pan. Broil 4 inches (10 cm) from the heat, to lightly warm the tuna, not cook it, about 1 minute, heating one side only.

6. Transfer the tuna to the serving platter, moisten with the remaining vinaigrette and serve immediately.

Yield: 4 servings

ARTICHAUTS A LA BARIGOULE LA NIÇOISE
LA NIÇOISE'S ARTICHOKES BRAISED IN WHITE WINE

Whenever I spy these fragrant braised artichokes on a menu, I order them first thing. A classic Provençal preparation, this soothing dish combines artichokes, herbs, vegetables, and white wine, and further enlivens it with a bright basil sauce, or pesto. It makes a wonderful first course, or it could serve as a main-course luncheon dish, with plenty of toasted whole-grain bread. The recipe comes from La Niçoise (see entry, page 121), where they use tiny, violet-hued chokeless artichokes. I have adapted the recipe to the more common globe artichokes.

Pesto:
4 large cloves garlic, peeled and halved, germ removed
Fine sea salt to taste
2 cups (50 cl) loosely packed fresh basil leaves and flowers
1 ripe tomato, peeled, cored, seeded, and chopped
About 1 cup (25 cl) extra-virgin olive oil
1 cup (3½ ounces; 100 g) freshly grated imported Parmigiano-Reggiano cheese.

1. Prepare the pesto: Place the garlic and salt in a food processor and process to a paste. Add the basil and process again. Add the tomatoes and oil, and process again. Stir in the cheese. Transfer to a small bowl. Serve immediately or store, covered, in the refrigerator for up to 1 day. Bring to room temperature, mix, and taste for seasoning just before serving.

2. Prepare the artichokes: Fill a large bowl with cold water. Halve and juice the lemon, adding both the juice and the lemon halves to the water. Rinse the artichokes under cold running water. Using a stainless steel knife to minimize discoloration, trim the stem of an artichoke to about 1½ inches (4 cm) from the base. Carefully trim and discard the stem's fibrous exterior. Bend back the tough outer green leaves, one at a time, and snap them off at the base. Continue snapping off

---

BRASSERIE STELLA
133 Avenue Victor-Hugo, Paris 16.
Tel: 47.27.60.54.
Métro: Victor-Hugo.
Continuous service, noon to 1:30 A.M.
No reservations.
Open daily.
Credit cards: AE, V.
Sidewalk terrace.
A la carte, 200 to 250 francs.

SPECIALTIES:
Brasserie: banc d'huîtres et de fruits de mer toute l'année (fresh oysters and shellfish, year-round), plats du jour (changing daily specials).

Brasserie Stella is an authentically old-fashioned sort of place that never went out of style. The glaring neon lights and helter-skelter decor are as tacky as they are nostalgically soothing, and the stylish clientele—squashed elbow to elbow along the faded banquettes—make this an ideal place to sit back and people-watch. In truth, Stella is just another neighborhood hangout, but when you consider the neighborhood—the very fashionable 16th—you understand its appeal. Service here is surprisingly democratic, the food is all right, and you can always find a table late at night, after other restaurants have closed their doors. I always order the *steak tartare*—which waiters prepare tableside with great flourish, served with decent *frites* or a simple green salad.

Artichokes:

1 lemon

4 large fresh artichokes

6 tablespoons (10 cl)
extra-virgin olive oil

4 carrots, peeled and
thinly sliced

3 white onions,
quartered, or 15 pearl
onions

1 cup (25 cl) dry white
wine, preferably a
Chardonnay

1 pound (500 g) ripe
tomatoes, peeled,
cored, seeded and
chopped

1 head of garlic,
unpeeled, halved
crosswise

A few stems of fresh flat-
leaf parsley

Salt and freshly ground
black pepper

leaves until only the central cone of yellow leaves with pale green tips remains. Lightly trim the top cone of leaves to just below the green tips. Trim any dark green areas from the base. Halve the artichokes vertically. With a small spoon, scrape out and discard the hairy choke. Vertically cut each trimmed artichoke half into 8 even slices. Place each slice in the acidulated water. Repeat for the remaining 3 artichokes. Set aside.

3. Drain the artichokes and pat them dry. In a large skillet, heat the oil over medium-high heat until hot but not smoking. Add the artichokes, carrots, and onions, and cook until the vegetables begin to soften, about 5 minutes. Add the wine and reduce, uncovered, over medium-high heat until most of the liquid has evaporated, about 10 minutes. Add the tomatoes, garlic, parsley, salt, and pepper. Add water to cover (about 2 cups; 50 cl), cover, and simmer over medium heat until the artichokes are fork tender, about 20 minutes.

4. With a slotted spoon, remove the solids from the pan. Separate and cut the artichokes and set aside; discard the remaining vegetables. Strain the cooking liquid through a fine-mesh sieve discarding any additional solids. Return the artichokes to the skillet and stir in the strained cooking liquid and about half the pesto. Garnish with parsley and pass the remaining pesto.

Yield: 4 to 6 servings

LE TIMGAD
21 Rue Brunel, Paris 17.
Tel: 45.74.23.70.
Fax: 40.68.76.46.
Métro: Porte-Maillot.
Reservations, noon to 2:30
P.M. and 8 to 11 P.M.
Open daily.
Credit cards: AE, DC, V.
Air-conditioned.
165-franc lunch menu.
A la carte, 300 to 350
francs.

SPECIALTIES:
North African: brick (various seasoned pastries, filled with lamb, tuna, eggs, salmon, or shrimp), tajine d'agneau (lamb stew, with almonds, prunes, olives, or artichokes).

Probably the second most popular French colonial cuisine in Paris is couscous in any guise. The most elegant Parisian spot for sampling couscous—the tiny semolina grain and the national dish of Morocco—is Le Timgad, a bright and beautiful restaurant not far from the Arc de Triomphe. Come with a big hunger, for here amid an airy decor of white plaster walls, chef Ahmad Laasri serves up platter after mounded platter of buttery couscous, garnished with steamed vegetables, raisins, chick peas and a fragrant sauce that you can season to taste with the peppery hot sauce known as *harissa*. With this, one samples spicy lamb sausage known as *merguez*, and a variety of carefully seasoned *tajines*, meat and poultry stews simmered slowly over a wood fire.

VIVAROIS
192 Avenue Victor-Hugo,
　Paris 16.
Tel: 45.04.04.31.
Fax: 45.03.09.84.
Métro: Pompe.
Reservations, noon to 2 P.M.
　and 8 to 10 P.M.
Closed Saturday, Sunday
　and August.
Credit cards: AE, DC, V.
Air-conditioned.
345-franc lunch menu.
　A la carte, 600 to 800
　francs.

SPECIALTIES:
Classic and contemporary:
bavorise de poivrons en coulis de
tomate crue (red pepper bavaroise
in raw tomato coulis), huîtres
chaudes au curry (warm oysters
in curry sauce), ravioli Rastellini
(lobster-filled ravioli), poularde
bressane au vinaigre (sautéed
chicken in vinegar sauce), parfait
aux marrons d'Ardèche (chestnut
parfait).

It's strange how restaurants—like fashion, music, design—swing in and out of vogue. During the past several years, almost no one spoke about Vivarois, the Parisian restaurant most gastronomes still put towards the very top of their lists. But Vivarois—the ultramodern temple of gastronomy in the fashionable 16th—is on people's minds again. And rightly so. My last meal there made me realize once again what a master we have in chef Claude Peyrot. But because his food is so subtle and so sophisticated, his culinary mastery is not instantly tangible or obvious to many diners. The menu is short, almost condensed, serving as a mere blueprint for what's to come. Peyrot's message is classic and consistent, and you have the feeling that he derives as much pleasure preparing the food, as you have in eating it. His *bavaroise de poivrons en coulis de tomate crue* has become a classic, with its essence of sweet red pepper married to deliciously acidic tomatoes, a dish that virtually sings of summer. I loved, as well, his voluptuous *raviolis de homard,* tender chunks of lobster encased in thin pockets of pasta. A pretty platter of mixed vegetables—an elegant rendering of *légumes à la grecque*—was both simple and sublime. Other "surprise" dishes that won my heart include a refined *flan de cervelles,* a delicate, complicated and satisfying flan of calf's brains, served with just a touch of cream and capers; and a stunning dish of thick filets of the freshest *rouget,* set on a bed of baby spinach and sprinkled with a thick julienne of black truffles. If a dish can be described as subtly explosive, this was, with its play of direct colors, flavors, and textures.

　　The modern decor—comfortable white chairs, shining gray marble, ample glassware and pleasant lighting—has stood the test of time. Service could not be friendlier, and be certain to follow the advice of the outgoing, chatty *sommelier,* Jean-Claude Vinadier. We did, and will never regret sampling Jacques Raynaud's Fonsalette *blanc,* or Jean Louis Grippat's soft and velvety, Saint-Joseph, a youthful wine with a lush texture, a lingering finish.

BELLEVILLE, SAINT-OUEN

19th and 20th arrondissements, Saint-Ouen

A LA COURTILLE
1 Rue des Envierges,
   Paris 20.
Tel: 46.36.51.59.
Métro: Pyrénées.
Reservations, 12:30 to 2:30
   P.M. and 8 to 11 P.M.
Open daily.
Credit card: V.
Menus at 70 and 100 francs
   (lunch only). A la carte,
   180 to 200 francs.

SPECIALTIES:
Bistro: concombre à la crème
(cucumbers in cream), moules
marinières (steamed mussels), foie
de veau à la lyonnaise (calf's
liver with onions), saucisson
lyonnais pistaché (poached pork
sausage stuffed with pistachio
nuts).

Few Paris neighborhoods have undergone such drastic upheaval as La Villette Belleville, on the city's eastern edge. Today, modern terraced gardens and monotone highrise apartments stand where once there were stockyards and passages filled with craftsmen and artisans that made for a lively neighborhood ambience far from the center of the city. Still, much of that provincial feel can be found, amid the gardens of the Parc des Buttes-Chaumont, the roving Thursday and Sunday produce market along the rue des Pyrénées, and at A la Courtille, a sparkling bistro-brasserie with a terrace and a view that overlooks the city of Paris. Wine bar enthusiasts will recognize the touch of Bernard Pontonnier, who once held court at the popular Left Bank wine bar, Le Café de la Nouvelle Mairie.

Decent food, great wines, a pleasant feeling, and good value make this a place to remember when you want to stretch your legs and expand your vision of Paris. The black and white Willy Ronis photographs of Paris past will tug at your heartstrings, and the well-priced menus will allow you to indulge in the matter at hand: well-selected, handmade wines. Amid a decor that's a mix of 1930 and 1990—eggshell colored walls and ceiling, comfortable green-leather banquettes and armchairs, paper table coverings and modern window blinds—diners tuck into solid bistro fare.

Although the food isn't great, it's generously portioned and good enough, with mounds of cucumbers tossed in thick cream, brilliant green and red salads of beets and lamb's lettuce, and a remarkable effilochée de queue de boeuf, strands of long-simmered oxtail set upon a bed of gently seasoned greens. Main courses include thick slices of calf's liver served with a mountain of sautéed onions, a rather undernourished guinea hen accompanied by plenty of shredded cabbage sautéed in butter, and an excellent pistachio-studded lyonnais sausage, served with a green salad and steamed, sliced potatoes. In a hurry, or on a strict budget? Try the *"formule rapide,"* a menu that includes a main course, along with a choice of either a first course, cheese, or dessert. Most wines are available by the glass: Last time we tried the sparkling Vouvray *pétillant*, Champalou, a pleasant aperitif; Corrine Couturier's well-muscled Côtes-du-Rhône, and Sylvain Bernard's lush red Saint-Joseph.

LAO SIAM
49 Rue de Belleville,
   Paris 19.
Tel: 40.40.09.68. and
   42.39.33.59.
Métro: Belleville.
Continuous service, noon
   to 11:30 P.M. No
   reservations.
Open daily except Chinese
   New Year.
Credit card: V.
Air-conditioned.
A la carte, 50 to 150 francs.

SPECIALTIES:
Laotian and Thai: poisson suprême (whole fish with spicy sauce), tourteau à la diable (sautéed crab with coconut-based sauce), caille sur hachis d'ail (deep-fried quail with garlic), liseron d'eau (fresh Thai greens sautéed with hot pepper).

There are restaurant menus that challenge me to a marathon. A marathon, that is, of sampling my way through the entire menu, from giant shrimp sautéed with ginger and chives, to such spirit-lifting dishes as *poulet soleil levant*, or "rising sun chicken," which is sautéed with a coconut-based sauce. Lao Siam, on the Rue de Belleville, is a bit like that, with a multi-page menu that offers foods of Laos, Thailand, Vietnam, and China. Run by two Thai brothers who opened the restaurant in 1985—Piekham is in the kitchen, Teme runs the front of the house—Lao Siam is one of dozens of Asian restaurants to crowd the changing 19th and 20th *arrondissements*, where new parks, high-rises, run-down cafés, wine bars, and now Asian shops and markets, vie for attention. With a varied cuisine that's based on very fresh, and largely inexpensive ingredients, Lao Siam is a favorite among the embassy crowds from all the Asian nations, including the Philippines, Singapore and Taiwan.

One dish not to miss here is the *tourteau au diable*, a whole crab that's cut up, then sautéed, and topped with a very thick coconut milk-based sauce seasoned with a flourish of hot pepper and strips of fresh celery. It's one of those ultimately satisfying and filling dishes, and one crab is easily enough to feed two as a main course. Also worth the Métro ride is the *cailles sur hachis d'ail*, a brace of whole quail that is chopped into bite-size pieces, quickly deep-fried, and topped with a crispy combination of garlic and onions. A good accompaniment is the classic sticky rice (*riz gluant*), a super-chewy and substantial rice that's actually eaten with the fingers, by pinching off walnut-sized lumps then rolling them into balls with one hand. Here, as in many Thai restaurants, the rice is served in beautiful covered handwoven baskets.

This is also the sort of place where everyone looks at what everyone else is eating, and if it looks good, an order is quickly placed for another serving of *boeuf mille épices* or *gambas au château*. On one visit, I counted no less than a dozen delicious-looking main dishes being served to the Laotian table of six next to us. A soothing dessert is the *citron givrée*, or a whole lemon that's carved out, filled with lemon sorbet, then frozen.

LAO THAI
34 Rue de Belleville,
 Paris 20.
Tel: 43.58.41.84.
Métro: Belleville.
Reservations, 11:30 A.M. to
 2:30 P.M. and 7 to 11 P.M.
Closed Monday.
Air-conditioned.
Credit card: V.
Menus at 47 francs (lunch
 only), 50, 98, 108, and
 118 francs. A la carte,
 50 to 150 francs.

S P E C I A L T I E S :
Laotian and Thai: saucisses thai
(spicy pork sausages), gigot en
sauce poivre et basilic (leg of lamb
in pepper and basil sauce),
crevettes fraîches à la citronnelle
(fresh shrimp seasoned with
lemongrass).

A bright, modern, pleasantly air-conditioned restaurant along the Rue de Belleville, offering the cuisine of Laos and Thailand. Open since 1988, this small and efficient restaurant offers good value: Try especially the saucisse thai, thin and lightly spicy pork sausage served with salad and herbs; refreshing Thai salads based on chicken, shrimp, or beef; and a gently spiced curry of lamb.

CHEZ LOUISETTE
(Richard & Armand)
130 Avenue Michelet,
 Marché Vernaison, Allée
 No. 10, 94300 Saint-Ouen.
Tel: 40.12.10.14.
Métro: Porte de
 Clignancourt.
Open Saturday, Sunday,
 and Monday, noon to 6
 P.M. only. No
 reservations.
No credit cards.
A la carte, 100 to 150
 francs.

When I'm in Paris for the weekend, my favorite Sundays begin with a long run in Parc Monceau, followed by an afternoon combing Paris' vast flea market at the Porte de Clignancourt. During my run, I think about the platters of mussels or the roast chicken and fries at Chez Louisette, and about the great Edith Piaf songs that Emmanuelle—a dark, buxom, energetic Piaf-style *chanteuse*—will sing that afternoon as she woos the very mixed group of regulars that crowd into this crazy-as-a-loon bistro. Chez Louisette is a riot, with its mix and match decor (made up, no doubt, of flea market rejects), and Christmas decorations that stay up year-round. The happy crowd

S P E C I A L T I E S :
Bistro: moules (steamed mussels),
poulet rôti (roast chicken), petit
salé aux lentilles (salt pork with
lentils).

is always just short of rowdy, and I find that I tend to order the same thing each time—giant bowls of steamed mussels, a dish that the Duchess of Windsor is said to have eaten here, ever so daintily, with her fingers. One 1950s guidebook to Paris notes: "Chez Louisette's is the only place in the flea market where you get your money's worth!" If you stay on well into the afternoon, you'll note there's barely a dry eye in the house as Emmanuelle (and others) sing on about *"La Vie en Rose."* You won't regret a thing. A scene, in the best, old-fashioned sense of the word.

RESTAURANTS: AN ALPHABETICAL LISTING
(WITH ARRONDISSEMENTS)

Ambassade d'Auvergne, Paris 3

L'Ambroisie, Paris 4

L'Ami Louis, Paris 3

Androuët, Paris 8

Apicius, Paris 17

Arpège, Paris 7

L'Assiette, Paris 14

Astier, Paris 11

Baracane-Bistrot de l'Oulette, Paris 4

Benoit, Paris 4

Le Boeuf sur le Toit, Paris 8

Brissemoret, Paris 2

La Butte Chaillot, Paris 16

La Cagouille, Paris 14

Le Caméléon, Paris 6

Campagne et Provence, Paris 6

Carré des Feuillants, Paris 1

Cartet, Paris 11

Caviar Kaspia, Paris 8

Chardenoux, Paris 11

Aux Charpentiers, Paris 6

Chiberta, Paris 8

La Cigale, Paris 7

Le Clos Morillons, Paris 15

Au Cochon d'Or des Halles, Paris 1

Contre-Allée, Paris 14

La Coquille, Paris 17

Le Bistrot d'à Côté–Flaubert, Paris 17

La Coupole, Paris 14

A la Courtille, Paris 20

Aux Crus de Bourgogne, Paris 2

Les Délices d'Aphrodite, Paris 5

Dodin Bouffant, Paris 5

Le Dôme, Paris 14

Bistrot du Dôme, 14

Le Duc, Paris 14

L'Ecaille de P.C.B., Paris 6

Erawan, Paris 15

Auberge Etchegorry, Paris 13

Bistro de l'Etoile–Lauriston, Paris 16

Fermette Marbeuf 1900, Paris 8

Brasserie Flo, Paris 10

La Fontaine de Mars, Paris 7

Les Fontaines, Paris 5

Chez Fred, Paris 17

Gaya, Paris 1

Chez Georges, Paris 2

Au Gigot Fin, Paris 10

Goumard-Prunier, Paris 1

Les Gourmets des Ternes, Paris 8

Le Grand Véfour, Paris 1

Le Grizzli, Paris 4

Le Bistrot d'Henri, Paris 6

Brasserie de l'Isle Saint-Louis, Paris 4

L'Impasse, Paris 4

Issé, Paris 2

Chez Janou, Paris 3

Jamin, Paris 16

Chez Jenny, Paris 3

Julien, Paris 10

Kim-Anh, Paris 15

Lao Siam, Paris 19

Lao Thai, Paris 20

Lescure, Paris 1

Brasserie Lipp, Paris 6

Louis XIV, Paris 1

Chez Louisette, Saint-Ouen

Aux Lyonnais, Paris 2

Le Machon d'Henri, Paris 6

Le Mâconnais, Paris 7

La Maison du Valais,
Paris 8

Chez Maître Paul, Paris 6

Manufacture, Issy-les-
Moulineaux

Le Bistrot de Marius, Paris 8

Marty, Paris 5

Miravile, Paris 4

Moissonnier, Paris 5

Moulin à Vent, Chez
Henry, Paris 5

La Niçoise, Paris 17

L'Oeillade, Paris 7

L'Oulette, Paris 12

Chez Paul, Paris 11

Chez Pauline, Paris 1

Perraudin, Paris 5

Le Petit Marguery, Paris 13

Pharamond, Paris 1

Chez Philippe, Paris 11

Au Pied de Cochon, Paris 1

Pierre au Palais-Royal, Paris 1

Pile ou Face, Paris 2

Port Alma, Paris 16

Le Relais du Parc, Paris, 16

Chez René, Paris 5

Le Roi du Pot-au-Feu, Paris 9

La Rôtisserie d'en Face, Paris 6

Royal Madeleine, Paris 8

Guy Savoy, Paris 17

Le Scheffer, Paris 16

A Sousceyrac, Paris 11

Brasserie Stella, Paris 16

La Table de Fès, Paris 6

Taillevent, Paris 8

Tan Dinh, Paris 7

Terminus Nord, Paris 10

Timgad, Paris 17

La Timonerie, Paris 5

La Tour de Montlhéry,
Paris 1

Le Train Bleu, Paris 12

Au Trou Gascon, Paris 12

Le Trumilou, Paris 4

Vaudeville, Paris 2

Jules Verne, Paris 7

Chez la Vieille, Paris 1

Le Vieux Bistro, Paris 4

Le Villaret, Paris 11

Vivario, Paris 5

Vivarois, Paris 16

Les Zygomates, Paris 12

RESTAURANTS LISTED BY ARRONDISSEMENTS

**Palais-Royal, Les Halles,
Madeleine, Opéra, Bourse**
1st and 2nd arrondissements

Brissemoret

Carré des Feuillants

Au Cochon d'Or des Halles

Aux Crus de Bourgogne

Gaya

Chez Georges

Goumard-Prunier

Le Grand Véfour

Issé

Lescure

Louis XIV

Aux Lyonnais

Chez Pauline

Pharamond

Au Pied de Cochon

Pierre au Palais-Royal

Pile ou Face

La Tour de Montlhéry

Vaudeville

Chez la Vieille

**République, Bastille,
Les Halles, Ile Saint-Louis**
*3rd, 4th, and 11th
arrondissements*

Ambassade d'Auvergne

L'Ambroisie

L'Ami Louis

Astier

Baracane-Bistrot de
l'Oulette

Benoit

Cartet

Chardenoux

Le Grizzli

Brasserie de l'Isle Saint-
Louis

L'Impasse

Chez Janou

Chez Jenny

Miravile

Chez Paul

Chez Philippe

A Sousceyrac

Le Trumilou

Le Vieux Bistro

Le Villaret

**Latin Quarter,
Luxembourg, Sèvres-
Babylone**
5th and 6th arrondissements

Le Caméléon

Campagne et Provence

Aux Charpentiers

Les Délices D'Aphrodite

Dodin Bouffant

L'Ecaille de P.C.B.

Les Fontaines

Le Bistrot d'Henri

Brasserie Lipp

Le Machon d'Henri

Chez Maître Paul

Moissonnier

Moulin à Vent, Chez Henry

Perraudin

Chez René

La Rôtisserie d'en Face

La Table de Fès

La Timonerie

Vivario

**Fauborg Saint-Germain,
Invalides, Ecole Militaire**
7th arrondissement

Arpège

La Cigale

La Fontaine de Mars

Le Maconnais

L'Oeillade

Tan Dinh

Jules Verne

**Madeleine, Saint-Lazare,
Champs-Elysées, Place de
Ternes**
8th arrondissement

Androuët

Le Boeuf sur le Toit

Caviar Kaspia

Chiberta

Fermette Marbeuf 1900

Les Gourmets des Ternes

La Maison du Valais

Le Bistrot de Marius

Royal Madeleine

Taillevent

**Grands Boulevards, Place
de Clichy, Gare du Nord**
9th and 10th arrondissements

Brasserie Flo

Au Gigot Fin

Julien

Le Roi du Pot-au-Feu

Terminus Nord

**Gare de Lyon, Daumesnil,
Gobelins**
*5th. 12th and 13th
arrondissements*

Auberge Etchegorry

Marty

L'Oulette

Le Petit Marguery

Le Train Bleu

Au Trou Gascon

Les Zygomates

**Montparnasse, Denfert-
Rochereau, Grenelle,
Porte de Versailles**
*14th and 15th arrondisse-
ments; Issy-les-Moulineaux*

L'Assiette

La Cagouille

Le Clos Morillons

Contre-Allée

La Coupole

Le Dôme

Bistrot du Dôme

Le Duc

Erawan

Kim-Anh

Manufacture

**Arc de Triomphe,
Trocadéro, Porte Maillot**
*16th and 17th
arrondissements*

Apicius

La Butte Chaillot

La Coquille

Le Bistrot d'à Côté–Flaubert

Le Bistrot de
l'Etoile–Lauriston

Chez Fred

Jamin

La Niçoise

Port Alma

Le Relais du Parc

Guy Savoy

Le Scheffer

Brasserie Stella

Le Timgad

Vivarois

**Saint-Ouen, La Villette,
Belleville, Père Lachaise**
*18th, 19th, 20th
arrondissements*

A la Courtille

Lao Siam

Lao Thai

Chez Louisette

Cafés
CAFES

Au Petit Fer à Cheval (see entry, page 145).

It is impossible to imagine Paris without its cafés. Parisians are sun worshippers, and the attraction of an outdoor sidewalk stopping place perfectly suits their inclination. Sometime around the first week of February, sunshine or not, café doors open wide, chairs and tables tumble out, and the season begins. The city has some 12,000 cafés varying in size, grandeur, and significance. As diverse as Parisians themselves, the cafés serve as an extension of the French living room, a place to start and end the day, to gossip and debate, a place for seeing and being seen.

No book on Paris literary, artistic, or social life is complete without details of café life, noting who sat where, when, and with whom—and what they drank. One wonders how writers and artists accomplished as much as they did if they really whiled away all those hours at sidewalk tables sipping *café au lait*, Vichy water, and *ballons* of Beaujolais.

When did it start? The café billed as the oldest in Paris is Le Procope, opened in 1686 by a Sicilian, Francesco Procopio dei Coltelli, the man credited with turning France into a coffee-drinking society. He was one of the first men granted the privilege of distilling and selling wines, liqueurs, *eaux-de-vie*, coffee, tea, and chocolate, with a status equal to a baker or butcher. Le Procope attracted Paris's political and literary elite, and its past is filled with history. It has been reported that it was there that Voltaire drank forty cups of his favorite brew each day: a blend of coffee and chocolate, which some credit with inspiring his spontaneous wit. When Benjamin Franklin died in 1790 and the French assembly went into mourning for three days, Le Procope was entirely draped in black in honor of France's favorite American. Even the young Napoleon Bonaparte spent time at Le Procope: When still an artillery officer, he was forced to leave his hat as security while he went out in search of money to pay for his coffee. Le Procope still exists at the original address, 13 Rue de l'Ancienne Comédie, but as a restaurant, not a café.

By the end of the 18th century, all of Paris was intoxicated with coffee and the city supported some 700 cafés. These were like all-male clubs, with many serving as centers of political life and discussion. It is no surprise to find that one of the speeches that precipitated the fall of the Bastille took place outside the Café Foy at the Palais-Royal.

By the 1840s the number of Paris cafés had grown to 3,000. The men who congregated and set the tenor of the times included journalists, playwrights, and writers who became known as *boulevardiers*. Certain cafés did have special rooms reserved for women, but in 1916 a law was passed that prohibited serving women sitting alone on the terraces of those along the boulevards.

Around the turn of the century, the sidewalk cafés along Boulevard du Montparnasse—Le Dôme, La Rotonde, and later, La Coupole—became the stronghold of artists; those along Boulevard Saint-Germain—Aux Deux Magots, Flore, and Lipp—were the watering holes and meeting halls for the literary. When the "lost generation" of expatriates arrived in Paris after World War I, they established themselves along both boulevards, drinking, talking, arguing, and writing.

Cafés still serve as picture windows for observing contemporary life. The people you see today at Aux Deux Magots, Café de Flore, and Lipp may not be the great artists of the past, but faces worth watching just the same. Linger a bit and you will see that the Paris stereotypes are alive and well: the surly waiters and red-eyed Frenchmen inhaling Gitanes; old men in navy berets; *clo-*

chardes (bag ladies) hauling Monoprix shopping bags holding all their earthly possessions; ultra-thin, bronzed women with hair dyed bright orange; and schoolchildren decked out in blue and white seersucker, sharing an afternoon chocolate with mother.

If you know how to nurse a beer or coffee for hours, café-sitting can be one of the city's best buys. No matter how crowded a café may be, waiters will respect your graceful loafing and won't insist that you order another round just to hold the table. Drinks are usually less expensive if you are willing to stand at the bar. At mealtime, if you see a table covered with a cloth or even a little paper placemat, that means the table is reserved for dining. If it is bare, you are welcome to sit and just have a drink. Note that the service charge is automatically added to all café bills, so you are required to pay only the final total and need not leave an additional tip, although most people leave any loose change.

LES HALLES, PONT-NEUF

1st arrondissement

LE COCHON A L'OREILLE
15 Rue Montmartre, Paris 1.
Tel: 42.36.07.56.
Métro: Les Halles.
Open 7 A.M. to 5 P.M. Closed
Sunday.
Hot meals at lunch only.

This is the most beautiful workingman's bar in Paris. It houses great murals, fresh flowers on the tiny bistro tables, workers in blue overalls five deep at the zinc bar, and peanut shells on the floor. If you happen to be up and about at 7 A.M., you may want to toss back a few drinks with the local merchants, who still keep this end of Les Halles busy in the early morning hours.

CAFE COSTES
4 Rue Berger, Paris 1.
Tel: 45.08.54.39.
Métro: Les Halles.
Open daily, 8 A.M. to 2 A.M.

Café Costes, which opened in 1984, has been billed "the first modern café in Paris." This huge peach-toned double-decker Art Deco space would look right at home in Los Angeles or Manhattan. Yet everything about Café Costes has that distinctly Parisian air, albeit the 1980s Les Halles version. The menu, thank goodness, could not be more classic (there's a pretty good *croque-monsieur* made with *pain Poilâne*), the light French music adds a romantic touch, and it appears that at last Paris has a café that bridges the gap between the classicism of Aux Deux Magots and the pinball atmosphere of the corner hangout.

Inside Aux Deux Saules.

AUX DEUX SAULES
91 Rue Saint-Denis, Paris 1.
Tel: 42.36.46.57.
Métro: Les Halles.
Open daily, 10 A.M. to
    midnight.

This is a popular spot for the young-and-chic-but-impoverished, and comes as a small breath of fresh air amid a sea of sex shops and fast-food eateries. Most of the action goes on outdoors—the trendy crowd hangs out at the large communal picnic tables set along this busy pedestrian *passage*. There are no longer any willows (*saules*) lining the Rue Saint-Denis, but the café serves a rather decent bowl of onion soup *gratinée* and drinkable red wine. Do save time for a trip inside: You can down a quick coffee at the bar, facing fabulous ceramic murals depicting life in old Les Halles.

UN CAFE, S'IL VOUS PLAIT

Cafés are, of course, for more than just coffee. Although café fare has not changed drastically since the early days, food, like fashion, goes in and out of style. During the 19th century, one popular drink was *fond de culotte* ("seat of your pants"), so named since supposedly it could only be drunk while sitting down. It was a mixture of gentian liqueur and *crème de Cassis*. During the same period, other popular drinks included the *mêle-Cassis*, half Cassis and half Cognac; the *bicyclette*, a blend of Champagne and vermouth; and the *pompier*, or "fireman," a blend of vermouth and Cassis.

Today, coffee, beer, and anise-flavored *pastis* are the staple drinks, along with various fruit juices sweetened with sugar. The *croque-monsieur*—a ham sandwich topped with grated cheese, then grilled—and the *sandwich mixte*—a thickly buttered *baguette* filled with Gruyère cheese and thin slices of *jambon de Paris*—are favorite café snacks. For larger meals, there are often meaty *plats du jour*, pork *rillettes*, pâtés, platters of raw vegetables known as *crudités*, *salade niçoise*, and even hot dogs.

Coffee and other hot drinks come in many forms. This small glossary should help you order what you want.

Café noir or *café express:* plain black espresso

Double express: a double espresso

Café serré: extra-strong espresso, made with half the normal amount of water

Café allongé: weak espresso, often served with a small pitcher of hot water so clients may thin the coffee themselves

Café au lait or *café crème:* espresso with warmed or lightly steamed milk

Grand crème: large or double espresso with milk

Décaféiné or *déca:* decaffeinated espresso

Café filtre: filtered American-style coffee (not available at all cafés)

Chocolat chaud: hot chocolate

Infusion: herb tea

Thé nature, thé citron, thé au lait: plain tea, tea with lemon, tea with milk

LA SAMARITAINE CAFE
19 Rue de la Monnaie,
Paris 1.
(Go to Magasin 2, 5th floor,
follow signs)
Tel: 45.08.33.33.
Métro: Pont-Neuf.
Café open 9:30 A.M. to 7 P.M.
(Tuesday and Friday
until 8:30 P.M.). Food
service begins at 11:30
A.M. Closed Sunday.

The popular slogan of this well-known department store is *"On Trouve Tout à La Samaritaine."* That "everything" includes one of the most spectacular views of the Paris cityscape. Visit on a sunny afternoon, order up a *citron pressé* (lemonade) or a beer, and relax before or after a visit to this mammoth, and confusing department store.

CHATELET, MARAIS, ILE SAINT-LOUIS, REPUBLIQUE

3rd, 4th, 10th and 11th arrondissements

CAFE BEAUBOURG
100 Rue Saint-Martin,
Paris 4.
Tel: 48.87.63.96.
Métro: Hôtel de Ville or
Rambuteau.
Open daily, 8 A.M. to 2 A.M.

The modern double-decker Café Beaubourg overlooks the circus-like atmosphere of the Centre Pompidou museum plaza, which year-round is filled with bagpipe players, guitarists, actors, and fat men who sit on beds of nails. Yet if you spend a few moments at one of the upstairs tables, you'll realize that the ultra-modern Café Beaubourg fills an age-old Parisian need, for cafés are places where you can be alone in public. Look around and you'll see table after table filled with lone individuals—puffing on a cigarette, drinking a beer, writing, reading, or carefully perfecting the art of doing nothing. And although at first glance the Café Beaubourg's decor is jarring—the adjectives that come to mind are giant, cold, overly

Cafés—for looking cool or for reading.

A BIT OF PARISIAN COFFEE HISTORY

When Louix XIV first tasted coffee in 1664, he was not impressed. But Parisian high society fell in love with the intoxicating brew, enjoying it at lavish and exotic private parties arranged by the Turkish ambassador, who arrived in 1669.

By 1670, the general public got a taste of the rich caffeinated drink when an Armenian named Pascal hawked it at the Saint-Germain fair in the spring. He hired formally dressed waiters to go out among the crowds and through the streets, crying as they went, *"Café. Café."* Later Pascal opened a little coffee boutique like those he had seen in Constantinople. It was not a smashing success, but he survived with the help of his wandering waiters, who even went door to door with jugs of the thick black brew. Their only competition was *"le Candiot,"* a cripple who sold coffee in the streets of Paris for a meager two *sous*, sugar included.

Then, as now, doctors discussed the merits and drawbacks of coffee. Those who favored the drink argued that it cured scurvy, relieved smallpox and gout, and was even recommended for gargling, to improve the voice. *Café au lait* was lauded for its medicinal qualities, and in 1688, Madame de Sévigné, whose letters record the life of the period, noted it as a remedy for colds and chest illness.

By the time the city's first café, Le Procope, opened in 1686, coffee was well on its way to winning the Parisian palate.

modern—the place works. The huge metal armchairs are surprisingly comfortable, the double-decker setting offers room to breathe in a neighborhood that can be utterly stifling, and the train-station voluminosity serves to shelter us and separate us from the world just outside the door. Food here is an afterthought: The generous *crudités* platter is fine, but sandwiches tend to be dreadfully dry. This can be remedied if you order a tomato salad on the side and create your own sort of city picnic, a great choice on a rainy Paris day when the colors of the brightly clothed crowd below jump out at you beneath the sobering gray sky.

MA BOURGOGNE
19 Place des Vosges, Paris 4.
Tel: 42.78.44.64.
Métro: Saint-Paul or Bastille.
Open daily, 8 A.M. to 1:30
A.M. Closed February.

The most active café in the Marais, Ma Bourgogne is set under the arcades of Paris's oldest square. Sit outdoors on the traditional beige and red rattan chairs absorbing the beauty of the architecture of buildings along the square that dates back to 1407. The café is calm in the morning and packed with local office workers at lunchtime. Come here for simple café standbys like salads, a glass of wine, or a bowl of Berthillon ice cream; the more complicated restaurant fare is expensive and unexceptional. The *pommes frites* are not bad, just ask for them *bien cuites*—well cooked. Writer Georges Simenon's inspector Maigret spent a lot of time here, perhaps inspecting the varied clientele, which ranges from old locals to tourists to the chic young residents of one of Paris's most sought-after addresses.

CAOUA
207 Rue du Faubourg
   Saint-Antoine, Paris 11.
Métro: Faidherbe-Chaligny.
Tel: 43.48.60.97.
Open 9 A.M. to 7 P.M. Closed
   Sunday and three weeks
   in August.

This calm, minimalist, modern coffee store/café comes as a pleasant surprise in the noisy bustle of the Rue du Faubourg Saint-Antoine. Come in the morning to relish superlative dark, rich coffee and frothy *café crème* served with a chocolatey sliver of bittersweet brownie on the side. At lunchtime, the spare metal chairs and tables fill up with local regulars: a mix of office workers and artists (whose work often hangs on the walls) and designers who take advantage of the neighborhood's cheap studio space. Marianne, the *patronne,* and her assistant, Eric, nourish them with some of the most beautiful homemade tarts in Paris: a sunny and savory *tarte provençale* and a fresh cherry tart popping with fruit. Salads come from the nearby open-air market, and the excellent sourdough bread comes from L'Autre Boulange (page 253). Later in the afternoon, Caoua calms down and transforms into a tea salon, where you can sip one of the dozen or so varieties of tea and coffee sold in the store with a slice of homemade fruit tart.

LE FLORE EN L'ILE
42 Quai d'Orléans, Paris 4.
Tel: 43.29.88.27.
Métro: Pont-Marie.
Open daily, 10 A.M. to 2 A.M.
Hot meals served
  continuously until 1 A.M.
Brunch served.

This combination café/restaurant/tea salon on the Ile Saint-Louis has expanded to offer a sidewalk terrace, where they serve extravagant Berthillon ice cream sundaes along with the original café menu. Le Flore en l'Ile offers fun, easy food to snack on while admiring the view: good but not great salads, *crêpes*, sandwiches and tarts. But who can complain about the breathtaking view of Notre-Dame? Inside, settle in at one of the marble-topped tables and enjoy the good *café crème* served in silver pitchers. Le Flore en l'Ile is especially cozy in blustery weather when you can gaze out the window at the willow trees swaying around Notre-Dame and warm yourself with a pot of freshly brewed, steaming hot tea. On weekends it's packed with tourists and Parisians who come here for a Parisian-style brunch: *croissants*, *café au lait*, fresh-squeezed orange juice, *oeufs brouillés*, and, unfortunately, cold toast. Ask for a *baguette* instead.

Tête-à-tête at Ma Bourgogne (see entry, facing page).

CAFE LOUIS-PHILIPPE
66 Quai de l'Hôtel de Ville,
  Paris 4.
Tel: 42.72.29.42.
Métro: Pont-Marie.
Open daily, 9:30 A.M.
  to 1 A.M.

Café Louis-Philippe—right across from the Pont Louis-Phillipe in the Marais—could be dubbed the Great Dane café, because of owner Gilles Girousse's mammoth gray Great Dane named Flore, who can be found snoozing beneath the spiral staircase or under one of the patio tables. At the foot of the Renaissance church of Saint-Gervais-et-Protée and across the street from the quays of the Seine, this shady, tree-filled terrace is one of the more pleasant in the city, assuming you secure a table away from the traffic. It makes a perfect midway stop between a visit to the Marais and a walk through the Ile Saint-Louis. On sunny, summer days, the terrace takes on a festive, holiday air, and in winter one can sit by the window at one of the upstairs tables overlooking the Seine.

Service here is friendly, and the young Parisian waiters look like they're having a great time. In addition to traditional café fare, such as steak piled high with caramelized sautéed shallots and garlicky, pan-roasted potatoes, Café Louis-Philippe serves homey specialties that are seldom found in cafés, such as creamy *oeufs brouillés* (scrambled eggs) thick with smoked salmon. Here they treat fish with an uncommonly light hand, serving brochettes of *lotte* and fresh, tender grilled salmon steaks barely brushed with butter. Salads—the traditional café standbys—could be better and fresher. And the desserts look tempting but taste tired. The strong, rich *café express* and frothy *café crème* come in pretty, bright-colored crockery cups, and are bracing enough to get you on your way.

CAFE DES MUSEES
49 Rue de Turenne, Paris 3.
Tel: 42.72.96.17.
Métro: Chemin-Vert or
  Saint-Paul.
Open daily 7 A.M. to 8 P.M.
  (10 P.M. Friday).

On the well-traveled tourist path between the Place des Vosges and the Picasso Museum, it comes as a happy surprise to find the Café des Musées, an authentic café/bistro filled with cheerful neighborhood regulars and delicious homemade food. At lunch the waitress brings you a handwritten menu scrawled with the *plats du jour*—classic café fare, such as *tarte provençale* with fresh salad, and fresh and copious platters of *crudités*. The only surprises here are good ones, such as reasonable prices and generous portions, good *café crème*, and the fact that the wine-loving *patron* bottles his own house wine, a light, fruity Côtes-de-Lyonnais. Try the generous *assiette de saumon cru mariné à l'aneth* (a kind of cross between gravlax and smoked salmon); a flavorful *steak tartare*, served with spicy, slivered onions, and fresh parsley and fresh herbs chopped into every bite. This turn-of-the-century café has been unbecomingly remodeled, but the cheerful ambience remains authentic and unspoiled.

**LE PETIT CHATEAU
D'EAU**
34 Rue du Château-d'Eau,
Paris 10.
Tel: 42.08.72.81.
Métro: République.
Open 7:45 A.M. to 8 P.M.
Closed Saturday, Sunday
and August.
Hot meals served at lunch.

This is a perfect working class neighborhood café, not far from Place de la République. The *patron* and *patronne* hold court with locals at the zinc-covered half-moon bar, serving forth good *café crème* and *orange pressé* (fresh-squeezed orange juice). Le Petit Château d'Eau also offers one of the city's classic interiors: Beveled glass doors lead to the spotless and cheery little café, with its fresh coat of paint and bright bouquets of market-fresh flowers. Large mirrors rimmed in antique green and white tiles make the room even cozier, as you sit back in an upholstered booth to read your daily newspaper.

AU PETIT FER A CHEVAL
30 Rue Vieille du Temple,
Paris 4.
Tel: 42.72.47.47.
Métro: Hôtel de Ville.
Open daily 9 A.M. to 2 A.M.
Hot meals served from
noon until 1 A.M.

A tiny, popular, and super-trendy neighborhood café that dates back to 1903, when the Combes family opened it as the Café de Brésil. Today the café still boasts a fabulous marble-topped horseshoe (*fer à cheval*) bar, mirrored walls, and the original patchwork tile floor. The *patron* has embellished the room a bit but retained a feeling of authenticity by adding another mirror, a giant chandelier, and shelves of glass and brick. The back room, always packed at lunchtime, boasts a giant Métro map and booths made up of old wooden Métro seats.

It's better to come during the day if you want to secure a table and enjoy the old-fashioned ambience, the eccentric waiters, and the good café fare. Blackboards above the tables indicate the daily specials, including the delicious *fer à cheval* salad of warm *chèvre* drizzled with olive oil on Poilâne toast with fresh salad greens and *magret de canard*, and one of the better cheesecakes to be found in Paris—light, creamy, and properly tart on a buttery graham cracker-like crust. In the evening, the crowd is three-deep at the bar and there's a free table once in a blue moon.

LE ROYAL BAR
19 Rue du Parc Royal,
   Paris 3.
Tel: 42.72.33.03.
Métro: Saint-Paul or
   Chemin-Vert.
Open approximately 11 A.M.
   to 7 P.M. Closed
   Tuesday. (Note: the
   patron keeps whimsical
   hours, depending on the
   weather and his mood.
   Sometimes he stays open
   later, sometimes he
   closes shop to go
   fishing.)

After a visit to the Picasso museum, stop into this tiny café to sip a "Période Rose"—a delicious pink fresh fruit frappe, made with a blend of strawberries, citrus fruit, pineapple, peaches, and more. The *patron*, Alain Sené, modestly admits that he's not a good baker, so instead he orders the delicious *tarte Tatin* and *tarte au citron meringuée* from Ladurée (not a bad choice, at all). Unfortunately he has added gimmicky paintings to keep in step with this gallery-glutted neighborhood, but when the café opens onto the sidewalk in nice weather, the art is easy to ignore. Civilized touches such as fresh flowers on the marble-topped tables, bentwood chairs, and pretty, old-fashioned tile floors belie the fact that this space originally served as the stables for the mansion across the street.

LE TEMPS DES CERISES
31 Rue de la Cerisae,
   Paris 4.
Tel: 42.72.08.63.
Métro: Bastille or Saint-
   Paul.
Open 7:30 A.M. to 8 P.M.
   Lunch served 11:30 A.M.
   to 2:30 P.M. Closed
   weekends and August.

Le Temps des Cerises is like a tiny *café du coin* in the countryside, filled with boisterous local workers and friendly *patrons*. The scene is democratic—with construction workers in their *"bleu de travail"* uniforms mixing with the white-collar crowd—and everyone seems happy to be here.

With a zinc bar, lace curtains, wooden tables, and 58-franc menu *"sur l'ardoise"* (written on a large chalkboard), Le Temps des Cerises hasn't changed in years and doesn't plan to. Fresh *baguettes* from the boulangerie across the street arrive in little baskets (whenever they run out, the waitress pops across the street to pick up a few more, so the bread is always fresh). Everyone orders the 58-franc menu (there is no *à la carte*).

Food here is simple, fresh, *fait maison*, and served in copious quantities without fanfare. No gastronomic wonders, but honest food meant to satisfy hungry workers. The *assiette de crudités*—mixed raw vegetable platter—is abundant and fresh in a light vinaigrette, and the *harengs pommes à l'huile* arrive as fat filets of herring paired with steamed potatoes. The chewy steak and overcooked green beans can be forgotten, but the hefty roast veal came medium rare and juicy, garnished with a pile of stewed chard. Order some reasonably-priced wine by the glass, carafe, or bottle, and opt for the good (if tiny) cheese plate over dessert.

CROQUE-MONSIEUR
GRILLED HAM AND CHEESE SANDWICH

The croque-monsieur *is the most Parisian of sandwiches. It's really no more than a grilled ham sandwich topped with grated cheese, but it appears in many different guises. One could spend weeks hopping from café to café, taking notes on variations and favorites. Sometimes a* croque-monsieur *is topped with a thick cheese* béchamel *sauce, or transformed into a* croque-madame *with the addition of an egg, but frankly, few Parisian cafés do justice to the sandwich. All too often, a* croque-monsieur *is made with airy, factory-made white bread, second-rate ham, and the cheese, well, it's not always Gruyère. (Parisian supermarkets even sell frozen* croque-monsieurs, *ready for popping in the oven or the microwave!) If you want a great* croque-monsieur, *make it yourself, with exceptional homemade* pain de mie, *the slightly buttery white bread that's been unjustly distorted by industrialization.*

3 tablespoons (1½ oz; 45 g) unsalted butter
12 thin slices homemade *pain de mie* (see recipe, page 243)
7 ounces (200 g) or 6 thin slices best-quality ham, cut to fit bread
4½ ounces (140 g) Gruyère cheese, grated

1. Preheat the broiler

2. Butter the slices of bread on one side. Place one slice of ham on 6 of the buttered sides, and cover with the remaining bread slices, buttered side out.

3. Place the sandwiches under the broiler, and grill on the buttered side until golden. Remove the sandwiches, turn, and cover each with grated Gruyère. Return to the broiler and grill until the cheese is bubbling and golden.

Yield: 6 sandwiches

Note: To transform a *croque-monsieur* into a *croque-madame*, grill a *croque-monsieur* until it is almost bubbling and golden, then cut a small round out of the top piece of cheese-covered bread, exposing the ham. Reserve the round. Break a small egg into the hole and place under the broiler for 2 or 3 more minutes. To serve, top the egg with the cheese-covered round.

One French cookbook even offers a recipe for a sandwich named after the food critic Curnonsky. To prepare a *croque-Curnonsky*, blend equal amounts of butter and Roquefort cheese, spread on thin slices of *pain de mie*, top with ham and another slice of bread, and grill on both sides.

LATIN QUARTER, LUXEMBOURG, SAINT-GERMAIN, SEVRES-BABYLONE, QUAI D'ORSAY

5th, 6th, and 7th arrondissements

CAFE BASILE
34 Rue de Grenelle, Paris 7.
Tel: 42.22.59.46.
Métro: Rue du Bac.
Open 7 A.M. to 8:30 P.M.
  Closed Sunday.

A perfectly banal-looking 1950s café—with white formica tables, mismatched tile floors, and waiters with thick mustaches—Café Basile is one spot in town to find Basil Kamir's delicious sourdough bread from the Moulin de la Vierge. Try any of the sandwiches with *pain Basile* (ham and cheese is the standard), or opt for their huge *salade composée*, really a mix of cubed ham, cubed cheese, and raw vegetables. Popular with students from the nearby "Science-Po" *(Fondation Nationale des Sciences Politiques)* this is an authentic neighborhood spot away from the hordes. Note the great fifties decor on the doors leading to the telephones and *toilettes*.

BRULERIE DE L'ODEON
6 Rue Crebillon, Paris 6.
Tel: 43.26.39.32.
Métro: Odéon.
Open 10 A.M. to 6:45 P.M.
  Tuesday through Friday;
  10 A.M. to noon and 1:45
  to 6:45 P.M. Saturday.
  Closed Sunday, Monday,
  and August.

One of Paris's oldest coffee roasting houses, this tiny coffee boutique and tasting spot is not a café per se, but for those of us in search of an honest cup of coffee (not a bitter compromise), this is the spot. Right off the Place de l'Odéon and near the Luxembourg Gardens, the Brûlerie de l'Odéon is an intimate, quiet corner to rest one's tired feet. There are just six little tables, where you can order about a dozen different brews and blends of coffee, plus an equal number of tea varieties. There's nothing flashy here—in fact, you may feel as though you're sipping tea in the cozy front room of a coffee warehouse. But it's a charming spot, really, decorated with great posters and displaying shelves filled with biscuits, honeys, and teas.

ALCOHOLIC DRINKS

Calvados: apple brandy

Marc de Bourgogne: pronounced "mar," an *eau-de-vie* distilled from pressed grape skins and seeds

Pippermint Get: bright green alcoholic mint drink

Cidre: hard apple cider

AUX DEUX MAGOTS
170 Boulevard Saint-
   Germain, Paris 6.
Tel: 45.48.55.25.
Métro: Saint-Germain-
   des-Prés.
Open daily, 8 A.M. to 2 A.M.
   Closed the second week
   in January.

The ultimate Paris café, great for observing the current fashion scene and restoring yourself with a steaming cup of good hot chocolate on a chilly afternoon. The menu boasts more than twenty-five different whiskies, and coffee is still served in thick white cups. In spring and summer, Aux Deux Magots offers one of Saint-Germain des Prés' most appealing and expansive terraces, while the interior is calm and pleasant, with its mahogany-red banquettes and brass-edged tables, walls of mirrors, and waiters attired in white floor-length aprons and neat black vests. Here you can sit in plain view of the famous wooden statues of the two Chinese dignitaries—the *deux magots* who gave their name to the café and still dominate the room. (The café's name does not, as some writers have suggested, translate as "two maggots"!) The owner recalls watching Jean-Paul Sartre write while smoking cigarette after cigarette from ten to twelve-thirty each day. Hemingway came, too, after World War I, for "serious talk" and to read aloud the poetry he'd written.

Aux Deux Magots.

CAFE DE FLORE
172 Boulevard Saint-
   Germain, Paris 6.
Tel: 45.48.55.26.
Métro: Saint-Germain-
   des-Prés.
Open daily, 7 A.M. to 1:30 A.M.

The rival of Aux Deux Magots next door, Café de Flore was a literary and artistic hangout, popular with Sartre, Simone de Beauvoir, and Albert Camus. During the Occupation, all the cafés in Montparnasse were full of German soldiers, but the Parisians preferred Flore, where there was even a small stove. After the war in the late 1940s, when most artists still gathered in Montparnasse, Picasso used to come here every night, sitting at the second table in front of the main door, sipping

Café de Flore.

a glass of mineral water, and chatting with his Spanish friends. Little has changed since, except the clientele, which is very high class and Left Bank, making it fertile people-watching ground. There's still the simple and classic Art Deco interior: red banquettes, walls of mahogany and mirrors, and a large sign suggesting that while pipe smoking is not forbidden, *"l'odeur de certains tabacs de pipe parfumés incommode la plupart de nos clients."* In other words, "courteous clients don't smoke pipes here." The Flore serves excellent *espresso* and *café crème*, the food is frightfully expensive but decent, and in the winter months, you can order up a platter of oysters and overpriced white La Doucette wine from the Loire.

CAFE DES HAUTEURS
(Musée d'Orsay)
62 Rue de Lille, Paris 7.
Tel: 45.49.47.03.
Métro: RER Quai d'Orsay
   or Solférino.
Open 10 A.M. to 5 P.M.
   Tuesday, Wednesday,
   Friday, and Saturday;
   until 9:45 P.M. Thursday;
   9 A.M. to 6 P.M. Sunday.
   Museum entry fee, about
   31 francs.

How many cafés—anywhere in the world—can boast of Toulouse-Lautrec murals on the wall and a view of the white domes of Sacré-Coeur in the distance? The rooftop café of the Musée d'Orsay (a lively museum fashioned out of a 19th century railroad station) is one of the finest spots for viewing the city. The café is situated right next to the museum's famed Impressionist collection, and through chunks of glass cut around a mammoth railway clock, one views a vast expanse of the cityscape, out over the slow-moving Seine, across to the Tuileries Gardens, and beyond to the hills of Montmartre. In good weather one can relax on the small outdoor terrace.

BRASSERIE LIPP
151 Boulevard Saint-
  Germain, Paris 6.
Tel: 45.48.53.91.
Métro: Saint-Germain-des-
  Prés.
Open daily, 8 A.M to 2 A.M.
  Nonstop restaurant
  service noon to 1 A.M.
  Closed mid-July to mid-
  August.

The terrace of this Left Bank institution is a bit airless, but if you must haunt the American hangouts of the 1920s, stop in any time of day for a coffee or snack of ham or cheese, and read your well-thumbed Hemingway.

CAFE DE LA MAIRIE
8 Place Saint-Sulpice,
  Paris 6.
Tel: 43.26.67.82
Métro: Saint-Sulpice.
Open 7 A.M. to 2 A.M. Closed
  Sunday.

This boasts one of my all-time favorite Parisian café terraces, a rambling expanse of wicker chairs and marble-topped tables facing the shady trees and roaring lion fountain of the pretty Place Saint-Sulpice. Inside the Café de la Mairie is noth-

SNACKS

The most popular café snacks are sandwiches, made either on the long and narrow *baguette*; on *pain de mie*, the square white bread; or on *pain Poilâne*, Paris's most popular country-style loaf. Poilâne's bread is often served as a *tartine*, an open-face sandwich with various toppings.

Here are some of the most popular sandwich ingredients, followed by other popular snacking items.

Jambon de Paris: cooked ham

Jambon de pays: country ham, usually salt-cured

Saucisson sec or *saucisson à l'ail:* dried sausage, plain or with garlic

Rillettes: soft, spreadable pork or goose pâté

Pâté de campagne: pork pâté

Sandwich mixte: Gruyère cheese and ham on a *baguette*

Cornichons: small French pickles or gherkins

Oeuf dur: hard-cooked egg

Carottes rapées: grated carrot salad, usually with vinaigrette dressing

Crudités: variety of raw vegetables in a salad, usually including grated carrots, beets, and tomatoes

Assiette de charcuterie: a combination plate of dried sausage, pâté, and *rillettes*

ing special, but on lazy summer afternoons, just settle into one of the chairs outside, sip a *citron pressé*, and watch *Le tout-Rive Gauche* walk by: mothers rolling their silver-wheeled, navy prams to the nearby Luxembourg gardens, chic women decked out in the latest Left Bank fashion, editors from the neighboring publishing houses, and a lively mix of students. Come early in the morning after picking up *croissants* and *pains au chocolat* from nearby Gerard Mulot (76 Rue de Seine) to enjoy a frothy *café crème* and the calm of the city as it wrestles from its slumber. If you're lucky, you might catch a glimpse of Catherine Deneuve, who lives on the *place*.

CAFE MOUFFETARD
116 Rue Mouffetard,
   Paris 5.
Tel: 43.31.42.50.
Métro: Censier-Daubenton.
Open 7 A.M. to 8:30 P.M.
   Closed Sunday afternoon
   and Monday.

The big sign outside reads *"Brasserie"* in bold burgundy lettering, but this rather earthy little spot set right in the middle of the busy Rue Mouffetard market is one of the homier cafés in Paris. A smoky little worker's hangout, it was brought to my attention by my friend Martha Rose Shulman, who was lured here by the homemade pastries, dense and buttery *croissants*, and delicious, almost creamy *brioches*. This is a rare café, where the patron and his wife make their *croissants* and *brioches*, as well as delicious whole-wheat half-*baguettes*, working through the night so the market workers will have something fresh and warm to sustain them through a long morning's labor. In wintertime, they also make little *chaussons aux pommes* and hot apple tarts, perfect for eating with a giant *café crème*.

LE NEMROD
51 Rue du Cherche-Midi,
   Paris 6.
Tel: 45.48.17.05.
Métro: Sèvres-Babylone.
Open 6:30 A.M. to 9:30 P.M.
   Saturday until 8:30 P.M.
   Closed Sunday, holidays,
   and two weeks in
   August.

Le Nemrod is a rambling corner café not far from Le Bon Marché department store and serves as a *"cantine,"* or mealtime meeting spot for the neighborhood. Food, service, and wine are above par here, for owners Richard and Michel Bonal are more attentive than most café owners. Their morning *croissants* come from Peltier around the corner (see Pastry Shops), they offer an assortment of cold sandwiches on Poilâne bread, and the ice cream comes from the famed Berthillion (see Specialty Shops). Best of all, here you'll find wines selected with care, such as Thevenet's Morgon, *cru*

Au Petit Fer à Cheval (see entry, page 145), a place for coffee and classical music.

POPULAR APERITIFS

Absinthe, the highly alcoholic anise-flavored drink invented by a Frenchman in 1797, was banned in 1915 because of its harmful effects on the nerves. It was quickly replaced by another popular though less dangerous drink, *pastis,* which has much in common with absinthe, but is lower in alcohol. Wormwood, the ingredient which caused absinthe to be banned, is omitted.

Pastis: anise-seed-flavored aperitif that becomes cloudy when water is added (the most famous brands are Pernod and Ricard)

Suze: bitter liqueur distilled from the root of the yellow mountain gentian

Picon and *Mandarin:* bitter orange-flavored drinks

Pineau des Charentes: sweet fortified wine from the Cognac region

Kir: dry white wine mixed with *crème de Cassis* (black currant liqueur)

Kir royal: Champagne mixed with *crème de Cassis*

Beaujolais, served out of clear glass carafes. Salads are good and copious, including a fine *salade Auvergnat,* chockablock full of walnuts, Cantal cheese, country ham, and greens.

LA PALETTE
43 Rue de Seine, Paris 6.
Tel: 43.26.68.15.
Métro: Mabillon.
Open 8 A.M. to 2 A.M. Closed Sunday, one week in February, and August.
Hot meals served at lunch until 3 P.M.

This picturesque artist's hangout is perfect on a sunny summer's afternoon, when the tables fill as much of the sidewalk as law and reason will allow. Everyone is in a light mood and seems to know everyone else, so La Palette has a particularly intimate Left Bank air. The *patron* wanders about shaking hands and chatting with the casually chic clientele, who look like they just stepped out of a Robert Doisneau photograph. They come for a drink and a snack of *"guillotines,"* open-face ham sandwiches on *pain Poilâne.* Don't forget to take a look inside to admire the brightly painted murals.

CONCORDE, OPERA, CHAMPS-ELYSEES, SAINT-AUGUSTIN

8th and 9th arrondissements

CAFE FLOTTES
2 Rue Cambon, Paris 8.
Métro: Concorde.
Tel: 42.60.80.89
Open daily, 7 A.M. to 2 A.M.

The former owners of the popular Café du Roy on the Rue Royale have moved to the Rue Cambon, right out the back door of W.H. Smith bookstore and a stone's throw from the Tuileries Gardens. Here the Flottes family has built the café of their dreams, decorated to the hilt in a *faux* Art Nouveau style, with marble-topped tables, comfy wicker chairs, and a long, molded zinc bar. J.J. Flottes holds court at the bar, his son, Olivier, oversees table service, while and his wife, Hugette, does a bit of both. This remains one of the better places in Paris to come for an honest cup of coffee and satisfying, authentic food that you could eat three times a day. Little details set Flottes apart from the rest of the cafés: rich espresso with bittersweet chocolate on the side; breakfast-time baskets of buttery *croissants* and *pains au chocolat* and pretty pots of homemade jam on the bar—perfect with a frothy *café crème* and a fresh *orange pressé*. And if you've never understood what all the fuss over a *croque-monsieur* sandwich was about, come here at lunch to taste a perfect rendition: grilled Gruyère cheese and ham on *pain Poilâne*. (Order it plain or "Royale" with tomato and a fried egg inside.) Vegetarians can ask for it without ham. The fresh *salade niçoise* with julienned roasted red peppers, tuna in oil, and crisp green beans remains one of the better Paris versions. Late on a cold winter's night stop in for a steaming porcelain crock of *soupe à l'oignon gratinée* and perhaps a plate of oysters. The café/brasserie formula is particularly convenient when one person is famished for a three-course meal and the other just wants a salad. This is a solid, democratic spot, where Parisiennes in couture suits toting Chanel bags sit side by side at the bar with businessmen and students in jeans.

LE FOUQUET'S
99 Avenue des Champs-
   Elysées, Paris 8.
Tel: 47.23.70.60.
Métro: George V.
Open daily, 8 A.M. to
   2 A.M.

This is one of the most popular Right Bank cafés, perfect for observing the ever-changing scene on the Champs-Elysées. Le Fouquet's is always making society news, as starlets and journalists talk and write about their rendezvous here. James Joyce used to dine at Le Fouquet's almost every night, and today well-known French chef Paul Bocuse stops in whenever he's in town. Most people don't come for the scene or the food, but to grab a snack before or after viewing one of the dozens of films playing at movie houses along the avenue. Sexism lives at Le Fouquet's, where a sign warns, *"Les dames seules ne sont pas admises au bar"* ("Women who are alone are not allowed at the bar"). The management insists that the sign, which has been up at the seven-stool bar since the restaurant opened at the turn of the century, was put there to protect women, not insult them. Most women see it otherwise. Incidentally, Le Fouquet's is pronounced to rhyme with "bets" not "bays," a remnant of the fashionable fascination with English early in the century.

A solitary café moment.

CAFE DE LA PAIX
12 Boulevard des
   Capucines, Paris 9.
Tel: 40.07.30.20.
Métro: Opéra.
Open daily, noon to
   1:15 A.M.

This open, expansive café near the Opéra represents a sort of gaiety of days past. The building has been declared a historic monument, and the café is not a bad place to sip your lemonade while sitting under the crisp green and white striped umbrellas that line the sidewalk. You should enjoy the spectacle of the passing show, which includes tourists, as well as Parisians.

BAR DES THEATRES
6 Avenue Montaigne,
   Paris 8.
Métro: Alma-Marceau.
Tel: 47.23.34.63.
Open daily 6 A.M. to 2 A.M.

Bar des Théâtres is one of those all-purpose cafés where one could take breakfast, lunch, and dinner, should one desire. With its paper tablecloths and friendly waiters, this is a rare, no-frills oasis in the highest rent district in Paris. If you do too much people watching—overly slim and beautiful models are always prancing past on their way to and from the fashion houses—you may lose your appetite for the simple, solid, café fare, including sandwiches and salads served in an atmosphere that's pure bustle, pure Paris. I've feasted on fresh oysters, sizzling snails, a giant *salade niçoise*, thick slabs of rosy lamb with mounds of white beans, and fruity sorbets. The café has been around since 1948: In other words, it's tried and true.

MONTPARNASSE

6th and 14th arrondissements

LA CLOSERIE DES LILAS
171 Boulevard du
   Montparnasse, Paris 14.
Tel: 43.26.70.50.
Métro: RER Port-Royal.
Open daily, 9 A.M. to 2 A.M.

The lilacs are long gone, but the romance of days when men like Henry James, Samuel Beckett, and Ernest Hemingway gathered here is still very much alive at this popular café/restaurant. You can sit outdoors beneath the colorful green and white awnings amid a garden of greenery, and sip coffee, or move to the enclosed terrace for an authentic *salade niçoise*. La Closerie des Lilas is still a hangout for French film stars and chic young Frenchmen, and a spot were one can linger while reading the copies of *L'Express* and *Paris Match* provided for the clients. Come late at night to sip fabulous Irish coffee topped with dollops of *crème fraîche* and to listen to the live jazz piano music. It's pure *Casablanca*.

LA COUPOLE
102 Boulevard du
  Montparnasse, Paris 14.
Tel: 43.20.14.20.
Métro: Vavin.
Open daily, 8 A.M. to 2 A.M.

This Montparnasse café/restaurant (see also Restaurants) is still a favorite meeting place for artists, models, and tourists, and the haunt of young Americans since its opening in 1927. Although today few artists can afford to live in this popular district, and the famous "coupole" (glass dome) has been covered over by a five-story building built above the café, this Paris institution still retains some of the Art Deco glitz and glamour of its heyday. The enclosed terrace café serves a daunting array of Hemingway era cocktails, as well as rich, dark espresso. It's a good place to stop before or after seeing a movie on Boulevard Montparnasse, but aside from pastries and *baguette* sandwiches, no food is served. However, one could make a meal of the enormous *tarte aux framboises*, a shortbread crown topped abundantly with jewel-like fresh raspberries. Mine looked so tempting that the people at the next table ordered one.

LE DOME
108 Boulevard du
  Montparnasse, Paris 14.
Tel: 43.35.34.82.
Métro: Vavin.
Open 8 A.M. to 1 A.M. Closed
  Monday.

When Le Dôme first opened at the turn of the century, it was just a drinking shack, and Montparnasse was a suburb of the Latin Quarter. Things change, and though Le Dôme has become a top-rate fish restaurant (see Restaurants), the rather elegant, fern-filled terrace is still a nice spot for lingering over coffee, or a *ballon de rouge*, or a *croque-monsieur* or *sandwich mixte*, both available on Poilâne's country bread. Every day (except Sunday), there is a daily fish special, priced at around 65 francs. I have lunched on a lovely plate of smoked salmon and fresh blinis, and a generous green salad. One can order a *plateau de fruits de mer*—platter of fish and shellfish—or an assortment of oysters.

LA ROTONDE
105 Boulevard du
  Montparnasse, Paris 6.
Tel: 43.26.68.84.
Métro: Vavin.
Open daily, 8 A.M. to 2 A.M..

Lenin and Trotsky sipped their *café crème* here in 1915, along with others of the international intelligentsia who made this café famous. It has been remodeled, and much of its charm has been lost, but in the afternoon La Rotonde gets the sun, so the Montparnasse crowd camps out here, sipping Ricard and smoking Gitanes. They serve a good *croque-monsieur*, available with *pain Poilâne*.

VICTOR-HUGO, ARC DE TRIOMPHE, PARC MONCEAU
16th and 17th arrondissement

LE COPERNIC
54 Avenue Kléber, Paris 16.
Tel: 47.27.87.65.
Métro: Kléber.
Open 7:30 A.M. to 8 P.M.
  Closed the last three
  weeks in August.

Few French customs offer greater satisfaction than the ritual of sitting down in a nice wicker café chair early in the morning, and ordering up a great cup of coffee and a buttery croissant to savor with your morning paper. At that hour, your palate is clean, highly receptive, and yet highly critical, so it will just say no to junk. At Le Copernic—an everyday café along Avenue Kléber, a five-minute walk from the Arc de Triomphe—your palate should be happy to wake up to the flat, crusty, chewy, *brioche*-like *croissants* that the owner makes fresh each day. Note that at lunchtime there's a great selection of sandwiches on Poilâne bread.

LE DOME DE VILLIERS
4 Avenue de Villiers,
  Paris 17.
Tel: 43.87.28.68.
Métro: Villiers.
Open daily, 6:30 A.M.
  to 2 A.M.

Take a stroll through one of the Right Bank's prettiest gardens—the romantic, old-fashioned, impeccably maintained Parc Monceau—then stop for a coffee, breakfast, lunch or dinner at one of the neighborhood's best-quality cafés. During the winter months you can be assured of fresh oysters, delicious *plats du jour* such as a sparklingly fresh cold *colin*, or cod, served with green salad, hard-cooked eggs and tomatoes. They also serve simple sandwiches and a variety of *croque-monsieurs*. (They even offer a vegetarian version with cheese and tomatoes). Service is friendly, and the café is outfitted with a cheery red and gold awning and comfortable wicker chairs, and is set back from the street. Before or after a visit, be sure to wander down the Rue des Levis market street.

BEER

Beer *(bière)* comes in many sizes and can be ordered by the bottle, *bouteille,* or on tap, *à la pression.*

Demi—8 ounces (25 centiliters)

Sérieux—16 ounces (50 centiliters)

Formidable—1 quart (1 liter)

A daily Parisian ritual.

LE VICTOR HUGO
4 Place Victor-Hugo,
Paris 16.
Tel: 45.00.87.55.
Métro: Victor Hugo.
Open 7 A.M. to 8:30 P.M.
Closed Sunday.

L e Victor Hugo is mentioned not because of its ambience, its history, or the people who have sipped here over the years. Rather, it's noted for its location and pleasant terrace, overlooking the fountains of the classic and well-heeled Place Victor-Hugo. I have to admit that, on Saturday afternoons, I love to position myself at a table, half trying to read the daily paper but all the while noticing the beautiful and fashionable folk who wander past. Here, in the heart of what journalist Richard Bernstein termed the "Deep Sixteenth," is one of the city's best seats for watching bourgeois Parisians stroll by in all of their cold, chic, and blasé glory. The *garçons* couldn't be more typical: They'll forget what you've ordered and are sure to disappear after you request the check, but if you can wait it out, they serve frothy *café crème* and delicious, buttery *croissant* twists in the morning.

PERE-LACHAISE

20th arrondissement

LE SAINT-AMOUR
2 Avenue Gambetta/
32 Boulevard Ménil-
montant, Paris 20.
Métro: Père-Lachaise.
Tel: 47.97.20.15.
Open 7 A.M. to 10 P.M.
  Meals served until 9 P.M.
  Closed Monday.

This sprawling café situated right on the edge of Père-Lachaise makes a wonderful stop for a snack or a meal after a visit to this famous cemetery. In the morning, baskets of croissants sit on the bar, accompanied by pretty pots of jam. But Le Saint-Amour's claim to fame rests on its hearty and happy selection of wines by the glass, mostly *côtes de Beaujolais*, including the namesake Saint-Amour. You can sample them at the long bar with *pain Poilâne casse-croûtes* (small, open-faced sandwiches) and Auvergnat specialties such as *saucisson sec* and cheese plates of Cantal, Saint-Nectaire, and Bleu d'Auvergne. Otherwise settle into one of the wicker chairs on the rambling terrace overlooking the busy boulevard and check out the interesting multi-ethnic neighborhood mix of old Paris and new immigrants. The friendly waiters love to play the guessing game of figuring out whose grave people have come to visit. Most of the time it's not too difficult, given the swarm of retroactive hippie tourists making a pilgrimage to the grave of Jim Morrison, The Doors' rock singer who died of a drug overdose in 1970. For ladies of a certain age, they'll suggest: "You aren't here to see Jim Morrison's grave are you? No, you must be here to see Piaf." The way to a lady's heart . . .

Salons de Thé
TEA SALONS

Gathering with friends at teatime.

Golden *pains au chocolat*, lush, ruby red strawberry tarts, and moist, dark chocolate cakes form a multicolored still life in the sparkling window. When gazing through, one senses an air of calm, repose, contentment. The door opens, revealing a mysterious blend of jasmine tea, vanilla-scented apple tart, and Haydn. At a far table, elderly women in veiled hats sit *tête-à-tête*, immersed in gossip and frothy hot chocolate, while nearby a well-dressed businessman flirts with a slender, chic Parisienne, who seems more involved in her *tarte abricot* than in his advances. This is the daily life of the Parisian *salon de thé*—cozy, intimate affairs designed to indulge France's insatiable sweet tooth and flair for guiltlessly whiling away hours at the table.

Though teatime is associated more closely with London, Paris supports dozens of full-fledged *salons de thé*, most of them distinctly French. Parisians don't fool around with frail cucumber sandwiches—they get right to the heart of the matter, dessert.

In Paris, as in London, tea salons reached the height of popularity at the turn of the century, providing matrons of standing with well-appointed surroundings for entertaining guests outside the home, and offering women a respectable career opportunity. During the 1920s, tea and dance salons became popular along the Champs-Elysées and in restaurants in the Bois de Boulogne: here aging *grandes dames* came alone, as did young men. They met, they danced, they drank tea, then went their separate ways.

Thanks to a renaissance during the 1970s, Paris now offers an unlimited variety of tea salons, each with a distinctive decor, menu, and ambience that follow the whim and passion of the owner. A cup of coffee or pot of tea will be more expensive here than in a run-of-the-mill café, but the atmosphere is usually calmer and the food generally superior. Lunch, and sometimes dinner, is available at most *salons de thé*, but more often than not, the food is an afterthought. An early morning or late afternoon visit for tea and pastry will, in the end, be more rewarding. Tea salons are, by the way, places where one feels perfectly comfortable alone.

PALAIS-ROYAL, LOUVRE

1st and 2nd arrondissements

ANGELINA
226 Rue de Rivoli, Paris 1.
Tel: 42.60.82.00.
Métro: Tuileries.
Open daily, 9:30 A.M. to
   7 P.M. Closed August.
Credit cards: AE, DC, V.

One almost expects a troupe of Proustian characters to wander into this turn-of-the-century salon just across the street from the Jardin des Tuileries. Up until 1948, this was the old and celebrated Rumpelmayers, where as a child A.J. Liebling downed ersatz American ice cream sodas and began his love affair with Paris. Today—with its green-veined, marble-topped tables and walls embellished with murals and mirrors—it's still snobbish, expensive, and so popular that often on weekends one has to wait at least half an hour to secure a table. But, this is one of the only places in town where they melt real chocolate bars for their *"Africain"*—a lethally rich, delicious hot chocolate.

MUSCADE
36 Rue de Montpensier,
   Paris 1.
Tel: 42.97.51.36.
Métro: Palais-Royal–Musée
   du Louvre.
Open daily: in summer,
   11 A.M. to 11 P.M; in
   winter, noon to 8:30 P.M.;
   tea, coffee, and desserts
   only from 3:30 to 7 P.M.
Credit card: V.

You don't have to book a table at the Grand Véfour to enjoy the romantic pink rose garden of the Palais-Royal. From May to September, Muscade expands to the garden terrace, and becomes one of the city's most tranquil, elegant outdoor spots for people watching or just resting weary bodies. It's a wonderful place to sip tea and watch the world go by. The Palais-Royal garden is an honest neighborhood park as well, filled with old ladies sharing their *baguettes* with the pigeons, maids and mothers pushing infants in pristine, navy prams, and children at play in the sandbox. Stop off before or after a visit to the Louvre or the Comédie Française, ignore the indifferent pastries and enjoy a *café crème* or a pot of tea under the elegant gray and white striped awnings.

THE S. F. (Schramm et Delhommeau)
Passage du Grand Cerf, 145 Rue Saint-Denis, Paris 2.
Tel: 40.28.08.76.
Métro: Etienne Marcel.
Open 9 A.M. to 7 P.M.
Closed Sunday and two weeks in August.
Credit card: V.

Off the dingy, sex-shop strewn Rue Saint-Denis, you can hardly believe your eyes when you look down the Passage du Grand Cerf, a recently restored turn-of-the-century arcade. Walking down this atrium-topped, wood-paneled hall is like stepping into an oasis of tranquility and comfort. Thé S.F.'s wooden tables and bentwood chairs spreading onto the tiled path practically beckon you to come sit down and have a drink. But you may also be tempted to try the loft-like upstairs dining room, with its cedar paneling and eclectic Art Deco decor, which includes a collection of 1920s movie theater speakers, radios and Victrolas.

Once you decide on a table, be prepared to peruse a list of forty-five teas from China, India, Taiwan, and Japan, supplied by Mariage Frères (see page 165) and Damman, two of Paris' most reputable tea merchants. Thé S.F. serves a few dessert specialties not always found in tea salons, such as *fontainebleau* (a creamy cloud of *crème fraîche* and *fromage blanc*); fresh fruit in a delicious and unusual syrup of honey, orange flower water, and orange zest; and *fouace aveyronnaise* (a sweet *brioche* from the *massif Central* region of France). Tea and pastries can also be purchased to take out.

VERLET
256 Rue Saint-Honoré, Paris 1.
Tel: 42.60.67.39.
Métro: Palais-Royal—
Musée du Louvre.
Open 9 A.M. to 7 P.M. Closed Sunday, Monday, and August.
No credit cards.

The rich aroma of freshly roasted coffee mingling with teas from China, Ceylon, India, and Japan draws passersby to the door of Verlet, one of the most reputable and helpful coffee and tea merchants in Paris. Here, not far from the Place du Palais-Royal and the Louvre's Musée des Arts Décoratifs, you enter a casual, cosmopolitan world, crammed with open sacks of roast coffee from all corners of the globe, mounds of dried fruits and nuts, and colorful tins of tea blended on the spot to your liking. There's almost always a line continuing outside the door for Verlet's products, but if there's some table space, settle down for a few minutes in this unadorned 1930s setting for its famous coffee or tea served from silver-plated teapots with handles covered by bright felt mittens. There are always four or five rich cakes and pastries made on the premises including a luscious apricot tart (see recipe, page 166) that goes so well with a warming cup of jasmine tea.

MARAIS, ILE SAINT-LOUIS

4th arrondissement

LA CHARLOTTE DE L'ISLE
24 Rue St. Louis-en-l'Ile, Paris 4.
Tel: 43.54.25.83.
Métro: Pont-Marie.
Open Thursday through Sunday 2 to 8 P.M.; Wednesday puppet shows 2:30 to 4 P.M. (by reservation); Tuesday poetry readings at 8:30 P.M., live pianist Friday afternoons.
Closed July and August
Credit Card: V.

From the outside, La Charlotte de l'Isle looks as if it might belong to the witch in Hansel and Gretel, with its whimsical window display of gingerbread houses, cookie ornaments, and chocolate sculptures in the shapes of animals and children. Inside the music, antique marionettes and, yes, even broomsticks hanging on the walls add to the sometimes strange, fairy tale ambience—one almost expects to be cast under a spell. Yet this enchanted world beckons with homey, delicious *florentines* (caramelized almond cookies coated with bittersweet chocolate), tarts and, above all, some of the best hot chocolate in Paris. Order a *chocolat chaud à l'ancienne* and be prepared to wait for a while in this funky tea salon while one of the two *patronnes* melts dark chocolate bars into liquid heaven. This is the ultimate happy ending for those who love super-thick rich hot chocolate.

Sometimes only café crème will do.

(Those who prefer frothy, leaner hot chocolate can ask for theirs to be diluted with warm milk.)

La Charlotte doubles as a kind of off-beat cultural center, with a literary club, and poetry readings on Tuesday nights, and puppet shows for children on Wednesday afternoons (reservations essential). Come in from the rain on a Friday afternoon, when there's a classical pianist, and it's like walking through the looking glass. Order one of the rich pastries, like the bittersweet chocolate *tarte de tantie* (a baked chocolate mousse with a fudgy chocolate glaze) and a steaming pot of tea in a pretty iron Japanese tea pot, listen to the raindrops and Chopin, savor the chocolate, and wait for the storm to abate in the sweetest and most civilized of ways.

Mariage Frères, a tea lover's paradise.

MARIAGE FRERES
30–32 Rue du Bourg-
  Tibourg, Paris 4.
Tel: 42.72.28.11.
Métro: Saint-Paul or
  Hôtel-de-Ville.
Open noon to 7:30 P.M.
  Closed Monday.
Hot meals served until
  3 P.M.
Credit cards: AE, V.

In the trendy yet still very old-fashioned Marais, one of France's oldest and most respected tea importers boasts a combination tea boutique and tasting salon. As you wander down the slightly scruffy Rue du Bourg-Tibourg you have no idea what is in store. But as soon as you approach Mariage Frères, your senses are transported to an appealing, pleasurable world. The aroma of exotic teas from China, Taiwan, Japan, India, and Brazil invades the senses, and sounds of classical music fill the air, as your eyes focus on a plant and wicker-filled neo-classical space bathed in delicate light and decorated in pale ochre and white.

TARTE ABRICOT VERLET
VERLET'S APRICOT TART

Verlet is a tiny tea and coffee shop that also serves good homemade pastries (see entry, page 163). Anyone who loves apricots will love this simple, homey pie, which takes about twenty minutes to make. Be sure to use fresh, not canned, apricots.

Pastry:
½ cup (4 ounces; 125 g)
   unsalted butter,
   melted
½ cup (100 g) sugar
2 cups (260 g) all-
   purpose flour (not
   unbleached)
1 teaspoon (5 g)
   unsalted butter, for
   buttering tart pan

Filling:
5 tablespoons *crème
   fraîche* (see recipe,
   page 279) or heavy
   cream, preferably not
   ultra-pasteurized
1 egg
¼ cup (50 g) sugar
1 tablespoon all-purpose
   flour
1 teaspoon vanilla
   extract
1 pound (500 g) fresh
   apricots, pitted and
   halved
1 tablespoon
   confectioners' sugar

1. Preheat the oven to 350°F (175°C).

2. Prepare the pastry: In a medium-size bowl mix the butter and sugar together thoroughly, then add the flour and knead by hand until well blended. The pastry will be very crumbly. Butter a 10½-inch (27-cm) tart pan. Using your hands, press the pastry into the buttered pan and bake in the preheated oven for 10 minutes.

3. Meanwhile, prepare the filling: In a small bowl combine the *crème fraîche* and egg, and mix until well blended. Add the sugar, mix well, then add the flour and vanilla. Pour the mixture into the prebaked pastry shell and arrange the apricots, cut side down, on top of the cream mixture.

4. Bake until a knife inserted in the cream comes out clean, about 45 minutes. Cool and serve at room temperature, preferably within an hour of baking. Sprinkle with confectioners' sugar just before serving.

Yield: One 10½-inch (27-cm) tart

There are some three hundred varieties of teas from twenty countries, as well as an astonishingly complete selection of tea paraphernalia, including about two hundred teapots, a charming individual tea services, even a series of wicker picnic sets that will make you want to pack up and take off at the next opportunity. Smokers and non-smokers are discreetly segregated, as smokers are directed to a second room upstairs. All the available teas are described in painstaking detail in the dictionary-like menu, and even tea experts are likely to feel overwhelmed. But one can always cop out and order one of the more familiar varieties, among them a delicately perfumed Darjeeling, a penetrating, flinty Keemun, a rich and pungent Assam, or the house specialty, a spicy, fruity blend called Christmas tea.

With such pleasant surroundings, it's a shame the food is a bit overpriced and not up to par. The salad combinations are simply silly, and tea-infused specialties barely have the taste of tea. Better to come at breakfast or teatime, for the flaky currant-filled scones, served with a variety of tea jellies, or the soothing *tarte aux fraises des bois* in season: excellent *pâte sablée* smothered with a blend of pastry cream and wild strawberries, all topped with a crackling caramel crust.

LUXEMBOURG, ODEON, ECOLE MILITAIRE

6th and 7th arrondissements

A LA COUR DE ROHAN
59–61 Rue Saint-André-des-Arts, Paris 6.
Tel: 43.25.79.67.
Métro: Odéon.
Open noon to 7:30 P.M.
Closed Monday and August.
No credit cards.

At first glance A la Cour de Rohan, in a *passage* near the Odéon Métro, looks more like a chic decorating boutique than a tea salon. But wander inside, and you'll find a cozy, English-country-style salon decorated in white and various shades of green. The comfortable chairs, aromas of Darjeeling and *gâteau Opéra* and the soothing sounds of classical music make you want to settle in for the afternoon. Although the cute atmosphere might become a bit cloying in warm weather, in winter this is a lovely place to escape the crowds of the Rue-Saint-André-des-Arts and to sip tea served in antique metal pots. Try their *Mille et un Nuits* tea, a light, flowery blend, nice for the afternoon. Unfortunately the desserts are almost sickly sweet and unexceptional.

DALLOYAU
2 Place Edmond-Rostand, Paris 6.
Tel: 43.29.31.10.
Métro: Luxembourg.
Open 9 A.M. to 9 P.M.

After a walk through the Luxembourg Gardens, settle in at Dalloyau, formerly Dalloyau-Pons, an aristocratic, old-world tea salon with a pleasant terrace facing the park greenery and the stunning fountain at Place Edmond-Rostand. The snooty young waitresses act as though they'd rather be elsewhere, but overlook that, because in the summertime this is one of the classiest people-watching spots in town. In winter, go at about 10 A.M., climb the curving stairway to the tearoom, take a table overlooking the gardens, order up a steaming cup of smoky Chinese tea or a *café crème* with a pitcher of frothy steamed milk on the side, and enjoy a yeasty little *brioche* in stately silence.

LES DEUX ABEILLES
189 Rue de l'Université, Paris 7.
Tel: 45.55.64.04.
Métro: RER Pont de l'Alma.
Open 9 A.M. to 7 P.M. Closed Sunday.
Sidewalk terrace.
Credit card: V.
Non-smoking section.

Voilà! Just a 10-minute walk from the Eiffel Tower, the tea salon of your dreams—with sprays of roses, fresh-baked smells wafting from the kitchen, and sideboards piled high with homemade temptations like apple-berry crumble, perfect lemon scones, *tarte Tatin*, and fresh fruit tarts. Les Deux Abeilles (the Two Bees) are Anne and Varelia Arella, mother and daughter, who chose this name because "we work like two busy bees together." Although many desserts have an Anglo-Saxon origin (the moist lemon scones are some of the best to be found on either side of the English Channel), Madame Arella has never visited Britain or the U.S. It's just that she prefers the simple—and sweet—authenticity of teatime fare such as crumbles, pies, and tea cakes to frilly French pastries. The happy result is food you want to dig into not just look at: If they have it that day, sample their remarkable raspberry *tarte* oozing with a thick layer of fresh berries and topped with a crisp meringue crust. The few items not made on the premises, like the bread (from Poilâne) and the jams (from a farm in the Cévennes mountains) are high quality.

The decor mirrors the food with an unfussy but completely feminine, soft, and tranquil space, decorated with antiques from the Arellas' country house. Tables don crisp, white linens and rose-patterned crockery to match the rose wallpaper, and the honeycomb ceramic tiles add a rustic touch. Country charm notwithstanding, at lunch this becomes the chic retreat of dressed-to-kill Parisiennes, including Catherine Deneuve and Isabelle Adjani, who come here for light but satisfying specialties such as white asparagus tarts, *ravioles aux herbes,* pretty salads and *pain Poilâne.* A single complaint: It's a pity the service is not more professional.

In addition to a fine selection of teas served in simple porcelain pots, Les Deux Abeilles offers an unusual selection of old-fashioned drinks such as ginger lemonade, *hydromiel* (or mead, a fermented honey-based liquor), and apple-cassis cider. Everything here can be ordered to take out.

MARIAGE FRERES
13 Rue des Grands
    Augustins, Paris 6.
Tel: 40.51.82.50
Métro: Mabillon or Odéon.
Open 10:30 A.M. to 7:30 P.M.
    Closed Tuesday.
Credit cards: AE, V.

Acouple of blocks away from the Pont-Neuf and down the street from Picasso's old apartment in the Rue des Grands Augustins, this *Rive Gauche* outpost of the tea salon Mariage Frères has a more decorated, less lived-in look than the original, colonial-style Marais shop. The high ceilings and high-backed mahogany chairs lend a kind of stiff formality to the tearoom, and they make it seem a little empty even when it's completely full. But

The tea boutique at Mariage Frères.

the trademark tea remains the same: a steaming Art Deco teapot filled with one of the dozens of varieties listed in the book-like menu, *"L'Art du Thé."* The ground-floor tea and gift boutique is more spacious and amenable to browsing than the Marais shop, and the service is friendlier and less hurried (See also entry, page 165).

LA NUIT DES THES
22 Rue de Beaune, Paris 7.
Tel: 47.03.92.07.
Métro: Rue du Bac.
Open noon to 7 P.M. Closed
   Sunday and August.
Credit card: V.

La Nuit des Thés is for those who love Paris in all its gilt-trimmed, frilly formality. The Louis XVI-style decor, the mirrors and marble floors, lend this tea salon a "let-them-eat-cake" ambience. Like Versailles, it's regal but not particularly comfortable. The succulent tarts, however, measure up to their sumptuous surroundings, and good tea is served steaming hot in metal, Art Deco teapots. The bird-like *propriétaire* looks as though she's never poked her head into the kitchen nor tasted her own delicacies (when asked if she made the desserts herself, she looked horrified and replied that she hired a chef to do all the cooking). But like any good ruler, she knows how to delegate: Worth a detour is the *tarte au fromage blanc caramelisée,* an ethereal, creamy cloud of Parisian-style cheesecake with a crackling caramel crust. And for chocolate lovers, the *dacquoise au chocolat* offers an elegant excuse to sample silky rich, sweet chocolate mousse in an edible meringue shell.

PRADIER
6 and 32 Rue de
   Bourgogne, Paris 7.
Tel: 45.51.78.36 and
   45.51.72.37.
Métro: Assemblée
   Nationale.
Open 9 A.M. to 7 P.M. Closed
   Sunday and Monday.
Credit card: V.

Stroll into this posh *pâtisserie* and tea salon in the heart of the seventh arrondissement for a close-up look at *"La Vieille France,"* with its emphasis on high quality, tradition, and aristocratic reserve. The curt waitresses in their frilly white aprons are of the old school and are likely to look you over before deigning to give you a seat. But the dainty and delicious *pâtisseries* and the *café crème,* served in a silver pitcher, will win you over. For those who want to take a piece of *"Vieille France"* home with them, stop into the Marie-Pierre Boitard shop (see page 353) across the street to admire the opulent array of tableware.

CONCORDE, MADELEINE, PIGALLE

1st, 8th and 9th arrondissements

LADUREE
16 Rue Royale, Paris 8.
Tel: 42.60.21.79.
Métro: Madeleine.
Open 8:30 A.M. to 7 P.M.
   Closed Sunday, holidays
   and August.
Hot meals served at
   lunch only.
Credit cards: MC, V.

Until I discovered the delights of Ladurée one day at ten in the morning, I could not have cared less about *croissants*. But after visiting some sixty *salons de thé* throughout Paris, it's the frothy cup of *café au lait* and the flaky, yeasty *croissants* of Ladurée near the Place de la Madeleine that return in my dreams.

Can there be any early morning atmosphere more elegantly Parisian in tone? There's the hushed and intimate turn-of-the-century decor, with pale olive wood-paneled walls, *trompe l'oeil* ceilings, straightback chairs, tiny marble-topped tables, and a clientele that's equally at home at Cartier and the Ritz. The air is not snobbish, just a bit blasé, and while the sandwiches wouldn't keep a bird alive, this is the place to rediscover what *croissants* should taste like. And I've never found a better cup of *café au lait* in Paris, served in a silver pitcher with a bite of bittersweet chocolate on the side. The pastries like the meltingly rich *croissant aux noix* and the *Kramich* (a puff pastry raisin twist) are deliciously fresh. The chewy, almondy, almost marzipan *financiers* (almond cakes) are a little taste of heaven, as are their famous macaroons: vanilla, chocolate, caramel, pistachio, and—a new addition—praline.

LE PENY
3 Place de la Madeleine,
   Paris 8.
Tel: 42.65.06.75.
Métro: Madeleine.
Open daily 8 A.M. to
   9 P.M. (until 10:30 P.M.
   in the summer).
Credit card: V.

The best tables at Peny (also known as Penny) spill out onto the shady sidewalk terrace facing the Place de la Madeleine. Although this popular summertime spot looks more like an ordinary café, it merits tea salon status thanks to the carts of homemade pastries, wheeled around by the waiters to tempt the innocent passerby. Although neither the pastries nor the coffee quite measure up to the perfect standards set by Ladurée across the street, the service is quicker, and those running late in the morning will be satisfied by the yeasty *croissants* and good *café crème* at the bar. Or, if you can handle it at that time of day, their famous *gâteau Peny à la noix de coco*, or coconut cake. Unfortunately, the lunchtime offerings are best avoided.

TEA FOLLIES
6 Place Gustave-Toudouze, Paris 9.
Tel: 42.80.08.44.
Métro: Saint-Georges.
Open noon to 7 P.M. Monday through Saturday; 12:30 to 7 P.M. Sunday.
Hot meals served at lunch only.
No credit cards.

Bright, friendly, casual, a stop at Tea Follies is like having afternoon tea on a front porch strewn with stacks of local newspapers and magazines and fresh flowers. The contemporary red, white, and gray tea salon opens out onto the tree-filled Place Gustave-Toudouze, and in good weather tables spread out onto the sidewalk—perfect for sunning and gossip over a cozy pot of tea. With such a lovely location and tea, what a pity that the scones and desserts are so disappointing.

SABLES A LA LAVANDE TEA FOLLIES
TEA FOLLIES' LAVENDER SHORTBREAD COOKIES

Fragrant, delicate, and delicious, these shortbread cookies are great to have around for snacking, for serving with ice cream or at teatime, which is what they do at Tea Follies, a very popular tea salon in the city's 9th arrondissement. If you don't have access to freshly dried lavender flowers (look for them at shops that sell herbes de Provence*), fresh, chopped rosemary leaves are a very worthy substitute.*

1¾ cups (250 g) unbleached all-purpose flour
½ cup (100 g) sugar
8 tablespoons (4 ounces; 120 g) unsalted butter, softened
1 egg
1 tablespoon dried lavender flowers, or fresh rosemary leaves
Pinch of salt

1. Preheat the oven to 400° F (200° C). Line 2 baking sheets with cooking parchment.

2. In a large bowl, combine the flour and sugar, then, using a pastry fork, slowly incorporate the softened butter, the egg, the lavender, and the salt, working the mixture into a soft dough. Transfer it to a floured work surface and knead into a ball. Roll the cookie dough to a ¼-inch (7-mm) thickness, then cut it into about thirty-six ½-inch (6-cm) cookies.

3. Transfer the rounds to the prepared baking sheets, place the baking sheets in the oven, and bake until evenly brown, 10 to 15 minutes. Transfer the cookies to a baking rack to cool.

Yield: About 36 cookies

TORAYA
10 Rue Saint-Florentin, Paris 1.
Tel: 42.60.13.00.
Métro: Concorde.
Open 10 A.M. to 7 P.M. Closed Sunday.
Credit cards: AE, DC, V.

The miniature pastries and handmade ceramics are displayed like diamonds in a jeweler's window; the spotless decor is a sober, modern blend of black, gray, and white. Toraya is an authentic contemporary Japanese tea salon, complete with white ceramic cups used for *matcha* (the ceremonial Japanese green tea), which is frothy, almost bitter, and whisked to a foam. To most Western palates the pastries look much better than they taste, but the adventuresome will want to try the tiny multi-colored variations made of *adzuki* bean purée, or the little leaf-wrapped balls of sticky rice. It's a lot cheaper than a trip to Tokyo, and a nice exotic touch for those with little enthusiasm for pastries laden with Western cream and sugar.

TROCADERO

16th arrondissement

CARETTE
4 Place du Trocadéro,
Paris 16.
Tel: 47.27.88.56.
Métro: Trocadéro.
Open 8 A.M. to 7 P.M. Closed Tuesday and August.
Hot meals served until 4 P.M. only.
No credit cards.

By nine in the morning this spacious, terraced tea salon facing the Trocadéro swarms with handsome male joggers who come for a little after-run nourishment. It's not unusual to see a trim, well-muscled Frenchman down two *pains au chocolat*, a couple of glasses of freshly squeezed orange juice, and a *café au lait* in record time, as he buries his nose in the French sporting journal *l'Equipe*. The *pain au chocolat* is yeasty and fresh and the smoky Chinese tea is first rate, but the *financier* is better left to someone else. Ignore the snooty service, and don't bother stopping by in the afternoons unless you enjoy being asphyxiated by a cigarette-induced haze.

COQUELIN AINE
67 Rue de Passy, Paris 16.
Tel: 45.24.44.00.
Métro: La Muette.
Open 9 A.M. to 7:30 P.M.
Closed Sunday afternoon.
Credit card: V.

Coquelin Aîné is to the 16th *arrondissement* what Pradier is to the 7th—prim, slightly snooty, and delicious despite it all. But this *pâtisserie*/tea salon has more of a neighborhood feeling, with local matrons stopping in for sustenance after doing their marketing and mothers parading infants in regal, navy prams. The terrace spreads out onto the charming square, and provides a good vantage point for watching the bustle of the nearby covered market of Passy and the Rue de l'Annonciation market street. Come here for a satisfying morning *café crème* or *chocolat chaud* and *croissant* or a sweet afternoon tea on the terrace.

TERNES, VILLIERS

17th arrondissement

CHOCOLAT VIENNOIS
118 Rue des Dames,
   Paris 17.
Tel: 42.93.34.40.
Métro: Villiers.
Open 10 A.M. to 10 P.M.
   Closed Saturday night
   and Sunday.
Hot meals served
   throughout the day.
Credit cards: AE, V.

This adorable tea salon not far from the Rue de Lévis market is worth a detour for anyone who loves great *café viennoise* (half whipped cream, half bracing black coffee), rich and beautiful *linzertorte*, warm and fragrant apple strudel. The waitresses are charming, speaking French with a lovely Austrian accent, and the salon itself is out of a fairy tale. It's especially beautiful at Christmastime, when the entire building is covered with lights and greenery.

Tea and snacks, very intense.

LE STUBLI
11 Rue Poncelet, Paris 17.
Tel: 42.27.81.86.
Métro: Ternes.
Pastry shop open 8:30 A.M.
   to 7:30 P.M. Tuesday
   through Saturday;
   10 A.M. to 12:30 P.M.
   Sunday. Tea salon open
   10 A.M. to 6:30 P.M.
   Tuesday through
   Saturday; 10 A.M. to
   12:30 P.M. Sunday.
   Closed Monday.
Credit card: V.

Many a morning I take my newspaper and my string bag to the Rue Poncelet, head for this quiet, very private tea salon overlooking the bustling street market below, and grab a few moments to myself. The coffee here is exceptional—always served with a miniature pitcher of cream—and the pastries are the sort that even the strongest among us must struggle to resist. I am in love with their mile-high cheesecake and the flaky, fruit-filled strudels. Diet watchers: don't let the creamy desserts scare you away. Le Stübli's brochure proudly notes that they are made with reduced (30 percent) fat cream and a minimum of butter and sugar (see also Pastry shops).

Bistros et Bars à Vin
WINE BARS

A toast to good times.

Enter into the land of bread and Beaujolais, cheese and *charcuterie.* Known as *bistros à vin* (wine bars), most of these cozy neighborhood spots open about the time much of Paris is rising for breakfast. From the exterior many resemble ordinary cafés, yet once you've entered and sipped a glass of silky, scented Fleurie or fresh and fragrant Sancerre, and sampled an open-face sandwich of garlic-and-thyme-flecked *rillettes* (spreadable pork or goose pâté) on thick sourdough bread, you understand the difference.

There is always food and conviviality, but more important, there is wine—by the glass, the carafe, the bottle. Light and fruity Beaujolais is king, but one also finds delicate Bourgueil from Touraine; young wines from Bordeaux, Chinon, and Côtes-du-Rhône; the Atlantic Coast's delicious Muscadet; the Jura's white and pleasant Arbois; and Provence's heady, vigorous Gigondas. Obviously, not every wine bar stocks every wine, but most offer from a dozen to thirty wines at from about 20 to 50 francs a glass, along with—at the very least—cold platters of cheese or *charcuterie* designed to complement the house selection. Most are casual affairs with no printed menu, but wine selections and daily specials are usually handwritten on blackboards set behind the bar.

Is there any reason to go to a wine bar rather than a café for a glass of wine? Categorically, yes. The wine sold in most cafés is mass-produced and banal, and much of it watery and undrinkable. The wine sold in wine bars is usually carefully chosen by the *bistrotiers* (owners), most often dedicated men who are passionate about wine. When not behind the bar, many of them are traveling the country in search of good little wines. Often their selections are shipped directly to the wine bar in barrels (it's cheaper that way) and the *bistrotier* bottles them himself, storing the excess in basementlike caves beneath the bar.

The food—simple and unpretentious as it may be—is chosen with the same care. Most offer platters of French cheese, several kinds of hams, sausages, pâtés, and bread, often either Lionel or Max Poilâne's famous country loaf (see recipe, page 246), redolent of sourdough and fresh from their huge wood-fired ovens. Sometimes, homey pâtés, *quiches,* or dessert tarts—all dishes chosen to go perfectly with the house wines—are prepared by the owner's wife. Some wine bars offer even heartier fare, such as wintry *daubes* (stews), platters of cooked sausages, and *confit d'oie* (preserved goose). As one *bistrotier* put it, "Wine is made to go with food. Tasting wine alone should be left to the experts."

Best of all, wine bars serve as a tasting and testing ground for wines yet to be discovered, as well as for familiar favorites. Since many wine bars offer little-known, small production wines by the glass, this is the time to acquaint oneself with those such as Montlouis or Quarts de Chaume, both whites from the Loire; or to sample several of the ten *cru* Beaujolais, perhaps a Moulin-à-Vent, a Juliénas, and a Chiroubles, side by side.

While years ago most wine bars specialized in the young, inexpensive quaffing wines, today the trendier, more formal "English style" wine bars—such as Willi's and L'Ecluse—offer a wider selection, including older vintages and those from more noble vineyards.

Dozens of wine bars pepper the streets of Paris. Here are a few special ones, a choice selection for a quick lunch, a pleasant afternoon interlude, or a late-night snack. They present a good alternative to a full-fledged meal. One should lunch well for 150 to 175 francs depending on selections. The most popular spots are crowded at lunchtime, but if you go early, at noon, or late, at 2:30, you're likely to get a seat and still enjoy the atmosphere.

LES HALLES, PALAIS-ROYAL, LOUVRE

1st arrondissement

A LA CLOCHE DES HALLES
28 Rue Coquillière, Paris 1.
Tel: 42.36.93.89.
Métro: Les Halles.
Open 8 A.M. to 10 P.M.
Closed Saturday evening and Sunday.
No credit cards.
Wine may be purchased to take home.

This well-known wine bar takes its name from the wooden bell that once rang out across Les Halles to signal the beginning and the end of the day's commerce in the old wholesale food market. The market has been gone since 1970, but the wine bar remains. Owner Serge Lesage (who won the "meilleur pot" award in 1986) offers delicious cold platters—such as ham cooked on the bone, *quiche lorraine,* and a good *tarte Tatin* in the winter months. Wines to sample include Beaujolais, Côtes-du-Brouilly, Moulin à Vent, and Fleury. A major spot for celebrating the arrival of Beaujolais *nouveau* the third Thursday in November.

JUVENILES
47 Rue de Richelieu, Paris 1.
Tel: 42.97.46.49.
Métro: Palais-Royal.
Open noon to 11 P.M.
Monday to Friday, noon to 2:30 P.M. and 7 to 11 P.M. Saturday.
Closed Sunday.
Credit card: V.
Wine may be purchased to take home.

Serious wine bar enthusiasts will not want to miss Tim Johnston and Mark Williamson's fine endeavor, Juveniles, the little brother of Willi's Wine Bar, just off the fashionable Place des Victoires. Juveniles is an unadorned café turned wine bar, and it has rapidly become a great place to get a quick, good bite to accompany sips of an astonishingly fine selection of wines. Their *tapas*—little snacks served at wine bars in Spain—may be a bit unorthodox, but delicious nonetheless. There's always a good selection of wines by the glass, as well as a variety of good, lesser-known wines by the bottle, at very good prices.

Raising a glass with a friend.

TAVERNE HENRI IV
13 Place du Pont-Neuf,
    Paris 1.
Tel: 43.54.27.90.
Métro: Pont-Neuf.
Open noon to 10 P.M.
    Closed Saturday, Sunday
    and the last two weeks
    of August.
Wines may be purchased
    to take home.
No credit cards.

Opposite the statue of its namesake, Henri IV, this tobacco shop offers a certain grubby, old-fashioned, Parisian charm, where men sit reading *Figaro* or *France-Soir* as they munch on *tartines* of goose *rillettes*, between sips and swallows of fruity Morgon, or stand at the bar to chat with the beefy, outgoing *patron,* Robert Cointepas. The menu here includes *tartines*, or open-face sandwiches, topped with such variations as warm goat cheese with herbs, ham and Comté, and platters of *foie gras* and toast. Wines available by the glass include Beaujolais, Bordeaux, and wines from the Loire and the Jura. This bar was a Meilleur Pot winner in 1960, which may seem like a long time ago. But I'm sure this tradition-bound spot could easily win it again today.

MEILLEUR POT

The annual "Meilleur Pot" award designates the elite in Parisian wine bars. The traveling trophy—named after the traditional half-liter (about 17-ounce) Beaujolais *pot*, or jug—is awarded to *bistrotiers* who carry on the tradition of searching out and buying good French wines direct from the producers. The *bistrotier* then bottles the wines himself and serves them over the counter, by the glass or by the bottle.

The award, begun in Paris in 1957, is given to the *bistrotier* himself, not his establishment. If he sells or moves on, the title goes with him, right into retirement. Only one award is given each year.

Judging takes place from April to December, when a jury of ten makes anonymous visits to various Parisian wine bars. At the end of December or beginning of January, a formal award ceremony is held and the current title holder relinquishes the trophy, handing it to the new season's winner.

You'll note that many wine bars received the awards decades ago, yet they continue to thrive, a testament to the award, the wine bars, and Parisian traditions.

LE RUBIS
10 Rue du Marché-Saint-
 Honoré, Paris 1.
Tel: 42.61.03.34.
Métro: Tuileries.
Open 7 A.M. to 10 P.M.
 Closed Saturday,
 Sunday, and August.
Wines may be purchased
 to take home.

A classic, happy sort of bustling wine bar, where lunch is a free-for-all as clients stand five and six deep at the bar, dodging waiters and nudging neighbors. In good weather you can lunch outside, standing at the huge wine barrels that serve as makeshift tables. A Meilleur Pot winner in 1963. Hot meals served at lunch only.

Le Rubis, a lunchtime portrait.

WILLI'S WINE BAR
13 Rue des Petits-Champs,
 Paris 1.
Tel: 42.61.05.09.
Métro: Palais-Royal or
 Bourse.
Open noon to 2:30 P.M., 7 to
 11 P.M. Closed Sunday.
Credit card: V.

Perhaps the most popular and most respected wine bar in Paris, Willi's is bright, airy, and pleasantly decorated with a highly polished wood bar and an always-chic clientele. This is the place to come for an introduction to the wines of the Côtes-du-Rhône, including the bold, rich, and well-balanced Hermitage of Gérard Chave, and Georges Bernard's fruity Tavel, the rosé many consider to be the best in the world. Food here varies, with a changing selection of hot daily specials, a good variety of salads, and delicious bread from one of Paris's best bakers, Jean-Luc Poujauran.

MARAIS, ILE DE LA CITE

4th arrondissement

LA TARTINE
24 Rue de Rivoli, Paris 4.
Tel: 42.72.76.85.
Métro: Saint-Paul.
Open 8:30 A.M. to 10 P.M.
  Closed Tuesday and
  Wednesday morning,
  and August.
No credit cards.

If La Tartine were situated in the United States, you might call it a luncheonette. But this is Paris and La Tartine (meaning an open-face sandwich) is a wine bar in the oldest sense of the word. In fact, it's been called a café for wine drinkers, for the place is often filled with regulars. At lunchtime, crowds come to share modest platters of paper-thin slices of *jambon de Paris*, the pale-colored ham that's cured in salt brine, then cooked. La Tartine offers a broad range of wines, with some thirty wines available by the glass, and a *cave* of some 3,000 bottles. Worth sampling here: firm and fragrant *crottin de Chavignol*, the famed goat cheese from the Loire Valley, best enjoyed with owner Jean Bouscarel's crisp white Sancerre. La Tartine is a nice place to visit before or after a tour of the Marais. This is the neighborhood once inhabited by Eastern European refugees, and Trotsky—who supposedly visited La Tartine in its café days—lived right around the corner, on Rue Ferdinand Duval. A Meilleur Pot winner in 1965.

> *"They drank with unbuttoned bellies."*
> Rabelais

HEART OF THE MATTER

Most Paris bars open early not just to brew espresso, but also to accommodate the nearly 5 percent of the population who indulge in a spiritous breakfast, a practice known as *tuer le ver*, or "killing the worm."

According to legend, a certain madame, the wife of Monsieur de la Varende, died suddenly as a result of a worm gnawing away at her heart. An autopsy was performed, the worm was still alive, and all attempts to kill the creature failed. Finally, someone doused the worm with white wine, bringing about its quick demise. Quite logically, the moral of the story is: A glass of wine early in the day will keep the worms at bay.

Jacques Mélac takes a break with the crew (see entry, page 187).

LE VALENCAY
11 Boulevard du Palais,
 Paris 4.
Tel: 43.54.64.67.
Métro: La Cité or Saint-
 Michel.
Open 11 A.M. to 11 P.M.
 Closed Sunday.
Credit Card: V.

A calm oasis in the neighborhood of Notre-Dame and the Place Saint-Michel, Le Valençay is the perfect spot to come for a quick—and well-chosen —glass of wine, a huge green salad tossed with walnuts, and a platter of lovely cheese, all served with freshly toasted *pain Poilâne*. At lunchtime, local businessmen come in shirt sleeves for the 60-franc *plat du jour*. On a recent visit, it was a copious meal that included green salad, pan-fried steak smothered with shallots, and potatoes cooked in delicious goose fat. One good daily special to try— if it's on the menu that day—is the plate of soft, young *crottin*, or goat cheese, sprinkled with white wine and heated, making for a hit-the-spot luncheon course. A good selection of wines from throughout France are available by the glass, carafe, or bottle. Service is swift, professional, and friendly.

LUXEMBOURG, SAINT-MICHEL, SEVRES-BABYLONE, ECOLE MILITAIRE

5th, 6th, and 7th arrondissements

**BISTROT DES
 AUGUSTINS**
39 Quai des Grands-
 Augustins, Paris 6.
Tel: 43.54.41.65.
Métro: Saint-Michel.
Open 10:30 A.M. to
 midnight.
Wines may be purchased
 to take home.

Wander into this minuscule wine bar right across from the book stalls on the *quai*, and you feel as though you've walked into a village bistro. The carved Art Deco oak bar is pure 1930s, the owner sports a well-worn apron from Chiroubles, a village in the Beaujolais, and the aroma of the *plat du jour* fills the air. On my last visit, it was a succulent platter of sautéed chicken, served with sautéed potatoes. Other good bets include simple tossed green salads topped with either grilled *crottin* goat cheese or the marvelous cow's milk cheese, Saint Marcellin. Around two in the afternoon, just as your thoughts turn to dessert, the owner sets down a hot-from-the-oven home-made apple tart, allowing it to cool near the window as you plan your future. The bread is Poilâne, and there are at least a dozen wines available by the glass, including selections from René Sinard's Côtes-du-Rhône, and a fine Saint-Amour, *cru* Beaujolais, from the Domaines des Ducs. A great spot to know about when you need to get away from the throngs of tourists that inhabit this popular *quartier.*

CAFE DE LA NOUVELLE MAIRIE
19 Rue des Fossés-Saint-Jacques, Paris 5.
Tel: 43.26.80.18.
Métro: Luxembourg.
Open 9:30 A.M. to 1 A.M. Monday to Friday, 11 A.M. to 6 P.M. Saturday. Closed Sunday.
Credit card: V.

There are few prettier or more Left Bank Parisian squares than the tiny Place de l'Estrapade, just steps from the Pantheon and the Luxembourg Gardens. Reserve a table at lunch at Café de la Nouvelle Mairie on a sunny day to look out on the tree-covered square and a lovely view of the fine, turn-of-the-century facade of La Boulangerie Moderne. Service here is hurried and the staff may appear aloof and sleepy-eyed, but turn the other cheek, order up a nice glass of Saumur-Champigny, a platter of *crudités* (various raw vegetables), and a plate of *carpaccio de canard* (thinly sliced, raw duck breast), and simply enjoy. The

Sampling the new Beaujolais at Au Sauvignon (see entry, page 184).

wine list offers just twelve wines, most of them choices from reliable vineyards in Chinon, Saumur-Champigny, Bourgeuil, or Sancerre, and there is a single hot *plat du jour* offered daily. The bread is Poilâne, and the neighborhood's the tops.

LES PIPOS
2 Rue de l'Ecole-
  Polytechnique, Paris 5.
Tel: 43.54.11.40.
Métro: Maubert-Mutualité.
Open 8 A.M. to 9 P.M.
  Monday to Friday,
  9 A.M. to 3:30 P.M. and
  8 P.M. to 2 A.M. Saturday.
  Closed Sunday.
No credit cards.

Wander into this little Left Bank wine bar, and you'll swear you've wandered into a small village café: Owner Jean-Michel Delhomme will tell you the pedigree of every wine you sample and do his enthusiastic best to sell you on the daily special, even if you're not in the mood for pork braised in beer. There are always salads and open-face sandwiches of ham or cheese, as well as pleasant cheese platters to sample with beer from the tap or wines from the Rhône, Loire Valley, or Bordeaux. The decor is pure nostalgia, with a wooden bar carved with grapes, red moleskin banquettes, and a true sense of neighborhood camaraderie you won't find many places.

SANCERRE
22 Avenue Rapp, Paris 7.
Tel: 45.51.75.91.
Métro: Ecole Militaire or
  Alma-Marceau.
Open 7:30 A.M. to 8:30 P.M.
  Closed Saturday night,
  Sunday, and the third
  week of August.
Credit card: V.
Wine may be purchased
  to take home.

This is a low-key, casual little wine bar with the folkloric decor of the pleasant wine village of Sancerre, about 125 miles from Paris. The dry, flinty white Sancerre wine from the Domaine la Moussière is featured here, along with its perfect mate, the dry, almost chalky *crottin de Chavignol* goat cheese. The wine bar is popular with workers from the French television studios located nearby, and features a quiet (if citylike) sidewalk terrace. (Architecture buffs should walk across the street to look at the fantastic Art Nouveau apartment building constructed in 1905 at 29 Avenue de Rapp).

AU SAUVIGNON
80 Rue des Saint-Pères,
   Paris 7.
Tel: 45.48.49.02.
Mètro: Sèvres-Babylone.
Open 8:30 A.M. to 11 P.M.
   Closed Sunday, two
   weeks in February, and
   August.
No credit cards.

Au Sauvignon certainly takes the award for the most chic wine bar in Paris, located right in the center of the city's affluent neighborhood inhabited by the B.C.B.G. (*bon chic, bon genre* crowd). If you're into people watching (and who isn't?), if you love a good *tartine* on Poilâne country bread, and enjoy a glass or two of Bourgueil, Muscadet, or Puligny-Montrachet, then stop in while you're in the neighborhood. Au Sauvignon offers no hot food, only assorted platters and sandwiches of cheese and meats, which are particularly great when time is limited and your stomach is empty. A Meilleur Pot winner in 1961.

L'ECLUSE

If you ever wondered whether members of a chain of any sort can remain charming, chic, and retain at least a semblance of authenticity, the answer is yes. Over the past several years, little L'Ecluse wine bars have popped up all over Paris, following the same formula that made the first L'Ecluse, on the Quai des Grands-Augustins, a success. The decor, menu, and style are the same in each and appeal to a largely well-heeled business clientele. Belle Epoque posters, converted gas lamps, a long wooden bar, and mirrored walls give L'Ecluse a turn-of-the-century atmosphere, though the food and wine are totally up-to-date. Note, however, that a meal here will not be cheap. Service tends to be slow, perhaps intentionally. The first glass of wine comes quickly, and it's likely to be consumed by the time your snack or meal arrives. So, if you think you might want more than one glass, order a bottle. It will likely be less expensive in the long run. Don't come here looking for Beaujolais; this is Bordeaux country. You may choose from more than seventy château-bottled Bordeaux, with some eighteen of these wines offered by the glass on a list that changes every three weeks. Good bets: a slice of *foie gras* and a glass of either Sauternes or Barsac; a plate of *carpaccio* with a young red Bordeaux; and then a slice of fudgy *gâteau au chocolat* with a cup of thick, black *express*. Open into the early morning hours, L'Ecluse is good for late-night snacks, especially after the theater, opera, or a film. Each L'Ecluse is open noon to 1:30 A.M. daily. Credit cards: AE, V.

"Wine is one of the most civilized things in the world and one of the natural things of the world that has been brought to the greatest perfection, and it offers a greater range of enjoyment and appreciation than possibly any other purely sensory thing which may be purchased."
    Ernest Hemingway

L'ECLUSE LES HALLES
120 Rue Rambuteau, Paris 1.
Tel: 40.26.30.73.
Métro: Les Halles.

L'ECLUSE SAINT-MICHEL
15 Quai des Grands-Augustins, Paris 6.
Tel: 46.33.58.74.
Métro: Saint-Michel.

L'ECLUSE FRANCOIS 1ER
64 Rue Francois 1er, Paris 8.
Tel: 47.20.77.09.
Métro: George V.

L'ECLUSE MADELEINE
15 Place de la Madeleine, Paris 8.
Tel: 42.65.34.69.
Métro: Madeleine.

L'ECLUSE BASTILLE
13 Rue de la Roquette, Paris 11.
Tel: 48.05.19.12.
Métro: Bastille.

CHAMPS-ELYSEES, GRAND BOULEVARDS

8th arrondissement

MA BOURGOGNE
133 Boulevard Haussmann,
Paris 8.
Tel: 45.63.50.61.
Métro: Miromesnil.
Open 7 A.M. to 8:30 P.M.
  Closed Saturday,
  Sunday, and holidays.
Credit cards: AE, V.
Wines may be purchased
  to take home.

Well-dressed businessmen and women stand elbow to elbow at the bar at lunchtime, when you won't be able to sit down without a reservation. This is a solid, serious wine bar. Serious, that is, about wine, but not about daily cares; the atmosphere is comfortable and happy, just the way you ought to feel when you're standing in a room filled with sausages and hams dangling from the rafters. The friendly, chatty *patron,* one Louis Prin, was a winner of the Meilleur Pot in 1962. Wines worth sampling here include Beaujolais, Mâcon, Sancerre, Pouilly-Fumé, and a small assortment of Bordeaux. There's always a warm *plat du jour,* such as *coq au vin* (chicken in red wine), *boeuf bourguignon* (beef in red wine, and *andouillette au Pouilly* (chitterling sausage in white wine).

LE VAL D'OR
28 Avenue Franklin D.
  Roosevelt, Paris 8.
Tel: 43.59.95.81.
Métro: Saint-Philippe-
  du-Roule.
Open 8 A.M. to 9 P.M.
  Closed Sunday.
Credit card: V.

Géraud Rongier's bustling wine bar off the Champs-Elysées is great any time of the year, but particularly fun from November 15 to the end of the year, because here one generally finds some of the best Beaujolais in town. Packed at lunch, when office workers line up at the bar, it looks like any ordinary café. But Rongier, who won the Meilleur Pot in 1973, makes Le Val d'Or worth a detour. He can be found each morning at the Rungis wholesale market on the outskirts of Paris, shopping for ingredients for the *plat du jour* he serves to the crowds of well-dressed businessmen in his small downstairs dining room. If the sturdy *boeuf bourguignon* is on the menu, go for it, or the platter of *saucissons* cooked in the full-bodied Côte-de-Brouilly. If the *tarte Tatin* is available, don't pass it up. The irresistible apple tart is prepared on the premises and served with thick *crème fraîche.* On the main floor, Rongier serves up a hearty ham and cheese *quiche,* abundant platters of excellent *charcuterie,* and *baguettes* filled with thick slices of superb *jambon à l'os* (a flavorful ham cured on the bone.). Besides Beaujolais, Rongier likes to show off his discoveries, including good selections of Mâcon-Clessé, Sancerre, Pouilly, and Chinon.

BASTILLE, NATION

11th and 12th arrondissements

CLOWN BAR
114 Rue Amelot, Paris 11.
Tel: 43.55.87.35.
Métro: Filles-du-Calvaire.
Open noon to 2:30 P.M.
  and 7 P.M. to 1 A.M.
Closed Sunday, and
  August.
No credit cards.

The Clown Bar—just a few steps from Paris's giant Cirque d'Hiver, or indoor circus—is a turn-of-the-century café turned wine bar that's worth a detour for its decor alone. The walls are covered with cute, kitschy, and beautiful circus-theme tiles, while circus posters and other related memorabilia form a stage set for a pleasant mealtime interlude. The food here is above average for wine-bar fare, and includes salads of thinly sliced ham layered with pears cooked in red wine and spices (a great play of sweet and sour), platters of poached, lightly smoked sausages from the Jura village of Morteau, and nicely grilled lamb chops. Clown Bar also offers traditional wine-bar platters

> **"I**t's a naive wine, without any breeding, but I think you'll be amused by its presumption."
>
> *James Thurber*

of sausages, *charcuterie,* or cheese. The wine list is decent, offering some good wines from the Loire, Burgundy, Rhône, the Southwest, and Corsica. I'm particularly fond of Alain Graillot's sturdy, finely balanced Crozes-Hermitage.

Jacques Mélac, a proud, outgoing patron.

JACQUES MELAC
42 Rue Léon-Frot, Paris 11.
Tel: 43.70.59.27.
Fax: 43.70.73.10
Métro: Charonne.
Open 9 A.M. to 7 P.M.
    Monday, 9 A.M. to
    midnight Tuesday
    through Friday. Closed
    Saturday, Sunday, and at
    Christmas.
Credit card: V.
Wines may be purchased
    to take home.

One of the most authentic and liveliest wine bars in Paris. Situated just west of the Place de la Bastille, this bar is run by Jacques Mélac, an outgoing, energetic *patron* devoted to wine and good times. With his handlebar mustache, this proud Auvergnat looks as though he walked right out of central casting. If there's any question about what you're to do here, there's a sign on the wall that tells you clearly: "If you want water, you must place your order the day before." Another reminds clients that the "water is reserved for cooking potatoes." Coffee is served reluctantly, and lemonade is reserved for children under 11 years of age.

At lunchtime, the wine bar takes on the frenzy of the stock exchange at the height of trading: Workers, businessmen, and secretaries crowd about the bar or vie for a rickety stool around one of the tables in order to partake of the day's meaty specials, as well as the fine selection of regional cheeses, including bleu des Causses, Saint-Nectaire, and Laguiole. Wine selections include Beaujolais, Chinon, Saint-Joseph, Muscat de Beaumes-de-Venise, Lirac, Vouvray, and Monsieur

Melac's own Lirac. Jacques Melac's is the only wine bar in Paris with its own "vineyard"—vines rise along the exterior walls of the bar, and a celebratory harvest is held each fall. A hot meal is served at lunch, and at dinner Tuesday through Friday. A Meilleur Pot winner in 1982.

LE PASSAGE
18 Passage de la Bonne-
   Graine, Paris 11.
Tel: 47.00.73.30.
Métro: Ledru-Rollin.
Open 8 A.M. to 10:30 P.M.
   Closed Saturday lunch
   and Sunday.
Credit card: V.
Wines may be purchased
   to take home.

Here it is, the wine bar of my dreams: Charles Jouget's Chinon; Alain Graillot's Crozes-Hermitage; Eloi Durrbach's Domaine de Trevallon; Burgundy from Domaine Rion; salads tossed with my favorite olive oil (from Mausanne-les-Alpilles in Provence); bouncy jazz music; and a staff that's cheery, helpful, and efficient. Add to that, a thoroughly varied menu—everything from a good *steak tartare* to a selection of pasta dishes to sample with Italian wines—great country bread from Boulangerie Féret around the corner, and respectable homemade desserts, such as a trio of *pots de crème,* or a rich chocolate tart. Hidden at the end of a rather dingy alley off the Faubourg-Saint-Antoine, Le Passage bustles day and night, offering a pleasant refuge, away from traffic and urban roar. The wine bar offers a list of more than seventy wines, champagnes, *eaux-de-vie* and sweet *vins liquoreux* to take home with you.

DENFERT-ROCHEREAU

14th arrondissement

L'ECHANSON
89 Rue Daguerre, Paris 14.
Tel: 43.22.20.00.
Métro: Gaîté or Denfert-
   Rochereau.
Open noon to 2:30 P.M.
   and 8 to 10:30 P.M.
   Closed Sunday, Monday,
   and August 10 to
   September 5.
Credit cards: MC, V.
Wines may be purchased
   to take home.

If you're looking for a spot for a good glass of wine and quick lunch or dinner near the Gare Montparnasse, L'Echanson is it. The welcome here is almost nonexistent, and be sure to double check the addition on your bill—but aside from that, the food is delicious and light and the wine selection is enormous, focusing on the Rhône and Loire valleys. Some of the fine dishes sampled here on a recent visit include well-seasoned salads topped with perfectly cooked artichokes or with a tender *confit* of duck gizzards, a refreshing gazpacho and thick slabs of beautifully cooked and expertly seasoned salmon.

LE RALLYE
6 Rue Daguerre, Paris 14.
Tel: 43.22.57.05.
Métro: Denfert-Rochereau.
Open 9:30 A.M. to 8 P.M.
   Closed Sunday, Monday,
   and August 1 to
   September 15.
Wines may be purchased to
   take home at adjacent
   boutique.

Stop in around 12:30 on a nice day, and settle on the terrace to watch the activity of the merchants along the bustling Rue Daguerre. The Péret family runs both Le Rallye and a serious wine shop next door, so be advised to take time to sample a few different wines by the glass (more than forty are available), then later select a few bottles to take home. Le Rallye offers classic wine bar fare: platters of cheese or sausage to go with their fine selections of wine, including well-priced Beaujolais, wines from the Loire valley, and small châteaux of Bordeaux.

ARC DE TRIOMPHE

17th arrondissement

CAVES PETRISSANS
30 bis Avenue Niel,
   Paris 17.
Tel: 42.27.83.84.
Métro: Ternes.
Reservations, noon to 2:30
   P.M. and 8 to 10 P.M.
   Closed Saturday,
   Sunday, holidays, and
   the first three weeks of
   August.
Credit cards: AE, V.
Wines may be purchased at
   the boutique to take
   home.

Now in its fourth generation—the Petrissans have sold wine here since 1895—the Caves Petrissans has expanded into a fine neighborhood wine bar/restaurant, where you will always be assured of very drinkable wines by the glass or bottle, plus a menu that changes every few weeks. At lunch, service is à la carte, with lovely main courses such as *lapin en gelée au basilic* (jellied rabbit terrine) served with ratatouille, as well as *steak tartare,* chopped raw beef, and daily specials such as lamb stew *(navarin d'agneau)* or rabbit with mustard *(lapin à la moutarde).* The 170-franc dinner

A wine bar lunch.

menu includes a first course, a main course, cheese, and dessert. The decor is pure 1930s—lots of glass, wood, and nostalgia—and the owners, Marie-Christian and Jean-Marie, are proud of their little establishment, as they should be. One of the best bets in the neighborhood.

MONTMARTRE, BELLEVILLE

18th and 20th arrondissements

BISTRO-CAVE DES ENVIERGES
11 Rue des Envierges, Paris 20.
Métro: Pyrénées.
Tel: 46.36.47.84.
Open noon to 8 P.M. Hot meals until 2 P.M. and Wednesday, Thursday and Friday nights. Closed Monday and Tuesday.
Wines may be purchased to take home at adjacent boutique.

Quintessential Paris! A glass of fruity red Chinon, a wicker basket of golden *baguette de campagne,* a plate of creamy, blue-veined Fourme d'Ambert and fresh chèvre, and a look-out on lively street life and the tree-tops of the Parc de Belleville beyond. Around 7:30 on a Sunday evening the wicker chairs of the Bistro-Cave des Envierges terrace fill up with locals returning from a stroll through the neighboring park; the men at the next table are embroiled in their chess game and glasses of Gamay de Touraine, while an artist at the corner table sketches his mistress smiling at him over her *café*. Meanwhile on the sidewalk, little boys patrol the street on bicycles, North African immigrant families stroll by in bright-colored robes, old ladies walk their dogs, laundry hangs out to dry. One has the feeling that this is what the Latin Quarter and Montmartre must have looked like years ago. Pass through the rose-colored awning and facade into this simple turn-of-the-century wine bar/café (an annex of La Courtille down the street; see Restaurants). You won't find any frills or fanfare here, just reasonably priced, good quality wine, cheese (perfectly fresh *chèvre* in season), and *charcuteries* for a happy local clientele with not too many francs to spare. The chewy, dense country *baguettes* come from the bakery down the street, so they're always fresh. The adjoining *cave* sells carefully selected and reasonably priced wine, mostly *vins de pays* and *crus bourgeois*.

BEAUJOLAIS

In Paris, the third Thursday of November—the first day of sale of Beaujolais *primeur,* the new Beaujolais—signals the beginning of a season-long fête that doesn't cease until after the holiday revelry has cleared sometime in January.

It really doesn't matter if the year's crop happens to be overabundant, short on acidity, or even lacking in that special fruitiness associated with Beaujolais. It doesn't matter that almost everyone in Paris agrees that the publicity surrounding the wine is out of proportion with its real worth. The fact is that Beaujolais is a "happy" wine, one that is there to enjoy; you don't have to take it too seriously.

In the wine bars that sell Beaujolais, it is available by the glass, year round. Although the terms *primeur* and *nouveau* are used interchangeably, technically *primeur* is served only from the third Thursday of November to December 15. The term *nouveau* is technically reserved for the wines released for sale December 15, to be drunk through the next November.

FLOGNARDE AUX FRAMBOISES CAVES PETRISSANS
CAVE PETRISSANS' RASPBERRY FRUIT FLAN

A flognarde *(also spelled* flaugnarde, flangnarde, *and* flougnarde*) is a traditional French fruit flan, similar to the better-known* clafoutis. *This recipe was shared with me by Marie-Christine and Jean-Marie Allemoz, owners of the outstanding Caves Petrissans (see entry page 189), where this dessert is made with raspberries, cherries, or pears, depending upon the season.*

1 teaspoon unsalted butter, for buttering the pan

5 eggs

¾ cup (150 g) granulated sugar

⅓ cup (45 g) all-purpose flour

Pinch of salt

1 tablespoon Cognac

2 cups (250 ml) heavy (whipping) cream

1 teaspoon vanilla extract

1 pound (500 g) fresh raspberries (about 4 cups)

Confectioners' sugar, for garnish

1. Preheat the oven to 400°F (200°C).

2. Generously butter a straight-sided 10½-inch round baking dish.

3. In the bowl of an electric mixer, combine the eggs, granulated sugar, and flour, and mix at low speed until thoroughly blended. Add the salt, Cognac, cream, and vanilla extract; mix again. Pour the batter through a fine-mesh sieve, into the prepared baking dish. Arrange the raspberries in a single layer over the batter.

4. Place in the center of the oven and bake until golden brown on top, (the batter puffs up around the fruit, enveloping it like a cloud) with the center custard-like and still trembling, 45 to 50 minutes. Transfer to a rack to cool. Serve at room temperature, sprinkling generously with confectioners' sugar just before serving. Cut into pie-shaped wedges, using a spatula to transfer the wedges to dessert plates.

Yield: 8 servings

AUX NEGOCIANTS
27 Rue Lambert, Paris 18.
(Across from 48 Rue Custine.)
Tel: 46.06.15.11.
Métro: Lamarck-Caulincourt.
Open noon to 7 P.M. Monday and Wednesday; noon to 10:30 P.M. Tuesday, Thursday, and Friday. Closed Saturday, Sunday, holidays, and August.
No credit cards.
Wines may be purchased to take home.

At the foot of Montmartre, this unpretentious and inexpensive neighborhood wine bar seems to have been spared the ravages of time and tourists that have attacked the Place du Tertre neighborhood farther up the hill. Waiting for a table at the old-fashioned zinc bar of Aux Négociants, observing the rowdy regulars walking up to the bar to refill their wine glass and yelling for *le patron* like children crying for their mother, one can easily imagine Toulouse-Lautrec coming in for a *ballon de rouge*. Le Patron, Jean Navier, who doubles as the chef and the waiter, quiets them with simple French home cooking, while Madame tends the bar. Every day they offer a different *plat du jour* marked on the chalkboard, such as Friday's *gigot*

At Au Sauvignon, it's smiles and toasts when the new Beaujolais arrives (see entry, page 184).

with white *haricot* beans simmered in cider and *poulet fermier rôti "au diable"* on Thursday, with terrines of pâté and crocks of *cornichons* and hearty *pain de campagne* to start. Be forewarned: The only hot meal is the daily special, and it sells out early. But Monsieur Navier will whip up a fluffy omelet and a green salad for latecomers. Do save room for dessert: the *sablée aux framboises* (a buttery, thick, short pastry crust overflowing with raspberries) is worth hiking up and down the hills of Montmartre for, and the cherry *clafoutis* is popping with fruit. Wines to look for include the Loire valley's Bourgueil and Jasnières as well as Cahors, Bordeaux, and a Gaillac rouge from the Southwest.

Marchés
MARKETS

Rue Mouffetard: a daily ritual (see entry, page 198).

Most mornings after an early jog around Paris's Parc Monceau, I extract a string bag from my sweatshirt pocket and head straight for Rue Poncelet, the lively open-air street market a few blocks away. Marketing is best in the morning, when the vegetable man is in good temper (and is sober), the crowds are thin, and the produce at its freshest.

The cluttered, colorful market—one of many scattered about Paris—opens precisely at 9 A.M., when most days the sky is thick, somber, and a dozen shades of gray, and the city is just beginning to wake up. A tour of Paris's markets offers a rare glimpse of an immensely important French ritual—one that should even be of interest to those not particularly passionate about food—since it allows one to examine the authentic fabric and texture of contemporary Gallic society.

Parisians devote a good part of their day to marketing, and it's obvious that what many of the French do between meals is make shopping lists, market, and talk about meals past and meals future. Daily marketing is still the rule in Paris, where everything from Camembert to cantaloupe is sold to be eaten that day, preferably within a few hours. I still smile appreciatively when the cheese man asks if the Camembert will be savored that afternoon, or perhaps that evening, then shuffles through his larder, touching and pinching to come up with one that's perfectly ripe and properly creamy.

Most of the merchants are fiercely proud people, and though some may be rough and peasant-like, they display a refined sense of aesthetics. The vegetable man admirably attacks his *métier* like an artist: Each morning, beginning around 7 A.M., he painstakingly arranges the fruits and vegetables in orderly rows, paying careful attention to shapes, textures, and shading. The result is a colorful, vibrant mosaic: fat stalks of celery rest next to snow-white cauliflower, the ruffled green leaves of Swiss chard stand beside them, followed by yellow-white Belgian endive, pale green artichokes, then—zap!—rosy tomatoes or ruby red peppers. Across the aisle, green Granny Smith apples line up alongside the sweet Italian blood oranges, called *sanguines* (favored for their juice, which runs the color of a brilliant sunset), while bananas from Martinique and walnuts from Grenoble fill out the palette.

Mastering the intricacies and etiquette of French marketing is no simpler than learning French, and easily as frustrating. And it requires patience. A serious marketing trip—which will only get you through the next meal—can take a good hour, and often takes more, if you want to do it right.

The selection at even the smallest markets is amazing. A large *rue commerçante* (merchant street) such as Rue Poncelet might include half a dozen *boulangeries* and *pâtisseries*; two supermarkets; a good dozen fruit and vegetable merchants; a coffee, tea, and spice shop; four poultrymen; two *triperies* for tripe, kidneys, sweetbreads, and liver; three *fromageries*; one butcher for horsemeat; five other *boucheries*; four *charcuteries* for cold cuts; two or three regional or foreign specialty shops; and at least half a dozen restaurants and cafés. Depending on the length of the lines and the merchants' chatter, each individual purchase can take 5 to 10 minutes.

French merchants, it must be noted, are not just merchants. They're philosophers, songsters, comics, tutors, and culinary counselors. Parisian housewives don't need cookbooks. The butcher, poultryman, and fishmonger all willingly dispense verbal recipes with each purchase. (Otherwise, merchants are not known for their generosity. The concept of a baker's dozen is not generally put into practice in France, though the fishmonger will, on occasion, throw in a bunch of dill with the salmon.)

Booming voices and shrill cries fill the air throughout the day as merchants hawk their finest produce, selling from rickety wooden puchcarts or narrow stalls. One piercing voice boasts of *"la très belle salade"* (very beautiful lettuce), while another shouts *"Jetez un petit coup d'oeil"* (take a little look) at the *"canette de barbarie extra"* (extra-special duckling). Another ruddy-faced butcher holds out a fresh, plump *boudin* (blood sausage) for a shopper to inhale, announcing that it offers *"une véritable symphonie"* of lively aromas.

Meanwhile, at one corner, you may trip over a donkey tended by a trader selling an exotic array of herbs and essences, while nearby a jazzy brass band plays on.

The chatter is often amusing. One fall, I looked on as a shopper requested a kilo of *raisins de Hambourg*, France's popular muscat grape. Then, by accident, she noticed that the plump, purple grapes came from Provence, in the south of France, not Germany. "But Madame," the merchant replied with a serious wink and a broad smile, "you know that in France, agriculture is very, very complicated."

I always begin at one end of the street—flanked by indoor and outdoor stalls—and tour the entire market before buying a thing, making mental notes of what's fresh, stopping to wave at the flower lady (who, due to my affinity for red tulips, calls me "Madame Tulipe"), reading the price and origin of each item chalked on little blackboards that dangle above the stalls.

Lots of things here work on what one friend calls the *"pas possible"* principle, meaning "it's done this way here, so tough luck for you if you want it otherwise." Merchants bristle at any atypical request, particularly from foreigners. One friend worked for weeks to get her pork butcher to cut the *poitrine fumée*, or smoked slab bacon, thin enough to fry American-style. The butcher finally won, insisting that if he sliced the bacon any thinner, she'd end up with lace.

Once I ordered two kilos of fresh jalapeño peppers for pickling, and the vegetable merchant looked as though he'd seen a mirage. He asked, "How do you eat them?" "Just like this," I responded, pretending to bite into a fiery raw pepper. The merchant smiled, turned to a colleague, and playfully whispered, "She comes by every morning, buys two kilos at a time!"

And it took a long time to wean myself of the democratic

American form of marketing: self-service. Here, the law is *ne touchez pas*—don't touch—and anyone caught selecting his own pears and peaches will be forcefully admonished.

The full flavor of the market varies according to the time of day. It's as much fun to tour markets at morning's close, promptly at 1 P.M., as it is when they first open. One o'clock is the hour when a sudden hush falls over all of Paris. Shoppers scurry home to lunch while merchants sing, chant, and shout like schoolchildren let free for recess. A few minutes later the streets are deserted, save for a few *clochardes* (bag ladies) rifling through the rejected produce that tumbled to the gutters.

Sometimes, the population density in markets can be just too much. On a rainy Saturday at around six in the afternoon, Poncelet is a veritable obstacle course. Families with strollers, slow-moving old ladies pulling metal shopping carts, dogs, and long lines make passage all but impossible.

But no matter the time of day, the season, or the market, Paris is ever a moveable feast.

The city's markets, like its neighborhoods, reflect a variety of cultures and classes, and a tour of one or several will tell you much about the daily life of the city, and of the habits of those who live in each neighborhood.

There are two basic sorts of markets worth visiting: The *rues commerçantes*, or merchant streets, are stationary indoor-outdoor street markets, generally large, rambling, and open six days a week. There are some fifty-seven *marchés volants*, or roving markets, which include more than 5,000 independent merchants moving from neighborhood to neighborhood on given days.

(The old-fashioned marchés-couverts, or covered markets, have basically not been able to withstand modern-day competition from supermarkets and other open-air markets and are far less interesting than in the past).

RUE COMMERÇANTES
Merchant Streets

Standard hours are 9 A.M. to 1 P.M. and 4 P.M. to 7 P.M. Tuesday through Saturday; 9 A.M. to 1 P.M. Sunday. Most are closed Monday, and the number of merchants is substantially reduced during the months of July and August.

1st arrondissement

RUE MONTORGUEIL
Beginning at the Rue
  Rambuteau.
Métro: Les Halles.

Les Halles, Paris's most famous market, is no more, but Rue Montorgueil remains. The city has made attempts to spiff up a rather grubby, and run-down market by adding a pleasant new cobblestone street, and many of the city's finest chefs still do their marketing here, sharing chores as one chef markets for all the fish, another goes after the group's meat, still another for the produce, then all meeting for coffee before heading back to their restaurants. Stop into Stohrer (No. 51; see Pastry Shops) for perfect pastries. While in the neighborhood, walk down the recently restored Passage du Grand Cerf and visit the majestic 16th-century Saint-Eustache church, where you will find a little chapel dedicated to the fruit and vegetable markets of Les Halles.

5th arrondissement

RUE MOUFFETARD
Beginning at Rue de l'Epée-
  de-Bois.
Métro: Censier-Daubenton
  and Monge.

Parisians complain of high prices, poor-quality produce, and too many tourists, but Rue Mouffetard remains one of the city's classic and most popular merchant streets. Begin at the top

Taking time for the news between sales.

of the market just before noon to get a feel of the spirit and texture of the street, which has an honest sort of beaten-down charm. There's a lot of hawking and jostling here as tough merchants sell out of wooden crates balanced on tattered wooden sawhorses. Stop in at Café Mouffetard (No. 116; see Cafés) for the dense and buttery *croissants*, homemade *baguettes*, and rich *brioches*. Also take a quick look at the Facchetti Italian market (No. 134) with its four-story mural of animals wandering through the forest. At the top of the Rue Mouffetard at 16 Place de la Contrescarpe, stop by Boulangerie Brusa (see Bakeries) for a tangy *baguette au levain*.

6th arrondissement

RUE DE SEINE/BUCI
Beginning at Boulevard
   Saint-Germain.
Métro: Odéon.

This is considered Paris's most expensive market street, and it is certainly one of the most densely populated. The Hamon Fromagerie (81 Rue de Seine) offers some of the best goat cheese in the neighborhood. It's also one of the few Paris *fromageries* to sell *fromage frais bien égoutté*, a fresh curd cheese and key ingredient in American-like cheesecake. Walk a few shops down to Carton Boulangerie/Pâtisserie (6 Rue de Buci; see Bakeries) for an excellent *tarte rustique* (pizza-like savory tart), and delicious fruit tarts and *viennoiseries*.

7th arrondissement

RUE CLER
Beginning at Avenue de la
   Motte-Piquet.
Métro: Ecole Militaire.

One of Paris's tidiest high-class markets, this broad pedestrian street allows for comfortable browsing. Since many Americans live in the quarter, merchants are used to curious stares and constant questioning about unusual items. Take a look at Charcuterie Gonin (No. 40; see Specialty Shops), a brilliantly spotless corner shop with a huge assortment of carry-out items, including *moussaka, coulibiac* of salmon, and tarts and Davoli (No. 34), one of the city's few real Italian markets, all mirrors and black marble, with an amusing clutter of hams and sausages. Off Rue Cler, at No. 12 Rue du Champ-de-Mars, Marie-Anne Cantin offers a remarkable selection of cheeses (see Cheese Shops).

"The air was laden with the various smells of the city and its markets: The strong smell of leeks mingled with the faint but persistent scent of lilacs, all carried along by the pungent breeze which is truly the air of Paris."

—Jean Renoir

RUNGIS WHOLESALE MARKET

France's largest food market—south of Paris, and near the Orly airport—covers some 440 acres of blacktopped surface, with 864 wholesalers and 1,050 producers selling everything from fresh fruits and vegetables to whole sides of rosy beef, to basket upon basket of fresh Brittany coast oysters. To feed the city's ten million inhabitants, the Rungis wholesale market annually processes some 700,000 tons of potatoes, 500 million eggs, 560,000 tons of meat, and 750 million liters of wine.

There's no question that Rungis, open since 1969, lacks the romantic, grubby charm of the old Les Halles market it replaced. The modern-day wholesale market is spacious and sanitary, with hangar upon hangar of sober gray buildings. Specialty markets open and close throughout the day and night, with fishmongers opening the market at 3 A.M., and flower merchants opening their stalls at 11 in the morning.

Rungis is open only to professionals, and casual onlookers are not welcomed openly. There are, however, two public tours offered daily, Monday through Friday.

One is offered by the Rungis market in French or in English, and must be arranged in advance. Groups must be at least fifteen, arriving in a tour bus or mini-van. This tour begins at 6:30 A.M., lasts at least two hours, and costs 35 francs per person. For reservations (two months in advance for July and August) contact Madame Gillot, Société Semmaris, 1 Rue de la Tour, 94152 Rungis Cedex. Tel: 46.87.35.35. Fax: 46.87.56.77.

The second public tour is conducted by the American Robert Noah, and it is one of the many personalized tours offered by his Paris en Cuisine cooking school. Tours are conducted in English, beginning at 5:30 A.M. and ending around 9 A.M. The tour takes visitors through all of the major markets and costs 425 francs per person. Write Paris en Cuisine, 49 Rue de Richelieu, 75001 Paris. Tel: 42.61.35.23.

9th arrondissement

RUE DES MARTYRES
Beginning at Rue Notre-
Dame de Lorette.
Métro: Notre Dame de
Lorette.

12th arrondissement

BEAUVEAU
Place d'Aligre.
Métro: Lédru-Rollin.

16th arrondissement

**RUE DE
L'ANNONCIATION**
Beginning at Place de Passy
and Rue de
l'Annonciation.
Métro: La Muette.

17th arrondissement

RUE DE LEVIS
Beginning at Boulevard
des Batignolles.
Métro: Villiers.

In 1787 this street boasted 25 auberges for 58 houses—that's about one eatery for every two houses! While this ratio has been substantially reduced, you won't go hungry here, especially if you stop into Terrier Charcuterie Lyonnaise (No. 58), or Fromagerie Molard (No. 48), a century-old *fromagerie* that still retains its original marble counters. It's about a 15 minute walk down from the Rue Lepic market street, and one could easily visit both in a morning.

The Place d'Aligre market is one of the city's liveliest, and worth visiting simply for its ambience. There's an old-fashioned feel, and the market serves as the social and commercial hub of this heterogeneous, working class, immigrant neighborhood. You can find everything here— French, Kosher, and Halal butchers—as well as Asian specialties and a traditional French covered market. While the quality is not always first rate, the prices are some of the lowest in town.

This cobblestoned street has a pristine, village-like character, and caters to well-heeled Passy residents. Shops to look into include Le Palais des Thés (No. 21; see Specialty Shops), tea merchants with an encyclopedic selection of teas and pretty tea pots and accessories; and Beurre et Cacao *pâtisserie* (No. 35; see Pastry Shops) for homey old-fashioned pastries. Walk through a quaint court-yard to Caves Châteauneuf (No. 23), a neighbor-hood wine shop with a good selection of Bordeaux. At the end of the street in the Place de Passy, sit down for coffee and a pastry at Coquelin Aîné, one of the best *pâtisseries* in Paris (67 Rue de Passy; see Pastry Shops and Tea Salons).

A lively market street not far from the tiny elegant Parc Monceau, where you can picnic on the market's offerings. Pick up a *pain paillasse*, a rustic sourdough loaf, at the Cousanon Boulangerie (No. 21, see Bakeries). Farther along, the Jean Carmès et Fils *fromagerie* (No. 24, see Cheese Shops) offers more than a hundred varieties of French cheese, all aged in its own cellars.

Flowers, anyone?

LES MARCHES BIOLOGIQUES
ORGANIC MARKETS

These are food markets unlike others in Paris—more like old-fashioned country farmers' markets. On weekends from thirty to fifty independent organic farmers set up stalls on Paris' Boulevard Raspail and along one of the main streets of Boulogne and Joinville, two Parisian suburbs. They sell organically grown fruits and vegetables, homemade breads, dried fruits and nuts, *charcuterie*, farm-raised chickens, ducks, and geese; and even wine that's guaranteed to be "natural." The organic, or *biologique*, movement in France is active and well-organized, and these markets are shining examples of its success. On a given weekend you might find one stand selling freshly made pizza and another rustic whole-wheat breads. There is also homemade apple or pear cider, a huge variety of artisanal goat cheeses, sausages, and beer, and even one merchant offering bright and glorious sprays of dried flowers. For all markets, it is best to go early in the day for a good selection.

Le Marché Raspail-Rennes, 1 Boulevard Raspail beginning at Rue de Rennes. Métro: Rennes. Every Sunday, 8:30 A.M. to 1 P.M.
Le Marché Boulogne, 140 Route de la Reine, 92 Boulogne-sur-Seine. Métro: Boulogne-Pont de Saint-Cloud, or accessible via Paris's No.72 bus. Open 8 A.M. to 4 P.M. first and third Saturdays of each month.
Le Marché Joinville-Le-Pont, Place Mozart, 94 Joinville. Métro: RER Line B to Joinville, then via the suburban No. 106 and 108N buses. Open 8:30 A.M. to 1 P.M. second and fourth Saturdays of each month.
Le Marché Sceaux-Robinson, Rue des Mouille-Boeuf. Rue Jules-Guesde, 92 Sceaux. Métro: RER Line B to Robinson. Every Sunday, 8:30 A.M. to 1 P.M.

For further information on these markets, call Nature and Progrès, Tuesday through Saturday, 2:30 to 7 P.M. at 47.00.60.36.

RUE PONCELET-RUE BAYEN

Beginning at Avenue des Ternes.

Métro: Ternes.

Highlights of this high-quality market street include La Fromagerie Alléosse (No. 13; see Cheese Shops), for its impeccable assortment of cheeses, Brûlerie des Ternes (No. 10; see Specialty Shops) for coffee and tea; and Le Stübli (No. 11; See Pastry Shops) with fairy tale sweets that make you dream of the Danube; and the fresh and astonishing assortment of fish and shellfish at Daguerre Marée (4 Rue Bayen). Stop into l'Epicerie Verte, a health food store at 5 Rue Saussier-Leroy for a tangy, dense, organic sourdough *baguette*. Around the corner on Avenue des Ternes (No. 16), the glass front of the Maison Pou shields one of the tidiest neighborhood *charcuteries*.

18th arrondissement

RUE LEPIC

Beginning at Place Blanche.

Métro: Abbesses or Blanche.

This somewhat grubby street that winds up the hill from Place Blanche to Place des Abbesses still retains an old-fashioned Montmartre charm, especially if you stop into the Lux Bar (No. 12), a neighborhood café with original tile murals and Art Nouveau woodwork from 1910. Les Petits Mitrons (No. 26) *pâtisserie* bakes some of the most beautiful homemade fruit tarts to be found in Paris. At the top of the hill, stop into J. Perrat at 36 Rue des Abbesses for fabulous *pain de seigle* made with chestnuts and almonds (see Bakeries). Le Sancerre (35 Rue des Abbesses), a lively wine bar/café, is a fun spot for a *tartine* and glass of wine on the terrace.

RUE DU POTEAU

Beginning at Place Jules-Joffrin.

Métro: Jules Joffrin.

Set high above Paris on the butte, or hill, of Montmartre along several winding streets, this pretty market is worth a detour simply to get an idea of what a real Paris neighborhood might have looked like a few decades ago. Start out early in the morning at Place Jules-Joffrin, then go to No. 81 Rue du Mont-Cenis, where, at Pâtisserie de Montmartre (see Pastry Shops), you'll find delicious and unusual *chaussons au citron* (lemon custard turnovers). Take your time peeking into the shops along the Rue du Poteau, where the spotless turn-of-the-century storefronts will amaze you. A real find is the Fromagerie de Montmartre (No. 9; see Cheese Shops), where you'll be certain to find something appealing among the forty varieties of goat cheese and a hundred other cow's and sheep's milk varieties. Just across the street, the Maistre Rôtisserie (No. 10), filled with churning rotisseries, offers unusual roasted meat specialties, such as quail, rabbit in mustard, porc with prunes, farm-raised chicken and spit-roasted lamb—all warm and ready to take home for dinner or a picnic.

MARCHES VOLANTS
Roving Markets

Note that these markets are open from 7 A.M. to 1:30 P.M. only on the days listed. These tend to be less expensive than the other markets, and you'll find fresher, more unusual produce here, but sometimes less variety. They are usually set up on sidewalks or along the islands of major boulevards and offer a full range of products, including fruits and vegetables, meats, poultry, fish, cheese, and fresh flowers. These markets often have a good deal of neighborhood character, and you'll also find a fine assortment of *maraîchers*, or market gardeners, who bring their produce in from farms in the Paris region. The following is a selection of the most interesting markets.

5th arrondissement

CARMES
Place Maubert.
Métro: Maubert-Mutualité.
Tuesday, Thursday, and
   Saturday.

This small, animated market square is best on Saturdays when you'll find organic produce, along with Jean-Yves Riaux, who sells an international assortment of breads, including a crusty, white *fougasse*. Make a special trip to the Le Soleil Provençale stall: Monsieur and Madame Brocker stock a tempting selection of Provençal specialties, such as a variety of extra-virgin olive oils, *tapenade, pistou, rouille, aioli*, homemade jams, and blocks of *savon de Marseille* sold by weight—all great for gifts. Celine Poppeville across the way offers beautiful wild mushrooms, fresh herbs, and unusual salad greens. Across the street, the Brûlerie de Maubert (3 Rue Monge) sells fresh roasted coffee and artisanal jams and has a coffee-tasting bar. La Pirée (47 Boulevard Saint-Germain) is a family-run

Greek deli offering fresh, high-quality salads, including excellent *tarama* (fish roe spread) and roasted red pepper and garlic dip, as well as garlic-flecked olives.

MONGE
Place Monge.
Métro: Monge.
Wednesday, Friday, and Sunday.

A lively market square with several excellent market gardeners. The *"Roi des Potates"* boasts of more than twenty potato varieties, including those you never knew existed. Pick up an excellent *baguette au levain* at S. Hervet (69 Rue Monge; see Bakeries). Celine Poppeville (who moves from market to market) offers beautiful wild mushrooms, fresh herbs, and unusual salad greens.

6th arrondissement

RASPAIL
Boulevard Raspail, between Rue du Cherche-Midi and Rue de Rennes.
Métro: Rennes or Sèvres-Babylone.
Tuesday and Friday. On Sunday this is an organic market.

The only street market in the neighborhood, and one that includes several market gardeners. Best on Sundays when it becomes Paris's only organic market. The produce is generally top rate and you'll find a great selection of grains, along with such items as homemade sauerkraut, sea salt, cultivated mushrooms, and organic wines.

An irresistible selection.

7th arrondissement

BRETEUIL
Avenue de Saxe, from
  Avenue de Ségur to
  Place Breteuil.
Métro: Ségur.
Thursday and Saturday.

A calm, genteel market behind Les Invalides. Gilles Chauvée brings products from the Sarthe and Ardèche regions, such as good country bread, sausages, pâté, and organic jam. Charcuterie Leconte offers a flavorful *terrine de cabillaud aux fines herbes* (cod terrine with *fines herbes*). Madame Verbel makes delicious homemade jams. Several market gardeners.

Marketing advice is ageless.

11th arrondissement

**BELLEVILLE-
  MENILMONTANT**
Beginning at Boulevard de
  Belleville and
  continuing to Boulevard
  de Ménilmontant.
Métro: Belleville or
  Ménilmontant.
Tuesday and Friday.

Make a special trip to this market near Père-Lachaise to find Madame Saint-Ellier, an *apicultrice* (beekeeper) who sells slices of acacia honeycomb fresh from her hives outside Paris. She's at the corner of Boulevard de Belleville and Rue de Ménilmontant next to Métro Ménilmontant (Her husband sells honey at Richard-Lenoir market.) Many stands sell African herbs, spices, and couscous ingredients.

RICHARD-LENOIR
Boulevard Richard-Lenoir,
  beginning at Rue
  Amelot.
Métro: Bréguet-Saban,
  Bastille, or Richard-
  Lenoir.
Thursday and Sunday.

In the shadow of the Bastille Opera, this is one of Paris's best, biggest (some two hundred merchants), and most heterogeneous markets, especially on Sundays. Madame Annie Boulanger presides over one of Paris's best market stands: a fantasy *charcuterie* with fresh salads such as ratatouille and *pipérade*, and first-rate specialties, including grilled peppers, cooked sea snails served with homemade mayonnaise, grilled sardines, fresh

Always the freshest produce.

pasta, smoked herring, *tarte provençale*, *pâté de foie au porto*, and much more. Pierre Lucien et Fils creamery stocks rounds of raw milk *fromage blanc* filled with garlic and *fines herbes*, as well as creamy Fontainebleau (see recipe, page 271) and rich, low fat (20 percent) and no-fat *fromage blanc*—better than any American cream cheese and perfect for cheesecake. At the end of the market near the Bastille, Monsieur Saint-Ellier sells fresh honeycomb.

13th arrondissement

GOBELINS
Boulevard Auguste-
   Blanqui, from Place
   d'Italie to Rue Barrault.
Métro: Place d'Italie.
Tuesday, Friday, and
   Sunday.

Maison Lorenian creamery stocks fresh goose eggs from February until the beginning of July. While in the neighborhood, walk down the village-like Rue de la Butte aux Cailles.

Look but don't touch.

At No. 16 Rue Montmartre, there's a curiously named alley, the Queen of Hungary Passage (Passage Reine de Hongrie). Sometime during the 18th-century reign of Marie Antoinette, the queen was passing through the alley and was handed a petition by a woman who ran a market stall. The queen commented on the merchant's likeness to the queen of Hungary, and soon the alley was renamed.

TO MARKET, TO MARKET

Paris's first food market was established during the 5th century, on what is now the Ile de la Cité. As the city expanded, other small markets were created, first at the city gates, then, beginning in the 13th century, at the old iron works between Rue Saint-Denis, Rue Saint-Honoré, and Rue Croix-des-Petits-Champs, the site of the present Forum des Halles shopping mall.

At the time, the big *halle*, or market, was shared by merchants, craftsmen, and peddlers offering an international array of goods. To encourage trade here, other city merchants and craftsmen were ordered to close their shops two days each week. It was not until the 16th century, when Paris had 300,000 inhabitants, that produce and other food-stuffs came to dominate the market.

By 1546, Paris boasted of four major bread markets and one live animal market. In the 17th century, the Quai de la Mégisserie along the Seine's Right Bank—then known as the "valley of misery," now the site of the live bird market—was the chicken, wild game, lamb, goat, and milk-fed pig market; Rue de la Poissonnière was established as the fish market; and the wine market was installed on the Left Bank's Quai Saint-Bernard.

The French Revolution of 1789 put an end to the royal privilege of authorizing markets, and transferred the power to the city. By 1860, Paris had fifty-one markets, twenty-one of them covered and the rest open-air affairs.

By the mid-19th century, the central Les Halles was badly in need of repair, so a new hall with iron girders and skylight roofs—reminiscent of the still-existing Gare de l'Est—was built by the architect Baltard between 1854 and 1866. The design, complete with vast underground storehouses and linked by roofed passages and alleys, became a model for markets throughout France and the rest of the world. As the city's population grew, the market space eventually became inadequate, and in 1969 the market was moved to Rungis, south of Paris, near Orly airport. Les Halles was torn down to make way for a major modern shopping complex, and the neighborhood is now frenetic with shops and restaurants, with gardens at the center.

BRUNE
Boulevard Brune,
  beginning at No. 49.
Métro: Porte de Vanves.
Thursday and Sunday.

Alively neighborhood market with at least half a dozen market gardeners, and good rye bread (*pain de siegle*) to be found at L'Epi Gaulois, 23 bis Boulevard Brune. Monsieur and Madame Lanie run an impressive cheese stand, stocking over thirty varieties of fresh *chèvres* in season, as well as a delicious Chablis-infused *Epoisses*. On Sundays, visit the nearby flea market at Porte de Vanves.

EDGAR-QUINET
Along Boulevard Edgar-
  Quinet, beginning at
  Rue de Départ.
Métro: Edgar-Quinet.
Wednesday and Saturday.

Asprawling boulevard market, particularly good on winter Saturdays when an oysterman from Bordeaux sells his *Marennes d'Oléron*. Several market gardeners.

Balancing a heavy load.

MONTROUGE
On the *place* between the
  Rues Brézin, Saillard,
  Mouton-Duvernet and
  Boulard.
Métro: Mouton-Duvernet.
Tuesday and Friday.

On a pretty square in front of the town hall of the 14th *arrondissement*. Monsieur and Madame Lanie run an impressive cheese stand, stocking over thirty varieties of fresh chèvres in season, as well as a delicious Chablis-infused *Epoisses*.

15th arrondissement

DUPLEIX
Boulevard du Grenelle,
  between Rue Loumel
  and Rue du Commerce.
Métro: Dupleix or La
  Motte-Piquet-Grenelle.
Wednesday and Sunday.

A picturesque market under the arches of the elevated métro line, especially nice on Sundays. The Cooperative Crémerie de Chatou sells raw milk, homemade yogurt, *fromage blanc,* and *chèvres* fresh from their farm outside Paris. They make salt-free and low-fat cheeses for the diet-conscious. There are several market gardeners. Le Soleil Provençale stall offers a good selection of oils, olives and soaps from Provence.

Prime produce from a small cart.

16th arrondissement

AUTEUIL
Place Jean-Lorrain.
Métro: Michel-Ange-
  Auteuil.
Wednesday and Saturday.

An adorable, tiny market square with excellent produce. Several market gardeners sell here, including one (across from Hédiard) who brings baskets of exotic salad greens and boutique vegetables, such as baby eggplant.

COURS DE LA REINE
Avenue Président Wilson,
  between Rue Debrousse
  and Place Iéna.
Métro: Alma Marceau or
  Iéna.
Wednesday and Saturday.

Several excellent market gardeners, with some organic produce. Madame Gallet sells English muffins, crumpets, and marmalade, as well as a good, dense country baguette. Madame Annie Boulanger, who roves with the markets, offers her fantasy *charcuterie* with fresh salads, including grilled peppers, cooked sea snails served with homemade mayonnaise, grilled sardines, and *tarte provençale.* Stop in to Patisserie Malitourne (30 Rue de Chaillot; see Pastry Shops) for a *téméraire* (rum-infused *crème pâtissière* in an almond crust wrapped in a nougatine shell), or a *chausson aux pruneaux.*

19th arrondissement

PLACE DES FETES
Métro: Place des Fêtes.
Tuesday, Friday, and
Sunday.

One of the city's loveliest, tree-shaded market squares, picturesque and sprawling. *Poissonerie* "Goia des Mers," has an especially good selection Sunday mornings. You'll find a few market gardeners, one who sells nothing but potatoes, another who sells nothing but mushrooms or chicken, and some nice cheese stands where the merchants bring in their own aged cheeses. You'll usually find some spectacular Brie and raw milk cheeses from just east of Paris. Stop into nearby Pâtisserie de l'Eglise (10 Rue du Jourdain; see Pastry Shops) for an after-market treat.

Side mirrors would be helpful.

Pâtisseries
PASTRY SHOPS

Demonstrating appropriate madeleine technique.

The Parisian pastry chef is truly a man to be admired. Imagine his responsibility. Day in and day out, season after season, he must attend to the care and feeding of the formidable Parisian sweet tooth.

Everywhere you turn in Paris, someone—man, woman, or child—seems to be either munching on a *pain au chocolat*, peering wide-eyed into the window of a pristine, wondrous pastry shop, savoring the last lick on an ice cream cone, or carrying, with admirable agility, a beribboned white box filled with the day's dessert.

Perhaps the city's per capita consumption of butter, sugar, cream, and eggs is not the highest in the world, but if a population won prizes simply on its level of enthusiasm for all things sweet and satisfying, I think that Parisians would win. I have watched reed-thin women heartily down three and four dessert helpings in a row—unashamedly, unabashedly, with no remorse. I have eaves-dropped as a pair of businessmen huddled at lunchtime, talking in hushed, animated tones. The subject was not politics, not the European Community, not racing cars, but chocolates. Chocolates! I have listened as one enthusiastic *pâtissier* explained "I love éclairs, but I don't make them in my shop. So when I visit my buddies, I have an éclair feast. Seven is my limit. And I usually meet my limit."

French regional and ethnic pastries, of course, are important in Paris. The cheese-filled Alsatian *gâteau au fromage blanc* and the just-sweet-and-buttery-enough *kougelhopf* are everywhere; from Basque country in the southwest comes the cream-filled *gâteau basque*; from Normandy, the simply perfect apple tart. Don't miss at least a visual tour of Rue des Rosiers, the main street of the Jewish quarter, where there are almost as many pastry shops as street numbers, or a peek inside one of Gaston Lenôtre's several elegant shops, where a look is just about (but not quite) as good as a taste.

Everywhere, one finds *croissants* (along with the chocolate-filled version known as *pain au chocolat); brioches* (the *mousseline* variety is more buttery and typically Parisian); the *madeleine* (a lemony tea cake that Proust made famous); and the *financier* (a personal favorite), the almondy rectangle that is part cake, part cookie, and absolutely satisfying when fresh and carefully made.

For many—Parisians as well as those passing through—a day in this town without a pastry is a day not worth living. Why this is so could be the subject of a major treatise, but suffice it to say that they climb the sweet mountain because it is there.

BASTILLE, ILE SAINT-LOUIS, MARAIS, LES HALLES

2nd and 4th arrondissements

PAUL BUGAT
5 Boulevard Beaumarchais, Paris 4.
Tel: 48.87.89.88.
Métro: Bastille.
Open 8 A.M. to 8 P.M. Closed Monday and August.

Steps away from the Place de la Bastille, Paul Bugat's modern, spacious pastry shop/tea salon excels at traditional desserts. The *crème brûlée* with its rich vanilla flavor and caramelized crust, merits a special trip. Don't miss the fruit *clafoutis*, simple apricot tarts, and excellent *pains au chocolat*. They also serve savory tarts, sandwiches, and salads. In nice weather, Bugat sets out tables on the terrace facing the Bastille, and this is a great place to get a quick bite before a performance at the Opéra de la Bastille. Paul Bugat's pastry cookbook—*Mastering the Art of French Pastry*—is a modern classic.

BRIOCHE MOUSSELINE DENIS RUFFEL

Paris bakeries offer many variations on the classic brioche, *a buttery, egg-rich yeast bread that's enjoyed for luxurious breakfasts or snacks, appearing in various forms and sizes. This* brioche, *known as* brioche mousseline *because it is richer in butter than* brioche ordinaire, *is incredibly golden and delicious.* Brioche mousseline *is typically Parisian, and the light and sticky dough is often baked in tin coffee cans. Denis Ruffel, from the Left Bank pastry shop* Pâtisserie Millet *(see entry, page 223), offers his personal version, baked in a rectangular loaf pan. Ruffel's special glaze gives all sweet breads a certain glow.*

Brioche:
1 tablespoon or 1 package active dry yeast
¼ cup (60 ml) lukewarm milk
⅓ cup (65 g) sugar
1 teaspoon salt
4 cups (560 g) unbleached all-purpose flour
8 eggs
1¼ cups (10 ounces; 310 g) unsalted butter at room temperature, plus 2 teaspoons unsalted butter for buttering the loaf pans

Glaze:
1 egg
1 egg yolk
Pinch of salt
Pinch of sugar
1 teaspoon milk

1. In the bowl of an electric mixer combine the yeast, milk, and sugar, stir by hand, and set aside for 5 minutes until the yeast has dissolved.

2. Stir in the salt, then with the mixer at low speed add the flour, cup by cup, then the eggs, one by one, mixing well after each addition.

3. Add the 1¼ cups butter, bit by bit, incorporating it smoothly into the dough. The dough will be very soft and sticky. Cover securely with plastic wrap and let rise, at room temperature, until doubled in bulk, about 1 hour.

4. With a wooden spoon, stir the dough to deflate it, cover again, refrigerate, and let rise until doubled in bulk, 1½ to 3 hours.

5. Preheat the oven to 350°F (175°C).

6. Stir down the dough again and pour equal portions of the dough into two well-buttered 6-cup (1.5-liter) loaf pans. The dough will remain very soft and sticky. Cover and let rise until almost doubled in bulk, about 1 hour. Don't worry if it doesn't double in bulk. It will rise more during the baking.

7. Combine the ingredients for the glaze and brush all over the top of the *brioches*. Bake until golden brown, about 35 minutes. Unmold immediately and cool on a rack. The *brioches* can easily be frozen.

Yield: 2 loaves

CALIXTE
64 Rue Saint-Louis-en-Ile,
Paris 4.
Tel: 43.26.42.28.
Métro: Pont-Marie.
Open 9:30 A.M. to 1:30 P.M.
and 4 to 7:30 P.M.
Monday through
Wednesday and Friday
and Saturday; until 6:30
P.M. Sunday. Closed
Thursday, August, and
holidays.

In the heart of the Ile Saint-Louis, Calixte seems strangely hidden from the fray of this well-traveled tourist path. The understated windows would never lead one to believe that here lie some of Paris's most perfect *croissants* and *pains au chocolat,* worth making a special trip to find (they only bake one batch and often run out by 11:30). The shop's small but select pastry display doesn't seduce you with fancy, gilt-covered cakes and mousses, but chef Bernard's creations are the real thing: rich and full of flavor, uncluttered by excess sugar and cream. If you have time to taste only one *mille-feuilles* (Napoleon) in Paris, come here for one so good that you truly believe it has a thousand layers of buttery puff pastry. Chef Bernard also bakes state-of-the-art renditions of classic desserts, such as the *Opéra,* truffle cake, and *mousse aux cassis.* Calixte is the secret address of a faithful local clientele, and many of the privileged neighborhood matrons order their entire dinner menu here, starting with the flavorful *terrine de poisson* (either plain or encased in a phyllo dough crust) and continuing straight through dessert.

SACHA FINKELSZTAJN
27 Rue des Rosiers, Paris 4.
Tel: 42.72.78.91.

and

**FLORENCE
FINKELSZTAJN**
24 Rue des Ecouffes,
Paris 4.
Tel: 48.87.92.85.
Métro: Saint Paul.
Open 10 A.M. to 1:30 P.M.
and 3 P.M. to 7 P.M.
Closed Monday,
Tuesday, and mid-July
through mid-August.

Sacha and Florence Finkelsztajn run the best of the many pastry shops that line Rue des Rosiers, the heart of Paris's Jewish quarter. The Finkelsztajns' cheesecake (better known as *vatrouchka*) rivals anything you'll find in New York, especially when it comes fresh and warm from the oven in the afternoon. Their *gâteau aux figues* helps you understand where the Fig

French fruit tarts: always luscious.

Newton began, and the shop's assortment—poppy seed cakes, hazelnut cakes, and strudels filled with apples and raisins, honey, and citrus peel, even dates—is enough to make one weep real tears. Finkelsztajn also has a deli counter filled with tempting specialties such as *tarama*, chopped herring, smoked fish, *fromage blanc hongrois*, and more. They also bake authentic Jewish rye bread and a rich, spicy onion bread. Throw discipline to the winds for a day and enjoy.

PATISSERIE POTTIER
4 Rue de Rivoli, Paris 4.
Tel: 48.87.87.16.
Métro: Saint Paul.
Open 8 A.M. to 1 P.M. and
3 to 7:30 P.M. Closed
Monday, Tuesday
(except in December),
and August.

Talented, ambitious young Christian Pottier is in love with his work, and it shows: The windows of this pristine, jewel-like shop not far from the Place des Vosges is filled with minor masterpieces. His cakes and pastries are always pure, fresh, sparkling and authoritative. Particular favorites include the shiny, buttery *brioche* that's made with only the best *beurre des Charentes;* the moist *quatrequarts* pound cake filled with Golden Delicious apples or enhanced with a twist of lemon; the light miniature fruit soufflé with a caramelized crust; and the house specialty: *Le Délice au Chocolat,* a dark, rich chocolate *ganache* with a macaroon filling. Monsieur Pottier, who works in a neatly organized kitchen beneath the store, also bakes particularly remarkable *viennoiseries*, including the unusual *"Danois,"* a Danish-shaped puff pastry filled with chocolate chips. He also prepares some 800 pure-butter *croissants* each day, brushing them lightly with a sugar syrup that, in baking, gives them a hint of almonds and hazelnuts. They come out of the oven at 8:15 each morning, so get in line.

STOHRER
51 Rue Montorgueil,
Paris 2.
Tel: 42.33.38.20.
Métro: Les Halles.
Open 7:30 A.M. to 8:30 P.M.
Closed the first two
weeks of August.

One of Louis XV's pastry chefs opened this shop in 1730, and it continues to thrill clients with its delicious individual *pithiviers*—cream-filled, flaky puff pastry decorated like a crown—little apricot or apple tarts, and superbly fresh *pains au chocolat*. Little elderly sales ladies seem to swarm about the tiny shop, eager to assist in your selection. Take time to walk through the neighboring Rue Mont-orgeuil market, which is slightly seedy but still retains the charm of old Les Halles.

TARTE FEUILLETEE A L'ANANAS JAMIN
JAMIN'S PUFF PASTRY PINEAPPLE TART

Pineapple is an often-ignored fruit in France, although it has been around since the 18th century. Louis XIV pricked his tongue the first time he tried pineapple (not knowing it should be peeled), but Louis XV loved the sweet fruit. At Restaurant Jamin (see entry, page 117), chef Joël Robuchon found that, at first, he had a hard time convincing diners that a simple little pineapple tart could be so delicious. Until, of course, they tasted it. It's especially easy to make if you've a stash of tart shells in the freezer. The tart must be assembled at absolutely the last minute, or it turns soggy and you lose the wonderfully fresh and fruity flavor of the pineapple. Monsieur Robuchon uses a very thin puff base for this tart, but any good homemade pastry crust may be used.

1 cup (250 ml) milk
2 egg yolks
¼ cup (50 g) sugar
3 tablespoons
  unbleached all-
  purpose flour
1 tablespoon cornstarch
2 teaspoons kirsch
  (cherry brandy) or
  other fruit-based *eau-
  de-vie*
1 prebaked 10½-inch
  (27-cm) pastry shell,
  cooled
6 slices fresh pineapple,
  each ½ inch (1½ cm)
  thick
2 tablespoons quince or
  red currant jelly

1. Place the milk in a small saucepan over medium-high heat and scald it.

2. Meanwhile, in the bowl of an electric mixer, combine the egg yolks and sugar, and beat until thick and pale yellow. Slowly incorporate the flour and cornstarch. Slowly blend the scalded milk into the egg mixture.

3. Return the mixture to the pan and bring it to a boil over medium heat, stirring constantly. Remove from heat and whisk in the kirsch. Spread the warm pastry cream over the pastry shell.

4. Cut the pineapple slices into wedges. Arrange the wedges in a sunburst pattern on the pastry cream, starting from the outside and working in.

5. In a small saucepan melt the jelly over low heat. Strain. Brush the warm jelly over the pineapple and serve the tart immediately.

Yield: One 10½-inch (27-cm) tart

LATIN QUARTER, SAINT-GERMAIN
5th and 6th arrondissements

PATISSERIE
   BOULANGERIE
   ALSACIENNE
   (Andre Lerch)
4 Rue du Cardinal Lemoine,
   Paris 5.
Tel: 43.26.15.80.
Métro: Cardinal-Lemoine.
Open 7:30 A.M. to 1:30 P.M.
   and 3 to 7 P.M. Closed
   Monday, Tuesday, and
   August.

André Lerch and his madeleines.

A jolly, super-active pastry chef/baker, André
Lerch brings the best of Alsace to Paris, with
his golden *kougelhopf* (see recipe, page 220), twenty
different kinds of simple, family-style fruit tarts
that vary with the seasons, giant rounds of fresh
cheesecake (*tarte au fromage blanc*), along with whatever new creation he dreamed up overnight. (When
Monsieur Lerch can't sleep, he picks up a cookbook
to inspire himself to try a new recipe the next day
in the shop!) He'd like nothing better than to be
able to spend four or five hours decorating a single
tart, but instead he lives realistically, and feeds
his creative urges by changing his repertoire with
the seasons. He's busiest from November to March,
when wintry Alsatian baked goods are most in
demand: *springerle, quiche Lorraine,* and the delicious spice bread, *pain d'épices,* are all there. Year-
round, he sells *kougelhopf* (along with the folkloric
ceramic molds for baking them at home) and
the famous plump tea cakes known as *madeleines.*
Pâtisserie Lerch is also a *boulangerie* and bakes a
dense, crusty baguette and *pain de campagne* with
stone-ground flour.

GASTON LENOTRE, THE PARIS PASTRY KING

One wonders how Gaston Lenôtre does it. He and his band of Lenôtre-schooled pastry chefs are all over France, turning out cakes and pastries, breads, chocolates and ice creams, four-course meals, and light snacks by the thousands. Yet throughout, everything stamped Lenôtre has that certain quality that's hard to top. His chocolates are still among the best in town, and no one makes a *gâteau Opéra* or meringue and chocolate mousse-filled *concorde* like Lenôtre's. His shops are great spots to know when you need a snack, a sandwich, a quick picnic, or meal. All are open daily, 9 A.M. to 9 P.M.

LENOTRE

44 Rue du Bac, Paris 7.
Tel: 42.22.39.39.
Métro: Rue du Bac.

3-5 Rue du Havre, Paris 8.
Tel: 45.22.22.29.
Métro: Saint-Lazare.

61 Rue Lecourbe, Paris 15.
Tel: 42.73.20.97.
Métro: Sèvres-Lecourbe.

193 Avenue de Versailles, Paris 16.
Tel: 42.88.53.39.
Métro: Mirabeau.

44 Rue d'Auteuil, Paris 16.
Tel: 45.24.52.52.
Métro: Michel-Ange/Auteuil.

49 Avenue Victor-Hugo, Paris 16.
Tel: 45.01.71.71.
Métro: Victor Hugo.

15 Boulevard de Courcelles, Paris 17.
Tel: 45.63.87.63.
Métro: Villiers.

121 Avenue de Wagram, Paris 17.
Tel: 47.63.70.30.
Métro: Wagram.

KOUGELHOPF ANDRE LERCH
ANDRE LERCH'S ALSATIAN COFFEE CAKE

In Paris, André Lerch, an outgoing Alsatian baker (see entry, page 218), runs a popular bread and pastry shop where he bakes forty to fifty kougelhopf *each day, using well-seasoned molds a half-century old. There's a curious story behind these molds: Apparently, before World War II there was an Alsatian bakery where his now is. The baker went off to war, leaving behind his molds, buttered and prepared with whole almonds. He never returned, and when Monsieur Lerch moved in decades later, he found the molds stashed behind the ovens. He insists that well-seasoned molds are the secret to good* kougelhopf. *"The mold isn't good until it's been used 200 times," he warns. Since most of us won't make 200* kougelhopf *in two and a half lifetimes, Monsieur Lerch offers a shortcut: Thoroughly butter a new mold, and place it in a low oven for several hours, re-buttering every fifteen minutes or so. The mold will take on a seductive essence of browned butter, and will be ready to produce fragrant, golden loaves.*

½ cup (80 g) white raisins
2 tablespoons kirsch (cherry brandy) or other fruit-based *eau-de-vie*
1 cup (250 ml) milk
1 tablespoon or 1 package active dry yeast
3¾ cups (525 g) unbleached all-purpose flour
2 eggs, beaten
½ cup (100 g) sugar
1 teaspoon salt
¾ cup (6 ounces; 185 g) unsalted butter, at room temperature
1 tablespoon (½ oz; 15 g) unsalted butter, for buttering the *kougelhopf* mold
½ cup (70 g) whole almonds
1 tablespoon confectioners' sugar

1. In a small bowl combine the raisins and kirsch.

2. Heat the milk to lukewarm, add the yeast, stir well, and set aside for 5 minutes.

3. Place the flour in a large bowl and make a well in the center. Add the dissolved yeast and milk, the eggs, sugar, and salt, mixing well after each addition. The dough will be quite sticky. Knead by hand for 10 minutes by slapping the dough against the side of the bowl, or knead by machine for 5 minutes. Add the butter, bit by bit, and knead until the dough is smooth or until the dough comes cleanly off the sides of the bowl. Drain the raisins and knead them into the dough.

4. Place the dough in a large clean bowl and cover securely with plastic wrap. Let rise at room temperature, about 1 hour. The dough will rise slightly.

5. Punch down, knead gently, cover, and let rise again, about 1 hour. The dough will rise slightly.

6. Preheat the oven to 350°F (175°C).

7. Heavily butter a 2-quart (2-liter) earthenware *kougelhopf* mold or bundt pan and place an almond in the well of each of the mold's indentations. Place the dough in the mold and let rise until it reaches the top, about 1 hour.

8. Bake 1 hour, or until *kougelhopf* is golden brown.

9. Unmold and when cool, sprinkle with confectioners' sugar. *Kougelhopf* tastes best the day after it's baked, when it's been allowed to "ripen."

Yield: 1 *kougelhopf*

JEAN-PIERRE CARTON
6 Rue de Buci, Paris 6.
Tel: 43.26.04.13.
Métro: Odéon or Mabillon.
Open 8 A.M. to 9 P.M. Closed
Monday.

Stop into this tempting, modern bakery in the Rue de Buci market street to try the earthy *tarte rustique*: a *fougasse*-like, savory tart on a thick, whole-grain crust topped with flavorful combinations of leeks and onions with rosemary and *crème fraîche*, chorizo sausage and goat cheese, or olives and anchovies. Many specialties here come in miniature sizes too, so you can sample *petit pains* filled with olives, Gruyère, onions, or bacon, and perhaps take home a bagful of miniature *pains au chocolat* and almond *croissants* without too many guilt pangs. For a special brunch, try the *baguette*-sized *pain aux lait aux pepites de chocolat*, a rich, golden bread bursting with bittersweet chocolate chips. Most of the standard breads here look better than they taste.

André Lerch's kougelhopf
(for recipe, see facing page.)

SEVRES-BABYLONE, ECOLE MILITAIRE, LA TOUR MAUBOURG

7th arrondissement

CHRISTIAN CONSTANT
26 Rue du Bac, Paris 7.
Tel: 47.03.30.00.
Métro: Rue du Bac.
Open daily, 8 A.M. to 8 P.M.

If you would like to see how *nouvelle cuisine* has influenced French pastries, stop in at Christian Constant's all-white, contemporary shop, where "exotic" kiwi tarts and tiny, boutique-sized chocolates fill the display windows. Not all of Monsieur Constant's creations inspire respect, but he does offer a few pleasing classics: His warm individual *tarte Tatin* goes down well in the morning with a bracing cup of thick *express,* and can be enjoyed in tranquility in the little tea salon that adjoins the shop.

DALLOYAU, SINCE 1802

Since 1802, when Napoleon ruled the republic, Dalloyau has done its best to satisfy the Parisian sweet tooth. Today, the company has five boutiques in Paris and five in Japan, and its activities are incredibly diverse, offering pastries, chocolates, *charcuterie*, and fully catered meals and banquets. Best bets, though, are the coffee macaroons and the cake mogador, composed of chocolate cake, chocolate mousse, and a fine layer of raspberry jam. All shops are open daily, 9 A.M. to 9 P.M.

99-101 Rue du Faubourg Saint-Honoré, Paris 8.
Tel: 43.59.18.10.
Métro: Saint-Philippe-du-Roule.

25 Boulevard des Capucines, Paris 2.
Tel: 47.03.47.00.
Métro: Opéra.

2 Place Edmond-Rostand, Paris 6.
Tel: 43.29.31.10.
Métro: Luxembourg.

63 Rue de Grenelle, Paris 7.
Tel: 45.49.95.30.
Métro: Rue du Bac.

69 Rue de la Convention, Paris 15.
Tel: 45.77.84.27.
Métro: Charles-Michel.

BERNARD DESGRIPPES
16 Avenue Rapp, Paris 7.
Tel: 45.51.66.39.
Métro: Ecole Militaire or
   Pont de l'Alma.
Open 7:15 A.M.to 8 P.M.
   Closed Sunday.

Make a detour to this *boulangerie-pâtisserie* not far from the Eiffel Tower for the delicious and unusual *"raissol" aux pruneaux*, a slipper of rich puff pastry filled with prunes, almost like a flat *baguette*. It makes a cozy and comforting breakfast or teatime treat. Breads here are just okay.

DUCHESNE
112 Rue Saint-Dominique,
   Paris 7.
Tel: 45.51.31.01.
Métro: Ecole Militaire or La
   Tour-Maubourg.
Open 8 A.M. to 8 P.M. Closed
   Sunday.

Duchesne could be called the "ballroom pastry shop" because of the glittering mosaic walls and the chandeliers hanging from the gilt-painted ceilings. Stop by to admire this pretty boutique near the Eiffel Tower, and across the street from the lovely Fontaine de Mars arcade. Then, if you're in the mood for something sinfully rich, pick up a *galette aux pommes de terre*, a puff pastry packet stuffed with chunks of potatoes, tart *crème fraîche* and *fines herbes*—it gives new meaning to sour cream and chive potatoes. The breads don't always live up to their surroundings.

Irresistible, buttery croissants.

PATISSERIE MILLET
103 Rue Saint-Dominique,
Paris 7.
Tel: 45.51.49.80.
Métro: Ecole Militaire or
La Tour-Maubourg.
Open 9 A.M. to 7 P.M.
Tuesday through
Saturday; 9 A.M. to 1 P.M.
Sunday. Closed Monday,
one week in February,
and August.

A classic, spotless pastry shop offering pure honey *madeleines*; almond-flavored *financiers*; buttery, egg-rich *brioche mousseline* (see recipe, page 214); some twenty different varieties of cakes and tarts; and twenty flavors of ice cream. Their *croissants* and *croissants aux amandes* are some of the best in town, and Denis Ruffel, Millet's energetic pastry chef, tucks two delicious sticks of chocolate into his remarkable *pain au chocolat*. Upstairs, behind the scenes, there's a good-size chocolate "factory," while on the main floor a small tea salon provides the perfect spot for sampling everything that tempts the palate.

A BAKER'S DOZEN

In the 17th century, butlers were charged with buying the wine and bread for their households. A contract would be signed with the local baker for a year's worth of bread. For every twelve loaves bought for the household, the butler got to keep the thirteenth for himself.

PELTIER
66 Rue de Sèvres, Paris 7.
Tel: 47.34.06.62. or
  47.83.66.12.
Métro: Vaneau.
Open 9:30 A.M. to 8 P.M.
  Monday through
  Saturday; 8:30 A.M. to
  7 P.M. Sunday.

Since 1961, the Peltier name has stood for quality pastry in Paris. Today, the family's spacious, pristine shop offers some of the most beautiful tarts and cakes in Paris, along with superb *croissants* and lovely frozen fruit *soufflés*. Sample their special cakes and tarts—one covered with seven different fresh fruits, another a mango-flavored *charlotte*—at the counter in the corner of the shop. Then take home a *princesse*, a meringue cake with almonds, vanilla cream, and grains of *nougatine*.

MADELEINES
LEMON TEA CAKES

While researching this book, I became fixated, absolutely fanatical, about madeleines, *the plump and golden tea cakes shaped like tiny scallop shells. They were something to boost my spirits on the days when I walked for miles sleuthing in search of culinary jewels. I tasted dozens of* madeleines, *but only a few that were "just right."*

The best, freshest madeleine *has a dry, almost dusty taste when taken on its own. One of my favorite versions is made by André Lerch, an Alsatian baker with a bread and pastry shop on the Left Bank.*

*To be truly appreciated—to "invade the senses with exquisite pleasure" as they did for Marcel Proust—*madeleines *must be dipped in tea, ideally the slightly lime-flavored* tilleul, *which releases the fragrant, flavorful lemon essence of the little tea cake. Special* madeleine *tins can be found in all the French restaurant supply shops, and in the house-wares section of department stores. The following is a recipe I developed.*

4 eggs
1 cup (200 g) sugar
Grated zest (peel) of
  2 lemons
1¼ cups (225 g) all-
  purpose flour (do not
  use unbleached flour)
¾ cup (6 ounces; 185 g)
  unsalted butter,
  melted and cooled,
  plus 1 tablespoon
  (½ oz; 15 g) unsalted
  butter, for buttering
  madeleine tins

1. Place the eggs and sugar in a large bowl, then using a whisk or electric mixer, beat until lemon colored. Add the zest. Fold in the flour, then the ¾ cup butter.

2. Refrigerate the batter for 1 hour.

3. Preheat the oven to 375°F (190°C).

4. Butter the *madeleine* tins, then spoon in the batter, filling each well about three-fourths full. Bake 10 to 12 minutes, or until *madeleines* are golden brown.

5. Remove the *madeleines* from their tins as soon as they're baked and cool them on a baking rack. Note: Wash tins immediately with a stiff brush and hot water but no detergent, so they retain their seasoning. The *madeleines* are best eaten as soon as they've cooled. They may, however, be stored for several days in an airtight container.

Yield: Thirty-six 3-inch (8-cm) *madeleines*

MADELEINE, PLACE DE CLICHY

8th and 9th arrondissements

FEYEUX
56 Rue de Clichy, Paris 9.
Tel: 48.74.37.64.
Métro: Liège or Place de
Clichy.
Open 7:30 A.M. to 7:30 P.M.
Closed Monday.

A combination tearoom, *pâtisserie-boulangerie*, and chocolate shop, this unpretentious boutique beckons you inside with the marvelous *croquembouche* sculpture in the window. There's a timeless array of Parisian fare, including rich *financiers*, doughnut-shaped *beignets aux pommes* (more like an apple-*brioche* fritter—no doughnut ever tasted so good!), and a modern chocolate-chip *brioche*.

LADUREE
16 Rue Royale, Paris 8.
Tel: 42.60.21.79.
Métro: Madeleine.
Open 8:30 A.M. to 7 P.M.
Closed Sunday and
August.

Ladurée remains one of Paris's most elegant and traditional shops—a tea salon and pastry shop of note. Press your nose against the window and dream on. The choice is not a simple one. Shall it be a buttery early morning *croissant*, an exquisite lunchtime strawberry or raspberry tart, or a mid-afternoon chocolate macaroon? And this doesn't even take into account some of the best classic cakes in Paris, perfect to order for a birthday or special occasion. If there's time—and a table free—also stop for a cup of *café au lait*, one of the best in the city. On your way out, buy a delicate *brioche mousseline* or a raisin-filled *brioche* called *cramique*, to lure you out of bed the next morning. (See also Tea Salons.)

PASTEUR

15th arrondissement

HELLEGOUARCH
185 Rue de Vaugirard,
Paris 15.
Tel: 47.83.29.72.
Métro: Pasteur.
Open 8:30 A.M. to 7:30 P.M.
Closed Monday and
August.

Several years ago I conducted a blind tasting, in search of the best Parisian *croissant*. Hellegouarch won hands down, and their *croissants*—when fresh from the oven around 9 A.M.—are still among the best in town. Their *pains au chocolat* are equally appealing: everything the buttery, flaky, chocolate-filled pastry should be, and even a little more.

FINANCIERS
ALMOND CAKES

The little rectangular almond cakes known as financiers *are sold in many of the best pastry shops in Paris. Perfect* financiers *are about as addictive as chocolate, and I'd walk a mile or two for a good one. The finest have a firm, crusty exterior and a moist, almondy interior, tasting almost as if they were filled with almond paste. Next to the* madeleine, *the* financier *is probably the most popular little French cake, common street food for morning or afternoon snacking. The cake's name probably comes from the fact that a* financier *resembles a solid gold brick. Curiously, as popular as they are,* financiers *seldom appear in recipe books or in French literature.*

The secret to a good financier *is in the baking: For a good crust, they must begin baking in a very hot oven. Then the temperature is reduced to keep the interior moist. Placing the tins on a thick baking sheet while they are in the oven is an important baking hint from the Left Bank pastry chef Jean-Luc Poujauran, who worked for months to perfect his* financiers, *among the best in Paris. The special tin* financier *molds, each measuring 2 x 4 inches (5 x 10 cm), can be found at restaurant supply shops. Small oval* barquette *molds or even muffin tins could also be used.*

1 cup (140 g) almonds
1⅔ cups (210 g) confectioners' sugar
½ cup (70 g) unbleached all-purpose flour
¾ cup (185 ml) egg whites (5 to 6)
¾ cup (6 ounces; 185 g) unsalted butter, melted and cooled, plus 1 tablespoon (½ oz; 15 g) unsalted butter, for buttering 18 *financier* molds

1. Preheat the oven to 450°F (230°C).

2. Toast the almonds on a baking sheet until browned, about 5 minutes. Remove but leave the oven on. When the almonds are cool, grind them to a fine powder in a food processor.

3. In a medium-size bowl, combine the sugar, ground almonds, and flour, then sift or force the mixture through a fine mesh sieve into a second bowl. The mixture should be very fine. Stir in the unbeaten egg whites until thoroughly blended, then stir in the ¾ cup butter until well blended.

4. Butter the *financier* molds (or *barquette* molds), then fill each mold almost to the rim. Place the tins on a thick baking sheet (or a broiler pan) and place in the center of the oven. Bake for 7 minutes, then reduce heat to 400°F (205°C) and bake another 7 minutes. Turn off the heat and let the *financiers* rest in the oven another 7 minutes.

5. Remove the *financiers* from the oven and unmold as soon as they've cooled. Serve with tea, coffee, ice cream, or *sorbet*. (Note: Wash molds immediately with a stiff brush and hot water but no detergent, so they retain their seasoning.) The *financiers* may be stored in an airtight container for several days.

Yield: Eighteen 2 x 4-inch (5 x 10-cm) *financiers*

VICTOR-HUGO, PASSY, AUTEUIL, TERNES
16th and 17th arrondissements

**PATISSERIE
ALSACIENNE**
(C. Brocard)
91 Avenue Raymond
Poincaré, Paris 16.
Tel: 45.00.56.55.
Métro: Victor Hugo.
Open 8 A.M. to 7:30 P.M.
Closed Monday and mid-
July through the first
week of September.

A fine little shop just off the Place Victor-Hugo for sampling superb Alsatian pastries, including a fresh and buttery *kougelhopf, quiche lorraine,* onion tarts, Christmas stollen, and anise bread.

BEURRE ET CACAO
35 Rue de l'Annonciation,
Paris 16.
Tel: 42.24.00.55.
Métro: La Muette.
Open 8 A.M. to 7:30 P.M.
Monday through Saturday,
8 A.M. to 1:30 P.M.
Sundays. Closed August.

A nice spot for homey, country style pastries, most filled with butter and chocolate, including such specialties as the *lingot,* a moist, brownie-like chocolate cake; *brioche aux pommes;* the *albicocche,* an apricot crumble tart; and a delightful *chausson aux pruneaux.*

COQUELIN AINE
1 Place de Passy, Paris 16.
Tel: 45.24.44.00.
Métro: La Muette.
Open 9 A.M. to 7 P.M.
Tuesday through
Saturday; 9 A.M. to 1 P.M.
Sunday. Closed Monday.

Take a break while visiting the Rue de l'Annonciation market and get in line with all the genteel ladies of this very chic *quartier.* They know where the good things are, such as fresh and yeasty *brioche, pain au chocolat* oozing with bittersweet chocolate, almond rich *financiers,* and dozens of other sweets to excite even the stoic. Their *puits d'amour,* or wishing wells (a puff pastry base topped with a rim of *choux* pastry, filled with pastry cream and a caramelized sugar topping), are among the best in town and merit a detour. The few tables in back are almost always taken, but if it's a warm and sunny day, sit outside on the terrace and enjoy the bustle of the Place de Passy. (See also Tea Salons.)

ICE CREAM WORTH WAITING FOR

The line stretches right around the corner, and neither subzero temperatures nor pouring rain can deter the hearty souls who queue up for a taste of Berthillon, Paris's finest ice creams, sorbets, and *granités*. There's always a lot of good-natured grumbling about the wait, while perfect strangers trade tales of past visits or argue passionately about which of the sixty-plus Berthillon flavors is best, purest, most authentic, most decadent.

There's always a lot of "place saving" as customers race up to the front of the line to check the list of current seasonal offerings. Once you reach the window you'd better have your choice well in mind—there is no time for hemming, hawing, asking advice, or questions. Will it be *glacé au chocolat amer*, bitter chocolate ice cream rich with cream and eggs, or maybe *nougat au miel*, a crunchy, heavenly blend of nuts and smooth, smooth honey? Or perhaps the glistening black currant sorbet *(Cassis)* that tastes so much like the real thing you can't believe you're not nibbling blackberries.

Berthillon, 31 Rue Saint-Louis-en-l'Ile, Paris 4. (43.54.31.61). Métro: Pont-Marie. Open 10 A.M. to 8 P.M.. Closed Monday, Tuesday, July, August and during Easter break.

If the thought of waiting in line is discouraging, don't despair. Berthillon ice cream and *sorbets* are sold in many Paris cafés:

Restaurant Cadmios, 17 Rue des Deux-Ponts, Paris 4. (43.25.50.93) (cones only).

Le Flore en l'Ile, 42 Quai d'Orléans, Paris 4. (43.29.88.27).

Lady Jane, 6 Quai d'Orléans, Paris 4. (44.33.08.36).

Le Mandarin, 148 Boulevard Saint-Germain, Paris 6. (46.33.98.35).

Le Petit Châtelet, 39 Rue de la Bûcherie, Paris 5. (46.33.53.40).

Le Reveille, 29 Boulevard Henri-IV, Paris 4. (42.72.73.26).

Rostand, 6 Place Edmond-Rostand, Paris 6. (43.54.61.58).

La Rotonde, 105 Boulevard Montparnasse, Paris 6. (43.26.68.84 and 43.26.48.26).

Sometimes one just isn't enough.

**LES DELICES DE
  LONGCHAMP**
150 Avenue Victor Hugo,
  Paris 16.
Tel: 47.27.99.52.
Métro: Pompe or Victor
  Hugo.
Open 7:30 A.M. to 8 P.M.
  Tuesday through
  Saturday. 8 A.M. to 7:30
  P.M. Sunday. Closed
  Monday and two weeks
  in August.

B rave the extremely snooty service at this posh, modern, formal *pâtisserie-boulangerie-traiteur*. Come for excellent *viennoiseries*, such as *pains au chocolat* melting with bittersweet chocolate, moist almond *financiers*, star-shaped almond *croissants*, and *pains aux pistaches et chocolat*. How these sour-faced ladies can make such sweet pastries is a mystery. The *flûte Mozart* is the specialty here—a dense, white *baguette au levain* made with organic flour, the best in the neighborhood. Also popular, the herb-filled *tarte Provençale*, and *tarte aux deux saumons*, prepared with both smoked and poached salmon.

MALITOURNE
30 Rue de Chaillot,
  Paris 16.
Tel: 47.20.52.26.
Métro: Iéna.
Open 8 A.M. to 2:30 P.M. and
  4 to 7:30 P.M. Closed
  Sunday afternoon and

The shop features original pastries created by Jean-Yves Malitourne, a *pâtissier* from the Sarthes region of France who worked in the kitchens of Roger Vergé at Moulin de Mougins in the south of France before opening his own *pâtisserie* in this posh Paris neighborhood. Try the *téméraire*, an almond biscuit topped with Cointreau-infused *crème pâtissière* and wrapped in hazelnut *nougat*; or the Savoureux, a chocolate biscuit topped with chocolate mousse. His raspberry tarts and prune turnovers are also lovely.

LE STUBLI
11 Rue Poncelet, Paris 17.
Tel: 42.27.81.86.
Métro: Ternes.
Open 8:30 A.M. to 7 P.M.
  Tuesday through
  Saturday and 8:30 A.M.
  to 1 P.M. Sunday.
  Closed Monday.

If you love classic and beautiful Austrian pastries—ultra-fresh crumb-topped cherry or rhubarb strudels, light cheesecakes—then this is the boutique for you. Note the tea salon upstairs and delicatessen across the street for a quick bite or carry-out. (See also Tea Salons.)

Always a crowd at Berthillon.

MONTMARTRE

17th and 18th arrondissements

**PATISSERIE DE
  MONTMARTRE**
81 Rue du Mont-Cenis,
  Paris 18.
Tel: 46.06.39.28.
Métro: Jules-Joffrin.
Open 9 A.M. to 7:30 P.M.

While visiting the charming Rue du Poteau market street, stop in at Pâtisserie de Montmartre for a crisp and buttery *croissant*, a tart lemon turnover (*chausson au citron*), or a hazelnut-scented *financier*. They also make several whole-grain specialty breads, including a ten-grain loaf topped with sunflower seeds, as well as their own jams in summertime.

PAINT YOUR OWN SUNDAE

When the line is longer than your patience at the famed Berthillon ice cream shop, head over to Damman's, a combination tea salon/ice cream parlor that also offers top-quality teas, as well as tarts and cakes. The real attraction here is some of the best ice cream in Paris, not overly sweet, and filled with pure fruit flavor. Damman's offers an original selection of ice cream and sorbet flavors, including bitter tangerine, amaretto, Bulgarian yogurt, even Pastis. Come especially for the palettes of ice cream, an original twist on ice-cream sundaes: They fill palette-shaped plates with scoops of ice cream and wells of sauce and *coulis*, so you can paint your own sundae, allowing your artistic and gastronomic fancies to go wild. Surprisingly reasonable prices.

DAMMAN'S
20 Rue Cardinal Lemoine, Paris 5.
Tel: 46.33.61.30.
Métro: Cardinal Lemoine.
Open 11:30 A.M. to 10 P.M. daily in summer. 11:30 A.M. to 7 P.M. in winter. Closed Sunday in winter.

VAUDRON
4 Rue de la Jonquière, Paris 17.
Tel: 46.27.96.97.
Métro: Guy-Moquet.
Open 7:30 A.M. to 7:30 P.M. Tuesday through Saturday; 7:45 A.M. to 2:30 P.M. Sunday. Closed Monday.

A large and spotless pastry shop dedicated to quality and simplicity at affordable prices. Vaudron has been around since 1931, catering to its faithful Parisian clientele and their births, baptisms, and weddings, generation after generation. Since 1969, Roland Indrière, now assisted by his son, Michel, has continued the tradition, aspiring to offer simple, unfussy, appealing cakes and pastries made with the highest quality ingredients. Try their chocolates, their honey-sweetened *financiers*, and their deliciously fresh buttercream-filled caramel macaroons. They prepare giant apple turnovers (*chaussons aux pommes*) each Wednesday and pear-filled pound cakes (*quatre-quarts aux poires*) each Thursday, not to mention *brioches, madeleines,* twenty flavors of ice cream, and other cakes and tarts.

BELLEVILLE, MENILMONTANT

20th arrondissement

PATISSERIE DE L'EGLISE
10 Rue du Jourdain,
Paris 20.
Tel: 46.36.66.08.
Métro: Jourdain.
Open 8 A.M. to 7:30 P.M.
Closed August.

A good place to know while in the neighborhood: Be sure to at least take a look at the beautifully restored ceiling of this 1887 boutique situated on a quiet, village-like square. If you're in the mood, try a good and flaky *pain au chocolat*, a rectangle of *tarte aux cerises* (watch out for pits!) made with state-of-the-art puff pastry, or the individual *clafoutis aux abricots*, ideal for eating out of hand.

Warm bread at any hour.

Boulangeries
BAKERIES

Fresh bread daily—in France it's a must.

Of the hundreds of Parisians I've interviewed over the years, I love the bakers best. In days past, they were most often roly-poly men in worn white T-shirts, who came to Paris from little French towns and villages to make their way. They were men who loved their wives, who never seemed to have enough time to sleep, and who were passionate—almost crazily, over-the-edge, off-the-wall passionate—about bread.

Today's French baker wears many hats—that of a baker, banker, entrepreneur. It could be said that the face of Paris changes with the face of its bread bakers. While historically, the price of a *baguette* was controlled by law (generally, a *baguette*, a litre of milk, and the daily newspaper all cost the same), those controls were lifted in 1988, changing forever the way bread is prepared, baked, and sold in Paris.

There are now two kind of bakers. One is the dedicated *boulanger* who cares about the flour, the water, the oven, the bread, and the consumer. The other is the entrepreneur who bakes without passion (often frozen dough that comes from a central factory) and is interested only in the bottom line. (Whenever I am in a neighborhood where I know there's great bread, and I see someone walking down the street with a flabby impostor, I am tempted to tap them on the shoulder and offer a bit of unsolicited gastro-

nomic advice.) Here, of course, we're interested in the first kind of
baker, the traditional baker who mixes, kneads, rises, and bakes
the bread on the premises. With love.

One of my greatest gastronomic Parisian treats is to walk
into a favorite *boulangerie* around noon, my stomach growling with
hunger. I order a crusty *baguette "bien cuite,"* and before I've set
down my few francs, I've bitten off the heel. Chewy, yeasty ecstasy.
Bread is life. It's food that makes you feel good, feel healthy; it's
food that goes with everything, and goes especially well with the
things we love most about France—fine cheese, great wine.

The responsibility of baking good bread is hard, tedious,
lonely work, and unfortunately few young Frenchmen still aspire
to be bakers when they grow up. Working through the night in
suffocatingly hot basements holds little glamour for them. The
truth is, the romantic image of the French baker slaving through
the night to provide breakfast fare is basically a memory these
days, although there do remain a few diligent souls who do labor
through the darkest hours.

How does one tell the good loaf from the bad, and what
makes the difference? The good French loaf is made with a respect
for the simple nature of the ingredients: wholesome, stone-milled
wheat or rye flour, fresh yeast (*levure*) or a fresh sourdough starter
(*levain*), pure water, and a minimum of salt. This is true whether
it's a thin, crisp, and golden *baguette* or *ficelle*; a plump, round,
country-style *pain de campagne*; or a made-to-eat-with-cheese loaf
studded with hazelnuts, walnuts, or raisins.

In the best bakeries, ovens are fired all day long, ensuring that
customers can purchase loaves just minutes old throughout the day.
(French bread often contains no fat and thus quickly goes stale.)
Most dough is now kneaded mechanically, but the best is done
slowly, so the flavor is not killed by over-kneading. Good dough is
allowed to rise slowly, several times, with plenty of rest between
kneadings. At the finest bakeries every loaf is formed by hand.
Good bread has a thick crust, a dense and golden interior with lots
of irregular air holes, and a fresh wheaty aroma and flavor.

About a decade ago, French bakers organized a nationwide
"good bread campaign," a loosely organized attempt to bring back
the kind of bread made before World War II brought modernization to the corner bakery. Today, that campaign seems to have

paid off in a renaissance of artisanal breads. Sourdough *baguettes* and crusty ryes now vie for space on some bakery shelves with such novelty breads as *pain à l'emmenthal et noix* (emmenthal and walnut bread), *fougasse* (ladder-like flat country bread), and *pain aux plantes* (whole-grain bread baked with herbs), not to mention ten-grain loaves baked with everything from flax seeds to pumpkin seeds. This artisanal trend has also spawned a bevy of brand-name breads, made from industrially patented flour. Bakeries buy the flour and the recipe that goes with it and bake loaves with wholesome sounding names, like Mannedor, Retrodor, Baguepi, and Pain Passion.

At the same time, the interest in all things natural and *biologique* (organic) is stronger than ever. The terms *"pain de campagne"* and *"paysanne"* (usually crusty white bread made with a portion of whole wheat or rye flours) have become bakery standards. What's positive is that the growing demand has pushed passionate bakers to create (or recreate) innovative variations on the country theme—*pains campagnotte, triple alliance, vieille France, paillasse, bucheron,* to name a few. Unfortunately, this is a phenomenon found only at the best bakeries, and is far from ubiquitous.

The downside of today's bakery trends is that it's getting harder and harder to find an honest, classic white *baguette.* Too often "modernization" takes the essential human touch—and the life—out of *baguettes.* They're made with poor quality industrial flour, they're over-kneaded (making for loaves that seem to dry out seconds after baking), or, what's worst, "baked off" from frozen, industrially prepared loaves. In short, the loving, patiently made, hand-formed loaf has become a relic of days past.

While bakers have yet to begin a full-scale war against one another, I sensed battle signs one day as I passed a little bakery in the 15th *arrondissement.* The sign on the door said:

INFORMATION DES CONSOMMATEURS:
UN TERMINAL DE CUISSON N'EST PAS
UNE BOULANGERIE TRADITIONELLE

meaning, a place that "bakes off" factory-made bread is not a traditional bakery.

While I can't promise you'll find great bread on every corner or even in every neighborhood, I've done my best to scour the city for the best breads that Paris has to offer.

LES HALLES, BOURSE, OPERA

1st and 2nd arrondissements

ANDRE CLERET
4 Rue des Lavandières-
  Sainte-Opportune,
  Paris 1.
Tel: 42.33.82.68.
Métro: Châtelet.
Open 7 A.M. to 8 P.M.
Closed Sunday, Monday,
  and either July or
  August.

André Cléret's is a bakery haven hidden on a side street near the frenetic Place du Châtelet, a *boulangerie* that's ideal for escaping from the neighborhood's lineup of fast-food joints. Local workers flock here for the incomparable selection of sandwiches: Westphalian ham and Gruyère on a raisin-rye bun; a chunky purée of radishes and *fromage blanc* on a whole-grain roll; rosemary-flecked goat cheese with tomatoes; feta cheese and salad; *brioche* "pockets" filled with tuna salad and tomatoes, and countless other combinations, all stacked in tidy piles behind the counter. The *boulangerie* is just around the corner from the Châtelet theaters, so stop off for a pre-performance bite, or for fortification before a visit to nearby Notre-Dame and the Ile de la Cité. Cléret also offers a solid selection of country breads, such as *baguettes au levain*; flat, golden disks of *pain à l'ancienne* with a slightly sour, fermented taste; and chewy Gruyère and onion *fougasse*, here a filled, oval-shaped flat bread.

BOULANGERIE JEANDRE
45 Rue de l'Arbre Sec,
  Paris 1.
Tel: 42.60.11.05.
Métro: Louvre or Pont-
  Neuf.
Open 7 A.M. to 8 P.M. Closed
  Saturday, Sunday, and
  holidays.

I first discovered this bakery's state-of-the-art *baguette* while lunching one day at Chez la Vieille, Adrien Biasin's homey bistro down the street (see page 26). When I left the restaurant, I stopped in to take a dense, heavy *baguette* home for dinner. As it turned out I didn't stay home that evening, but there the *baguette* was, fresh as ever, for breakfast the next day. For those who can't decide between a buttery *croissant* or wholesome, fresh bread in the morning, the shop offers a scrumptious chance to have your cake and eat it too: the special *pain feuilleté aux seigle et raisins*, a tulip shaped rye bread made with buttery puff pastry. Peel off a petal-like mouthful and sigh on.

J.P. LE LEDIC
16 Rue des Petits-Carreaux,
Paris 2.
Tel: 42.36.54.29.
Métro: Sentier.
Open 6:30 A.M. to 8 P.M.
Closed Sunday and
Monday.

Just an ordinary-looking bakery offering superb *pain paillasse*—huge, inflated country loaves—great for tucking under your arm as you wind your way through the crowded market street. This tangy, moist bread tastes a bit like a San Francisco sourdough. Tasting Monsieur Le Ledic's loaf, I got excited about bread once again!

MAX POILANE
42 Place du Marché
St-Honoré, Paris 1.
Tel: 42.61.10.53.
Métro: Tuileries.
Open 8:30 A.M. to 7:30 P.M.
Closed Sunday.

One of Paris's best-kept secrets is that there is more than one Poilâne: famous brother Lionel, and less famous brother Max. Working with the same ingredients and huge wood-fired ovens, they produce essentially the same large, round country loaf with slight variations: Max's tastes less acidic, and he also bakes breads that can't be found *chez* Lionel, like a white *levain* bread and *petits pains aux noix* and *au seigle et froment* (mini-nut breads and rye wheat breads). Lean, intense, and poetic, Max Poilâne is a fanatic about bread: "I love bread, I eat bread with bread. One day I even found myself eating bread with sorbet—that was too much." When he goes to restaurants, he brings a little sack of his own bread with him. Like Lionel, he has managed to keep his operation streamlined and homey, despite the fact that five huge, wood-fired ovens are kept going twenty-four hours a day. Large, personalized *pain décoré* (decorated country loaf) can be ordered several days in advance.

PETITS PAINS PARISIENS JAMIN
JAMIN'S CRUSTY OVAL-SHAPED ROLLS

These rolls are so favored at Jamin (see entry, page 117), the popular restaurant on Rue de Longchamp, that each diner consumes an average of three rolls per meal. Chef Joël Robuchon bakes them fresh for both lunch and dinner, in a small convection oven fitted with a vaporizing attachment to help develop a good crust. Equally good results can be obtained at home.

2½ cups (625 ml)
  lukewarm water
2 tablespoons or 2
  packages active dry
  yeast
6 to 7 cups (840 to
  980 g) unbleached
  all-purpose flour
2 teaspoons salt

1. Combine the water, yeast, and 1 cup (140 g) of the flour in a large mixing bowl, and set aside for 5 minutes to dissolve the yeast.

2. Once the yeast has dissolved, add the salt; then begin adding the remaining flour, cup by cup, until the dough is too stiff to stir. Place the dough on a lightly floured wooden board and begin kneading, adding additional flour as necessary. The dough should be fairly stiff and firm. Knead until the dough is smooth and satiny, 10 to 15 minutes. Place the dough in a bowl, cover securely with plastic wrap, and let rise at room temperature until doubled in bulk, about 1 hour.

3. When the dough has doubled, punch down and let rise again, covered, until doubled in bulk, 1 hour.

4. Punch down again, then separate the dough into 18 equal portions, each weighing about 3 ounces (95 g). Form into neat ovals, and place on a baking sheet. Mist with water (a household flower mister works well), cover with a clean cloth, and let rise until almost doubled in bulk, about 45 minutes.

5. Preheat the oven to 450°F (230°C). Just before putting the rolls in the oven, place a shallow baking pan filled with 2 cups (500 ml) boiling water on the bottom of the oven to create a steamy atmosphere for baking, which will give the rolls a good crust.

6. Bake until the rolls are a rich golden brown, 20 to 25 minutes. Mist with cold water several times during the first 3 minutes of baking.

7. Remove the rolls from the oven and transfer to a cooling rack. Because there is no fat in this recipe, the rolls will not stay fresh for long. They should, ideally, be consumed within two hours of baking. (Alternatively, the rolls, once baked, may be frozen. To serve, take the rolls directly from the freezer, place unwrapped in a cold oven, set oven to 400°F (205°C), and bake 15 to 20 minutes to thaw and refresh.)

Yield: 18 rolls

BOURSE, REPUBLIQUE, MARAIS

2nd, 3rd, and 4th arrondissements

ESPACE GOURMAND
27 Rue des Archives,
Paris 4.
Tel: 42.72.93.94.
Métro: Hôtel de Ville or
Rambuteau.
Open 7:30 A.M. to 8 P.M.
Closed Sunday and
August.

This airy, new *boulangerie-pâtisserie-café* is a real find in this neighborhood, where wholesale boutiques and art galleries are squeezing out quality food shops. Come in for the special, modern-day, thyme-flecked *fougasse*, filled with *béchamel* and combinations such as tomatoes and *herbes de Provence*; or the *campagnarde*, stuffed with bacon, *béchamel*, and potatoes, or Roquefort, leeks, olives, and anchovies. The *fougasse* also comes in cute, cocktail-size versions. For a festive touch to any table or picnic, try the daisy-shaped sourdough *"marguerite,"* with sesame and poppy seeds sprinkled over the crisp, golden crust. At lunchtime the Espace Gourmande serves sandwiches and fresh salads to take out or to sample at the shop's café. Pick up some bread and then poke your head into the nearby 18th-century Archives Nationales, an impressive mansion just down the street.

ONFROY
34 Rue de Saintonge,
Paris 3.
Tel: 42.77.56.46.
Métro: Filles-du-Calvaire.
Open 8:15 A.M. to 1:30 P.M.
and 3 P.M. to 8 P.M.
Closed Saturday
afternoon, Sunday, and
mid-July through
August.

This is one baker I almost wish I could keep a secret. I am wild about rich, sour rye bread, the sort of hearty Eastern European loaf on which you could survive forever. And this is exactly what comes out of Fernand Onfroy's old-fashioned, wood-fired oven. This unflappable baker from Normandy—whose first childhood memory is of the Americans landing on Omaha beach—works quietly and diligently, also producing a fine *baguette biologique* from organically grown flour, a whole-wheat *baguette complète*, as well as the every-day *baguette*. The excellent breads here surpass the pastries. When Monsieur Onfroy opened his modest little shop not far from Place de la République in 1965, he discovered the remains of an old underground Roman oven, then a more recent, though still ancient, oven at another level. Rue de Saintonge was first created in 1628, and most likely there's been a bakery at No. 34 for several centuries.

AU PANETIER LEBON
10 Place des Petits-Pères,
Paris 2.
Tel: 42.60.90.23.
Métro: Bourse.
Open 8 A.M. to 7 P.M. Closed Saturday, Sunday, and either July or August.

By 8 A.M. most mornings there's a line of customers streaming in to buy Bernard Lebon's *baguette au levain* (sourdough baguette), still baked in a sturdy, wood-fired, brick-lined oven built around the turn of the century. Up at 5 A.M. each day, he travels just a few floors from his apartment above the shop to a flour-dusted but impeccably tidy cellar, where his assistant has been working since midnight. Monsieur Lebon gets right to work, ready to greet the first crackling batch of bread as it comes from the oven at 6 A.M. Working steadily, he continues to mix, knead, and form additional loaves for later bakings at 9 A.M. and noon. The 250 *baguettes* they produce each day are crisp and chewy, and like the baker, authentic and honest. But Monsieur Lebon and his wife, Yvette, don't stop there: They offer some fifty different shapes of bread (not all of them available each day), including giant *couronnes* (rings) of wheat and rye, special *baguettes moulées* baked in molds to yield even crispier crusts, in all preparing eight different kinds of dough. What's the hardest thing about his job? "Getting the various breads to rise evenly, so they're ready for baking at the same time," says the agile, square-jawed baker. Does he love his own bread? He eats it three meals a day. Plus every afternoon he enjoys one of his pastry chef's apple tarts, warm from the oven. Decorated breads can be made to order. At lunchtime the bakery often offers a wonderful *galette de pommes de terre* (puff pastry tart filled with potatoes, herbs, and crème frâiche) and there is always a good variety of sandwiches and savory tarts.

RACHINEL
87 Rue Saint-Antoine,
Paris 4.
Tel: 48.04.81.51.
Métro: Saint-Paul.
Open 6:30 A.M. to 8:30 P.M.
  Tuesday through
  Saturday, 5 A.M. to 8:30
  P.M. Sunday. Closed
  Monday.

Rachinel is the only bakery in Paris that makes *fougasse* stuffed with salmon and Gruyère, a delicious, if unusual combination. This oval-shaped flat bread has a split top to show off the various fillings, ranging from olives and anchovies, to ham, Gruyère, and mushrooms. Baked four times each day, the *fougasse* is a crowd-pleaser for the hordes of hungry *lycée* (grammar-school) students and neighborhood workers who clamor into the shop. So if the one you want is sold out, just take a walk through the bric-à-brac shops of the nearby Village St. Paul and come back later.

SAINT-GERMAIN, LATIN QUARTER, PLACE D'ITALIE
5th and 13th arrondissements

GERARD BEAUFORT
(AU COIN GOURMAND)
6 Rue Linné, Paris 5.
Tel: 47.07.10.94.
Métro: Jussieu.
Open 7:30 A.M. to 8 P.M.
Closed Saturday, Sunday,
  and August.

An ordinary-looking bakery near the Rue des Boulangers, offering a marvelous assortment of serious breads: wonderful *baguettes au levain*, and *"Benoitons,"* rich, moist, rye bread chock full of honey, raisins and nuts. These breads are delicious plain or spread with a creamy Camembert or fresh chèvre. In addition to classic bakery fare—such as ultra-buttery *croissants* and *pains au chocolat*—Beaufort is always inventing new delicacies. When he offers *pain aux pépites de chocolat* (rich brioche spirals filled with chocolate chips), don't pass it up. Also try the *"weekend au citron,"* a round, *financier*-like cake, perfect in nice weather, as a sweet snack in the neighboring Jardin des Plantes.

BOULANGERIE
  BEAUVALLET &
  JULIEN
6 Rue de Poissy, Paris 5.
Tel: 43.26.94.24.
Métro: Maubert-Mutualité.
Open 7:15 A.M. to 8 P.M.
  Closed Wednesday and
  August.

A simple, old-fashioned boulangerie with a great *baguette* (a classic, with gentle crust and a delicious interior, or *mie*) and good *pain rustique*. Beauvallet supplies several neighborhood restaurants, including Dodin-Bouffant, Timonerie, and Vivario, down the street.

MICHEL BRUSA
16 Rue Mouffetard, Paris 5.
Tel: 47.07.06.36.
Métro: Censier-Daubenton
or Cardinale-Lemoine.
Open 7:30 A.M. to 7:30 P.M.
Closed Sunday afternoon
and Monday.

A short walk up from the Rue Mouffetard market, this tiny bakery on the Place de la Contrescarpe bakes tangy, moist sourdough *baguettes*,
the best in the neighborhood. Other breads here
are nothing special.

BOULANGERIE GARCIA
52 Boulevard Saint-
Germain, Paris 5.
Tel: 43.54.48.78.
Métro: Maubert-Mutualité.
Open 7 A.M. to 8 P.M. Closed
Sundays and either July
or August.

B oulangerie Garcia could be nick-named the
"Mitterrand bakery," for it's just down the street
from the medieval Rue de Bièvre, where the president of the Republic keeps an apartment. While
the president may not have time to buy his daily
bread, Madame Garcia did confide that a member
of President Mitterrand's staff comes in to buy the
dense, dark, crispy, extra-sour *baguette à l'ancienne*.
Pick one up to nibble on while strolling through
the market in Place Maubert (Tuesday, Thursday,
and Saturday; see Markets.) Be forewarned: They
always run out by 6 P.M., earlier on market days.
Aside from a delicious, lattice-topped mushroom
tart, the pastries here are unexceptional.

*Poujauran's special boutique
(see entry, page 251).*

PAIN DE MIE DENIS RUFFEL
DENIS RUFFEL'S SANDWICH LOAF

This is France's firm, fine-grained sandwich loaf: milky, just slightly sweet, and delicious when fresh and toasted. Denis Ruffel, from Pâtisserie Millet (see entry, page 223), the Left Bank pastry shop, manages to turn a single loaf of pain de mie *into an entire buffet, making dozens of tiny, highly decorated, open-face sandwiches. He'll top some with caviar or smoked salmon and lemon triangles, others with a blend of Roquefort, walnuts, and butter, and still others with thin slices of sausages topped with piped butter rosettes. The* mie, *by the way, is the crumb, or non-crusty portion of any bread, and since this bread has virtually no crust, it's called* pain de mie. *Some Paris bakers advertise* pain de mie au beurre, *to distinguish their bread from those made with margarine. The loaf is usually made in a special pan fitted with a sliding cover, which helps mold the bread into a tidy rectangle. The molds are available at many cookware shops, although the bread can be made in any straight-sided loaf pan. To obtain a neat rectangular loaf, cover the dough-filled loaf pan with foil and a baking sheet, then weight the sheet with a brick or other heavy object and bake.*

1 cup (250 ml) lukewarm milk

3 tablespoons unsalted butter (1½ oz; 45 g), at room temperature, plus 1 tablespoon (½ oz; 15 g) for buttering the bowl and loaf pan

1 tablespoon or 1 package active dry yeast

2 tablespoons sugar

2 teaspoons salt

2¾ cups (385 g) unbleached all-purpose flour

1. In a large bowl, combine the milk, the 3 tablespoons butter, yeast, and sugar, stir, and set aside for 5 minutes to proof the yeast.

2. Once proofed, stir in the salt, then add the flour, cup by cup, mixing well after each addition. Knead by hand for 2 or 3 minutes, or until the dough forms a smooth ball. Place in a well-buttered, large bowl (use some of the remaining 1 tablespoon butter) and cover securely with plastic wrap. Let rise in a warm place until double in bulk, approximately 1 to 1½ hours.

3. Butter a 6-cup (1.5-liter) loaf pan, or the mold and cover of a 6-cup (1.5-liter) *pain de mie* pan. If using a loaf pan, butter a piece of aluminum foil to use as a lid. Punch down the dough, knead for 1 minute, then transfer it to the pan or mold. Press down the dough smoothly, being sure it fills the corners, and cover. Let rise until double in bulk, another 1 to 1½ hours.

4. About 30 minutes before the dough is ready to be baked, preheat the oven to 375°F (190°C).

5. Bake until the loaf is golden brown, about 45 minutes. (If using a loaf pan cover with buttered foil and a baking sheet, then weight the sheet with a brick or other heavy object.) Unmold immediately and cool on a rack. The bread will stay fresh for several days, wrapped and stored at room temperature. *Pain de mie* also freezes well.

Yield: 1 loaf

**BOULANGERIE SYLVAIN
  HERVET**
69 Rue Monge, Paris 5.
Tel: 43.31.27.36.
Métro: Monge.
Open 7 A.M. to 8 P.M.,
  7 P.M. on Sundays.
Closed Monday and
  August.

An employee at a nearby bakery once confided that the best *pain au levain*—traditional sourdough bread—could be found "chez Madame Hervet". And on market days, the long line streaming out the door of this pretty *boulangerie* attests to the fact. If it is possible for a bakery to be frustrating, this one is, because the vast assortment of artisanal breads are all but hidden from view until you get right to the front of the line. And then you have to make your choice *"tout de suite"* or risk being scolded by the customer behind you. How to choose between a *baguette au levain* or one of their specialty breads, like the crusty *pain paillasse* or the *pain aux dix céréales*? Have it both ways: tuck the *baguette* under your arm and then pick a bagful of *petit pains* in every variety to sample on a walk through the Place Monge market. Stick with the bread here, the *croissants* are much better across the street at Pâtisserie Morin.

**BOULANGERIE
  MODERNE**
16 Rue des Fossés Saint-
  Jacques, Paris 5.
Tel: 42.54.12.22.
Métro: Cluny-la-Sorbonne
  or Luxembourg.
Open 7 A.M. to 8 P.M.
  Closed Saturday
  afternoon, Sunday, and
  Christmas week.

There's nothing modern about the Belle Epoque storefront of this tiny neighborhood *boulangerie* set on the active Place de l'Estrapade near the Panthéon. They sell an "American-style" *baguette* that tastes as though it's made with gluten-rich American flour. It's a neighborhood favorite, with a crisp crust and a denser than average, chewy interior.

**PLACE MAUBERT
MARKET**
Stall at Place Maubert.
Métro: Maubert-Mutualité.
Open 7 A.M. to 1 P.M.
Thursday and Saturday.

The Frenchman who tends this bake stand has never been to Portugal, but his stall offers unusual Portuguese specialties like crusty corn-bread and *"natas,"* tiny custard tarts with puff-pastry shells, made by Portuguese bakers outside Paris. This is also one of the only places in Paris to find German *folkenbrot*, a dense, almost wet whole-grain rye that keeps for days and is made from black rye flour imported from Germany. In addition to this international assortment, he also sells white *fougasse* and *pain de campagne*.

MAISON PLANE
53 bis Boulevard Arago,
Paris 13.
Tel: 47.07.14.58.
Métro: Glaçière.
Open 7:30 A.M. to 8 P.M.
Closed Wednesday and
Thursday.

Try to get here right about lunchtime, when the crisp and crunchy *petits pains* are fresh from the oven. Make a special trip to taste the *pain aux plantes*, a pungent, slightly crunchy, whole-grain bread seasoned with a range of herbs, including fennel, basil, chamomile, and thyme. This little neighborhood bakery also bakes beautiful *kougel-hopf*, a brand-name organic loaf, and good, if slightly underdone, *fougasse* and *baguette au levain*. And the helpful shopkeepers will put up with a barrage of questions about the multitude of breads.

J.C. VANDERSTICHEL
31 Boulevard Arago,
Paris 13.
Tel: 47.07.26.75.
Métro: Gobelins.
Open 6:30 A.M. to 8 P.M.
Closed Sunday, Monday,
and either July or
August.

Wonderful organic loaves come out of the oven around 11:00 A.M. at this simple, straightforward bakery, which also offers beautiful, classic *baguettes* and *ficelles*. Try the hearty, crusty *baguette biologique*—you won't regret it. They stuff their rich *pain au chocolat* with three bars of choco-lat instead of the usual two.

VIALARD
14 Rue Monge, Paris 5.
Tel: 43.54.31.21.
Métro: Maubert-Mutualité.
Open 7 A.M. to 8 P.M.,
7 A.M. to 7 P.M. on
Sunday. Closed Monday.

Young, friendly Chantal and Jean-Michel Vialard turn out a lovely assortment of hand-formed breads in their quaint, turn-of-the-century *boulangerie* and tea salon. Try the dense loaves of *pain au levain* (plain and with onions and bacon) and the *pain Rivaud*, a mix of rye and stone-ground whole wheat flour. Their *tarte à l'oignon*, spilling out with caramelized onions and *crème fraîche*, is one of Paris's best. For a rich switch from a *croissant*, try the *tresse au beurre,* a buttery braid of puff pastry.

PAIN POILANE AU LEVAIN NATUREL
POILANE'S NATURAL SOURDOUGH BREAD

I don't know anything that makes me prouder as a cook than to succeed with a fragrant, densely crusted loaf of sourdough bread, made—miraculously—with nothing but flour, water, and salt.

This is the recipe that Paris's most famous baker, Lionel Poilâne (see entry, page 250), created for the French housewife, and the closest I've come to re-creating his superb and popular loaf at home. I also call it "Patience Bread," because it takes almost a week to make the first batch of this natural, slightly sour loaf.

To bakers accustomed to the fast-acting whoosh one gets from yeast doughs, Poilâne's dough is a real sleeper. This dough really takes its time expanding, but the reward for your patience is a very fine-grained, mildly acidic, gentle loaf. It's the most subtle and delicious bread I know, at once sophisticated and countryish. When you bite into it, you'll say, "Now, this is bread!" A great crust, with a moist, chewy, wheaty-brown interior.

This newly updated recipe should offer a consistent loaf, with a vibrantly acidic interior and an irresistibly thick and chewy crust. If you love good bread, invest in a baking stone, and get into the habit of spraying the oven for the first few moments: The added humidity, along with the baking stone, works to create a beautifully dense crust and gives the bread better keeping qualities. Also, do not be fearful of baking in a very hot oven, for it's that initial high heat that helps the bread rise during the first 15 minutes.

Once you become comfortable with the process of sourdough bread, you can improvise, adding whole grains, a bit of whole-wheat flour, or other ground grains and flour, including rye, semolina, or cornmeal. Just be sure not to overdo it, or your starter will become heavy and less active. And no matter how many times you make sourdough bread, remember that no two loaves are ever exactly alike: That's part of their eternal charm.

Sourdough starter:
1 cup (250 ml) water, at
    room temperature
2 cups (280 g) bread flour

The final loaf:
3 cups (750 ml) water,
    at room temperature
1 tablespoon fine sea salt
5½ to 6 cups (980g to
    1 kg 120 g) bread
    flour

1. Days 1 to 4: In a small bowl combine ¼ cup (65 ml) of water and ½ cup (70 g) flour and stir until the water absorbs all of the flour and forms a soft dough. Transfer the dough to a lightly floured work surface and knead into a smooth ball. It should be fairly soft and sticky. Return the starter to the bowl, cover with plastic wrap and set aside at room temperature for 24 hours. The starter should rise slightly and take on a faintly acidic aroma. Repeat this for 3 more days, each day adding an additional ¼ cup (65 ml) of water and ½ cup (70 g) flour. Each day the starter should rise slightly and should become more acidic.

2. Day 5: You are ready to make bread. Transfer the starter to a large, shallow bowl, add the 3 cups (750 ml) of water, the 1 tablespoon salt, and, with a wire whisk, stir for about 1 minute to thoroughly dissolve the starter. Add the flour, a bit at a time, stirring well after each addition. After you have added about 5 cups (650 g) of flour, the dough should be firm enough to knead. Lightly flour a large, clean work surface, and transfer the dough to the floured surface. (If your bowl

is large and shallow enough, you can knead the bread right in the bowl, reducing cleanup later.) Begin kneading, at first folding the dough over itself to incorporate air (it may actually be too soft to knead), adding additional flour until the dough is nicely elastic and soft, but still firm enough to hold itself in a ball. Knead for a full 10 minutes. (Set a timer, to be sure there's no cheating!).

3. Form the loaf and reserve the starter: Pinch off a handful of dough, about 1 cup (250 g), to set aside for the next loaf. Transfer this starter to a medium-size covered container (see Note). Shape the remaining dough into a tight ball by folding it over itself. Place a large floured cloth in a round, shallow bowl or basket—one about 10 inches (25½ cm) wide works well—and place the dough, smooth (top) side down, in the cloth-lined bowl or basket. Loosely fold the cloth over the dough. Set aside at room temperature for 6 to 12 hours. (You have a lot of flexibility here. A 6-hour rise is the minimum, but I often prepare bread in the evening and bake it the next morning, allowing the dough to rise for up to 12 hours. I have even forgotten the bread, baking it 24 hours later, and it was deliciously light and airy.) The dough will rise very slowly, but a good loaf should just about double in size.

4. At least 40 minutes before placing the dough in the oven, preheat it—with a baking stone—to 500°F (260°C).

5. Lightly flour a baking peel or paddle (or a flat baking sheet), invert the loaf onto the peel, and slash the top of the bread several times with a razor blade to a depth of about ¼ inch (7 mm), so it can expand regularly during baking. With a quick jerk of the wrists, propel the bread onto the baking stone. Spray the bottom and sides of the oven with water. Spray 3 more times during the next 6 minutes. (The spray will help give the loaf a good crust, and will give the dough a boost during rising). The bread will rise very slowly, reaching its full height during the first 15 minutes of baking. Once the bread begins to brown nicely—after about 15 minutes—reduce the heat to 425°F (220°C) and continue baking until the crust is a deep, golden brown and the loaf sounds hollow when tapped, 35 to 40 minutes total. Transfer to a baking rack to cool. Do not slice the bread for at least 1 hour, for it will continue to bake as it rests. For best results, store the

bread in a paper or cloth bag once it is thoroughly cool. Plastic will tend to soften the dense crust you worked so hard to create. The bread should remain deliciously fresh for 3 to 4 days.

Note: After you have made your first loaf and have saved the starter, begin at step 2 for subsequent loaves. Proceed normally through the rest of the recipe, always remembering to save about 1 cup of the starter. The starter may be stored at room temperature (in a covered plastic container or in a bowl covered with a damp cloth) for 1 or 2 days, or refrigerated for up to 1 week. Reactivate the starter every week by adding ¼ cup (65 ml) of water and ½ cup (70 g) of flour. Do not use more than 1 cup (250 g) of starter per loaf. (If you find you can't bake bread every week and you end up with more than 1 cup starter, offer the excess to a friend, add it to a yeast dough, or—as a last resort—discard it.) If refrigerated, remove the starter from the refrigerator at least 2 hours before preparing the dough. Although starter can be frozen, I find it takes so long to reactivate, one might just as well begin with a new starter.

Yield: 1 loaf

The hearty Poilâne loaf.

SAINT-GERMAIN-DES-PRES, SEVRES-BABYLONE, LA TOUR-MAUBOURG

6th and 7th arrondissements

G. ABOT
(Les Delices de Sevres)
70 Rue de Sèvres, Paris 7.
Tel: 47.34.65.88.
Métro: Duroc or Vaneau.
Open: 6:30 A.M. to 9 P.M.
  Closed Monday.

In the 18th century, France's famed storyteller La Fontaine used to walk through this neighborhood to read fables to his *patronnesse*, Madame de la Sablière. Her nearby *hôtel particulier* has since been destroyed, but Monsieur Guy Abot, whose modern workshop occupies its former courtyard, seems to have inherited the storytelling tradition. He loves to talk about his bread, and the sheer variety of *baguettes* here makes a story in itself. His latest creation, the *baguette aux olives de Nyons*, boasts a thick, brown crust and airy inside stained with black olives macerated in olive oil. This joins ranks with a golden, crisp, classic white *baguette*, a wholewheat *baguette* and two different kinds of *baguette au levain*—one white and one with stone-ground flour. Anyone tempted to try everything can sample most of the breads in pretty *petit pains*, which also come topped with hazelnuts, Gruyère, cumin, or poppy seeds. Once Monsieur Abot finds a great thing, he can't seem to get enough of it: He also turns out three different kinds of *pain de mie*—plain white, "enriched" with butter, and an airy *pain feuilleté*, perfect for cocktail canapés. Olive fans should also sample the moist rye loaf stuffed with black olives. If you're not too overloaded with bread, head down the street to the Maison du Fromage at No. 62 Rue de Sèvres for one of the better cheese selections in Paris, and you'll be set for a perfect picnic. (See Cheese Shops.)

GERARD MULOT
76 Rue de Seine, Paris 6.
Tel: 43.26.85.77 or
  46.33.49.27.
Métro: Odéon.
Open 7 A.M. to 8 P.M.
  Closed Wednesday and
  either July or August.

Gérard Mulot has moved his marvelous bakery around the corner—from Rue Lobineau to more spacious quarters in the Rue de Seine—but the quality hasn't budged an inch. This is the place to find what may be Paris's best *brioche*, almost muffin-like, topped with caramelized brown sugar and popping with raisins. They often run out before noon, so be there early, and take home a crusty loaf of *pain au levain* (sourdough bread made with natural yeast) for later in the day. Unlike many *pains au levain*, this bread has a light, airy texture that doesn't weigh you down. The pretty *baguette rustique*, however, doesn't live up to its earthy exterior. Opt instead for the crusty, moist rye raisin buns. Mulot's buttery *croissants* and *pains au chocolat* are so good that they're the breakfast of senators at the nearby Senate in the Palais du Luxembourg.

LIONEL POILANE
8 Rue du Cherche-Midi,
Paris 6.
Tel:45.48.42.59.
Métro: Sèvres-Babylone or
Saint-Sulpice.
Open 7:15 A.M. to 8:15 P.M.
Closed Sunday.

The line flows out the door at Poilâne.

Pain Poilâne . . . need one say more? There is no question that Lionel Poilâne makes the most famous bread in France, perhaps the world. Thousands of Parisians buy his moist sourdough loaf every day. It's sold at more than 600 shops around Paris and more than 300 restaurants. Each day, airplanes take off for Manhattan and Tokyo, delivering fresh-baked loaves for those willing to pay a very steep price. Each giant, round, wholesome loaf is made with a pungent sourdough starter, all-French flour, and fragrant sea salt. Each is formed by hand, rising in rustic—yet practical—fabric-lined wicker baskets. The loaves are baked in wood-fired ovens, one of which was built by the *patron* himself. But Poilâne bread is far from perfect, as Monsieur Poilâne readily admits. "People complain that it is uneven," he notes, suggesting that "with *levain*, that's the name of the game. No two batches are ever the same; a simple storm can ruin an entire baking." And he's right. There are days Poilâne bread is so dry, so lacking in authority and flavor, you know something's gone wrong. I've also tasted the bread so rich, dense, so properly acidic and authoritative, that every other loaf, before or after, pales by comparison. Criticism aside, no one's yet attempted to meet the Poilâne challenge. Rarely imitated—never successfully—he remains *"le roi du pain."* The Poilâne loaf has set the contemporary standard for bread, the loaf against which almost all others are judged (see recipe, page 246). Other delicacies include some of the best apple *tartelettes* in Paris—caramelized apples in a rich cloud of buttery puff pastry—and buttery baby *sablés* in a basket at the front of the shop.

Visitors to the family shop on Rue du Cherche-Midi are almost always welcome to visit the wonderfully fragrant, flour-dusted cellar, to watch the famous bread being mixed, kneaded, and baked in the ancient wood-burning oven set beneath the street. Large and personalized *pain décoré* can be ordered several days in advance. On busy Saturday afternoons, the proprietors often pass out butter cookies to soothe those waiting in line!

POUJAURAN
20 Rue Jean-Nicot, Paris 7.
Tel: 47.05.80.88.
Métro: La Tour-Maubourg.
Open 8:30 A.M. to 8:30 P.M.
  Closed Sunday and
  Monday.

Baker Jean-Luc with his antique delivery truck.

Jean-Luc Poujauran—an energetic, idealistic baker—claims he was the first in Paris to turn out a *baguette biologique*, made with organically grown, stone-ground, all-French flour. That was years ago, and his honey-colored, dense, and chewy *baguette* is unquestionably one of the best in Paris, a standard against which all others can be judged. A native of the rich and rustic southwest, Monsieur Poujauran is always trying new ideas: He once made a *biologique croissant*, using organic eggs, butter and flour, in memory of his grandmother, who brought him up on pure and healthy foods. He's the sort of young man who inspires confidence: When he was first starting out and had little money, faithful customers chipped in to help him buy his first bread mixer. Try Poujauran's earthy sourdough *pain de campagne*, along with the delightful and delicious pastries that fill this charming turn-of-the-century *boulangerie*. High-quality French pastry and bread flour can also be purchased in the shop.

LES GRANDS BOULEVARDS
8th and 9th arrondissements

CARON
26 Rue du Faubourg
  Montmartre, Paris 9.
Tel: 47.70.33.70.
Métro: Le Peletier or Rue
  Montmartre.
Open 7 A.M. to 7:30 P.M.
  Closed Wednesday,
  Thursday, and August.

Stop by as much for the show as for the bread at this cute bakery with beamed ceilings and a kitschy, country look. Caron is one of the few bakeries in Paris with a wood-burning oven right in the shop, so you can watch the baker slit *baguettes* and then slide them off his *pelle* into the fire. Piles of wicker bread baskets add to the ambience. Pick up an organic, whole-grain baguette or a pretty *couronne* of *pain au levain* and then walk to the nearby shop, La Mère de la Famille for some old-fashioned jams and chocolates. (See Specialty Shops.)

JULIEN
73 Avenue Franklin D.
  Roosevelt, Paris 8.
Tel: 43.59.78.76.
Métro: Saint-Philippe-
  du-Roule.
Open 7:30 A.M. to 7:30 P.M.
  Closed Saturday.

There's always a line out the door at this popular bakery and pastry shop, where office workers of the *quartier* seem to spend a good portion of their day, lunching in the back room or waiting to sample the breads or pastries. Their superbly classic *baguette* is dense, chewy, properly crisp (one could easily polish off a loaf without noticing it was gone). Stop in for a crisp, buttery *croissant* or *pain au chocolat*, fresh from the oven several times a day and delicious with a strong *café crème* at the bar. I'm also a big fan of their delightful lemon tart, *tarte au citron*.

BAGUETTES

The crackling-crisp, slender *baguette*—the name comes from the French for wand—is not as old as some people think. And it wasn't born; it evolved essentially out of consumer demand. According to Raymond Calvel, one of France's more respected bread experts, the *baguette* came into being just before World War I, when the classic French loaf had two shapes: the round *miche,* weighing about 5 pounds (2.5 kilos), and the *pain long,* an 8-inch by 30-inch (20.5-cm by 76-cm) loaf of the same weight. The *mie,* or interior, of the *pain long* was dense and heavy, the crust crisp and flavorful. Most consumers preferred the crust and bakers accommodated, making the bread thinner and thinner to obtain maximum crust, reducing the loaf's volume until they came up with the traditional 30-inch (760-cm) *baguette,* weighing 8 ounces (250 grams).

Other historians suggest that the *baguette* evolved from the *viennois,* a long, thin Austrian-type loaf popular around the turn of the century. The loaf has the same form as the *baguette,* but the dough is sweetened with sugar and softened with milk.

FAUBOURG SAINT-ANTOINE, BASTILLE, REPUBLIQUE

11th and 12th arrondissements

L'AUTRE BOULANGE
43 Rue de Montreuil,
Paris 12.
Tel: 43.72.86.04.
Métro: Faidherbe-Chaligny
or Nation.
Open 7:30 A.M. to 1:30 P.M.
and 4 to 7:30 P.M.
Monday through
Saturday. Closed
Saturday afternoon,
Sunday, and August.

Take a trek down this dingy side street to *pain au levain* heaven. Monsieur and Madame Cousin offer a mind-boggling array of breads, all *au levain,* fresh from the wood-fired oven in the back of this cozy shop (they'll let you take a look if they're not too busy). In addition to baking crusty, super-sour *pain au levain* and rye bread, they turn out exceptional specialty breads found nowhere else in Paris, like a state-of-the-art sourdough bread with Emmenthal cheese and walnuts: a moist *brioche* egg dough practically melting with an Emmenthal crust and a cheesy, nutty interior— it's amazing toasted. Also sample the whole-wheat prune and raisin bread, a perfect *roquefort fougasse* (it also comes plain and with olives, onions, bacon, and other whims of the baker), organic whole-wheat bread, or rye with orange zest to name a few. These hearty breads keep well for several days, so don't worry about buying too much! At lunchtime you can choose from the list of thirty different sandwiches served on a variety of specialty breads. An aspiring baker from the United States came here to learn how to use a wood-fired oven, and in return, she taught the Cousins how to make delicious, not-too-sweet chocolate chip cookies—just in case you're feeling homesick.

JACQUES BAZIN
85 bis Rue de Charenton,
    Paris 12.
Tel: 43.07.75.21.
Métro: Ledru-Rollin.
Open 7 A.M. to 8 P.M. Closed
    Wednesday, Thursday,
    and August.

A ten-minute walk from the ultra-modern Opéra Bastille, this turn-of-the-century bakery reassures you that *"la vieille Paris"* is still alive and well. Bazin bakes a beautiful and unusual medley of breads (all *au levain*), like rye with almonds, hazelnuts, walnuts, and raisins; *petits-pains* filled with apple or mimolette cheese; and a moist, crusty whole-grain *pain bûcheron*, baked with a crunchy mix of rye and whole-wheat flours and sunflower seeds. It's a short walk away from the lively street market in the Place d'Aligre. (See Markets.) The tiny, historic bakery is so beautiful, it's even appeared as a stage set in French advertisements.

JACQUES DUBOS
103 Avenue Parmentier,
    Paris 11.
Tel: 42.57.53.27.
Métro: Parmentier.
Open 7 A.M. to 8 P.M.
    Closed Sunday.

If you're looking for a great, classic *baguette*—dense, chewy, heavy—to go with your *charcuterie*, to prepare a ham and cheese sandwich, or simply to eat "as is," stop by this solid neighborhood boulangerie. This is also the place to find a lacy, flour-dusted *fougasse*. The *baguette campagnotte* (sourdough), *pain de seigle au froment* (rye and whole wheat) are delicious when fresh, but they get soggy later in the day.

BOULANGERIE FERET
149 Rue du Faubourg
    Saint-Antoine, Paris 11.
Tel: 43.46.02.08.
Métro: Ledru-Rollin.
Open 7 A.M. to 8 P.M.
    Closed Sunday and
    either July or August.

An ordinary bakery offering fabulous country loaves, or crusty and soul-satisfying *pain de campagne*, which I discovered while lunching at Le Passage, a nearby wine bar worth the detour. (See Wine Bars).

This *boulangerie* between Place de la République and the Bastille turns out some of the prettiest *baguettes au levain* (sourdough *baguettes*) in Paris— flour-dusted, golden brown, and shaped like a blade of wheat. Tear off one of the corners, bite into this tangy bread, and you won't be disappointed. Monsieur Pascal Robert also bakes a moist, chewy sourdough rye loaf and a panoply of specialty breads including *pain aux algues* (seaweed bread) and sourdough bread with onions or bacon. The *gougères* here merit a detour. At most bakeries these Gruyère cheese puffs (a specialty of Burgundy) come out dry, airy, and lifeless, but here they are dense, moist, and cheesy on the inside with a crisp crust of grated cheese.

DECORATED BREAD

One of the most beautiful and festive breads in Paris is the *pain décoré*, generally a large, round, decorated loaf that is personalized with one's name, a favorite symbol or saying, or most classically, a bunch of grapes or sheaves of wheat. The following *boulangeries* will prepare decorated breads to order, though all must be ordered in advance. The breads, by the way, are not simply decorative, they're edible when fresh.

Lenôtre, 3 and 5 Rue du Havre, Paris 9. (45.22.22.59); 49 Avenue Victor-Hugo, Paris 16. (45.01.71.71); 44 Rue d'Auteuil, Paris 16. (45.24.52.52); 121 Avenue de Wagram, Paris 17. (47.63.70.30). Three days in advance.

Lionel Poilâne, 8 Rue du Cherche-Midi, Paris 6. (45.48.42.59). Two days in advance.

Max Poilâne, 87 Rue Brançion, Paris 15. (48.28.45.90). Two days in advance.

BIR-HAKEIM, MONTPARNASSE, PORTE DE VANVES, PLAISANCE

14th and 15th arrondissements

L'EPI GAULOIS
23 bis Boulevard Brune,
    Paris 15.
Tel: 45.39.34.18.
Métro: Porte-de-Vanves.
Open 8 A.M. to 8:30 P.M.
    Tuesday through Saturday
    and 9 A.M. to 8:30 P.M.
    Sunday and Monday.
    Closed in August.

LE MOULIN DE LA
    VIERGE
105 Rue Vercingétorix,
    Paris 14.
Tel: 45.43.09.84.
Métro: Pernéty or
    Plaisance.
Open 7:30 A.M. to 8 P.M.
    Closed Sunday, Monday,
    and August.

This funny little modern shop, opening out onto the busy Boulevard Brune, offers a great rye bread—dense, crusty, chewy—and a good six-cereal bread, *pain aux six céréales*. Worth a visit on market day, each Thursday and Sunday along the boulevard.

A passion for bread is the only explanation for Basile Kamir's extraordinary and creative variety of bread. A bite into one of his sourdough loaves reminds you that this is what bread should taste like: moist and slightly tangy on the inside, surrounded by a thick, earthy crust. Monsieur Kamir's delicious, dense, golden country bread, baked with organically grown wheat is some of the best in town. Come here to find a perfect *fougasse*—crispy and golden on the outside with a rich, olive and anchovy interior (it also comes plain and with a variety of other fillings). The moist sourdough rye bread dons a crater-like crust that seems to erupt with walnuts and flour (it also comes plain and with raisins). Do try the simple and unusual provincial pastry specialties like the *carré dijonnaise*, a sandwich of brown-butter *sablés* that resemble rich graham crackers filled with raspberry jam; the *galette charentaise* (an overgrown wheel of melt-in-your-mouth butter *galette* doused with almonds) or the *canelé* (sweet miniature molded butter cakes, a specialty of Bordeaux). There is nothing fancy here and there doesn't need to be. The old-fashioned, turn-of-the-century bakery sits as a historical monument in the middle of block after block of impersonal, modern high-rise buildings at the southern edge of town. Don't give up trying to find it!

LE MOULIN DE LA VIERGE
82 Rue Daguerre, Paris 14.
Tel: 43.22.50.55.
Métro: Gaîté.
Open 8 A.M. to 7:30 P.M.
Closed Sunday, Monday, and August.

Monsieur Kamir's shop along the Rue Daguerre occupies a pretty, old-fashioned bakery a few blocks down from the popular Rue Daguerre market.

LE MOULIN DE LA VIERGE
166 Avenue de Suffren, Paris 15.
Tel: 47.83.45.55.
Métro: Cambronne.
Open 7:30 A.M. to 8 P.M.
Closed Sunday and August.

See above listings.

A BREAD MUSEUM

The Musée Français du Pain, installed in the *grenier* (grain loft) of a still active flour mill just southeast of Paris at the edge of the Bois de Vincennes, is like a toy store for bread lovers. Thousands of bread-related trinkets and memorabilia line the spotless rooms that are filled with cartoons and drawings, carefully preserved bread boards and knives, wicker rising baskets and shiny copper molds—all there to celebrate the nobility of bread in history. There are façades and signs from Belle Epoque bakers; Saint-Honoré, the 7th-century "patron saint" of bakers, is represented paddle in hand; there are 17th-century metal molds, designed for making hosts used for religious celebrations; fascinating tin spice-cookie molds, ancient bread-related manuscripts, as well as miniature models of brick-lined, wood-fired ovens.

Musée Français du Pain, 25 bis Rue Victor-Hugo, 94220 Charenton-le-Pont. (43.68.43.60). Métro: Charenton-Ecoles. Open 2 to 4 P.M. Tuesday and Thursday. Closed July and August.

LIONEL POILANE
49 Boulevard de Grenelle,
    Paris 15.
Tel: 45.79.11.49.
Métro: Bir-Hakeim or
    Grenelle.
Open 7:15 A.M. to 8:15 P.M.
Closed Monday.

MAX POILANE
87 Rue Brancion, Paris 15.
Tel: 48.28.45.90.
Métro: Porte de Vanves.
Open 7:15 A.M. to 8 P.M.
    Monday through
    Saturday. Closed
    Sunday. In July and
    August; 7:30 A.M. to
    1:30 P.M. Saturday.

S ee listing, 6th *arrondissement*.

M ax Poilâne's original 15th *arrondissement* bakery is worth a detour: The charming turn-of-the-century shop, with its marble floors, glistening chandelier, and beautiful, crusty loaves arranged like still lifes in wicker baskets around the room, is one of the most romantic little *boulangeries* in town.

*A Ganachaud assortment
(see entry, page 265).*

THE DAILY LOAF

T he following are just a few breads—of various sizes, flours, *fantaisie* shapes—found in the Parisian *boulangerie*.

Baguette: in Paris, this is legally a loaf weighing about 8 ounces (250 grams) and made from flour water, and yeast. It may also contain fava bean flour and ascorbic acid, or vitamin C. *Baguettes* dusted with flour may be sold as *baguette de campagne, baguette à l'ancienne,* or *baguette paysanne.* There are also two "brand name" *baguettes,* the Belle Epoque and the Banette, sold in various bakeries. The bakers guarantee that these are made without the addition of fava bean flour or ascorbic acid, and are made according to old-fashioned methods.

Baguette au levain: (also sold by other names, sometimes called **baguette à l'ancienne**): sourdough *baguette.*

Boule: ball, or round loaf, either small or large.

Chapeau: small round loaf, topped with a little *chapeau,* or hat.

Couronne: ring-shaped *baguette.*

Le fer à cheval: horseshoe-shaped *baguette.*

Ficelle: very thin, crusty *baguette.*

Fougasse: generally, a crusty, flat rectangular-shaped, lacy bread made of *baguette* dough; can be filled with onions, herbs, spices, or anchovies, or can be made of puff pastry dough.

Miche: large round country-style loaf.

Pain de campagne: there is no legal definition for the country loaf, which can vary from a white bread simply dusted with flour to give it a rustic look (and fetch a higher price) to a truly hearty loaf that may be a blend of white, whole wheat, and perhaps rye flour with added bran. It comes in every shape, from a small round individual roll to a large family loaf.

Pain complet: bread made partially or entirely from whole-wheat flour, with bakers varying proportions according to their personal tastes.

Pain de fantaisie: generally, any odd or imaginatively shaped bread. Even *baguette de campagne* falls into the *fantaisie* category.

Pain de mie: the rectangular white sandwich loaf that is nearly all *mie* (interior crumb), and very little crust. It is made for durability, its flavor and texture developed for use in sandwiches. Unlike most French breads, it contains milk, sugar, and butter, and may contain chemical preservatives.

Pain aux noix and *pain aux noisettes:* bread, most often rye or wheat, filled with walnuts or hazelnuts.

Pain polka: bread that is slashed in a criss-cross pattern; usually a large country loaf cut in this manner.

Pain aux raisins: bread, most often rye or wheat, filled with raisins.

Pain de seigle: bread made from 60 to 70 percent rye flour and 30 to 40 percent wheat flour.

Pain de son: legally, a dietetic bread that is quality-controlled, containing 20 percent bran mixed with white flour.

Pain viennois: shaped like a *baguette*, with regular horizontal slashes, this loaf usually contains white flour, sugar, powdered milk, water, and yeast.

MAX POILANE
29 Rue de l'Ouest, Paris 14.
Tel: 43.27.24.91.
Métro: Montparnasse
    or Gaîté.
Open 8:30 A.M. to 7:30 P.M.
    Closed Sunday.

Sophie Poilâne, daughter of Max, has opened a boulangerie on the modern Place Constantin Brancusi. Her shop is a lovely place to come for breakfast before or after the train at the Gare Montparnasse. Despite the jarringly modern neighborhood, this bakery makes every effort at old-fashioned charm—from the marble tables and good *café crème* served with pitchers of steamed milk to the little gourmet gifts like homemade jams, apple cider, bon-bons and boxes of *madeleines de Commercy*. They also serve sandwiches on *pain Poilâne*, perfect to take away for a snack on the train.

Lacy fougasse on display.

SAIBRON
4 Place Constantin
Brancusi, Paris 14.
Tel: 43.21.76.18.
Métro: Montparnasse
or Gaîté.
Open 7:30 A.M. to 7:30 P.M.
Closed Sunday and
Monday.

Located just across the street from Max Poilâne, Monsieur Saibron knows he has stiff competition and makes the extra effort that pays off in high-quality bread. So if you only have a few minutes before or after catching a train at nearby Gare Montparnasse, stop in to sample their *pains fermiers*: breads prepared with stone-ground flour and natural yeast. In addition to their specialty, an olive oil "enriched" *fougasse*, they bake an excellent sourdough *baguette au levain*; moist, mini-triangles of rye-raisin bread; whole-wheat *baguettes*; and crisp, flour-dusted *couronnes* (rings) of *pain de campagne*. The oven is in the shop, so if you have time to spare, you can watch the bakers at work.

VICTOR-HUGO, AUTEUIL

16th arrondissement

LA GRIGNOTIERE
84 Rue de Lauriston,
Paris 16.
Tel: 47.27.90.21.
Métro: Boissière or
Victor Hugo.
Open 7 A.M. to 8 P.M. Closed
Saturday afternoon,
Sunday, and July or
August.

The *pain "Vieille France"* at La Grignotière is a fancified, 16th *arrondissement* name for what other bakeries call *pain paillasse*, a crusty, whitish, country sourdough bread. This is one of the few bakeries in Paris to offer pretty, meringue-coated lady finger *vacherin* molds, ready to take home and fill with ice cream, fruit, chocolate mousse, or whatever combination you may dream up—a great idea for a party.

ARC DE TRIOMPHE, PORTE MAILLOT, VILLIERS

17th arrondissement

AUX ARMES DE NIEL
29 Avenue Niel, Paris 17.
Tel 47.63.62.01.
Métro: Ternes.
Open 6:30 A.M. to 8:30 P.M.
Monday, and
Wednesday through
Saturday; 6:30 A.M. to
1:30 P.M. and 4 to 8 P.M.
Sunday. Closed Tuesday
and August.

For a good, solid sourdough *baguette* ask for a *ficelle au levain* with a deep and dark brown crust, a yeasty aroma, and honey-colored interior. They also sell huge, round, beautiful decorative loaves made to order.

Satisfied customer, Moulin de la Vierge (see entry, page 256).

BOULANGERIE BELEM
47 Rue Boursault, Paris 17.
Tel: 45.22.38.95.
Métro: Rome.
Open 10 A.M. to 8 P.M.
  Closed Monday and
  August.

The Portuguese make some of the most mar-velous bread in the world, and here, tucked away in a working-class corner of the 17th *arrondissement*, you'll find some classic Portuguese corn bread—dense, delicious round loaves, great to slice for grilling and coating with sweet butter. Take note: The corn bread is baked only on Friday, Saturday, and Sunday. The ordinary bread here is unexceptional. But if you arrive on a non-corn bread day, don't leave without trying the delicious *natas*, miniature puff pastry tartlets filled with lemon vanilla custard. The cute, tiled shop displays maps of Portugal and bottles of Porto for sale.

BOULANGERIE COUASNON
21 Rue de Lévis, Paris 17.
Tel: 43.87.28.27.
Métro: Villiers.
Open 7 A.M. to 8 P.M.
Tuesday through
Saturday; 7 A.M. to
1:30 P.M. and 3 to 7:30 P.M.
Sunday. Closed Monday
and either July or
August.

T he loaves of incredibly crusty *pain paillasse* (an unmolded, stone-shaped country bread) piled high in the front window beckon you inside and don't disappoint—break open the golden, crisp shell to reveal a moist, white sourdough interior.

GOUDENHOOFT
59 Avenue des Ternes,
Paris 17.
Tel: 45.74.27.14.
Métro: Ternes.
Open 7 A.M. to 8 P.M. Closed
Wednesday and either
July or August.

G oudenhooft has crossed over to the Right Bank from its old Rue de Grenelle shop. Now located in between the Place des Ternes and Porte Maillot, it makes a welcome addition to a neighborhood where there aren't enough good bakeries to go around. Their *baguettes au levain* are beautiful and crusty. Also try their specialty, *pâte bourbonnaise:* This picture-perfect *tarte* filled with potatoes, *crème fraîche* and chives (or filled with mushrooms) on buttery *pâte feuilletée.*

MONTMARTRE, BARBES-ROCHECHOUART
18th arrondissement

BLONDEAU
(La Petite Charlotte)
24 Rue des Abbesses,
Paris 18.
Tel: 46.06.18.77.
Métro: Abbesses.
Open 6:30 A.M. to 8 P.M.
Closed Sunday
afternoon, Monday, and
August.

A t the foot of Montmartre, walk down the bustling street market along Rue Lepic to Blondeau for hearty homemade breads that will fill you with enough energy to climb the hill up to Sacré-Coeur. Their *pain sportif* mixes at least ten different grains, including soy-bean flour, pumpkin seed, and linseed into a whole-wheat base filled with raisins and nuts. They also bake a homey *"triple alliance"* loaf, a wheat bread mixed with linseed and sesame seeds. On weekends they offer specialties such as olive bread.

Blondeau may not bake the best bread in Paris, but this is definitely the best in the neighborhood. The pastries and tea salon fare, however, are soggy and unexceptional. Do take the time to admire the nearby Place des Abbesses, which boasts one of Paris's last remaining Art Nouveau

Métro stations designed by Hector Guimard. Despite the hordes of tourists, this sunny neighborhood overlooking all of Paris retains an old-fashioned feeling.

AU PAIN D'ANTAN
2 Rue Eugène Sue, Paris 18.
Tel: 42.64.71.78.
Métro: Marcadet-
  Poissonniers.
Open 7 A.M. to 1 P.M. and
  3:30 to 7:30 P.M. Monday
through Thursday;
7 A.M. to 7:30 P.M. Friday
and Saturday. Closed
Sunday and August.

Literally "bread from bygone days," this homey *boulangerie* is run by Jacques Sousa, who bakes the best bread in the 18th *arrondissement* and some of the best sourdough bread in Paris. His brick-lined oven, dating from the 1920s, turns out a small but delicious selection of hearty, old-fashioned breads: dark, crusty loaves of sourdough and rye sourdough rounds with or without nuts and raisins. Try their specialty: *fouace aveyronnaise*, a butter-enriched *brioche* from the center of France.

BOSTOCK BERNARD GANACHAUD

Bostock is a terrific way to recycle day-old brioche, *which on its own is already quite marvelous. Bernard Ganachaud, one of my favorite Parisian bakers, now retired, kindly shared the recipe for this kirsch-and-almond-flavored pastry. Superb fresh from the oven, bostock is still delicious a few days later. Eat it for breakfast or dessert. (See Ganachaud entry, facing page.)*

1¼ cups (170 g) whole
  almonds
1 cup (250 ml) water
1⅜ cups (275 g) sugar
10 slices day-old *brioche*
2 large eggs
3 tablespoons kirsch *eau-*
  de-vie (cherry brandy)

1. Preheat the oven to 375°F (190°C).

2. Toast the almonds on a baking sheet until browned, about 5 minutes. Remove but leave the oven on. When cooled, grind ¾ cup (100 g) of the almonds to a fine powder in a food processor. Coarsely chop the remaining almonds.

3. In a medium-size saucepan over medium heat, combine the water and ⅝ cup (125 grams) sugar and stir until dissolved. Remove the syrup from the heat.

4. Dip the slices of *brioche* in the syrup and drain them on a wire rack. Once drained, arrange the slices on a baking sheet.

5. In a small mixing bowl combine the eggs, finely ground almonds, and remaining sugar and blend to a thick paste. Spread the mixture on the *brioche*.

6. Sprinkle the *brioche* with kirsch, then the coarsely chopped almonds. Bake for 15 minutes or until golden brown.

Yield: 10 servings

MENILMONTANT, PYRENEES

20th arrondissement

A LA FLUTE GANA
226 Rue des Pyrénées,
    Paris 20.
Tel: 43.58.42.62.
Métro: Pyrénées.
Open 7:30 A.M. to 1:30 P.M.
    and 2:30 to 8 P.M. Closed
    Sunday, Monday, and
    July or August.

Isabelle and Valérie Ganachaud—daughters of Bernard Ganachaud, one of the city's legendary bakers—offer an incredible assortment of first-class bread. Try the *"flûtes Gana,"* which are irresistibly crusty and thin *baguettes*, breads stuffed with raisins and hazelnuts, country breads enriched with wheat germ, and an assortment prepared with organic, or *biologique*, flours.

GANACHAUD
150–154 Rue Ménil-
    montant, Paris 20.
Tel: 46.36.13.82.
Métro: Pelleport.
Open 2:30 to 8 P.M.
    Tuesday; 7:30 A.M.
    to 8 P.M. Wednesday
    through Saturday; 7:30
    A.M. to 1:30 P.M. Sunday.
    Closed Monday and
    August.

The great Bernard Ganachaud has retired, but his successor, Monsieur Jeudon, continues in a fine tradition, offering more than thirty different breads, all kneaded by hand. Definitely worth a detour.

Bread by the armful is almost a one-day supply for an enthusiastic eater.

Fromageries
CHEESE SHOPS

Fromagerie de Montmartre (see entry, page 283).

If all France had to offer to the world of gastronomy was bread, cheese, and wine, that would be enough for me. Of the trinity, it is cheese that links one to the other. I cannot imagine a more understated, unified French meal than one perfectly fresh *baguette*, a single Camembert, so ripe and velvety it won't last another hour, and a glass or two of young, fruity, well-balanced red wine. And I can't imagine a better place to discover French cheese than in Paris, where dozens of *fromageries* line the streets, each shop as different and distinctive as the personality of its owner, each offering selections that vary with the seasons.

Only the French produce so many varieties of cheese, so graphically reflecting their regional landscape and the many kinds of soil, climate, and vegetation. From the milk of cows, goats, and sheep; from the green, flat lands of Normandy, the steep mountain Alps, and the plains of Champagne east of Paris comes a veritable symphony of aromas, textures, colors, and forms. Cheese fresh from little farms and big cooperatives, cheese to begin the day and to end it. The French consume a great deal of cheese—about forty-two pounds per capita per year, compared to the American's twenty pounds—and of all the varieties, Camembert is the undisputed favorite.

How many varieties of French cheese are there, really? The French are not a people given to simple agreement. When Winston Churchill said, "A country that produces 325 varieties of cheese can't be governed," he was, undoubtedly, responding to a bit of cheese hype. The real figure, say experts, is more like 150 to 200 serious varieties, with perhaps an additional 100 cheeses that are minor variations.

There's an old *New Yorker* magazine cartoon that describes the confusion perfectly: An elderly woman is sitting on the sofa, poring over maps of France. She looks up at her husband and says: "Has it ever occurred to you, dear, that most of the villages and towns in France seem to have been named after cheeses?"

Don't let anyone convince you that the cheese you eat in France and the French cheese you eat in the United States are necessarily the same. A major reason they don't taste the same has to do with United States Department of Agriculture regulations barring the importation of cheese made from unpasteurized milk that has been aged less than sixty days. Pasteurization may make cheese "safe," but in the process it kills all the microbes that give the cheese its character and flavor, that keep it a live, ever-changing organism. There is no question that pasteurized milk produces uniformly bland, "dead" cheese. The regulation rules out the importation of France's finest fresh young cheese, including raw-milk Camembert and Brie, and the dozens of varieties of lively, delicate goat cheese, although on occasion a few may slip through.

Yet even in France, cheese made from pasteurized milk is increasingly common. For instance, less than 5 percent of the 160,000 tons of Camembert produced in France each year is made from raw milk. The advantage, of course, is that cheese made with pasteurized milk can be made available year-round, and will have more stable keeping qualities. When in France, take the time to get a true taste of fresh French cheese: Specify raw-milk cheese by asking for *fromage fermier* or *au lait cru*. These cheeses are produced in limited quantities, the result of traditional production methods.

Paris has dozens of *fromageries* that specialize in raw-milk cheese, with some shops offering as many as 200 different varieties. Before living in Paris I thought that cheese merchants only bought and sold cheese. Wrong. The best, most serious cheese people actually age the cheese they sell. That is, they buy the cheese ready-made from the farmer, then, following a sensitive and tricky aging process, they take the cheese from its young, raw state to full maturity, refining the cheese in underground cellars that are usually humid and cold. The process is called *affinage*, and it can last from days to months, depending on the cheese. As each cheese matures, it takes on its own personality, influenced by the person responsible for its development. Maturing cheese needs daily attention: Some varieties are washed with beer, some with a blend of salt and water, some with *eau-de-vie*. Some are turned every day, moved from one cellar to another as the aging process continues. Each merchant has his own style of aging, and there are varying opinions on how cold and how humid the cellar should be; whether the cheese should be aged on clean straw or old straw, paper, or even plastic; or whether the cheese should be turned daily or just every now and then. And each merchant has a different opinion on when a cheese is ripe, and thus ready to be put on sale.

I adore watching the dedicated *fromagers*, whose love for cheese is totally infectious. In their cellars they are in heaven, as they vigorously inhale the heady, pungent aromas that fill the air and give the cheese little "love taps," the same way bakers give their unbaked loaves a tender touch before putting them in the oven. Now, having toured most of the various aging cellars that exist beneath the streets of the city, I see what a single individual can do to change the course of a cheese's life, ultimately determining taste and texture. Henry Voy's cheese, from La Ferme Saint-Hubert, has a lusty, almost over-the-hill quality about it that at times can be quite appealing. Cheeses from Alléosse are refined and elegant, always in perfect, presentable shape.

A few words on selecting cheese: Be sensitive to the seasons. For instance, don't expect to find Vacherin in the middle of summer. When in doubt, ask to know the seasonal specialties in a given shop. In selecting cheese for a *dégustation* (a cheese tray or sample selection for tasting) either at home or in a restaurant, choose three or four varieties, generally including a semi-soft cheese, a goat cheese, and a blue. Eat the mild cheese first, then move on to the stronger varieties.

Be wary of cheese wrapped in plastic. Like us, cheese has to breathe to maintain life and vigor. Don't be afraid of a bit of mold. Generally the bluish film on goat's milk cheese is a sign that the cheese is made with raw milk and has been ripened on fresh straw. Cheese that won't mold, and won't spoil, is already too dead to bother about.

Be open-minded and adventurous. The first months I lived in Paris I rarely bought Brie or Camembert—I'd had so many disappointing pasteurized-milk varieties that I lost my enthusiasm for these wonderful cheeses. Then one day, I happened to sample a perfect Camembert and "click," I instantly understood what the fuss was all about.

OPERA, PALAIS-ROYAL

1st arrondissement

LA MAISON DU BON FROMAGE
35 Rue du Marché Saint-Honoré, Paris 1.
Tel: 42.61.02.77.
Métro: Pyramides or Tuileries.
Open 9 A.M. to 2 P.M. and 4:15 to 8:30 P.M. Closed Sunday, Monday, and August.
Credit card: V.

Owners Michèle and Alain Eletufe are true perfectionists, and that perfection shows even before you enter their tiny *fromagerie*, boasting of some two hundred varieties of cheese. Look out for their lovely *chèvres* (all guaranteed to be made with fresh, never frozen, goat's milk), the superb Reblochon from the Savoie, an exceptional Brie de Meaux, and an aged Brillat-Savarin, with its rosy, reddish glow. They also offer a good selection of breads, perfect for a picnic in the Tuileries Gardens.

Two types of Emmental, first Savoyard, then Swiss, and two types of Comté cheese from the Jura region of France, first aged, next to it, young.

SCENTS OF PARIS

It was the Camembert above all that they could smell. The Camembert with its gamey scent of venison had conquered the more muffled tones of Maroilles and Limbourg. . . . Into the middle of this vigorous phrase the Parmesan threw its thin note on a country flute, while the Brie added the dull gentleness of damp tambourines. Then came the suffocating reprise of a Livarot. And the symphony was held for a moment on the high, sharp note of an aniseed Gérôme, prolonged like the note of an organ."
—Emile Zola, *Le Ventre de Paris.*

CHEZ TACHON
38 Rue de Richelieu,
   Paris 1.
Tel: 42.96.08.66.
Métro: Palais-Royal.
Open 9:30 A.M. to 1:30 P.M.
   and 4 to 7:30 P.M. Closed
   Sunday, Monday, July,
   and August.
No credit cards.

A truly classic, old-fashioned *fromagerie*, near the Louvre and the Palais-Royal. Little handwritten signs tell you about the origin and history of many cheese varieties, and there is even an advisory list noting which ones are currently at their best. Tachon presents some wonderful finds, including many small-production farm cheeses: great Burgundian Epoisses from the Laiterie de la Côte in Gevrey-Chambertin; superb Swiss Tête de Moine du Bellelay; an above average farm-fresh Saint-Nectaire, mild, sweet, and tangy, and aged a full two months on beds of rye straw; and Livarot, from Normandy farms, a cheese that's strong, spicy, and elastic, the sort of cheese that sticks agreeably to your teeth. Also, try the Roquefort Maria-Grimal, the Camembert from the Coopérative d'Isigny, and the earthy, smoked pork sausages from the French Alps.

ILE SAINT-LOUIS

4th arrondissement

LA FERME SAINT AUBIN
76 Rue Saint-Louis en l'Ile,
   Paris 4.
Tel: 43.54.74.54.
Métro: Sully-Morland or
   Pont-Marie.
Open 8:30 A.M. to 1 P.M. and
   4 P.M. to 7:45 P.M. Closed
   Sunday afternoon and
   Monday.
No credit cards.

Tidy, spotless, fragrant, and welcoming—what more can one ask of a cheese shop? The only problem here is limiting one's choice: Ask what's good that day and Madame Odette Jenny will, according to the season, offer you a flawless and aromatically spicy Langres cow's milk cheese from the Champagne region, a beautifully aged and pungent Livarot cow's milk cheese from Normandy, or a dry and clean sheep's milk (brebis) cheese from the Auvergne. In the winter months—November through March—try the sweet little cakes of castagnolu, prepared with chestnut flour. Also a thorough selection of Poilâne breads, including the hearty rye loaves, perfect for pairing with well aged cheeses. Madame Jenny does much of her own aging in the 17th-century caves beneath the boutique, and will happily prepare special tasting platters—plateaux-dégustation—for parties and special events.

FONTAINEBLEAU

This creamy, white, succulent dessert cheese is found, from time to time, in Paris fromageries. *Usually sold in little white containers lined with cheesecloth, the fresh cheese takes its name from the town of Fontainebleau, south of Paris. Although Fontainebleau is far from rare, this elegant cheese is seen less and less frequently in Paris shops: It stays fresh for just twenty-four hours, and it is not economical for most cheese shops to handle. But since this appealing dessert is easy to make, there's no reason not to serve it often. In France, Fontainebleau is made at home with* fromage blanc, *sort of a "curdless" cottage cheese, but I found that yogurt is an excellent substitute. This version is similar to* coeur à la crème, *but since it is lightened with egg whites, Fontainebleau is less rich. It is an ideal dessert for a large group because the recipe can easily be doubled or tripled. And since it is made in advance, it takes no last-minute preparation. Fontainebleau is particularly beautiful when made in a white ceramic* coeur à la crème *mold, but it can be formed in a strainer as well. I serve Fontaine-bleau with a fresh raspberry sauce and the little almond cakes,* financiers *(see recipe, page 226). It is also delicious with strawberries, fresh figs, or blueberries.*

2 cups (500 ml) whole
 milk yogurt
1 cup (200 g) sugar
2 cups (500 ml) heavy
 cream (preferably not
 ultra-pasteurized) or
 crème fraîche (see
 recipe, page 279)
3 egg whites

1. In a large mixing bowl, combine the yogurt and all but 2 tablespoons of the sugar.

2. In a second bowl, whip the cream or *crème fraîche* until stiff and fold into the yogurt mixture.

3. In yet another bowl, whip the egg whites until stiff, add the reserved 2 tablespoons of sugar, and whip until glossy, about another 20 seconds. Gently fold the egg whites into the yogurt-cream mixture.

4. Transfer mixture to a 6-cup (1.5-liter) cheesecloth-lined, perforated mold (or use two or more smaller molds). Cover the mold, and place it in a bowl in the refrigerator. Refrigerate for 24 hours, draining off the liquid from time to time. The cheese should become fairly firm and dry, almost like a whipped cream cheese.

5. To serve, unmold the Fontainebleau onto a platter, unwrap, and surround with a colorful fresh fruit sauce or fresh berries. Serve immediately.

Yield: 8 to 10 servings

BAC, SEVRES-BABYLONE, ECOLE MILITAIRE

7th arrondissement

BARTHELEMY
51 Rue de Grenelle, Paris 7.
Tel: 45.48.56.75.
Métro: Rue du Bac.
Open 8:30 A.M. to 1 P.M. and
4 to 7:30 P.M. Tuesday
through Friday; 8:30 A.M.
to 1:30 P.M. and 3 to
7:30 P.M. Saturday.
Closed Sunday and
Monday.
Credit card: V.

Everyone from the president of the French Republic to actress Catherine Deneuve shops here, and even without that recommendation, this Paris landmark demands a visit. Barthélémy offers some of the finest Swiss Vacherin you're ever likely to find (from October to March only), well-aged Epoisses, Camembert from the Coopérative d'Isigny, as well as Gabriel Coulet's exceptional Roquefort.

CHEESE TO GO

If you are planning to tuck a selection of French cheese into your suitcase for your welcome-back meal in the United States, be careful. U.S. Customs observes very strict government rules on foods coming into the country. Technically, no cheese, unless it is commercially sealed, can be brought by tourists into the U.S. This rules out virtually all French cheese.

MARIE-ANNE CANTIN
12 Rue du Champ-de-Mars,
Paris 7.
Tel: 45.50.43.94.
Métro: Ecole Militaire.
Open 8:30 A.M. to 1 P.M. and
4 to 7:30 P.M. Closed
Sunday afternoon and
Monday.
Credit card: V.

One of Paris's prettiest cheese boutiques, just off the bustling Rue Cler open-air market. Marie-Anne is the daughter of Christian Cantin, whose cheese shop at 2 Rue de Lourmel, in the 15th *arrondissement*, has long been a Paris landmark. She and her husband, Antoine Diaz, offer some eighty to a hundred remarkably well-aged selections, and you'll find their cheeses at such illustrious restaurants as Joël Robuchon's Jamin. The two are passionate about cheese, and that excitement carries over into the neatly organized, appealing little store. They're especially proud of the aging cellars beneath the shop, with one for goat cheese (very dry) and one for cow's milk (very humid). The floor of the cow's milk cellar is lined with pebbles, which are watered regularly to insure proper humidity. All cheese is aged on straw, and varieties such as Munster and Maroilles get a daily rub-down with beer or salt water, to transform mild, timid little discs into cheese loaded with character.

The true cheese lover, says Monsieur Dias, is someone who invariably selects Camembert, Brie, or Livarot as part of his cheese course. And the best varieties sampled here include a classic and elegant Camembert; a dusty, creamy little *bouton-de-chèvre* (a farm-fresh button of goat cheese); and a remarkable Charolais goat cheese: refined, clean, and full-flavored. If you are in the mood for a mercilessly pungent cheese, try the northern Vieux Lille ("old Lille"): Strong and rugged, it's a cheese that almost attacks your palate. More soothing and cheddar-like is Salers, the mild and nutty cheese from the Auvergne, and Comté, France's version of the well-known Swiss Gruyère. And do not leave the shop without a superbly runny Saint-Marcellin, aged as in Lyons.

Browsing at Marie-Anne Cantin's.

LA MAISON DU FROMAGE
(Alain Quatrehomme)
62 Rue de Sèvres, Paris 7.
Tel: 47.34.33.45.
Métro: Vaneau or Duroc.
Open 8:45 A.M. to 1 P.M. and 4:15 to 7:45 P.M.
(Saturday open 8:45 A.M. to 7:45 P.M.) Closed Sunday and Monday.
Credit cards: DC, V.

This popular Left Bank shop supplies some of the better restaurants in town. Look out for superb Beaufort from the Savoie; a Parmesan that's aged two and a half years; the cow's milk Saint-Marcellin, as creamy and runny as you'll find in Lyons. Also try the Swiss Fribourg, a superb cheese to sample with sweet wines of the Jura; and from November to March, the Swiss Vacherin.

STREET NAME MENU

It should come as no surprise to find that in Paris, a city so devoted to food, dozens of street names have a food connection. Here are a few, with the *arrondissement,* or neighborhood, in which they are now located:

Rue des Boulangers, 5th *arrondissement*: When the street was named in 1844, it was lined with numerous bakeries. Today there's not a loaf of bread for sale on "Bakers' Street."

Passage de la Brie, 19th *arrondissement*: named for the region east of Paris known for its wheat, pastures, butter, and of course, cheese.

Rue Brillat-Savarin, 13th *arrondissement*: named in honor of the gastronome and author of the famous *Physiology of Taste.*

Rue Brise-Miche, 4th *arrondissement*: During the Middle Ages, it was on this street that clergymen distributed bread to the needy. *Brise-miche,* named in 1517, literally means "break bread."

Rue Curnonsky, 17th *arrondissement*: named in memory of the gastronome Maurice-Edmond Sailland, who took on the Russian-sounding pseudonym around the turn of the century, when everything Russian was fashionable in Paris. The author of the multi-volume *La France Gastronomique* died in 1956, and the street was later named in his honor.

Rue des Eaux, 16th *arrondissement*: In 1650, when this road was opened in the Passy district, workers had discovered the area's mineral waters. (Passy is now one of the more fashionable Paris neighborhoods.) The source dried up during the 18th century, but the name, "Street of the Waters," remained. Who knows, if the source still existed, we could all be drinking Passy water instead of Perrier.

Rue de la Faisanderie, 16th *arrondissement*: A pheasant preserve, or *faisanderie,* once existed here, near the *château* of the Muette.

Rue des Fermiers, 17th *arrondissement*: There are no farmers, or *fermiers,* left here today, but in the 1800s there were still a few farms in this now-citified neighborhood not far from Parc Monceau. The street was named in 1840, when the area became part of Paris.

Rue des Jeûneurs, 2nd *arrondissement*: The name perhaps comes from a sign that hung above one of the houses in 1715, during the reign of Louis XV. It read: "Aux Déjeuners," or "Lunches Here."

Rue des Maraîchers, 20th *arrondissement*: During the 18th century, vegetable garden markets, or *maraîchers,* bordered the region. The street was named in 1869.

Impasse Marché aux Chevaux, 5th *arrondissement*: There are many Paris streets named after past or still-existing markets, but this is one story I particularly enjoy. Beginning in 1687, this was a major market site. Early each Wednesday and Saturday, pigs were brought to market for sale, then later in the day mules, donkeys, and horses (*chevaux*) were sold, giving the street its name. On Sundays, they sold wagons and dogs.

Rue des Meuniers, 12th *arrondissement*: The street of the millers takes it name from the flour mill that existed here during the 18th century. Today there's no sign of a mill.

Rue des Morillons, 15th *arrondissement*: Morillon is the name of a grapevine that flourished in the Parisian climate at a time when Parisians and those living on the outskirts still had room to grow grapes. The path that led from the vineyard was declared a road in 1730 and a street in 1906. Vineyards have once again been planted in the nearby Parc Georges-Brassens, but they're of the Pinot Noir variety, not Morillon.

Impasse de la Poissonnerie, 4th *arrondissement*: This street was built in 1783 when the Sainte-Catherine market first opened. It bordered a fish shop, thus its name.

Boulevard Poissonnière, 2nd and 9th *arrondissements*: Opened at the beginning of the 17th century, this street served as a *passage* for fish merchants coming direct from the Port of Calais, delivering their fish to the Paris central market, Les Halles. It was named in 1685.

THE RIND

The million dollar question: Should you eat the rind or shouldn't you? Even the experts don't agree. According to *Larousse des Fromages*, the French cheese bible, it is all a question of personal taste. Larousse advises, however, not to leave a messy plate full of little bits of crust. Pierre Androuët, the former dean of Paris cheese merchants, is more definite. Never eat the rind, he says, because it harbors all the cheese's developing molds and yeasts and can emit an alkaline odor. The truth? It's really up to you, though let logic rule. The rinds of soft-ripened cheese such as Brie and Camembert are definitely edible, and when the cheese is perfectly ripe, the thin, bloomy *croûte* adds both flavor and texture. However, with another soft cheese, Vacherin, the rind is always removed, and the creamy cheese is scooped out with a spoon. The rinds of semi-soft cheese, such as Reblochon, can have a very nutty flavor. The crust is always discarded when eating hard mountain cheese, such as Emmenthal, Gruyère, and *tête-de-moine.*

GARE SAINT-LAZARE, MADELEINE

8th arrondissement

ANDROUET
41 Rue d'Amsterdam,
   Paris 8.
Tel: 48.74.26.90.
Métro: Liège.
Open 8 A.M. to 7 P.M.
   Closed Sunday.
Credit cards: AE, DC, V.

In Paris, the name Androuët (pronounced ahn-drew-ETT) has been synonymous with cheese since the shop on Rue d'Amsterdam opened its doors in 1909. The boutique changed hands several years ago, and though this is still the place to go to create a lovely cheese tray, a picnic, or a package of cheeses to take home with you, the selection is not nearly as spectacular as it was years ago. The lovely assorted boxes of cheeses—ready-made cheese trays with a fine, seasonal variety, all labeled and ready to serve—are still available, but what you'll now see displayed in the windows is not the real thing, but plastic models!

When I first moved to Paris, Androuët was my cheese university: I'd come every Saturday to sample half a dozen new-found varieties. Today there are still some Androuët cheeses I count among my favorites, including the triple-cream Lucullus; the smooth and sunset orange Soumaintrain, full of character and flavor; and the Arôme au Gêne from the region of Lyons, pungent discs washed with *marc de Bourgogne*, an *eau-de-vie* distilled from pressed grape skins and seeds. In the fall, sample the Munster, aged for several months at large farms and given a daily splash of white wine; Pierre-Qui-Vire, an elegant, smooth, Burgundian cow's milk cheese, full of character and aged two months in cool, humid cellars; Epoisses, brushed with *marc de Bourgogne* to give it a rare pungency and a rind the color of fresh fall leaves; and Rollot, the smooth and spicy cow's milk cheese from Picardy, aged two months and washed daily with a salty brine.

FROMAGE DE CHEVRE MARINE A L'HUILE D'HERBES
GOAT CHEESE MARINATED IN OIL WITH HERBS

This is a traditional method of storing and extending the life of a goat cheese, particularly useful for chèvre that has become very firm and dry. It's great to have on hand for days when you haven't had time to market. After the cheese has been consumed, you can continue adding more cheese and herbs to the oil, or use it for cooking or for salad dressings.

6 small goat cheese
   (Picodon, Crottin, or
   Cabécou)
1 clove garlic, peeled
1 teaspoon fresh thyme
   leaves
1 sprig fresh rosemary
2 bay leaves
12 whole black
   peppercorns
12 whole white
   peppercorns
12 whole coriander seeds
2 cups (500 ml) extra-
   virgin olive oil

1. Cut each cheese in half horizontally. In a wide-mouth pint (500-ml) jar place the cheese, then the garlic and herbs and spices. Cover with oil. Close securely and store in a cool place for at least 1 week.

2. To serve, remove the cheese from the jar, and drain off the oil. Broil the cheese just until warm, and serve with a tossed green salad and slices of fresh bread. Use cheese within 2 weeks.

Yield: 12 servings

CREPLET-BRUSSOL
17 Place de la Madeleine,
Paris 8.
Tel: 42.65.34.32.
Métro: Madeleine.
Open 9 A.M. to 7:30 P.M.
Tuesday through Friday
and 2 to 7 P.M. Saturday
and Monday.
Closed Sunday.
Credit card: AE, V.

Because of its location—near the famous Fauchon and Hédiard food shops—this is one of the city's better known *fromageries*. The windows are filled with a lot of processed cheese, but inside there is a solid, classic collection, including a fine raw-milk Camembert from the Isigny Cooperative in Normandy, nicely aged Brie, and a good variety of cheeses from northern France. On my last visit, many of the goat cheeses were not well aged and were simply over the hill. They've added a few stools and a slim bar for sampling cheese in the shop.

LA FERME SAINT-
HUBERT
21 Rue Vignon, Paris 8.
Tel: 47.42.79.20.
Métro: Madeleine.
Open 8:30 A.M. to 7:30 P.M.
Closed Sunday and
Monday morning.
Credit cards: AE, DC, V.

Just around the corner from Fauchon, this small, compact shop offers a remarkable cheese selection, including what's probably the best and most carefully selected Roquefort in Paris; a spectacular Beaufort, aged at least two years in special cellars; and a vigorous Maroilles, from Flanders, aged for four months and bathed daily with a healthy dose of beer. Owner Henry Voy also offers the Swiss *tête-de-moine*, so named because the fruity cylinder resembles the round, bald head of a monk. It's a cheese full of punch, depth, and character, a must for fans of Gruyère. Also worth sampling are the delicate, pale, goat's-milk butter and a good goat's milk yogurt. Monsieur Voy's palate goes toward cheeses that are rough and rustic, and sometimes aged just a bit too long, thus losing their charm. (See also Dégustation box, page 284).

PORTE DE VERSAILLES

15th arrondissement

FIL O' FROMAGE
4 Rue Poirier-de-Narçay,
Paris 14.
Tel: 40.44.86.75.
Métro: Porte d'Orléans.
Open 8:30 A.M. to 1 P.M. and
4 to 8 P.M. Closed
Sunday morning,
Monday, and August.
Credit card: V.

This beautifully restored *fromagerie*—with marble counters and bright sprays of flowers—reflects good intentions and a sense of pride. Owners Sylvie and Chérif Bourbrit offer an excellent assortment of goat cheeses, and specialties from all over France. Try their well-aged sheep's milk cheese from Corsica—*brebis Corse*—a delicately earthy cheese that's great on toasted rye bread.

CREME FRAICHE

Where would French cuisine be without crème fraîche, *that thick and slightly tangy cream that lies somewhere between heavy cream and sour cream? Every* crémerie *in France sells* crème fraîche *in bulk, usually ladled out of giant round crockery bowls. It's versatile and nearly indispensable, showing up in hot and cold sauces, and is perfect for whipping with a touch of sugar to dab on a mound of fresh wild strawberries.*

2 cup (250 ml) heavy (whipping) cream (you cannot use ultra-pasteurized)

1 cup (250 ml) sour cream

1. Mix the heavy cream and sour cream together in a medium-size bowl. Cover loosely with plastic wrap and let stand at room temperature overnight, or until fairly thick.

2. Cover tightly and refrigerate for at least 4 hours, to thicken it even more. The *crème fraîche* will keep for up to 1 week in the refrigerator, where the tangy flavor will continue to develop.

Yield: 2 cups (500 ml)

LA FERME DU HAMEAU
223 Rue de la Croix-Nivert, Paris 15.
Tel: 45.32.88.70.
Métro: Porte de Versailles.
Open 8:30 A.M. to 1 P.M. and 3:30 to 7:30 P.M. Closed Sunday, Monday, and July.
No credit cards.

A tidy cheese shop that offers a little bit of everything, from delicious-looking *cassoulet* or *poule au riz* in glass jars, to lovely packages of macaroons. In the cheese department, they offer a superb Coulommiers—a creamy cow's milk cheese that is generally overshadowed by the often-bland neighbor, Brie. Here the Coulommiers is a delight, well-aged, and tasting faintly of almonds. Brie's "little brother," this bloomy, fat disc of cow's milk cheese is worth going out of the way to find. Other cheeses of note: a rare Beaufort *d'alpage*, a nicely aged Saint-Nectaire, and in the fall and winter months, Vacherin Mont d'Or.

VICTOR-HUGO

16th arrondissement

LILLO
35 Rue des Belles-Feuilles, Paris 16.
Tel: 47.27.69.08.
Métro: Victor-Hugo.
Open 8 A.M. to 1 P.M. and 4 to 7:30 P.M. Closed Monday.
Credit card: V.

An elegant, sparkling little shop near the Place Victor-Hugo, on one of Paris's most chic market streets, Rue des Belles-Feuilles. This is a neighborhood where quality is taken for granted, and no one need worry about Monsieur Lillo letting his clients down. Though few cheeses are actually aged here, many of the two hundred or so varieties are "finished" for five or six days in the neat cellars beneath the shop. Almost all are raw-milk, small-production cheeses, and among the best varieties sampled are the raw-milk Brie, Munster, and Roquefort.

COURCELLES, VILLIERS

17th arrondissement

ALLEOSSE
13 Rue Poncelet,
   Paris 17.
Tel: 46.22.50.45.
Open 9 A.M. to 1 P.M. and
   4 to 7:15 P.M. Closed
   Sunday afternoon and
   Monday.
Credit card: V.

Say "cheese," it's Alléosse.

The hard-working, outgoing, and thoroughly professional Alléosse family run the best cheese shop in Paris. The father, Roger Alléosse, travels throughout France, searching out the best farm cheeses, the best *laiteries* or dairies, the best cheese agers in each region. Their wide selection of cheeses from France, Italy, Greece, and the Netherlands is astonishing, and serve as a mini cheese university. I always come home with more cheeses than I'd planned to buy, but somehow every last morsel gets devoured. The Alléosse cheeses are aged in a series of *caves* beneath the store. Some special cheeses to note include always perfect raw milk Camembert; beautifully aged Langres, a soft, smooth, pungent cheese from the Champagne area; a smoother and super-rich *brebis fermier*, or farm-made sheep's milk cheese from the Pays Basque; and a supple, raw-milk, blue-veined Forme d'Ambert, aged with a dose of sweet Sauternes wine. There is generally a good selection of very fresh and young goat cheeses from Burgundy; always a well-aged Beaufort, delicious Coulommiers, and at times a well-aged Saint-Marcellin.

Creamy blocks of butter.

BUTTER

France produces 10 percent of the world's butter, most of it unsalted. Though Normandy, with its shining green pastures and fawn-colored cows, produces a high-quality product, the best butter comes from Charentes, in the southwest of France. Charentes butter, sold in packets under the label *"beurre d'Echiré"* or *"beurre de Ligueil,"* is favored by French pastry chefs because it is firmer and less watery than other varieties and makes superior pastry.

In cheese shops you often see huge creamy blocks of butter behind the counter. They are usually labeled *"beurre des Charentes," "beurre de Normandie,"* or *"beurre demi-sel." Demi-sel* is Brittany's lightly salted butter. Rarely used in cooking, it finds its place on the table. (While the bulk butters look good and fresh, beware: They sit all day absorbing the mingled odors of the cheese and are not always terribly fresh.)

The French don't usually butter their bread, so whether or not the butter appears on the home or restaurant table is really a matter of personal taste. Butter is always served with *charcuterie* (cold cuts), with radishes, anchovies, sardines, and with the rye bread that comes as part of any order of oysters or other shellfish. If you don't see butter on a restaurant table, it is perfectly proper to ask for it, though in more casual restaurants you may be charged a *supplément* of a few francs. Butter is usually included with the cheese course, and is used to soften the effect of strong and salty cheese such as Roquefort.

JEAN CARMES ET FILS
24 Rue de Lévis, Paris 17.
Tel: 47.63.88.94.
Métro: Villiers.
Open 8 A.M. to 1 P.M. and
    4 to 7:30 P.M. Closed
    Sunday afternoon,
    Monday, and August.
Credit card: V.

Situated right in the middle of the hectic Rue de Lévis market, Carmès is a big, open, family-run cheese shop with Jean Carmès behind the cash register while son, Patrick, rushes about with a nervous sort of vigor, keeping an eye on incoming deliveries, and checking out the progress of the two hundred or so varieties of cheese aging in the humid *caves* below the shop. These people are passionate about cheese, taking the care to label each variety, happy to help you select a single cheese or an entire platter. Eighty percent of their cheeses are bought fresh from the farm. Most varieties spend an average of three to four weeks in the Carmès cellars, aging on fresh, clean straw mats until the cheese is ready to be put on sale. Some specialties here include l'Ecume, a triple-cream cheese so rich it easily replaces butter; Tanatais goat cheese, much like a Charolais, dry and delicious with a bloomy crust; and a Petit-Suisse *"comme autrefois"*, a fragile cheese that stays fresh for just four or five days. Real fresh *crème Chantilly* (sweetened *crème fraîche*) and Fontainebleau (a creamy dessert cheese) are sold here as well.

ALAIN DUBOIS
79 Rue de Courcelles,
Paris 17.
Tel: 43.80.36.42.
Métro: Courcelles.
Open 8:30 A.M. to 1 P.M. and
4 to 7:30 P.M. Closed
Sunday, Monday
morning, and August.
Credit card: V.

There's always a line out the door at this tiny, spotless, traditional shop—taken over a few years ago by Alain Dubois—where raw-milk Camembert, Pyramide goat cheese, and Saint-Marcellin, are generally in excellent form. For my taste, most of the cheeses are underaged, that is, sold before they're properly *affiné*. But since many clients prefer cheese with less character, that's the way it's sold here. The staff could be a bit cheerier and also more helpful about informing customers.

Cheese from the moutains, an Alléosse assortment (see entry, page 280).

ALAIN DUBOIS
80 Rue de Tocqueville,
Paris 17.
Tel: 42.27.11.38.
Métro: Villiers.
Open 7:30 A.M. to 1 P.M. and
4 to 7:30 P.M. Tuesday
through Saturday; 9 A.M.
to 1 P.M. Sunday. Closed
Monday.
Credit card: V.

Young Alain Dubois turned the family *crémerie* into a full-fledged *fromagerie* in the early 1970s. The shop is artfully and tastefully arranged, and Dubois is proudest of his Epoisses de Bourgogne, washed with *marc de Bourgogne* every day or so and aged according to his own "secret" process; his Fribourg, a softer Swiss Gruyère, aged in cellars in the Jura region for at least two years; and his Swiss Vacherin Mont d'Or, still made in chalets and available from the end of fall into the early spring. Dubois offers some seventy varieties of goat cheese, according to the season. Dubois and his wife love visiting farms in search of good cheese and are avid restaurant-goers, feeling that one can't be a good *fromager* without being a dedicated gastronome.

MONTMARTRE

18th arrondissement

FROMAGERIE DE MONTMARTRE
9 Rue du Poteau, Paris 18.
Tel: 46.06.26.03.
Métro: Jules-Joffrin.
Open 8:45 A.M. to 12:30 P.M. and 4 to 7:30 P.M. Closed Sunday and Monday.
No credit cards.

If you just love looking at beautiful cheese displays, don't miss this spacious *fromagerie*, typical of the pretty food shops along the Rue du Poteau. Fromagerie de Montmartre offers a sparkling variety of farm-fresh raw-milk cheeses from all over France, and the owner, Madame Delbey, is happy to let you "window shop" as you wander about the well-organized store, examining the flawless selection of cheese displayed on trays of straw and aged in her own cellars. Goat cheese is one of their strongest features—they offer more than forty different varieties. Outstanding cheeses sampled here include a beautifully aged Comté from the Jura, Auvergnat Cantal aged more than eighteen months, and their creamy Fontainebleau *maison*.

> "*The Roquefort, with its blue and yellow marbling, looks diseased, like rich people who have eaten too many truffles.*"
> —Emile Zola,
> *Le Ventre de Paris*

DEGUSTATION

A favorite way to enjoy French cheese is to take a tour of France through a *dégustation* (tasting) of the country's more than 180 varieties of cheese. The following restaurants, most of which are also *fromageries,* offer a *dégustation* of cheese on their menus.

Androuët, 41 Rue d'Amsterdam, Paris 8. (48.74.26.93). Métro: Liège. Restaurant open noon to 2:30 P.M. and 7:30 to 10:30 P.M. Closed Sunday and holidays. Credit cards: AE, DC, V. 200-franc *dégustation.* Reservations advised.

Once one of my favorite spots for sampling cheese—in seven heavenly courses—Androuët has changed ownership and style. The cozy, rustic dining room has been transformed into a cold, modern restaurant. The seven-course *dégustation* is still on the menu, and though it's not nearly up to the quality of years past, it's still the biggest show in town. Be sure to come with a very hearty appetite, and plenty of time!

La Boutique à Sandwiches, 12 Rue du Colisée, Paris 8. Métro: Franklin-D.-Roosevelt. (43.59.56.69). Open 11:45 A.M. to 1 A.M. Closed Sunday and August. About 100 to 150 francs. Credit card: V.

For an unusual cheese experience, wander up to the first floor of this simple delicatessen to sample *raclette,* a hearty, filling Swiss dish that includes firm, buttery melted cheese, potatoes boiled in their skins, pickled onions, and *cornichons.* Huge wheels of several varieties of Swiss cheese are split in half, then the exposed portion is placed under a special *raclette* broiler. As the cheese melts, it is scraped off—crispy, bubbling brown crust and all—and brought to the table. You will hardly be able to finish the tangy melted cheese before the waiter is back, ready to scrape another serving onto your plate. With the *raclette,* savor the delicate white Apremont wine, from the Savoie.

La Ferme Saint-Hubert, 21 Rue Vignon, Paris 8. (47.42.79.20). Métro: Madeleine. Restaurant open 11:30 A.M. to 3 P.M. and 6:45 to 9:45 P.M. Closed Sunday and Monday. 67-franc *dégustation.*

Next door to La Ferme Saint-Hubert *fromagerie* you'll find a tiny, casual little lunchroom serving

A selection of Cantal.

abbreviated *dégustations* suited to cheese enthusiasts with limited time. Their most popular platter is made up of seven varieties, representing the seven major types of French cheese. At La Ferme Saint-Hubert, they are aged to the borderline of perfection, while reflecting the owner's preference for ripe, full-flavored cheese. Platters of goat cheese and salads are also available. There's a small wine selection, and little pots of pure white goat's-milk butter are served with a fresh country loaf from baker Lionel Poilâne. The cheese is not labeled, so you'll have to make good mental notes, then slip into the shop next door after the meal to identify the cheese you have just tasted. *Raclette* is served every evening.

Les Miss, 4 Rue des Fossés-Sainte-Jacques, Paris 5. (43.54.90.02). Métro: Luxembourg. Open noon to 3 P.M. and 6 to midnight. Credit Card: V. 46- and 92-franc *dégustations*.

A lively, skylit neighborhood lunch spot, with a simple cheese-based menu featuring savory *crêpe tourtes;* salads that combine greens, goat cheese, and walnuts; and nicely labeled *dégustation* platters served with the fabulously crusty *baguettes* from the nearby Boulangerie Moderne. The melted Swiss Raclette cheese is served with tiny boiled potatoes and slices of delicious smoked ham. There's a small wine list, including an excellent Côtes-du-Rhône.

La Maison du Valais, 20 Rue Royale, Paris 8. (42.60.23.75). Métro: Madeleine. Open noon to 3 P.M. and 7:15 to 10:30 P.M. Closed Sunday and three weeks in August. *Raclette*, 90 francs. Credit cards: AE, DC, MC, V.

My favorite spot in Paris for sampling platter after platter of warm, creamy-white Swiss *raclette*. Here, in a rustic chalet-like setting, the superb—and filling—*raclette* is served with plenty of boiled potatoes and a marvelously piquant condiment of onions and mustard, as well as puckery *cornichons*. With it sample a light white Swiss Fendant from—where else—Valais.

Charcuteries
PREPARED FOODS
TO GO

Decisions are easy if you know what you want.

To lovers of all things earthy, hearty, rib-sticking, and aromatic, the Paris *charcuterie* is a touch of heaven. Literally meaning the shop where you buy *chair cuite*—cooked meat—the city has hundreds of them. Some are museumlike with carved marble counters and hanging brass racks, others are modern and spotless, with products displayed like diamonds in a jeweler's window. You can buy fragrant sausages and mosaic pâtés, salted and smoked hams, and strange-sounding items such as *gratton, fritons, rillettes,* and *rillons.* Who else but the French could manage to make so much of the lowly pig? And where else but in Paris can you find one shop with eighteen different varieties of *boudin* sausage made right on the premises, another with more than a dozen different varieties of ham, still others that sell not only pork products, but also caviar, *foie gras,* fresh country breads, smoked salmon, and even the vodka, Champagne, or Sauternes to go with them?

You need not go beyond Paris to sample the wonders of the French world of *charcuterie*—my favorite regional shops feature products from the rugged Auvergne region in south-central France, and offer farm-fresh goat and sheep's milk cheeses, a heady

Bleu d'Auvergne, dozens of kinds of ham, sausages, pâtés of so many different names, colors, and shapes it makes the head spin. There are also Alsatian-owned shops redolent with the pungent warmth of cooked sauerkraut, mounds of pork chops, and colorful assorted sausages, plus some of the finest farm Munster cheese.

Shops with a Breton accent are likely to feature Brittany's prune-filled flan known as *far breton,* while those from the Savoie region bordering Switzerland will offer hams and sausages cured in the mountain air, as well as local white wines, such as the pale, delicate, Apremont or the fizzy, light, Crépy.

The size and selection available will vary widely from shop to shop, neighborhood to neighborhood. Run-of-the-mill *charcuteries* make only a small portion of the products themselves, but the finest shops, such as those mentioned here, either produce most of their own sausages and hams, pâtés, and *terrines,* or buy them direct from independent farmers in various regions of France.

Many, but not all, Paris *charcuteries* also offer hot meals at lunch and dinner time, a carry-out concept that to most of us seems distinctly modern. It's not. For ever since *charcuteries* were established in 1475, their very reason for existence was to sell cooked pork products. In days when a large percentage of Parisians lived without even rudimentary cooking facilities (and many still do), the *charcuterie* served as a kitchen away from home.

Along with the hundreds of different meat products, most *charcuteries* also sell *escargots* (snails) ready for popping in the oven, a variety of pastry-topped *pâtés* or *terrines* to be eaten warm or at room temperature, pizzas, *quiches,* and dozens of salads, ranging from those of ivory-colored celery root or bright red beets to a julienne of carrots showered with vinaigrette. Condiments such as olives, pickles, and *cornichons* can almost always be found, along with many kinds of regional packaged cakes, cookies, and pastries. The modern-day Parisian charcuterie also takes note of the modern palate and a desire for lighter fare, and such Asian specialties as the Vietnamese spring roll *(rouleau de printemps)* have become part of the standard *charcuterie* repertoire. And should one be too concerned about all that fat, listen to what one French doctor has to say about *boudin,* that savory, steaming sausage made with pork blood: "*Boudin* is so full of iron and vitamins, it should be reimbursed by social security!"

Today, the Parisian definition of *charcuterie* is a broad one, and major shops such as Fauchon, Lenôtre, Dalloyau, Hédiard, and Flo Prestige (all listed elsewhere in this guide) perform the services of *charcuterie* and caterer, offering, as well, pastries, breads, chocolates, wines, liquors, and condiments. What follows here, is a choice selection of the smaller shops, most of them family run, with personalities of their own. In each case, a sampling of this, a slice of that will make a picnic lunch or snack a true Parisian feast.

TUILERIES

1st arrondissement

CHEDEVILLE
12 Place du Marché-Saint-
  Honoré, Paris 1.
Tel: 42.61.04.62.
Métro: Tuileries.
Open 8 A.M. to 1:30 P.M. and
  2:30 to 6:30 P.M. Closed
  Saturday afternoon,
  Sunday, and August.
Credit cards: AE, V.

One of the city's major—and rather industrial— *charcuteries*, famous for the pâtés, fresh and dried sausages, *foie gras* and hams that find their way into some of Paris's better restaurants. It is place full of character, where you are welcome to watch the half dozen butchers hard at work preparing for the day's labors. Their *andouillette*, or chitterling sausage, is considered the best in Paris.

MARAIS, BASTILLE

4th and 11th arrondissements

**LA GALOCHE
D'AURILLAC**
41 Rue de Lappe, Paris 11.
Tel: 47.00.77.15.
Métro: Bastille.
Open 10 A.M. to midnight.
  Closed Sunday, Monday,
  and August.
No credit cards.

This always lively local bistro also sells regional hams, sausages, breads, cheese, and wine. It is a nice spot to know about late at night when other neighborhood *charcuteries* tend to be closed.

Sausage and frites.

ORDERING CHARCUTERIE

The best way to visit a Paris *charcuterie* is armed with a little knowledge and a hearty appetite. The following are some of the most commonly found products:

Andouille: cold smoked chitterling (tripe) sausage.

Andouillette: smaller chitterling (tripe) sausage, usually served grilled.

Ballotine: usually poultry, boned, stuffed and rolled.

Boudin blanc: white sausage of veal, chicken or pork.

Boudin noir: pork blood sausage.

Cervelas: garlicky cured pork sausage.

Confit: duck, goose, or pork cooked and preserved in its own fat.

Cou d'oie farci: neck skin of goose, stuffed with meat and spices, much like a sausage.

Crépinette: small sausage patty wrapped in caul fat.

Fritons: coarse pork *rillettes,* or a minced spread, that includes organ meats.

Fromage de tête: headcheese, usually pork.

Galantine: cooked, boned poultry or meat stuffed and rolled, classically glazed with gelatin, and served cold.

Grattons: crisply fried pieces of pork, goose, or duck skin; cracklings.

Hure (de porc or *de marcassin):* a headcheese prepared from the head of a pig or boar.

Jambon (ham)

> *d'Auvergne:* salt-cured ham.
>
> *de Bayonne:* raw dried, salt-cured ham.
>
> *de Bourgogne:* also *persillé:* cold cooked ham, cubed and preserved in parsleyed gelatin, usually sliced from a *terrine.*
>
> *cru:* any raw cured ham.
>
> *cuit:* any cooked ham.
>
> *fumé:* any smoked ham.
>
> *de montagne:* any mountain ham.
>
> *á l'os:* ham with the bone in
>
> *de Paris:* pale, lightly salted, cooked ham.
>
> *de Parme:* Italian *prosciutto* from Parma.

du pays: any country ham.

persillé; also *de Bourgogne;* cold cooked ham, cubed and preserved in parsleyed gelatin, usually sliced from a terrine.

sec: any dried ham.

de Westphalie: German Westphalian ham, raw-cured and smoked.

de York: smoked English-style ham, usually poached.

Jambonneau: cured ham shank or pork knuckle.

Jésus: smoked pork sausage from the Franche-Comté.

Lard: bacon

Lardons: cubes of bacon.

Merguez: small spicy sausage.

Museau de porc: vinegared pork muzzle.

Oreilles de porc: cooked pig's ears, served grilled, with a coating of egg and bread crumbs.

Pâté (seasoned, chopped meats that are molded, baked, and served hor or cold)

de campagne: coarse country-style.

de canard: of duck.

de chevreuil: of venison.

en croûte: baked in pastry.

de foie: of liver.

de grive: of thrush, or songbird.

de lapin: of rabbit.

de liévre: of wild hare.

maison: in the style of the house or *charcuterie.*

d'oie: of goose.

Pied (foot)

de cochon: pig's foot.

de mouton: sheep's foot.

de porc: pig's foot.

Poitrine fumée: smoked bacon.

Poitrine d'oie fumée: smoked goose breast.

Rillettes (d'oie): minced spread of pork (goose); also can be made with duck, fish, or rabbit.

Rillons: pork belly, cut up and cooked until crisp, then drained of fat; can also be made of duck, goose, or rabbit.

" Drink wine when you eat ham.
Soup is for ordinary hunger; roasts make a meal festive.
Venison pâté is too good for disobedient children."
—Lesson from a 17th-century French schoolbook.

Coils of boudin.

Rosette (de boeuf): dried pork (or beef) sausage, usually from Beaujolais.

Saucisse (most often, small fresh sausage, which is cooked in liquid and/or broiled, and eaten warm)

   chaude: warm sausage.

   de Francfort: hot dog.

   de Morteau: smoked pork sausage from the Franche-Comté.

   de Strasbourg: red-skinned hot dog.

   de Toulouse: mild country-style pork sausage.

Saucisson (most often, a large air-dried sausage, such as salami, eaten sliced as a cold cut. When fresh, usually called *saucisson chaud*—hot sausage)

   à l'ail: garlic sausage, usually to be cooked and served warm.

   d'Arles: dried, salami-type sausage.

   de campagne: any country-style sausage.

   en croûte: sausage cooked in pastry crust.

   de Lyon: air-dried pork sausage, flavored with garlic and pepper, and studded with chunks of pork fat, sometimes flavored with pistachio nuts or truffles.

   sec: any dried sausage or salami.

Terrine (actually the earthenware container used for cooking meat, game, fish, or vegetable mixtures. It also refers to the pâté served in the vessel. It differs from a pâté proper in that the *terrine* is actually sliced out of the vessel, while a pâté has been removed from the terrine)

   d'anguille: eel.

   de caille: quail.

   de campagne: country-style.

   de canard: of duck.

   du chef: in the chef's special style.

   de faisan: of pheasant.

   de foie: of liver.

   de foies de volaille: of chicken liver.

   de grives: of thrush, or songbird.

   maison: in style of the *charcuterie* or house.

   de perdreau: of partridge.

   de volaille: of chicken.

PRODUITS HONGROIS
11 Rue de Sévigné, Paris 4.
Tel: 48.87.46.06.
Métro: Saint-Paul.
Open 9 A.M. to 1 P.M. and 3
to 7 P.M. Closed Sunday,
Monday, and mid-July to
the end of August.

A tiny, tidy Eastern European shop not far from the trendy Place des Vosges, which offers fresh, aromatic, and delicious Hungarian sausages. Pro-propriétaire Anna Suba specializes in smoked *charcuterie*, and her beef and pork sausage seasoned with hot peppers is a special treat.

LE SAVOYARD
39 Rue Popincourt,
Paris 11.
No telephone.
Métro: Saint-Ambroise.
Open 9:30 A.M. to 9 P.M.
Closed Monday, August,
and the first week of
September.

This out-of-the-way *charcuterie* is worth a detour. Perfectly aged Reblochon; Beaufort prepared with high-mountain summer milk; rye bread baked in wood-fired ovens; fresh and dried sausages from the mountains of the Savoie, prepared with both donkey and goat meat, or with pork and fresh juniper-smoked sausages filled with *chanterelle* wild mushrooms. They offer twenty different Savoie wines, and even a little bar at which to enjoy them.

A LA VILLE DE RODEZ
22 Rue Vieille-du-Temple,
Paris 4.
Tel: 48.87.79.36.
Métro: Saint-Paul.
Open 8 A.M. to 1 P.M. and
3 to 7:30 P.M. Closed
Sunday, Monday, and
mid-July through
August.

The long, hearty loaves of country bread come up from Aurillac in south-central France four times a week, while the fragrant sausages and hams that hang from the rafters of this spotless shop all have the wholesome Auvergnat stamp. You will also find buckwheat flour for earthy *crêpes*; *fouace* (an extra-buttery regional *brioche* studded with candied fruits); *boudin noir* (blood sausage); rough, red regional wines; and that delicate, straw-yellow Cantal-like cheese, Laguiole. You can select an entire picnic or a simple snack, then buy a handmade wicker basket in which to carry your treasures.

Carefully slicing into a terrine.

SAINT-GERMAIN-DES-PRES, ODEON, SEVRES-BABYLONE

6th and 7th arrondissements

CHARCUTERIE
ALSACIENNE
10 Rue de Buci, Paris 6.
Tel: 43.54.93.49.
Métro: Odéon.
Open daily, 9 A.M. to 10 P.M.
Closed Monday.
Credit cards: AE, DC,
MC, V.

Oh boy, sausage-lovers' heaven! I'm a real fan of Alsatian food, especially the incredible collection of sausages one finds in this charming, fragrant boutique, a new offshoot of the company founded in Mulhouse back in 1876. Try the cumin-flecked pork sausages, the *boudin* blood sausages, or the slender smoked Montbéliard sausages from the Jura, to the south of Alsace. The word "cute" must have been coined to describe the interior of this cheery and modern shop, decorated with woodwork painted with bright, folkloric floral designs.

CHARCUTERIE CHARLES
10 Rue Dauphine, Paris 6.
Tel: 43.54.25.19.
Open 9 A.M. to 1 P.M. and 4
to 7 P.M. Closed Saturday
and Sunday.
Métro: Odéon.
and
135 Rue Saint Dominique,
Paris 7.
Tel: 47.05.53.66.
Métro: Ecole Militaire.
Open 9 A.M. to 1 P.M. and 4
to 7 P.M. Closed Saturday
and Sunday.

A grand and award-winning specialist of *boudin blanc*, white pork and veal sausage, including those seasoned with truffles, hazelnuts, pistachios, wild *cèpe* mushrooms, prunes, corn, as well as the "plain" variety. Also good blood sausage, or *boudin noir*, and hams.

CHARCUTERIE
COESNON
30 Rue Dauphine, Paris 6.
Tel: 43.54.35.80.
Métro: Odéon.
Open 8:30 A.M. to 1:15 P.M.
and 3 to 8 P.M. Closed
Sunday, Monday, one
week at Easter, and
August.

One of the city's most respected family *charcuteries*, run by the friendly Coesnon family, who came to Paris from Normandy during the 1950s. Their specialties include homemade French sausages, with more than eighteen different varieties of *boudin*, including *boudin noir* (blood sausage)—some filled with raisins, chestnuts, apples, or herbs—and *boudin blanc* (pork and veal sausage), along with *andouillettes* (chitterling sausages). In the winter months, the *boudin* is made fresh each Tuesday and Thursday. Also game *terrines*, home-smoked bacon, and *foie gras cru* (fresh fattened goose and duck liver), are sold all year round.

VIGNEAU-DESMAREST
105–107 Rue de Sèvres,
  Paris 6.
Tel: 42.22.23.23.
Métro: Sèvres-Babylone.
Open 9:30 A.M. to 8 P.M.
  closed Sunday.

Vigneau-Desmarest, founded in 1920, remains one of the city's last *grandes charcuteries*, with many of their pork products prepared from farm-raised pigs, or *porc fermier*. The shop also serves as a full-scale delicatessen, where you can buy fruits and vegetables, wines, and prepared foods to carry-out.

VICTOR-HUGO, ARC DE TRIOMPHE, VILLIERS
16th and 17th arrondissements

**CHARCUTERIE
  ALSACIENNE**
37 Rue de Belles-Feuilles,
  Paris 16.
Tel: 47.27.33.74.
Métro: Victor-Hugo.
Open 9 A.M. to 8 p.m.
  Closed Monday.

See listing, 6th *arrondissement*.

Oh là là!

CORDIER
129 Avenue Victor-Hugo,
  Paris 16.
Tel: 47.27.97.74.
Métro: Victor-Hugo.
Open 9 A.M. to 1:30 P.M. and
  3:30 to 7:30 P.M. Closed
  Sunday.
Credit cards: AE, V.

Cordier is a solid, traditional neighborhood *charcuterie,* with a touch of luxury. Here fine smoked salmon and fresh raw fatted duck and goose liver, *foie gras cru,* is sold at holiday time, for preparing your own *terrines* of *foie gras* or for sautéeing in thick, dense slices.

DIVAY
4 Rue Bayen, Paris 17.
Tel: 43.80.16.97.
Métro: Ternes.
Open 8 A.M. to 1 P.M. and 4
  to 7 P.M. Closed Sunday
  afternoon and Monday.
Credit card: V.

Divay—a large and dependable *charcuterie*—likes to advertise as having the cheapest *foie gras* in Paris. It *is* less expensive than others, and both their duck and goose *terrines* are delicious. Also excellent are the hams, sausages, carry-out salads, and much of the year, raw foie gras for preparing one's own homemade *terrines*.

FOIE GRAS

*F*oie gras—a crown jewel of French gastronomy—
is the smooth and buttery liver from a fattened
duck or goose. Seasoned lightly with salt and pepper,
then cooked gently in a white porcelain terrine,
this highly perishable delicacy demands no further
embellishment than a slice of freshly toasted country
bread and a glass of chilled sweet Sauternes. At its
best, *foie gras* is one of the world's most satisfying
foods. Earthy and elegant, a single morsel of it melts
slowly on the palate, invading one's senses with an
aroma and flavor that's gracefully soothing, supple,
and rich, with a lingering, almost organic aftertaste.
Depending on its origin and length of cooking time,
the color of *foie gras* ranges from a slightly golden
brown to a peach-blushed rose. Rich in calories, *foie
gras* is best enjoyed slowly and parsimoniously—it is
also expensive.

What is better, goose or duck liver? It is
purely a matter of preference. Fattened goose liver
(*foie gras d'oie*) is less common and more expensive
than fattened duck liver (*foie gras de canard*) because
its production requires more intensive care and feeding. Geese are very susceptible to disease or pertur-
bation in their daily routine, so the casualty rate is
high. Ducks are more hardy and less demanding, and
during the past twenty years the fattened duck liver
has gained popularity, as French restaurateurs and
consumers have also developed a strong appetite for
the breast of the fattened duck, the *magret de canard*.
As for taste, goose liver is slightly subtle and mild,
duck liver more forward-tasting and a bit more
acidic.

What does one look for in *foie gras*? Ideally, a
slice of *foie gras* should be the same color throughout,
a sign that it is from the same liver and has been
carefully and uniformly cooked. It should always
have a fresh, appealing, liverlike aroma.

Serve *foie gras* slightly chilled, but not too cold.
If possible, remove it from the refrigerator fifteen to
twenty minutes before serving. When too cold, flavors are masked. When too warm, *foie gras* can turn
mushy, losing its seductive charm.

The following are the legal French definitions
and preparations for *foie gras*. When purchasing it
preserved, look for products packed in terrines or

glass jars, rather than tins, so you can see exactly what you are buying. The best *foie gras* has a fresh color, slices neatly, is generally free of blood vessels, and is not heavily surrounded with fat. Many shops also sell *foie gras* by the slice, cut from a larger terrine. This should be refrigerated, and is best eaten within a few hours. *Foie gras* that can legally enter the United States must have been sterilized—cooked at a temperature of 230°F (110°C)—and is generally marked *foie gras de conserve.*

Foie gras cru: Raw liver. If of good quality, this is the ultimate in *foie gras*. Usually found only at select Paris *charcuteries* around the end of the year, it is delicious sliced raw and spread on warm toasted bread; it can also be preserved in a terrine at home. Often sold vacuum-packed. The best are the smallest, a little over 1 pound (500 to 600 grams) for goose, a little under 1 pound (400 grams) for duck. Lobes should be supple, round, smooth rather than granular, and without spots. A good buy when purchased from a reputable merchant.

Foie gras mi-cuit or nature: The lightly cooked preserved *foie gras* of connoisseurs, and the best way to sample *foie gras* for the first time. Ideally, only the highest-quality livers are preserved in this manner. The terms *mi-cuit* and *nature* are used interchangeably with *foie gras frais*, denoting that the livers have been pasteurized at 175 to 200°F (80 to 90°C). Next to raw, this is the best way to enjoy *foie gras*, for it is barely cooked, retaining its pure, agreeably rich flavor. Sold in terrines, vacuum packed, in aluminum foil-wrapped rolls, or in a can or jar, it requires refrigeration. Depending on packaging, it will last several days to several months.

Foie gras entier: Entire lobes of the fattened liver, lightly seasoned and generally cooked in a terrine or glass jar. If the container is large, additional pieces of another liver may be added to fill it in. Sold fresh (*frais*), which requires refrigeration and must be consumed within a few weeks or months (depending on length of cooking time); and *en conserve*, which requires no refrigeration and will last several years.

Foie gras en conserve: Fattened livers, whole or in pieces, that have been seasoned, then sterilized in a jar or can at 230° to 240°F (108 to 115°C). Requires no refrigeration. Carefully conserved, high-quality *foie gras* will actually ripen and improve with age. It should be stored in a cool, dry place and turned from time to time, and could be kept for up to ten years. A good buy when purchased from a reputable merchant.

Bloc de foie gras: By law, composed of either 50 percent fattened duck liver or 35 percent goose liver that must be obviously present in chunks, held together by *foie gras* that has been mechanically blended. Not the best buy, for there is also a 10 percent allowance for pork barding fat.

Foie gras truffé: *Foie gras* with at least 3 percent truffles. A bad buy, for the flavor of the expensive truffle is totally lost, the price greatly inflated.

Foie gras parfait: A mechanically mixed blend of usually mediocre-quality *foie gras* surrounded with stuffing of pork, veal, or chicken meat, then wrapped in barding fat. A bad buy.

Foie gras pâté, galantine, or purée: Various products with a base of *foie gras.* Usually composed of lowest-quality livers mixed with pork, chicken, or veal, surrounded by barding fat. The word *gras* may be missing, but the mixtures must contain a minimum of 50 percent *foie gras,* with added stuffing mixture and pork barding fat. A bad buy.

L'ENTRACTE
46 Rue de Lévis, Paris 17.
Tel: 42.27.88.19.
Métro: Villiers.
Open 9 A.M. to 1 P.M. and 4 to 7 P.M. Closed Sunday and Monday.

In her seventies the earthy Louisette still sells *charcuterie* out of a little kiosk attached to a café. Specialties from Brittany and the Auvergne include a *mousse de canard* and an assortment of artisanal honeys.

JEAN-CLAUDE ET NANOU
46 Rue Legendre, Paris 17.
Tel: 42.27.15.08.
Métro: Malesherbes.
Open 8:30 A.M. to 1 P.M. and 4:15 to 8 P.M. Closed Sunday afternoon (all day during summer months), Monday, and August.

Chic, friendly, and outgoing, Jean-Claude and Nanou Clement run a tidy family *charcuterie,* where they bring in marvelous products from their native Auvergne, including very firm and flavorful hams that have been aged for a full eight months and many farm cheeses from Laguiole and Saint-Nectaire, including the sheep's milk cheese from the Benedictine Abbaye de Belloc. Also excellent are the sausages which have been dried the old-fashioned way in huge barrels of cinders.

BOUCHERIE LAMARTINE
172 Avenue Victor-Hugo, Paris 16.
Tel: 47.27.82.29.
Métro: Victor Hugo or Rue de la Pompe.
Open 7 A.M. to 7:30 P.M.
Closed Saturday afternoon, Sunday, and August.

Boucherie Lamartine, one of the finest butcher shops in Paris, also sells the products made near Lyons by René Besson, better known as Bobosse. They carry his delicate *quenelles de brochet*, or pike dumplings, and the famous pistachio-studded pork sausage, *saucisson de Lyon*. Other offerings include beef aged a full 21 days, *pré-salé* lamb in September, and spring baby lamb and baby veal.

MAISON POU
16 Avenue des Ternes, Paris 17.
Tel: 43.80.19.24.
Métro: Ternes.
Open 9:30 A.M. to 1:15 P.M. and 3:30 to 7:15 P.M.
Closed Sunday and Monday.
Credit cards: DC, V.

A "press-your-nose-against-the-window" shop: Elegant, upscale, and spotless, it is filled with fragrant sausages, steaming sauerkraut, and hams, not to mention a wide selection of wines, cheeses, preserved and dried wild mushrooms, fresh truffles in season, and preserved truffles year-round. They also sell a fabulous and beautiful selection of pâtés.

SCHMID
36 Rue de Lévis, Paris 17.
Tel: 47.63.07.08.
Métro: Villiers.
Open 8:30 A.M. to 7:30 P.M.
Closed Sunday afternoon and Monday.
Credit cards: MC, V.

Almost as good as a trip to Alsace: Here the windows are filled with heart-shaped Alsatian spice cookies, golden, farm-aged Munster, sausages for slicing or poaching, wines, liqueurs, and *foie gras* from the region.

Today's specials.

Chocolatiers
CHOCOLATE SHOPS

The *allure of chocolate.*

The way the French fuss over chocolate, you might think they had invented it. They didn't, but as in so many matters gastronomic, the French inspire envy. They have refined the art of fine chocolate making, coaxing and coddling their sweets into existence, working carefully until they've produced some of the smoothest and strongest, richest, most intoxicating, and flavorful candies to be found anywhere in the world.

The French chocolate-buying public is discriminating, and *chocolatiers,* or chocolate makers, are fortunate to have a clientele willing to pay a premium price for confections prepared with the finest South American cocoa beans, the best Madagascar vanilla, the freshest Sicilian pistachios, the most expensive Dutch cocoa butter.

But chocolate is not without its trends. Today, the French palate has gone crazy for *"le gout amer,"* the bittersweet taste of chocolate high in cocoa butter and low in sugar. But beware, a low sugar content is not necessarily a sign of quality. The best bet is to buy in small quantities, and judge for yourself.

Before there was chocolate as we know it today—in bars and in flavored squares and rounds, enjoyed as a snack or dessert—chocolate was prepared as a drink. As the brew became popular in Europe during the 17th century, it also became the subject of discord. Was chocolate healthy? Was it lethal? Was it a dangerous aphrodisiac? The famous 17th-century letter writer, Madame de Sévigné, wrote her daughter at the time: "It flatters you for a while, it warms you for an instant; then it kindles a mortal fever in you." But when her daugher moved from Paris, she worried how she could "get along" without a *chocolatière,* or chocolate pot.

Paris's first chocolate shop—situated on the Rue de l'Arbre Sec in what is now the 1st *arrondissement*—was opened in 1659, when Louis XIV gave one of Queen Anne's officers the exclusive privilege to sell chocolate.

Chocolate soon became the rage of the French courts. It was served at least three times a week at Versailles, and it is said that Napoleon preferred chocolate to coffee as a morning pick-me-up. In Voltaire's later years, he consumed twelve cups a day, always between five in the morning and three in the afternoon. He lived to be eighty-four-years old. Brillat-Savarin, the French 18th-century gastronome, put it concisely: "Chocolate is health."

In the early 1800s, two very clever Parisians figured a way around the still-raging dispute over the merits of chocolate. They sold it as medicine. A certain Monsieur Debauve, a *chocolatier,* and a Monsieur Gallais, a pharmacist, teamed up and opened an elegant shop at 30 Rue des Saints-Pères, just off the Boulevard Saint-Germain. Soon the nervous, the sickly, the thin, the obese, were going to Debauve and Gallais for "the chocolate cure." It's no surprise to find that the chocolate preparations became bigger business than other pharmaceuticals, and Debauve & Gallais—where chocolates are still sold in the same shop today—soon became the most important chocolate shop in Paris.

Today in France, chocolate remains synonymous with *gourmandise* and comfort. There is even a *Club des Croqueurs de Chocolat,* a private Parisian group of chocolate loving connoisseurs that meets regularly to taste and judge the latest chocolate creations. Still, the French display a great deal of discipline when it comes to their beloved chocolate. They actually eat less chocolate than their neighbors—the French consume about eleven pounds of chocolate per person, compared to twenty-two for the Swiss and fifteen for the Belgians (the Americans consume about nine pounds). But when they eat chocolate, they want plenty of it, and fast: 80 percent of all the chocolate sold in Paris is sold during the final three weeks of December!

BOURSE

2nd arrondissement

DEBAUVE & GALLAIS
33 Rue Vivienne, Paris 2.
Tel: 40.39.05.50.
Métro: Bourse.
Open 10 A.M. to 7 P.M.
 Closed Sunday and
 August.

This former *confiserie* of the Duc de Praslin has been transformed into an annex of the famed Left Bank establishment. The same ravishing chocolates, without crossing the river. (See also 6th *arrondissment.*)

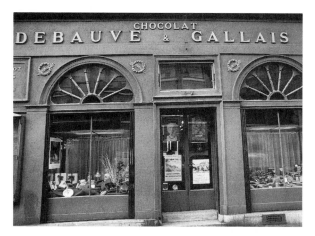

SAINT-GERMAIN DES PRES, SEVRES-BABYLONE, ECOLE MILITAIRE

6th and 7th arrondissements

MICHEL CHAUDUN
149 Rue de l'Université,
 Paris 7.
Tel: 47.53.74.40.
Métro: Invalides.
Open 9 A.M. to 7 P.M. Closed
 Sunday and Monday.

Michel Chaudun's fragrant little shop offers some truly spectacular chocolates: I'm particularly in love with his super bittersweet chocolate bars, or *tablettes*. He's also famous for his *esmeralda* (bittersweet truffles), *veragua* (chocolates filled with praline and caramel), and dark, rich, chocolate cakes. The windows are often decorated with chocolates in the form of big capital letters, perfect gifts for the person who has everything, but . . .

DEBAUVE & GALLAIS
30 Rue des Saint-Pères,
   Paris 7.
Tel: 45.48.54.67.
Métro: Saint-Germain-des-
   Prés.
Open 10 A.M. to 7 P.M.
   Closed Sunday, Monday,
   and August.
Credit cards: AE, DC,
   MC, V.

An old shop with a bright new interior, this little jewel began life in 1800 as a pharmacy that dispensed chocolate. The counter is now covered with glass amphoras filled with hazelnut pralines and chocolate truffles dusted with cocoa. Chocolates are handled as though they were precious gems, and no matter how small your order, it will be wrapped, ribboned, and decorated with a lovely gold seal. The chocolates here are dark, intense, and masculine. On a sunny day, the sun shines through the shop's elegant *cosse d'orange* windows, arranged to form an elegant orange wedge.

CANDIED CHESTNUTS

Candied chestnuts, *marrons glacés,* are fall and winter specialties sold at most of the better chocolate shops in town. They appear around the beginning of November, when the first fresh chestnuts begin arriving from the Ardèche, in southeastern France. They generally disappear at the close of the season, around the middle of January. The process of turning fresh raw chestnuts into little candied jewels is painstakingly slow, and requires immense patience.

The fresh chestnuts are first boiled several times to free them from their shells and skins. If any bits of skin remain, they are removed by hand. The chestnuts are then wrapped in cheesecloth to prevent them from falling apart during the next process—a three- to seven-hour stint in a pressure cooker. Next, they are cooked again, this time for 48 hours in a vanilla sugar syrup over very low heat. The chestnuts are often delivered to shops in this form, conserved in syrup. They are then glazed in small quantities by sprinkling them with water and baking them, a process which gives the chestnuts their characteristic sugary appearance. Finally they are wrapped in the traditional shiny gold foil paper.

An exquisite display.

JEAN-PAUL HEVIN
3 Rue Vavin, Paris 6.
Tel: 43.54.09.85.
Métro: Vavin.
Open daily, 10 A.M. to
7:30 P.M.

and

16 Avenue de la Motte
Picquet, Paris 7.
Tel: 45.51.77.48.
Métro: La Tour-Maubourg.
Open daily, 10 A.M. to
7:30 P.M. Closed in
August.
Credit card: V.

Jean-Paul Hévin is one of the new, young generation of chocolate makers who sell their wares in modern shops that resemble jewelry stores, where the saleslady acts as though you're about to steal the family gems and also wishes you wouldn't bother her with your presence. Although the assortment is beautiful and varied, I find his chocolates just so-so. In fact, the *florentins* I sampled on the last visit resembled squares of chocolate topped with stale rice crispies. A better bet are the *palets amers,* tiny squares of bittersweet chocolate that melt oh-so soothingly. But chocolate lovers, go see for yourself. Hévin is young, and perhaps just needs to mature. There are also tea, coffee, sandwiches, *croissants,* cakes, and chocolate bars, or *tablettes.*

PUYRICARD
27 Avenue Rapp, Paris 7.
Tel: 47.05.59.47.
Métro: Ecole Militaire or
   Alma-Marceau.
Open 9:30 A.M. to 7:30 P.M.
   Tuesday through
   Saturday; 2 to 7:30 P.M.
   Monday. Closed Sunday
   and August.

A sober, old-fashioned shop selling handmade chocolates from Aix-en-Provence—rich and creamy, with the intensity of good South American chocolate. Try as well the famed *calissons d'Aix,* and the nougatine filled with pine nuts, or *pignons.*

RICHART
258 Boulevard Saint-
   Germain, Paris 7.
Tel: 45.55.66.00.
Métro: Solférino.
Open 10 A.M. to 7 P.M.
   Tuesday through Friday
   and from 11 A.M.
   Saturday and Monday.
   Closed Sunday.

A lovely, modern, elegant chocolate shop, featuring delicious *tablettes,* or chocolate bars, made with Venezuelan chocolate, as well as an exceptional sorbet of chocolate and cinnamon, *chocolat-cannelle.* Their sampling collection, "*grignotage,*" features some twenty different handmade chocolates, flavored with everything from *marc de Gewürztraminer* from Alsace, to a *coulis* of pineapple.

MADELEINE, ROND-POINT, ARC DE TRIOMPHE

8th and 9th arrondissements

BOISSIER
46 Avenue Marceau,
   Paris 8.
Tel: 47.20.31.31.
Métro: Alma-Marceau.
Open 10 A.M. to 7 P.M.
   Closed Saturday and
   Sunday.
Credit card: V.

B oissier always makes me think that someone is having a very exclusive bake sale, with little trays of perfect cakes and chocolates all lined up for inspection. Even though wealthy families in the neighborhood may have full-time cooks, the lady of the house still comes in here to select the evening's dessert!

LA BONBONNIERE
   SAINT-HONORE
28 Rue de Miromesnil,
   Paris 8.
Tel: 42.65.02.39.
Métro: Miromesnil.
Open 10 A.M. to 7 P.M.
   Closed Saturday and
   Sunday.
Credit cards: MC, V.

T his pristine, family-run shop is the sister boutique of the charming and fragrant Bonbonnière de Trinité (see page 308). It offers, of course, the same deep, dark, fresh-tasting chocolates, as well as a healthy assortment of packaged regional candies (or *bonbons*), cakes, and cookies. I'm partial to their fragile discs of bittersweet chocolate for serving with coffee. Also pretty rows of homey-looking jams and jellies, and tins of regional cakes and cookies.

LA MAISON DU
   CHOCOLAT
225 Rue du Fauborg Saint-
   Honoré, Paris 8.
Tel: 42.27.39.44.
Fax: 47.64.03.75.
Métro: Ternes.
Open 9:30 A.M. to 7 P.M.
   Closed Sunday and
   August.
Credit cards: MC, V.
Will ship internationally.

and

52 Rue Francois-1er,
   Paris 8.
Tel: 47.23.38.25.
Métro: Franklin-D-
   Roosevelt.
Open 9:30 A.M. to 7 P.M.
   Closed Sunday.
Credit cards: MC, V.

and

8 Boulevard de la
   Madeleine, Paris 9.
Tel: 47.42.86.52.
Métro: Madeleine.
Open 9:30 A.M. to 7 P.M.
   Closed Sunday.
Credit cards: MC, V.

Robert Linxe, chocolatier at
La Maison du Chocolat (above).

A chocolate-lover's dream: chocolate-colored façade, chocolate-colored blinds, even the *chocolatier,* Robert Linxe, in a chocolate-colored apron. You feel as though you'll gain a pound or two just breathing the air in his marvelous trio of shops. Monsieur Linxe is the undisputed king of chocolate in Paris, selling a sophisticated, handmade assortment of delights prepared in the neat little basement workshop on the Rue du Faubourg Saint-Honoré. He's rightly proud of his *framboise* (raspberry-flavored chocolate), and his creamy *palets d'or* melt in your mouth. Other excellent creations include *rigoletto* (filled with a caramel butter), *la bohème* (milk chocolate), and *roméo,* with an interior of fresh-brewed arabica coffee. He also experiments with fillings flavored with fresh-brewed tea, and with ginger.

At the cool, pristine, chocolate-hued boutique on Rue Francois 1er, you can sit at the marble-topped bar or around low, round tables and indulge in one of the world's greatest passions. One scorching summer's day I was miraculously invigorated by a *Guayaquil frappé,* a tall glass of perfect iced chocolate, a whipped blend of bitter chocolate ice cream and rich melted chocolate. The menu here offers no less than five variously flavored hot chocolates, chocolate mousses, sorbets, and ice creams. Chocolates, pastries, and cakes can be purchased to sample in the shop or take home. The diminutive menu offers a sampling of appropriate gastronomic sayings, including a pertinent warning from Saint Ignatius of Loyola, founder of the Jesuit order: "Gourmandise is a capital sin. So therefore, my brothers, let us guard against being gourmands. Let's be gourmets."

GRANDS BOULEVARDS, TRINITE, LE PELETIER, GARE SAINT-LAZARE

8th and 9th arrondissements

DENISE ACABO/
  A L'ETOILE D'OR
30 Rue Fontaine, Paris 9.
Tel: 48.74.59.55.
Métro: Blanche.
Open 10:30 A.M. to 8 P.M.
  Closed Sunday and
  August.
Credit card: V.

How does a chocolate lover visit Paris and yet manage to sample all the best homemade chocolates from all over France? The answer is a simple Métro ride to the Blanche station, then a swift, anticipatory walk down Rue Fontaine until you reach the charming, old-fashioned storefront of Denise Acabo. She's round and pigtailed, with an obvious passion for chocolate. Show a little interest, and, no questions asked, she'll take you on a guided tour of her fragrant boutique, where you'll travel to Lyon for a selection from the Bernachons, to Nice for the Auer family's, to La Clayette for

Bernard Dufoux's offerings, and to Voiron for Monsieur Bonnat's. Her selections are pure, honest, invigorating. If you have time for only one chocolate shop in Paris, make it this one. I assure you, it won't disappoint.

CHOCOLATE FOR ALL SEASONS

In Paris, chocolate is always in fashion. Throughout the year, the sparkling windows of the city's shops serve as a calendar, announcing each holiday, beginning with Valentine's Day when thousands of chocolate hearts are broken.

Spring is ushered in as shop windows are aswim with chocolate fish in anticipation of *Poisson d'Avril,* April Fool's Day. Large fish with bows around their tails are filled with schools of *fritures,* tiny chocolate minnows. And little boxes filled with milk chocolate "sardines" appear everwhere.

At Easter time chocolate bunnies, chicks, ducks, and puppies frolic in displays. They are surrounded by chocolate eggs wrapped with silvery, glittery, magical paper. On the Place de la Madeleine, Fauchon's huge, lacy chocolate egg sits in regal splendor, stopping pedestrian traffic for weeks.

Easter has hardly passed when tiny chocolate pots of *muguets,* lilies of the valley, appear as the traditional French symbol for the first of May. They keep company with the hearts and flowers that burst forth for *Fête des Mères,* Mother's Day.

Although the summer heat signals a slowdown for chocolates in Paris, chocolate shops refuse to give up. Windows are full of summer symbols, all nicely molded in chocolate—pails and shovels for playing in the sand, starfish, and shells.

Fall comes in with blustery days that announce the season for chocolate mushrooms and luscious, creamy truffles. All of this is a fanfare to Christmas, when chocolate shops split their attention between the candied chestnuts known as *marrons glacés* and *bûches de Noël,* or Christmas log cakes, homey reminders of times past, when guests offered their hosts a real log to keep the fire burning.

**LA BONBONNIERE DE
  LA TRINITE**
4 Place d'Estienne d'Orves,
  Paris 9.
Tel: 48.74.23.38.
Métro: Trinité.
Open 10 A.M. to 7 P.M.
  Closed Sunday.
Credit cards: MC, V.

See La Bonbonniere Saint-Honore, page 304.

A LA MERE DE FAMILLE
35 Rue du Faubourg
  Montmartre, Paris 9.
Tel: 47.70.83.69.
Métro: Montmartre or
  Cadet.
Open 8:15 A.M. to 1:30 P.M.
  and 3 to 7 P.M. Closed
  Sunday, Monday
  morning, and August.
Credit cards: MC, V.

This shop comes right out of a fairy tale. Stop in late in the afternoon, as the children are getting out of school, and watch the owners spoil the entire neighborhood with their incredible variety of sweets from all over France. In the chocolate department, sample the little *barquettes* of dark chocolate filled with *cassis* (black currants) or *framboise* (raspberry).

BASTILLE
11th arrondissement

LA PETITE FABRIQUE
12 Rue Saint-Sabin,
  Paris 11.
Tel: 48.05.82.02.
Métro: Bastille.
Open 10 A.M. to 7:30 P.M.
  Closed Sunday.
Credit card: V.

Wandering into La Petite Fabrique from the exhaust-fumed streets of Paris is like falling right into chocolate heaven. The aromas that envelop you are intoxicating, and you can watch as workers temper their chocolates and mold specialties. I wouldn't call these the best tasting chocolates in Paris, but they're delicious, and the boutique is worth visiting if you're in the neighborhood.

VICTOR-HUGO
16th arrondissement

BOISSIER
184 Avenue Victor-Hugo,
  Paris 16.
Tel: 45.04.87.88.
Métro: Victor-Hugo.
Open 9 A.M. to 7:30 P.M.
  Monday through Friday;
  10 A.M. to 7 P.M.
  Saturday and Sunday.
Credit card: V.

See listing, 8th and 9th *arrondissements*.

MACARONS CREOLES
CHOCOLATE MACAROONS

One day I was exhausted and a friend suggested that what I needed was chocolate. Not just any chocolate, but something special from La Maison du Chocolat, one of the best chocolate shops in Paris (see page 305). Fortunately, it just happens to be at the end of my street. I bought a chocolate-filled chocolate macaroon and was instantly cured. In gratitude and greed, I created this recipe the very next day, and have never found anyone who'd turn them down.

Macaroons:
1 cup (140 g) almonds
3½ ounces (110 g) bittersweet chocolate (preferably Lindt or Tobler brand)
1 teaspoon vanilla extract
2 large egg whites (2½ ounces; 80 g)
¾ cup (150 g) sugar
1 tablespoon (½ oz; 15g) unsalted butter, for buttering the baking sheet

Filling:
1¾ ounces (50 g) bittersweet chocolate
2 tablespoons *crème fraîche* (see recipe, page 279) or heavy (whipping) cream (preferably not ultra-pasteurized)

1. Preheat the oven to 275°F (135°C).

2. Toast the almonds on a baking sheet until browned, about 5 minutes. Remove, but leave the oven on. When cool, grind the almonds to a fine powder in a food processor.

3. In a small saucepan over very low heat, melt the 3½ ounces (110 g) chocolate with the vanilla.

4. In the bowl of an electric mixer on slow speed, mix the egg white, almonds, and sugar until well blended. With the machine still running, add the melted chocolate mixture, and continue beating until thoroughly blended.

5. Butter a baking sheet (or line with cooking parchment paper, then butter the paper). Spoon the batter onto the baking sheet, allowing 1 heaping tablespoon of batter for each macaroon.

6. Bake just until the macaroons are set, 15 to 18 minutes. They should be slightly firm but not dry. Transfer the macaroons to a rack to cool.

7. Meanwhile, prepare the filling. In a small saucepan over very low heat, melt the 1¾ ounces (50 g) chocolate. Add the *crème fraîche* or heavy cream and stir until well blended. Set aside to cool.

8. When the macaroons and the filling have cooled, spread a heaping tablespoon of the filling on half the macaroons, and cover each with a second macaroon, making a sort of sandwich. The macaroons may be served immediately, though they are best if they sit for a few hours.

Yield: 10 to 12 filled macaroons

Spécialités
Gastronomiques
SPECIALTY SHOPS

The exotic world of Izraël (see entry, page 313).

The specialty shops of Paris, ranging from old-fashioned, family-owned candy and spice shops to slick and rambling food emporiums, offer a potpourri of good things at your fingertips. Whether you're looking for the freshest black truffle; whether you want to taste thirty different kinds of honey, sample *foie gras,* or try mustard made with Saint-Pourçain wine; or whether you just want to purchase a little sack of licorice to nibble on as you wander about Paris, the following should offer some guidance. From the exotic to the commonplace, here is a hint of the things of which dreams are made.

PALAIS-ROYAL, OPERA, TUILERIES, LES HALLES

1st and 2nd arrondissements

LE COQ SAINT-HONORE
22 Rue Gomboust, Paris 1.
Tel: 42.61.52.04.
Métro: Opéra or Pyramides.
Open 8 A.M. to 1 P.M. and
4 to 7 P.M. Closed
Saturday afternoon and
Sunday.
Credit cards: MC, V.

Even if you aren't going to buy, wander past this incredible butcher shop—perhaps the best in Paris—to press your nose against the glass. If it's poultry or meat and is raised in France, you'll find it here: baby lamb from the southwest and salt-marsh lamb from the Atlantic coast; beautiful chicken from Bresse, the Landes, and Périgord; farm-raised turkeys, Challans ducks; and in season, fabulous French game. Monsieur André-Mary Josse, the owner, is a charming man and runs a serious shop; his clients include all the best chefs in Paris.

DETOU
58 Rue Tiquetonne, Paris 2.
Tel: 42.36.54.67.
Fax: 40.39.08.04.
Métro: Etienne Marcel.
Open 8:30 A.M. to 6 P.M.
Monday through Friday;
8:30 A.M. to noon
Saturday. Closed
Saturday afternoon
and Sunday.
No credit cards.

The source of Parisian pastry chefs' best ingredients: Valrhona chocolate, almonds from Spain, pure cocoa butter, and dried fruits. Also dried mushrooms, nut oils, smoked salmon and *foie gras*. Baker Gérard Mulot is one of the shop's better customers, and this is where he buys chocolates for his lovely "chocolate chip" *pains au chocolat*.

GARGANTUA
284 Rue Saint-Honoré,
Paris 1.
Tel: 42.60.63.38.
Fax: 42.61.49.81.
Métro: Tuileries.
Open 7:30 A.M. to 9 P.M.
Closed Sunday.
Credit cards: AE, V.

As the name suggests, everything here is king-size. Enjoy quality *croissants, pains au chocolat*, and oversize puff pastry *palmiers*—all big enough to feed a family of four—at the small counter tucked in back of the shop. The place is casual and colorful, with a wide selection of *charcuterie,* wines, liquors, and salads, ready to take home, or on a picnic or a plane.

**TETREL EPICERIE/
CONFISERIE**
44 Rue des Petits-Champs,
Paris 2.
Tel: 42.96.59.58.
Métro: Pyramides.
Open 9 A.M. to 5:30 P.M.
Closed Sunday.
No credit cards.

A pristine little shop for fine foodstuffs, with polished wood counters and sparkling windows all crowded with tins of candies, *confit*, and sardines. This is a good place to experience old Paris and pick up some old-fashioned sweets or a small gift reminiscent of the 19th century.

FLO PRESTIGE

One of Paris's more trustworthy carry-out food shops, Flo Prestige offers a bright and fresh selection of raw-milk cheeses, beautiful smoked salmon, assorted *charcuterie, foie gras*, and salads. Everything can be purchased in individual portions (there's even *pain Poilâne* by the slice), so put together a picnic and head for the Tuileries Gardens (or the nearest useful address). Wine and pastries are also available. Flo delivers (for a healthy price), and these are useful addresses to keep in mind for late-night hunger pangs. Shops are open 8 A.M. to 11 P.M. (Printemps boutique 9:30 A.M. to 9 P.M. Closed Sunday). Credit cards: AE, DC, V.

42 Place du Marché Saint-Honoré, Paris 1.
Tel: 42.61.45.46.
Métro: Pyramides.

Au Printemps: 64 Boulevard Haussmann, Paris 9.
Tel: 42.82.58.82.
Métro: Havre-Caumartin.

36 Avenue de La Motte-Picquet, Paris 16.
Tel: 45.55.71.25.
Métro: Latour-Maubourg.

211 Avenue Daumesnil, Paris 11.
Tel: 43.44.86.36.
Métro: Daumesnil.

354 Rue Lecourbe, Paris 15.
Tel: 45.54.76.94.
Métro: Balard.

61 Avenue de la Grande-Armée, Paris 16.
Tel: 45.00.12.10.
Métro: Argentine.

102 Avenue Président Kennedy, Paris 16.
Tel: 42.88.38.00.
Métro: Passy.

VERLET
256 Rue Saint-Honoré,
 Paris 1.
Tel: 42.60.67.39.
Métro: Palais-Royal.
Open 9 A.M. to 7 P.M. Closed
 Sunday, Monday, and
 August.
No credit cards.

For common and uncommon coffees and teas fresh from the world over. A block away from the Palais-Royal, this cozy shop filled with open sacks of coffee is a great spot for a pick-me-up. The tea room is homey and aromatic and the friendly proprietors love to discuss the merits and differences of each coffee variety. They also serve a good *croque-monsieur* and fine fresh desserts, including a delectable apricot tart (see recipe, page 166.)

MARAIS

3rd and 4th arrondissements

IZRAEL
30 Rue François-Miron,
 Paris 4.
Tel: 42.72.66.23.
Métro: Saint-Paul.
Open 9:30 A.M. to 1 P.M. and
 2:30 to 7 P.M. Tuesday
 through Friday; 9:30
 A.M. to 7 P.M. Saturday.
 Closed Sunday, Monday,
 and August.
Credit card: V.

Some years ago, a friendly, robust man named Israel married a woman named Izrael, hence the name of the shop. That doesn't quite make the patron Israel Izrael, but he does have a great sense of humor about it. The shop opened nearly fifty years ago, specializing in North African products. Today, the cluttered, delicious-smelling store features more than 3,000 products from all over the world—everything from guava paste to American corn chips, delicious Polish buckwheat to woven African baskets. There's a marvelous assortment of grains, rice, flours, dried fruits, and nuts, all sold out of giant sacks.

Chock-full at Izraël.

MAISON DES BONBONS
46 Rue de Sévigné, Paris 3.
Tel: 48.87.88.62.
Métro: Saint-Paul.
Open 10 A.M. to 7 P.M.
   Tuesday through Friday,
   2:30 to 7 P.M. Saturday
   and Sunday. Closed
   Monday.
Credit cards: MC, V.

A fantasy shop for children, as well as those with childhood memories of giant glass jars filled with chocolates, hard candies, caramels, wands of licorice (*reglisse*), you name it. This sweet boutique also carries an assortment of colorful tin boxes and some of France's best chocolate bars, from the Maison Bonnat.

A L'OLIVIER
23 Rue de Rivoli, Paris 4.
Tel: 48.04.86.59.
Métro: Saint-Paul or Hôtel
   de Ville.
Open 9:30 A.M. to 1 P.M.
   and 2 to 7 P.M.
Closed Sunday and Monday.
Credit card: V.

This bright, old-fashioned shop offers every kind of oil imaginable, from olive, walnut, and hazelnut for the table to palm oil for frying and almond oil for massages. Although the quality of the oil is not extraordinary, the nicely packaged products make fine gifts.

THANKSGIVING
20 Rue Saint-Paul, Paris 4.
Tel: 42.77.70.83.
Métro: Saint-Paul or
   Bastille.
Open daily 10 A.M. to 8 P.M.
Credit cards: MC, V.

Anyone in search of dark brown sugar for chocolate chip cookies, pancake mix, baking soda, pecan pie, or carrot cake in Paris will truly give thanks for this tiny American food shop in the Marais. As the name suggests, the shop will cater Thanksgiving meals. Its fresh seasonal products include, pumpkins, cranberries, yams, squash, and fresh corn.

LATIN QUARTER, SAINT-GERMAIN, INVALIDES, EIFFEL TOWER

5th, 6th, and 7th arrondissements

**L'AMBASSADE DU
   SUD-OUEST**
46 Avenue de la
   Bourdonnais, Paris 7.
Tel: 45.55.59.59.
Métro: Ecole Militaire.
Open daily 10 A.M. to
   11 P.M.
Credit cards: MC, V.

Foie gras frais, mi-cuit and cuit (fresh, semi-cooked and cooked), *pâté, rillettes, terrine, tourte Landaise* (a puff-pastry apple tart), *eaux-de-vie*, and all the earthy bounty of the French southwest can be found a couple of blocks from the Eiffel Tower. Open daily until 11 P.M., L'Ambassade du Sud-Ouest makes a convenient stop for last-minute gifts or picnic provisions for a feast in the Champs de Mars. You can sample foie gras sandwiches, *brouillades aux cèpes* (scrambled eggs with mushrooms), *cassoulet*, and other specialties in their café.

SARDINES

Decades ago, most self-respecting French gourmands tucked tins of fine and delicate Brittany sardines away in their *caves* (cellars), sometimes aging the tender little fish for a decade or more. Vintage, or *millésime*, sardines are again the rage in Paris, where most fine specialty shops offer a mixed assortment, tinned and carefully dated. Once they're taken home, the tins must be stored in a cool spot and turned every three or four months. As the rich, chewy sardines age, they become softer, more refined and delicate, ready to be consumed with a slice of crusty bread.

Sardines destined for *millésime* stardom bear no resemblance to the cheap garden-variety canned fish. Vintage sardines are always preserved fresh, while most ordinary sardines are frozen, then fried and processed. To prepare vintage sardines for processing, the fish are usually washed, grilled, and quickly deep-fried before being packed, by hand, into small oval tins. Generally the head, skin, and central backbone are removed from sardines packed for aging. Oil—usually the finest virgin olive oil—is added, perhaps a touch of spice or simply salt, then the tins are sealed and stored. They are turned regularly to ensure even aging, then put on the market one or two years after processing.

Many tins of vintage sardines include the words *première catégorie* or *extra* on the label, assuring that the sardines were prepared fresh, not frozen. Check for the processing date stamped into the bottom of the tin, so you know how long to keep them. Experts recommend the sardines be kept no more than four years.

The following are just a few of the shops offering vintage sardines. The tin or wrapper will bear the processing date.

Hédiard, 21 Place de la Madeleine, Paris 8. Tel: 42.66.44.36.

Fauchon, 26 Place de la Madeleine, Paris 8. Tel: 47.42.60.11.

Au Verger de la Madeleine, 4 Boulevard Malesherbes, Paris 8. Tel: 42.65.51.99.

HEDIARD

Tea, spice, and everything nice, Hédiard is one of the more chic groups of gourmet shops in town, with one-stop shopping for everything from their famous spices to exotic blends of vinegar or oil, great canned tuna and sardines, as well as chocolates, carry-out deli items, and exotic fruits and vegetables. Many visitors make annual visits simply to stock up on a few of Hédiard's thirty varieties of tea. Their freshly roasted coffee beans are also top quality (I love the Colombian *Maragogype*). Their wine cellars offer an extensive selection of Bordeaux at high prices. Good to know on off hours, when you want a quick pastry, *charcuterie*, a house gift. All shops open at 9:15 A.M. and are closed Sunday. Credit cards: AE, DC, V.

21 Place de la Madeleine, Paris 8.
  Tel: 42.66.44.36.
  Métro: Madeleine.
  Open until 10 P.M.

126 Rue du Bac, Paris 7.
  Tel: 45.44.01.98.
  Métro: Rue du Bac.
  Open until 9 P.M.

70 Avenue Paul-Doumer, Paris 16.
  Tel: 45.04.51.92.
  Métro: Trocadero or Muette.
  Open until 10 P.M.

6 Rue Donizetti, Paris 16.
  Tel: 40.50.71.94.
  Métro: Michel-Ange-Auteuil.
  Open until 9 P.M.

106 Boulevard de Courcelles, Paris 17.
  Tel: 47.63.32.14.
  Métro: Courcelles.
  Open until 10 P.M.

CAVIAR PETROSSIAN
18 Boulevard La Tour-
Maubourg, Paris 7.
Tel: 45.51.38.74.
Métro: La Tour-Maubourg
or Invalides.
Open 9 A.M. to 8 P.M. Closed
Sunday.
Credit cards: AE, V.

As Armen Petrossian says, "We sell dreams." And dreams are made of Russian caviar, smoked salmon, *foie gras*, truffles, and Sauternes. Everything here is of high quality, but the prices are competitive—I rarely buy caviar anywhere else in Paris. The Petrossians make regular trips to the Caspian Sea to monitor its processing. Other specialties include Russian pastries, fresh blinis, assorted herrings, vodka, and delicious black Georgian tea, along with Petrossian's own line of French products from the Périgord.

THE GENERAL STORE
82 Rue de Grenelle, Paris 7.
Tel: 45.46.63.16.
Métro: Rue du Bac.
Open 10 A.M. to 7 P.M.
Closed Sunday.
Credit cards: AE, DC, V.

After sampling your fill of *caviar, foie gras, croissants,* and chocolate truffles, if what you're really craving is Hershey bars and corn chips, brownies, and chocolate chips, this shop is the ticket to your dreams. The General Store is a sparkling boutique full of star-spangled goodies, all cheaper than a one-way ticket to the United States.

**LES HERBES DU
LUXEMBOURG**
3 Rue de Médicis, Paris 6.
Tel: 43.26.91.53.
Métro: Odéon or RER
Luxembourg.
Open: 9:30 A.M. to 7 P.M.
Tuesday through Friday,
11 A.M. to 2 P.M. and
3 to 7 P.M. Monday, and
11 A.M. to 7 P.M.
Saturday. Closed
Sunday.
Credit cards: MC, V.

I like to call this shop the health food general store. It offers everything from dried herbs and oils, fruits and nuts, honeys, jams, and fresh whole-grain breads each Wednesday, to organic baby foods and teas, all with an eye toward health and well-being. Some special items of note: the line of l'Olivier oils, sea salt from Brittany, an assortment of miniature soaps, shampoos, and toiletries for travel, and lily or cedar-scented paper for lining drawers.

TRUFFLES

Delicate, earthy, and increasingly rare, the prized black Périgord truffle symbolizes the *grand gastronomic* life of Paris, past and present. The writer Colette, who devoted one day each year to eating truffles, said it best: "If I can't have too many truffles, I'll do without truffles."

The Périgord truffle—in appearance a rather inelegant, wrinkled black nugget generally the size of a walnut, although it can be as small as a pea or as large as an orange—is perhaps the world's most mysterious food. A fungus with a capricious personality, it stubbornly refuses to be cultivated. (As one Frenchman observed, "Growing truffles is not farming, it's luck.") And its flavor is just as elusive. No one has succeeded in adequately describing the taste of a truffle. Some say it's licorice-like, others find a hint of black pepper. But it is the truffle's rich, pungent, and pervasive aroma that makes its flavor so singular. Eating fresh truffles makes me think of a quiet walk in the autumn woods under a slow drizzle, of freshly upturned black earth, of hazelnuts, of luxury, and of pleasure.

The traditional truffle comes primarily from the southwest of France, in the Quercy and Périgord regions east of Bordeaux, though in recent years the crop has been slowly moving farther south. Truffles are also found in the Tricastin area of the Rhône Valley, and a small quantity of the truffles processed in France come from Italy and Spain.

Truffles grow three inches to a foot underground, in stony, porous soil near the roots of scrub oak trees. Gathered from November to March by farmers using dogs or pigs trained to scent out and unearth the elusive tuber, the truffle reaches its peak of flavor toward the month of January. Truffles thrive on a rainy summer and autumn, and their presence sometimes can be spotted by the burned patch around the base of the tree—the truffle's way of ensuring enough air for itself by killing the undergrowth—or by the presence of a swarm of truffle flies that hover above where the tuber is growing.

Fresh truffles (*truffes fraîches*), are sold in Paris specialty shops from mid-November through March. An average-size fresh truffle weighs about 3 ounces, or about 100 grams, and though one truffle can't be

Someone who's tall and lanky is known as a "bean pole" in English, "une asperge" or asparagus in French.

considered an avalanche, it's enough for a gastronomic adventure.

At Paris's La Maison de la Truffe, which sells more than 600 pounds (about 300 kilos) of fresh and preserved truffles each year, fresh truffles arrive every two or three days from November to mid-March direct from the Périgord or the Vaucluse. Still encrusted with soil, the fragrant gems are placed unwrapped in small wicker baskets, so they can breathe during the four to five-hour train ride. A fresh truffle will last only three or four days, losing about one twentieth of its weight by evaporation each day after it is unearthed. Meanwhile, its flavor fades rapidly. Guy Monier, owner of La Maison de la Truffe, suggests that if a fresh truffle must be kept longer than three or four days, it should be gently washed, then buried in goose or duck fat and refrigerated; otherwise it is likely to mildew. It may be stored in fat for up to six months. A fresh truffle can also be refrigerated for two or three days, locked tight in a glass jar with several raw eggs still in their shells. The pungent truffle aroma will permeate the eggs, which can then be used to prepare a truffle-laced omelet, perhaps the best way to first experience a truffle.

For most of the world, the only known truffle is a preserved one. Although fresh is best, well-preserved truffles are better than no truffles at all. What does one look for in buying a preserved truffle? First, only buy preserved truffles in a glass container, so you can see what you're getting, and buy only:

Truffes brossées au naturel: truffles that have been sterilized in water and salt with no alcohol or spices used to mask or heighten their flavor. For the closest thing to a fresh truffle, try the whole preserved *truffe extra*, the top-grade truffle that is uniformly black and firm. If available, ask for a truffle of *premier ébullition*, that is, a truffle that has been brushed, salted, placed in its container, then sterilized. Since a truffle loses 25 percent of its weight during cooking, the weight of the *premier ébullition* truffle cannot be verified on the label. Thus, processors are required to underestimate on the label the true weight of the truffle. Most common are truffles of *deuxième ébullition*. In this process, the truffle is sterilized, removed from its container to verify its weight, then sterilized. All preserved truffles should be consumed within three years of being processed.

The following are other truffle gradings and other truffle preparations found on the market:

Truffes premier choix: small, irregularly shaped truffles that are more like pieces than whole truffles, and are more or less black. Not particularly good buys.

Truffes en morceaux: broken pieces of truffle that must be at least ¼ inch (5 mm) thick. Considered equal in quality to premier choix, and generally lower in price. Not particularly good buys.

Truffes en pelures: truffle peelings or shavings. Generally not worth the price.

Truffes préparées: truffles sterilized in water and salt, with liquor, alcohol, or wine added. A bad buy.

Jus de truffe: truffle juice. Not worth the price.

LAGRANGE EPICERIE A PARIS
15 Rue Lagrange, Paris 5.
Tel: 43.29.82.85.
Métro: Maubert-Mutualité.
Open daily 10 A.M. to 1 P.M. and 3 to 11 P.M.
Credit cards: MC, V.

Near Notre-Dame and open daily until 10 P.M., Epicerie Lagrange qualifies as a gourmet convenience store, offering fresh *charcuterie* preparations, tins of *foie gras, cassoulet,* and other regional specialties, as well as British and American packaged goods. The friendly *patron* of this new shop hands out samples of chocolate and other treats, and stocks a good selection of reasonably priced Bordeaux, as well as an earthy, artisanal wholegrain mustard from the Auvergne, made with Saint-Pourçain wine.

LE MARCHE DU BAC
69 Rue du Bac, Paris 7.
Tel: 45.44.05.70.
Métro: Rue du Bac.
Open daily 9 A.M. to 9 P.M.
No credit cards.

This Asian market arcade tucked into a *passage* off the Rue du Bac features exotic fruits, herbs, vegetables, and spices, as well as a Vietnamese take-out *charcuterie* and specialty store. Although for the flavor and price, Le Marché du Bac is not quite up to a Chinatown standard, it is a real find in this neighborhood.

MADELEINE, LE PELETIER, GARE DU NORD

8th, 9th, and 10th arrondissements

BETJEMAN AND BARTON
23 Boulevard Malesherbes, Paris 8.
Tel: 42.65.86.17.
Métro: Madeleine.
Open 9:30 A.M. to 7 P.M.
Closed Sunday.
Credit cards: AE, V.

A shop for Anglophiles almost across the street from Burberrys. You can stock up for afternoon tea here: They offer an excellent selection of teas, both classic varieties and seldom seen flower and herbal mixtures, as well as old-fashioned biscuits, and even scones (be forewarned, they often run out by the afternoon). To accompany all this, you may be tempted to buy one of the whimsical teapots shaped like animals and houses, among other things. Their extra-sour lemon drops can't be beat.

CAVIAR KASPIA
17 Place de la Madeleine, Paris 8.
Tel: 42.65.33.52.
Métro: Madeleine.
Open 9 A.M. to midnight.
Closed Sunday.
Credit cards: AE, DC, V.

A neat, simple, little boutique on the Place de la Madeleine, offering an excellent assortment of quality caviar, superb smoked salmon, and delightfully fresh blinis to take with you. There is also a cozy restaurant upstairs, where you can sample the house specialties on the spot. (See also Restaurants.)

FAUCHON
26 Place de la Madeleine, Paris 8.
Tel: 47.42.60.11.
Métro: Madeleine.
Open 9:40 A.M. to 7 P.M.
Closed Sunday.
Credit cards: AE, DC, V.

A visit to Fauchon is better than going to the theater. Many people even find their several shops on the Place de la Madeleine more fascinating than the Louvre. Fauchon's pristine glass windows, filled with expensive and exotic fruits and vegetables from every corner of the world, still stop traffic. Even the most jaded palates are tempted by the sheer quantity of food: more than 20,000 products including pastries, a mammoth international selection of fresh and packaged goods, coffee, tea, spices, and a complete *charcuterie*. This is the best-known food shop in town, but not always the friendliest and not always the best. Fauchon has recently expanded to add a fishmonger, bakery, and pastry shop. And in the lower level they've created a café and a self-service cafeteria (a handy place to know about at lunchtime) for sampling some of the goods they sell above.

CORNICHONS
TINY TART PICKLES

The cornichon, *a tiny tart pickle, is ubiquitous in France.* Cornichons *arrive at the table in squat white crocks, ready to be served with pâtés,* rillettes, *slices of salty country ham, or with* pot-au-feu. *The first time I made cornichons was in New York City. Picking through a bin full of garden-fresh cucumbers at the farmer's market on Union Square, I was able to come up with enough tiny cucumbers to make one precious quart. Now, frankly, I'm spoiled, for each August, the fresh cucumbers appear in abundance in Paris's open-air markets, ready for "putting up" with tiny white onions and plenty of fresh tarragon. I like them spicy and hot, so I add plenty of garlic and hot peppers.*

60 to 70 2-inch (5-cm) pickling cucumbers (about 2 pounds; 1 kg)

1/4 cup (65 g) coarse (kosher) salt

1 quart (1 liter) cold water, plus an additional 1½ cups (375 ml)

3 cups (750 ml) best-quality white wine vinegar

1 tablespoon sugar

12 small white pickling onions, peeled but with ends intact

4 large sprigs fresh tarragon

6 cloves garlic, peeled

8 small hot red peppers (fresh or dried)

½ teaspoon whole black peppercorns

2 bay leaves

1. Trim off stem ends of the cucumbers, then rinse and drain. In a large bowl combine the salt with 1 quart (1 liter) water. Stir until the salt is dissolved, add the cucumbers, and let stand in a cool place for 6 hours.

2. Scald two 1-quart (1-liter) canning jars, lids, and rings with boiling water and drain well.

3. Drain the cucumbers, discarding the salted water.

4. In a medium-size saucepan over medium heat combine the vinegar, 1½ cups (375 ml) water, and the sugar, and bring to a boil.

5. Layer the jars with the drained cucumbers, the onions, herbs, and spices, making sure to divide the ingredients evenly between the jars.

6. Pour the boiling vinegar, water, and sugar mixture into the jars, letting a bit of the liquid overflow the jars; this helps seal the lids well. Wipe the rim of each jar and seal. Let stand until cool. Store in a cool place for at least three weeks before serving. Refrigerate after opening.

Yield: 2 quarts (2 liters) *cornichons*

LE FURET-TANRADE
63 Rue de Chabrol,
Paris 10.
Tel: 47.70.48.34.
Métro: Gare de l'Est or
Poissonière.
Open 8 A.M. to 10 P.M.
Closed Sunday and two
weeks in August.
Credit cards: AE, V.

For those who miss the *confitures* of Tanrade—that extraordinary shop that once graced Rue Vignon in the 8th *arrondissement*—here you can find the old-fashioned smooth *confitures*, or jams (such as the *confiture poires passées*), that are truly honey-like, liquidy, but smooth and spreadable, and are designed for sweetening your morning bowl of thick and creamy yogurt. Try the *confiture/yogurt* combination, and you'll be hooked for life! Also artisanal pastries, chocolates, and honey.

LA MAISON DU MIEL
24 Rue Vignon, Paris 9.
Tel: 47.42.26.70.
Métro: Madeleine.
Open 9:30 A.M. to 7 P.M.
Tuesday through
Saturday; 9:30 A.M. to
6 P.M. Monday. Closed
Sunday.
Credit card: V.

Even if you're not passionate about honey, put this shop on your list. The "House of Honey" is one of the few stores in the world devoted totally to honey and honey products, and it's been at Rue Vignon since 1908. The fantasy-like tile decor—buzzing with bees and colorful hives—has not changed since then, nor has the founding family, the Gallands. They tend their own hives throughout France and buy selectively around the world. They sell some fifty-three tons of honey a year, producing about one-fourth of it themselves. Personal favorites include the hearty, rust-toned heather (*bruyère*), and the delicate, mellow linden tree blossom (*tilleul*). Tastings are offered in the shop, and most varieties are available in miniature jars, allowing one to sample several. Unfortunately, service can be cold and unfriendly. Honey-based soaps and health products are also sold.

**LA MAISON DE LA
TRUFFE**
19 Place de la Madeleine,
Paris 8.
Tel: 42.65.53.22.
Métro: Madeleine.
Open 9 A.M. to 8 P.M.
Closed Sunday.
Credit cards: AE, DC, V.

From November to March, come for the best fresh truffles to be found in Paris. Year-round, there are preserved truffles, goose and duck *foie gras*, exotic fruit, smoked salmon, a variety of *charcuterie*, and a respected assortment of wines and liqueurs.

ALBERT MENES
41 Boulevard Malesherbes,
Paris 8.
Tel: 42.66.95.63.
Métro: Saint-Augustin.
Open 10 A.M. to 7 P.M.
Tuesday through
Saturday. Closed
Monday morning, and
Sunday.
Credit cards: AE, V.

This pretty, wood-paneled shop, dating from 1921, looks like a room in a doll's house. Albert Ménès specializes in old-fashioned dry goods, such as its famous *galettes bretonnes* (rich butter cookies), jams, conserved flower petals, and an extensive selection of oils and vinegars—all great for gifts. Try the *vinaigre de xérès* (sherry vinegar) and exotic condiments, such as garlic *confit*, curry sauces, and a hot pimento purée. At Christmastime the shop sells pretty gingerbread ornaments (better for hanging on the tree than for eating).

A LA MERE DE FAMILLE
35 Rue du Faubourg
Montmartre, Paris 9.
Tel: 47.70.83.69.
Métro: Le Peletier or Cadet.
Open 8 A.M. to 1:30 P.M.
and 3 to 7 P.M. Closed
Sunday, Monday, and
August.
Credit cards: MC, V.

Walking into this spotless, sparkling candy shop—which dates back to 1791—is like wandering into the midst of a *naïf* painting. The window display and exterior are worth a trip on their own: The colorful, decorative boxes of *bonbons*, sugar candies, biscuits, and artisanal jams change with the seasons, but there's always a sense of organized clutter inside and out. You'll find products from all over France, including boxes of *Madeleines de Commercy* (perfect for gifts) and caramel-coated *Pralines de Montargis*.

PASTEUR

15th arrondissement

LE COMPTOIR
  CORREZIEN
8 Rue Volontaires, Paris 15.
Tel: 47.83.52.97.
Métro: Volontaires.
Open 9 A.M. to 1:30 P.M. and
  3 to 8 P.M. Closed
  Sunday and Monday
  morning.
Credit card: V.

This tidy shop just steps from the Volontaires metro, will make you feel as though you've taken a trip to the southwest: fresh wild mushrooms most of the year, excellent dried mushrooms year-round, top-quality hazelnut and walnut oils (from the Moulin de la Tour in Sainte-Nathalène, near Sarlat), delicate *cabecous* goat cheese, plus a huge variety of wine and packaged goods. Don't miss it, especially for the ultra-fresh nut oils.

TROCADERO, TERNES

16th and 17th arrondissements

BRULERIE DES TERNES
10 Rue Poncelet, Paris 17.
Métro: Ternes.
Tel: 46.22.52.79.
Open 9:30 A.M. to 1 P.M. and
  3:30 to 7:30 P.M. Tuesday
  through Saturday.
Closed Sunday afternoon
  and Monday.
Credit cards: MC, V.

With more than 24 different varieties of coffee beans freshly roasted right in the shop, the Brûlerie des Ternes is the Cartier of coffee roasters in Paris. I'm a diehard fan of their *maragogype*, big fat, lightly roasted Colombian beans that are low in caffeine but deliver a consistent flavor that's smooth and oh-so-satisfying. Tea drinkers are not ignored here, either, with more than 70 varieties of teas and herbs for brewing, plus all the tea and coffee-drinking paraphernalia one might desire.

AU COEUR DES LANDES
33 Rue Boissière, Paris 16.
Tel: 45.53.78.52.
Métro: Boissière.
Open 10 A.M. to 2:45 P.M.
  and 5 to 8:30 P.M. Closed
  Sunday.
Credit card: V.

This cheerful, tiny shop specializes in products from the Landes and the Basque country; in other words, it's yet another excuse for a *foie gras* shop. But this one has a twist: in addition to several different kinds of fresh *foie gras* (supplied to the restaurant Jean de Chalosse, among others), Au Coeur des Landes also offers smoked salmon-style trout; Basque specialties such as superb Serrano, Reebo, and Bellota hams from Spain; excellent sheep's milk cheese; delicately spicy peppers from Espelette; and delicious *gâteau Basque*. To go with all this, they stock wines from the southwest and serve sandwiches on crusty country rolls.

GANDOM
16 Rue Franklin, Paris 16.
Tel: 46.47.54.01.
Métro: Trocadéro.
Open 10 A.M. to 8 P.M.
  Closed Sunday and
  August.
Credit card: V.

If you've ever dreamed of creating a banquet out of "A Thousand and One Nights", stop into Gandom, near Place du Trocadéro. You can feast on rose petal *gelée* with delicate and seldom seen Persian pastries made from rice, almond, and chick-pea flour. They stock Iranian caviar and fresh and packaged specialties, including basmati rice, saffron, and Turkish delights. Gandom also serves as Paris's Maison de la Pistache, offering the best roasted nuts in the capital.

THE GENERAL STORE
30 Rue de Longchamp,
  Paris 16.
Tel: 47.55.41.14.
Métro: Trocadéro.
Open 10 A.M. to 7:30 P.M.
  Closed Sunday.
Credit cards: AE, DC, V.

See listing, 7th *arrondissement.*

VIVE LES SUPERMARCHES!

Supermarkets serve as windows on a culture— what better way to see how locals really live? Parisian department stores are home to some of the world's most luxurious and well-stocked supermarkets. Spacious, and open late, many even deliver. Finicky Parisians stop by after work and fill their shopping cart up with *foie gras,* ripe cheese and produce, smoked salmon, even a bottle of Château Petrus. Here are some of the best addresses:

LA GRANDE EPICERIE DE PARIS
Bon Marché
38 Rue de Sèvres (Magasin 2, main floor),
  Paris 7.
Tel: 44.39.81.00.
Métro: Sèvres-Babylone.
Open Monday to Saturday 8:30 A.M. to 9 P.M.,
  until 10 P.M. Saturday. Closed Sunday.
Credit cards: MC, V.

It's the Left Bank Fauchon, and though this fairly new supermarket lacks the tradition and history of the classic establishment on the Place de la Madeleine, La Grande Epicerie de Paris is a dream of a modern supermarket. Every packaged good you can imagine (from the most ordinary to the most exotic), a good choice of Italian cheeses, sausages, and carry-out items, a wine shop, a bread shop, an extensive frozen-food department, as well as a special delivery service for those in the neighborhood.

LAFAYETTE GOURMET
48 Boulevard Haussmann, first floor, Paris 9.
Tel: 48.74.46.06.
Métro: Chausée-d'Antin or Havre-Caumartin.
Open Monday through Saturday 9 A.M. to
    8 P.M. Closed Sunday.
Credit cards: AE, V.

Part of the grand Galeries Lafayette department store, this is a supermarket to rival the food halls of London, with special butcher shops, wine, fish and cheese shops, counters for sitting and sipping a glass of Champagne, a coffee, or an aquavit with your caviar or smoked salmon, plus a great selection of fresh produce and packaged items from around the world. Also special departments run by such names as Lenôtre and Petrossian.

MARKS & SPENCER
35 Boulevard Haussmann, Paris 8.
Tel: 47.42.42.91.
Métro: Chausée-d'Antin or Havre-Caumartin.
Open Monday through Saturday 9:30 A.M. to
    7 P.M.; Tuesday, 10 A.M. to 7 P.M.
Closed Sunday.
Credit cards: MC, V.

British jams, smoked fish from Scotland and Ireland, an astonishingly good, fresh (and expensive) assortment of hard-to-find baby vegetables, great apples from England, cottage cheese, typically British biscuits, crackers, and cookies, English muffins, and a fine assortment of top-quality sandwiches make this a favorite stop among Parisians, French and otherwise.

Vins et Alcools
WINE AND
LIQUOR SHOPS

Wine, an indispensable part of a meal.

In Paris, wine and liquor shops are not designed for popping in and out of quickly. Like almost everything gastronomic in France, wine is selected with great care, after conversation and contemplation. Wine shop owners are much like restaurant *sommeliers*. Passionate about their chosen field, they love to discuss, to advise, to help clients select just the right wine for a perfect little meal. Many of the shops listed here are small and specialized, reflecting the personal tastes of their owners. They are not wine supermarkets, so don't expect to find an infinite selection. Rather, think of each visit as a step toward a greater understanding and appreciation of wines and spirits.

CONCORDE, BOURSE

1st and 2nd arrondissements

JEAN DANFLOU
36 Rue du Mont-Thabor
(at the back of the
courtyard, second floor),
Paris 1.
Tel: 42.61.51.09.
Fax: 42.61.31.62.
Métro: Concorde.
Open 9 A.M. to 1 P.M. and
2 to 6 P.M. Closed
Saturday, Sunday, and
the first two weeks of
August.
Credit cards: AE, V.

Set aside a long and languid afternoon for sampling the wide assortment of Jean Danflou's fine fruit-based liqueurs, Calvados, Armagnac, and Cognac. This is a wine and spirits shop, yes, but also an elegant, friendly tasting salon set in a tiny apartment just off the Rue de Rivoli. Pierre-Glotin Danflou, a descendant of the man who founded the Paris-based company in 1925, is warm and welcoming, offering sample after sample of his exquisite, clear *eaux-de-vie*, including a fine Poire William, made only from the freshest Rhône Valley pears. (More than sixteen pounds of fruit go into preparing each bottle of Danflou's Poire William.) Sample, too, the raspberry (*framboise*), cherry (*kirsch*), yellow plum (*mirabelle*), and purple plum (*quetch*) liqueurs, all distilled east of Paris in the Vosges. Along with the tasting, you will learn some history and take a lesson in *eau-de-vie* etiquette (drink it at room temperature, not chilled, but from a chilled glass). Call or stop by for an appointment. Their motto, taken from Jean Cocteau, is *"La tradition c'est une statue qui marche."* "Tradition is a statue that walks."

LEGRAND FILLE & FILS
1 Rue de la Banque, Paris 2.
Tel: 42.60.07.12.
Fax: 42.61.25.51.
Métro: Bourse or Palais-
Royal–Musée du Louvre.
Open 8:30 A.M. to 7 P.M.
Tuesday through Friday,
8:30 A.M. to 1 P.M. and 3
to 7 P.M. Saturday.
Closed Sunday and
Monday.
Credit cards: MC, V.

There are at least two reasons to go out of your way to visit this lovely, well-stocked wine shop. One reason, of course, is the carefully chosen selection of French wines (many from small, independent growers in little-known wine-growing regions, such as Savoie and Languedoc-Roussillon) and liquors. The other is to examine the perfectly retained decor of this 19th-century *épicerie fine*, dating from 1890 and packed to the ceiling with candies, coffees, teas, and chocolates. Despite its renown, Legrand lacks pretension; the friendly *patronne* Francine Legrand-Richard, daughter of the original *patron* Lucien Legrand, will just as happily sell you a few chocolates as a vintage Bordeaux.

LATIN QUARTER, RUE DU BAC

5th and 7th arrondissements

JEAN-BAPTISTE BESSE
48 Rue de la Montagne
Sainte-Geneviève,
Paris 5.
Tel: 43.25.35.80.
Métro: Maubert-Mutualité.
Open 11 A.M. to 8 P.M.
Tuesday through
Saturday, 11 A.M. to
1:30 P.M. Sunday. Closed
Monday and August.
No credit cards.

Jean-Baptiste Besse, who has been at this tumble-down corner grocery since 1932, is a charming, modest little man with a permanent smile and most humble manner. If he has time, he'll talk your head off about Cognac and Armagnac, perhaps even about Bordeaux. Come here when you've plenty of time to chat or wait in line, or look on as he stumbles about the store in search of your request. (Treasures here are not always obvious.) Monsieur Besse can be trusted. You won't be sorry when you buy a gem he suggests.

THE QUINTESSENTIAL WINE GLASS

Getting the most out of a good wine involves more than just uncorking the bottle and pouring it into a glass. If the wine is good enough to merit attention, it merits a special wine glass for tasting. The Institut National des Appellations d'Origine (I.N.A.O.) in Paris responded to this need by designing what it considers the perfect tasting glass, as complementary to the wine as it is agreeable to the taster.

The glass has a wide base, a short stem, and an elongated egg-shaped cup that embraces the wine, carefully guarding its bouquet. Made of lead crystal, it is simple and undecorated, holding 1 cup (25 cl).

What are the qualities of a good wine glass? It should allow the wine to breathe without losing its strength, to develop without becoming faint; and it must permit the wine to show its deep, rich colors with no cuttings or etchings to interfere. The stem should be long enough to allow the wine to be swirled without being warmed by one's hand, and bowl itself should be longer than it is wide, so the bouquet is gently contained.

The I.N.A.O. glass is available in Paris at L'Esprit et Le Vin, 81 Avenue des Ternes, Paris 17 (45.74.80.99), and at Simon, 36 Rue Etienne-Marcel, Paris 2 (42.33.71.65).

RYST-DUPEYRON
79 Rue du Bac, Paris 7.
Tel: 45.48.80.93.
Métro: Rue du Bac.
Open 10 A.M. to noon and 1
to 7 P.M. Closed Sunday
and August.
Credit cards: MC, V.

This fine, classic old wine shop makes a good Left Bank spot for searching out vintage Armagnac, whisky, and port, as well as fine Bordeaux or great Champagne. They will even personalize bottles for special occasions—to celebrate a birthday, anniversary, wedding, or birth. Gift certificates are also available.

CHAMPS-ELYSEES, MADELEINE, GRANDS BOULEVARDS
8th and 17th arrondissements

CAVES AUGE
116 Boulevard Haussmann,
    Paris 8.
Tel: 45.22.16.97.
Métro: Saint-Augustin.
Open Tuesday through
    Saturday 9 A.M. to 8 P.M.,
    Monday 1 to 8 P.M.
    Closed Sunday and
    Monday.
Credit card: AE, V.

An elegant, classic wine shop, offering not just a carefully-chosen selection of wines, but also a fine assortment of vintage and non-vintage port, Cognac, Armagnac, and Champagne. This old-fashioned, wood-paneled shop has a gentleman's-club air about it, but despite the formality, Augé offers many reasonably priced wines and the sales ladies dispense good advice when helping you to select a wine for that evening's dinner.

FAUCHON
26-30 Place de la
    Madeleine, Paris 8.
Tel: 47.42.60.11.
Métro: Madeleine.
Open 9:40 A.M. to 7 P.M.
    Monday through
    Saturday. Closed
    Sunday.
Credit cards: AE, DC,
    MC, V.

This is a well-stocked *cave*, particularly if you're shopping for a fine Armagnac or Cognac. Prices are on the high side. But I like to save up my *centimes* for an occasional bottle of their fabulous wild-raspberry brandy, *eau-de-vie de framboise sauvage*. (See also Specialty Shops.)

PARISIAN VINEYARDS

Vineyards in Paris? Their history dates back to the Middle Ages, when abbey vineyards dotted the city and the wines they produced found their way to the noblest tables. (It was, in fact, the white claret from the suburb of Suresnes that François I said was "as light as a tear in the eye.")

Today the heritage continues as each year a little more than 1,000 bottles of authentic Parisian wines are carefully, ceremoniously bottled.

Tucked away in the hills of Montmartre, hidden among the narrow houses and car-filled sidewalks, there is a minuscule vineyard that annually produces just 500 bottles of a red wine simply labeled "Clos Montmartre." The harvest *fête*, a traditional celebration full of pageantry, takes place the first Saturday of October. For the harvest itself, the basement of the 18th *arrondissement mairie* (town hall) is turned into a wine cellar, and later some 300 bottles are sold there for about 300 francs each. The remainder is sold at auction. The wine does not lay any claims to greatness: It is more of an historical amusement than a gustatory treasure.

A second vineyard lies in the suburban community of Suresnes, west of Paris. Once considered the best in the Ile-de-France, the Suresnes vineyard was replanted in 1965. Now the local rugby team turns out to harvest the grapes, and the community celebrates the event on the first Sunday in October. Most of the 2,000 or so bottles of Clos du Pas-Saint-Maurice are sold on the last Saturday of September and the first Sunday of October at the Suresnes *cave municipale*. (It is also sold at Lucien Legrand and Au Verger de la Madeleine wine shops in Paris.)

In 1983, in an apparent effort to revive its illustrious wine heritage, the city of Paris planted another 700 vines of Pinot Noir grapes on the south side of Georges-Brassens Square, in the 15th *arrondissement* park built on the site of the former stockyards. In 1985, neighborhood children, members of the Lions Club, and the elderly helped pick the first Clos des Morillons harvest, which produced a total of 300 bottles of red wine, carefully aged in oak casks. The wine is sold at auction each December 15th at the 15th *arrondissement mairie*.

For more information about the harvests and wine sales, contact:

Montmartre: *Mairie* of the 18th *arrondissement*, 1 Rue Jules-Joffrin, Paris 18. Tel: 42.52.42.00. Métro: Jules Joffrin.

Suresnes: *Cave Municipale*, 28 Rue Merlin-de-Thionville, 92150 Suresnes. Tel: 45.06.32.10. Accessible via the No. 244 bus from Porte Maillot, the No. 144 bus from Pont de Neuilly, or the suburban train from Gare Saint-Lazare. The stop is Suresnes-Mont Valérin.

Clos de Morillons: *Mairie* of the 15th *arrondissement*, 31 Rue Péclet, Paris 15. Tel: 48.28.40.12. Métro: Vaugirard.

CAVE HEDIARD
21 Place de la Madeleine, Paris 8.
Tel: 42.66.04.84.
Métro: Madeleine.
Open 9:30 A.M. to 8 P.M.
Closed Sunday.
Credit cards: AE, DC, V.

An expansive *cave* offering perhaps the largest selection of Bordeaux wines in Paris. Also a large selection of Armagnac, Calvados, and Cognac. Prices are on the high side. (See also Specialty Shops.)

CAVES PETRISSANS
30 bis Avenue Niel, Paris 17.
Tel: 42.27.83.84.
Métro: Ternes.
Open 10:30 A.M. to 8 P.M. Tuesday through Friday, 9:30 A.M. to 1:30 P.M. Monday and Saturday. Closed Sunday and August.
Credit cards: AE, V.

A small, old-fashioned family operation, offering fine selections of Burgundy and Bordeaux. A wine bar/restaurant adjoins the shop, if you should decide to sample on the spot. (See also Wine Bars.)

A thoughtful selection.

When someone has had too much to drink, we say they're plastered, while the French are "beurré," or buttered.

CURNONSKY

Curnonsky, the 20th-century French food critic named "prince of gastronomes" by his peers, designated the five best white wines in France, perhaps the world:

Château d'Yquem: "The matchless sweet wine: true liquid gold."

Château-Chalon: "The prince of the Jura yellow wines, full-bodied, with the penetrating bouquet of walnuts."

Château-Grillet: "The legendary wine of the Côtes-du-Rhône, with a stunning aroma of violets and wild flowers; as changing as a pretty woman."

Montrachet: "The splendid lord of Burgundy, which Alexander Dumas counseled to drink, bareheaded, while kneeling."

Savennières Coulées de Serrant: "The dazzling dry wine from the vineyards of the Loire."

LES CAVES TAILLEVENT
199 Rue du Faubourg
  Saint-Honoré, Paris 8.
Tel: 45.61.14.09.
Fax: 45.61.19.68.
Métro: Charles-de-Gaulle–
  Etoile or Ternes.
Open 9 A.M. to 7 P.M.
  Monday through
  Saturday. Closed Sunday
  and the last week in July
  through the third week
  in August.
Credit cards: MC, V.

Without batting an eye, I would stand behind anything that Jean-Claude Vrinat supported. He's a remarkable man, and everything he touches has the mark of perfection and authenticity. Since the wine list at his family's restaurant, Taillevent, is one of the finest and most fairly priced in town, it comes as no surprise to find that his wine shop offers some 450,000 bottles, including 350 different wines, as well as 150 different *eaux-de-vie*, liqueurs, and excellent house Cognac, port, and sherry, dating back to 1848. Note that all of his wines are stored in a *cave* kept at—what else—perfect temperature and humidity. Monsieur Vrinat's daughter Valérie runs the shop along with wine expert Didier Bordas, and they couldn't be more helpful or informative. When you stop in, ask about the regularly scheduled wine tastings. Their motto: "A client is first of all, a friend."

AU VERGER DE LA MADELEINE
4 Boulevard Malesherbes, Paris 8.
Tel: 42.65.51.99.
Fax: 49.24.05.22.
Métro: Madeleine.
Open 10 A.M. to 1 P.M. and 3 to 8 P.M. Closed Sunday and two weeks in August.
Credit card: V.

Need a 1788 Madeira, an 1820 Cognac, an 1893 Sauternes, or a 1922 Lafite-Rothschild? Jean-Pierre Legras will be happy to oblige. Since 1937, the Legras family has operated one of Paris's *grandes épiceries fines*, and today they specialize in old bottles, odd bottles, new bottles, miniature bottles. Just give them a special date—birthday, anniversary, wedding—within the last 100 years and they should come up with an appropriate bottle to help you celebrate. Jean-Pierre is crazy about wine, and loves digging up dust-covered relics from the spacious underground *caves*. They offer more than ninety vintages of Armagnac, twenty-five of Calvados, and more than forty vintages of Madeira. He's proud of their collection of Sauternes old and new, of the fine and rare white Nuits-Saint-Georges from Henri Gouges, the straw-colored *vin de paille* of the Jura, not to mention his exclusive right to sell wine from Liechtenstein. He also carries the famous Paris wines from the vineyards at Montmartre and Suresnes, as well as the dry and fruity Louwber/Maastricht, a wine made in the Netherlands to commemorate meetings of the European union.

VINS RARES—PETER THUSTRUP
30 Avenue de l'Opéra, Paris 8.
Tel: 46.33.83.53.
Métro: Opéra.
Open 10 A.M. to 7 P.M. Closed Sunday.
Credit cards: AE, DC, V.

A wine merchant who deals in antiques? That's it. Swedish wine expert Peter Thustrup's passion for rare vintage wines has grown into a business, and now he offers more than 5,000 bottles— what he calls *"les introuvables,"* or wines that are virtually impossible to find. If you're searching for special bottles of Romanée Conti, Mouton Rothschild, Yquem, or vintage Champagnes, this is the place to look. His growing stock also includes younger wines, including American vintages.

Librairies Spécialisées: Gastronomie
FOOD AND WINE BOOKSHOPS

Paris bookstores are havens for books on food and wine. The following are just a few suggestions for finding old and new cookbooks, guidebooks, and historical, food-related volumes.

LES HALLES, OPERA, CONCORDE

1st and 8th arrondissements

AU BAIN MARIE
10 Rue Boissy d'Anglas, Paris 8.
Tel: 42.66.59.74.
Fax: 42.66.45.08
Métro: Concorde.
Open 10 A.M. to 7 P.M.
　Closed Sunday.
Credit cards: AE, DC, MC, V.

Along with tableware, linens, and antique bric-a-brac, Aude Clément offers a sometimes strange and always amusing collection of new and used cookbooks in English and in French. You will also find, from time to time, old guidebooks and collections of antique wine catalogs from the Paris wine shop, Nicolas.

BRENTANO'S
37 Avenue de l'Opéra, Paris 2.
Tel: 42.61.52.50.
Métro: Opéra.
Open 10 A.M. to 7 P.M.
　Closed Sunday.
Credit cards: MC, V.

This English-language bookshop offers a huge selection of cookbooks, in both American and British editions. A good place to go for food and wine related guidebooks in both English and French. Also a good spot to find current American or British magazines on food and the home.

GALIGNANI
224 Rue de Rivoli, Paris 1.
Tel: 42.60.76.07.
Métro: Tuileries or Concorde.
Open 10 A.M. to 7 P.M.
　Closed Sunday.
Credit cards: MC, V.

Since 1802 this neat-as-a-pin, old-fashioned, and professional shop along the arcades of the Rue de Rivoli has fascinated and pleased bibliophiles from around the world. Courteous service, a fabulous selection of English, American, and French tomes makes this a must stop for book lovers.

M.O.R.A.
13 Rue Montmartre,
    Paris 1.
Métro: Les Halles.
Tel: 45.08.19.24.
Fax: 45.08.09.05.
Open 8:30 A.M. to 5:45 P.M.
    Monday through Friday.
    Closed Saturday
    afternoon and Sunday.
Credit cards: MC, V.

A professional cookware shop that features a small but complete assortment of professional books devoted to breads, pastries, general cooking, and hotel and restaurant cooking. (See also Pour la Maison).

W.H. SMITH
248 Rue de Rivoli, Paris 1.
Tel: 42.60.37.97.
Métro: Concorde.
Open 9:30 A.M. to 7 P.M.
    Closed Sunday.
Credit cards: MC, V.

W.H. Smith offers a small selection of English-language books on food, wine, and travel, most of them British. Also a good selection of current British and American magazines.

LATIN QUARTER, SAINT-MICHEL, LUXEMBOURG

5th and 6th arrondissements

M.G. BAUDON
Bookseller at Box 11, Quai
    de Montebello, Paris 5.
Tel: 42.60.27.50.
Métro: Saint-Michel.
Flexible hours, depending
    upon weather: generally
    open 11 A.M. to 7:30 P.M.
    Closed Sunday and
    Monday.

The friendly, outgoing Madame Baudon is herself a passionate collector of old French cookbooks, and many of them find their way into her little wooden stall along the *quai*. A fine place for book browsing in the shadow of Notre-Dame.

GIBERT JEUNE
5 Place Saint-Michel,
    Paris 5.
Tel: 43.25.70.07.
Métro: Saint-Michel.
Open 9:30 A.M. to 7:30 P.M.
    Closed Sunday.
Credit card: V.

Gibert Jeune is one of the city's largest bookstores, specializing in both new and used books, mostly in French but also in English. Food and wine books are scattered about the second and third floors.

COOKING AND WINE SCHOOLS

The following are the most popular cooking and wine schools in Paris. If you plan to visit any of the schools, write or call for a brochure first, so you know what to expect. In many cases, custom-tailored courses can be arranged for groups of ten or more.

Le Cordon Bleu, 8 Rue Léon Delhomme, Paris 15. Tel: 48.56.06.06; Fax: 48.56.03.96. Métro: Vaugirard.

This famous classic French school has been instructing students in French cooking and pastry since 1895. Visitors may reserve a few days ahead for a single afternoon demonstration, and menus are available in advance for each month's program. Courses are ongoing, in French (with English translations), and the number of students varies according to the program. The Cordon Bleu also gives night courses in basic French cuisine starting at 7:30 P.M. and followed by a light snack of the course's preparation. (U.S. Connection: 1-800-457-CHEF).

Centre d'Information et de Documentation, Dégustation, Découverte de Vin/Alain Ségelle, 45 Rue Liancourt, Paris 14. Tel: 43.27.67.21.; Fax: 43.20.84.00. Métro: Gaîté.

Alain Ségelle is an outgoing young Frenchman with a passion for wine. His classes are serious affairs, in which he discusses in depth a variety of wine subjects. Many different courses are offered, ranging from a beginner's on the principles of wine tasting, to more specific classes on wines from the most important wine regions in France. Courses are in French (though classes in English are available on request.) Students sample and discuss three or four wines during each session. The C.I.D.D. also sponsors a year-round schedule of evening tastings and open houses.

Ecole de Gastronomie Ritz-Escoffier, 15 Place Vendôme, Paris 1. Tel: 42.60.38.30. Fax: 40.15.07.65. Métro: Opéra.

The famed Ritz Hotel and restaurant opens its kitchens and shares its chefs' expertise with students interested in French cuisine. Gregory Usher, former director of two well-known cooking schools—La Varenne and Le Cordon Bleu—has organized a

We say "the good old days," while the French call those lovely times of days past "les temps de cerise," the days of cherries.

multi-faceted cooking course, offering everything from weekday afternoon demonstration classes to twelve-week diploma courses. For many of its classes, the school draws upon the talents of Ritz executive chef Guy Legay, *sommelier* Georges Lepré, and the hotel's master baker, Bernard Bruban. The new, spotless kitchens are outfitted with the best in professional cookware and equipment. For groups, courses can be custom-tailored to fit requests.

Ecole Lenôtre, 40 rue Pierre-Curie, Boîte Postale 6 78373 Plaisir Cedex. Tel: 30.81.46.34. or 35. Fax: 30.55.14.88. Accessible by train from the Montparnasse station or by car.

This is where the best pastry chefs of France go for "refresher" courses. Gaston Lenôtre is one of the most respected and successful pastry chefs in France, and his school in the suburbs of Paris is open to professionals only. Ongoing full-participation courses are offered in pastry, chocolate, breadbaking, ice cream, *charcuterie,* and catering. A knowledge of French is important.

Ecole de Cuisine Princesse Ere 2001, 18 Avenue de la Motte-Piquet, Paris 7. Tel: 45.51.36.34. Fax: 43.47.38.68. Métro: Ecole Militaire.

Marie-Blanche de Broglie is an outgoing enthusiastic woman offering a number of courses in her well-appointed Paris apartment, in her Normandy château, and in trips to Champagne country. In Paris, she offers weekday participation classes in the harmony of wine and foods, pastry, and French regional cooking. Students can choose from single-day classes, or sessions from one week to up to twenty intensive classes. In her Normandy château, she offers weekend and week-long demonstration and participation classes for groups of five to fifteen. These include regional tours, wine tastings, and a visit to a Calvados distillery. Special summer programs can be organized. Courses may be arranged in English, French, or Spanish, with translations when necessary. (U.S. Connection: (404) 252-6497.)

Paris en Cuisine, 49 Rue de Richelieu, Paris 1. Tel: 42.61.35.23. Fax: 42.60.39.96. Métro: Palais-Royal–Musée du Louvre.

Robert Noah, a friendly, well-informed American in Paris, offers a variety of food-related tours of Paris. He arranges private or group visits to the Rungis wholesale market, tours of top restaurant kitchens, wine or cheese tastings, visits to Paris *charcuteries,* pastry, or bread shops, and even longer excursions into the countryside of France. The tours are particularly useful for those who do not speak French, for groups are kept to a maximum of ten, and Mr. Noah is a clear and careful translator. Paris en Cuisine also sponsors a professional cooking program, in English, which qualifies students to take an exam for the French *Certificat d'Aptitude Professionnel* (CAP), at the Centre de Formations Technologiques Ferrandi. One-week courses in pastry and cuisine can be organized. Mr. Noah also publishes a highly informative newsletter, and offers a reservation service for restaurants, hotels, theaters, and other travel arrangements in Paris and the rest of France. (U.S. Connection: P.O. Box 50099, Saint Louis, MO 63105).

Ecole de Cuisine La Varenne.

LIBRAIRIE GOURMANDE
4 Rue Dante, Paris 5.
Tel: 43.54.37.27.
Fax: 43.54.31.16.
Métro: Saint-Michel.
Open 10 A.M. to 7 P.M.
    Monday through
    Saturday, 3 to 7 P.M.
    Sunday.

This "branch" of the Quai de Montebello bookselling family, Baudon, is a most pleasant shop on a charming Left Bank street. One can spend hours browsing amidst the collection of cookbooks, tomes recounting the history of the table, assorted food-related antiques, as well as posters, lithographs, and drawings.

**LA LIBRAIRIE DES
  GOURMETS**
98 Rue Monge, Paris 5.
Tel: 43.31.16.42.
Fax: 43.31.60.32.
Métro: Censier-Daubenton.
Open 10:30 A.M. to 7 P.M.
  Closed Sunday, Monday,
  and August.
Credit card: V.

Walk past the threshold of this cheery, ochre-colored storefront and you open the door to literary, gastronomic heaven, a bookstore devoted exclusively to food and wine, with more than 2,500 titles, mostly in French, but some English-language offerings as well. Owner Anne Brunneau used to run a hotel in the Auvergne, but decided to try her hand at this for a change of pace. A must for bibliophiles.

LIBRAIRIE GUENEGAUD
10 Rue de l'Odéon, Paris 6.
Tel: 43.26.07.91.
Métro: Odéon.
Open Tuesday through
  Saturday 9:30 A.M. to
  12:45 P.M. and 2 to
  6:30 P.M. Closed Sunday,
  Monday, and August.

Owners Jean-Etienne and Edmonde Huret specialize in antiquarian books about the French provinces and have an abundant collection of hard-to-find books about French regional cooking and wine, as well as cookbooks. Each month they concentrate on a different region, so their selection is always changing.

**LIBRAIRIE JACQUES
  LANORE**
4 Rue de Tournon, Paris 6.
Tel: 43.29.43.50.
Fax: 43.54.97.81.
Métro: Odéon.
Open Tuesday through
  Saturday 10 A.M. to
  1 P.M. and 2 to 7 P.M.,
  Saturday until 6 P.M.
  Closed Sunday and
  Monday.

A tiny shop that caters to the French hotel and restaurant trade, with a delightful, broad selection of books devoted to every aspect of cooking. It includes many seldom-found tomes, such as professional works on French baking, pastry, *charcuterie,* and catering. Worth a detour for those hard-to-find books.

LE VERRE ET L'ASSIETTE
1 Rue du Val-du-Grâce,
  Paris 5.
Tel: 46.33.45.96.
Métro: Port-Royal.
Open 10 A.M. to 12:30 P.M.
  and 2 to 7 P.M. Closed
  Sunday, Monday morn-
  ing, and two weeks in
  August.
Credit cards: AE, DC, V.

This is one of the city's most fabulous cookbook shops, with a vast and esoteric collection of some 3,000 French and English books devoted to food and wine. There is also an assortment of wine-related paraphernalia, including corkscrews, wine glasses, vineyard maps, and wine thermometers.

BOOKS, AND MORE: FNAC

FNAC is a mammoth stereo/record/camera/ book-shop that always includes extensive selections of French books on food, wine, and travel. Prices are competitive. General hours: Open 10 A.M. to 7:30 P.M. Tuesday through Saturday; 1 P.M. to 7:30 P.M. Monday. Closed Sunday. Credit cards: AE, V.

FNAC-FORUM LES HALLES
1 Rue Pierre Lescot, Paris 1.
Tel: 40.41.40.00.
Métro: Les Halles.

FNAC-RENNES
136 Rue de Rennes, Paris 6.
Tel: 49.54.30.00.
Métro: Montparnasse-Bienvenue.

FNAC-ETOILE
26-30 Avenue des Ternes, Paris 17.
Tel: 44.09.18.00.
Métro: Ternes or Etoile.

SAINT-GERMAIN, ODEON, SEVRES-BABYLONE

6th and 7th arrondissements

REMY FLACHARD
9 Rue du Bac, Paris 7.
Tel: 42.86.86.87.
Métro: Rue du Bac.
Open 10 A.M. to noon and 2 to 6 P.M. Closed Saturday, Sunday, and August.

A small, tranquil shop devoted to old and rare books on the subject of gastronomy. Monsieur Flachard's collection includes books dating back to the 15th century, with prices ranging from 100 to 30,000 francs. I wouldn't mind being locked in this shop for hours, examining books on making honey, old tomes on how to care for your sensitive stomach, and ancient and beautifully illustrated books on winemaking. You'll find a bit of everything here, from a 1946 edition of the *Better Homes and Gardens Cookbook*, a biography of Madame Veuve Clicquot-Ponsardin of Champagne fame, original editions of Brillat-Savarin's *Physiologie du Goût*, and an 1840 manual for bread bakers. Menu collectors will also find a large assortment of menus from restaurants, banquets, and clubs in America, Germany, and France, dating from the 1870s to the 1920s.

LA MAISON RUSTIQUE
26 Rue Jacob, Paris 6.
Tel: 43.25.67.00.
Métro: Saint-Germain-des-Prés.
Open 10 A.M. to 7 P.M.
Closed Sunday.
Credit cards: AE, V.

This forest-green bookstore provides a bucolic haven in the heart of Saint-Germain-des-Prés. Maison Rustique, with more than 18,000 books in stock, specializes in all things related to the countryside: in particular, gardening, design, and *art de vivre*. In addition to a good cookbook collection (with some English titles), they stock how-to books on everything from beekeeping to raising dairy cows and sheep, jam-making, organic gardening and wine-making. I'm a particular fan of the La Rustica series that includes tomes on home preserving, and cooking with herbs or with edibles found in the wild. Ignore the cool service.

TEA AND TATTERED PAGES
24 Rue Mayet, Paris 6.
Métro: Duroc.
Tel: 40.65.94.35.
Open 11 A.M. to 7 P.M.
Closed Sunday.

There are more than 10,000 books in English, including many new and used cookbooks, in this combination tea-salon/bookstore run by American Kristi Chavane. Also brownies, fudge cookies, snacks, quilts, mugs, and teapots.

Pour la Maison
KITCHEN AND TABLEWARE SHOPS

Papeterie Moderne for any sign you desire (see entry, page 347).

If you have been searching for long-wearing cotton chefs' uniforms, odd-size baking tins, antique Champagne glasses, or that extra gadget to make cooking more practical and fun, you need look no more. These, plus lovely pastel-toned turn-of-the-century oyster or asparagus plates, sparkling contemporary glassware, antique silver *porte-couteaux* (knife rests), and sturdy copper pots are just a few of the hundreds of particularly French kitchen and table items found in the following shops. Note that some are small and sometimes casually run, so that opening and closing hours may not always be followed to the letter.

LES HALLES, PALAIS-ROYAL, PLACE DES VICTOIRES
1st and 2nd arrondissements

LA BOVIDA
36 Rue Montmartre,
Paris 1.
Tel: 42.36.09.99.
Métro: Les Halles.
Open 7:30 A.M. to 6 P.M.
Closed Saturday
afternoon and Sunday.
No credit cards.

A kitchen equipment shop for professionals, La Bovida has an impressive inventory of stainless steel, copper, porcelain, and earthenware, as well as serving platters, a variety of spices in bulk, and paper doilies in more than a dozen shapes and sizes. Service can be cool indeed.

LE CEDRE ROUGE
22 Avenue Victoria, Paris 1.
Tel: 42.33.71.05.
Fax: 40.26.46.78.
Métro: Châtelet.
Open 10 A.M. to 7 P.M.
Closed Sunday and two
weeks in August.
Credit cards: AE, MC, V.

A fabulous fantasy shop for home and garden. Most of the items here—garden furniture and umbrellas, gigantic bowls and pots—will be too big to fit into your suitcase, but this is a lovely shop for dreamers. And you're certain to go home with an idea or two.

E. DEHILLERIN
18-20 Rue Coquillière,
Paris 1.
Tel: 42.36.53.13.
Fax: 45.08.96.83.
Métro: Les Halles.
Open 8 A.M. to 12:30 P.M.
and 2 to 6 P.M. Closed
Sunday.
Credit cards: MC, V.

A fascinating, though often overwhelming, clutter of professional cookware, covering every inch of available wall, floor, and ceiling space. The remarkable selection of copper cooking items, baking pans, and unusual kitchen tools include copper tabletop potato warmers for raclette and *crémaillères* (hanging pots) to hang from the hearth. Some English is spoken by the helpful, if gruff, salespeople, and merchandise catalogs are available. They're experts at retinning copper, but it takes two to three weeks. The store will mail purchases.

**DUTHILLEUL ET
MINART**
14 Rue de Turbigo, Paris 1.
Tel: 42.33.44.36.
Métro: Etienne Marcel.
Open 9 A.M. to 7 P.M. Closed
Sunday.
No credit cards.

A rtisans' uniforms designed around 1850, natural-fiber work clothes; café waiters' vests, shirts, and ties; jewelers' smocks; meat deliverers' hooded robes; animal purveyors' blouses in red, black, and tan; and professional chef outfits, tailored to fit— they're all here. They also have an extensive selection of professional-quality cotton and linen dish towels.

**MURIEL GRATEAU
 BOUTIQUE**
29 Rue Valois, Palais-Royal,
 Paris 1.
Tel: 40.20.90.30.
Métro: Palais-Royal–Musée
 du Louvre.
Open 10 A.M. to 7 P.M.
 Closed Sunday.
Credit card: V.

Under the arches of the Palais-Royal, Muriel Grateau has created a shop for dreamers. Her opulent, richly colored (and priced) brocade table linens look as if they're part of a banquet scene in a Veronese painting. She designs them herself and has them made in Venice. She also sells at least a dozen shades of simple linen table sets, as well as fine hand-painted reproduction and antique porcelain in rarely seen designs.

GALERIE LAGUIOLE
1 Place Saint-Opportune,
 Paris 1.
Tel: 40.28.09.42.
Fax: 40.39.03.89.
Métro: Châtelet-Les Halles.
Open 10:30 A.M. to 7:30 P.M.
 Closed Sunday. Closed
 for lunch in August.
Credit card: V.

French designer Philippe Starck created this spare, knife-blade colored shop to go with his updated design for the classic Laguiole knives of the Auvergne, in central France. Although the French equivalent of the Swiss army knife was intended for cattle farmers in the 19th century, the sleek Laguiole pocket knife has become a "must" for the modern Frenchman. Here you can find it with both the traditional metal blade (it oxidizes with wear) and a modern stainless steel version. Different sizes and models of this foldable knife come with an assortment of blades and corkscrews. The ecology-minded can breathe easily: The handcrafted horn handles that mold perfectly to the shape of the hand come from cattle (the horns are cut in a procedure which does not harm the animal).

M.O.R.A.
13 Rue Montmartre,
 Paris 1.
Tel: 45.08.19.24.
Fax: 45.08.49.05.
Métro: Les Halles.
Open 8:30 A.M. to 5:45 P.M.
 Closed Saturday
 afternoon and Sunday.
Credit cards: MC, V.

This is another in the group of cookware shops near Les Halles, still frequented by professionals. M.O.R.A. has a large assortment of tools, baking tins (including several sizes of *pain de mie* molds), large *baguette* pans, cake molds, ice cube trays shaped like chocolates, and linen-lined wicker bread-rising baskets. They also stock the oblong *baguette* baskets one often sees on the arms of waiters carrying fresh bread back to their restaurants. (Be sure to come with dimensions of your oven: Many objects are oversize, made to fit large professional ovens.) They also have a good professional cookbook selection. (See Food and Wine Bookshops.)

PAPETERIE MODERNE
12 Rue de la Ferronnerie,
Paris 1.
Tel: 42.36.21.72.
Métro: Châtelet-Les Halles.
Open 9 A.M. to noon and
2 to 7 P.M. Monday
through Thursday and
Saturday, 10:30 A.M.
to 7 P.M. Friday. Closed
Sunday; vacation closing
varies.
No credit cards.

When you see this simple shop, unchanged for decades, you'll know the source of the city's myriad signs. They're everywhere—all the signs you have ever dreamed of—stashed into corners, piled on counters, hanging from the wall and the ceiling, on nails and thumbtacks. There are street signs for cheese, butter, sausages, beef tongue, and headcheese, along with café menus, bakery price lists, requests for people to stop smoking or spitting, even French "beware of dog" and "post no bills" warnings. Custom-made signs take about ten days.

A. SIMON
36 Rue Etienne Marcel and
48 Rue Montmartre,
Paris 2.
Tel: 42.33.71.65.
Métro: Les Halles.
Open 8:30 A.M. to 6:30 P.M.
Closed Sunday and
holidays.
Credit cards: AE, V.

This sedate establishment has professional serving dishes, porcelain, crystal, china, salt and pepper grinders, mustard jars, lovely white terrines, a wide variety of paper doilies, wicker cheese trays, and bread baskets. At their annex across the street (enter at 48 Rue Montmartre and walk through a passageway to the shop), there's professional cookware from copper pots to baking molds, scales to cookie cutters, along with the attractive marble-base Roquefort cheese cutters used in the best restaurants.

MARAIS, BASTILLE, ILE SAINT-LOUIS
3rd and 4th arrondissements

L'ARLEQUIN
19 rue de Turenne, Paris 4.
Tel: 42.78.77.00.
Métro: Saint-Paul.
Open 2:30 to 7 P.M. Closed
Sunday, Monday, and
August.
No credit cards.

Ancient and beautiful glassware on dusty shelves that reach from floor to ceiling. Liqueur glasses, Champagne *coupes*, wine glasses, juice glasses. The perfect place to compose your own mixed or matched set. A few vases as well.

Beautiful tableware beautifully displayed is always tempting.

LES GRANDS MAGASINS

The *grands magasins* (department stores) have been a Parisian tradition since Galeries Lafayette opened its doors in the late 19th century. While shopping at the original Galeries Lafayette store in the 9th *arrondissement*, do take a moment to admire the painted cupola and circular, rotund design. La Samaritaine's original building facing the Pont-Neuf also merits a visit for its Art Deco design and the superb view of Paris from the café at the top.

Department stores offer large selections, convenience, and efficiency that smaller boutiques often lack, and their housewares departments are loaded with can't-live-without gadgets. If you want to buy *jacquard* table linens, a set of Lunéville faïence, or Havilland porcelain, for example, it will probably be simplest to make your purchase at one of these stores. A few stay open at least one night per week and most have excellent sales in July. Shop around before making a large purchase—not all stores offer competitive prices.

B.H.V. (BAZAAR DE L'HOTEL DE VILLE)
52 Rue de Rivoli, Paris 4.
Tel: 42.74.90.00.
Métro: Hôtel de Ville.
Open 9:30 A.M. to 7 P.M.; until 9:45 P.M.
Wednesday. Closed Sunday.
Credit cards: AE, V.
Art de la table department on third floor.
Almost every contemporary kitchen tool or piece of equipment ever invented is available on the third floor of this enormous, catch-all department store, as well as china and crystal, baskets, table linens, and everyday kitchen products.

AU BON MARCHE
22 Rue de Sèvres, Paris 7.
Tel: 45.49.21.22.
Métro: Sèvres-Babylone.
Open 9:30 A.M. to 6:30 P.M. Closed Sunday.
Credit card: AE, V.
Art de la table department on third floor.
Au Bon Marché prides itself on its slogan—*"l'Esprit Rive Gauche"*—and to its credit stocks an original, boutique-like selection of tableware. Also an excellent selection of linens for the kitchen and table.

GALERIES LAFAYETTE
40 Boulevard Haussmann, Paris 9.
Tel: 42.82.34.56.
Métro: Chaussée-d'Antin.
Open 9:30 A.M. to 6:45 P.M. Closed Sunday.
Credit cards: AE, V.
Art de la table department in basement.
The doyenne of department stores, Galeries Lafayette
stocks a classic selection of kitchen products and
tableware that no proper French home should be
without: porcelain, crystal, crockery, and a Mariage
Frères tea boutique.

AU PRINTEMPS
64 Boulevard Haussmann, Paris 9.
Tel: 42.82.50.00.
Métro: Chaussée-d'Antin.
Open: 9:35 A.M. to 7 P.M. Closed Sunday.
Credit cards: AE, V.
Art de la table department on second floor of the
"Magasin de la Maison," 64 Boulevard Haussmann.
Au Printemps's convenient and spacious housewares/
tableware department offers no surprises, but I always
love wandering through for that extra kitchen hot
pad, the latest gadgets for grating or slicing, and an
always appealing selection of tableware and glassware.

LA SAMARITAINE
19 Rue de la Monnaie, Paris 1.
Tel: 40.13.87.20.
Métro: Pont-Neuf.
Open 9:30 A.M. to 7 P.M.; Tuesday and Friday
until 8:30 P.M.
Credit cards: AE, V.
Art de la table department on third floor of
building 1.
One of my favorite spots for that hard-to-find
kitchen gadget, whether it's a state-of-the-art timer,
a bundt cake pan, knives, unique coffeemakers,
graters, or canning materials.

LES CARRELAGES DU
MARAIS
46 Rue Vieille du Temple,
Paris 4.
Tel: 42.78.17.43.
Métro: Saint-Paul or
Hôtel-de-Ville.
Open 10 A.M. to 6:30 P.M.
Closed Sunday, Monday
morning, two weeks in
August, and Christmas
week.
No credit cards.

A multitude of square glazed tiles in every shade of nearly every color make this a personal favorite. (My kitchen counters in Provence are covered with their lovely, timeless tiles in varied shades of ochre). Also a fine selection of traditional, handmade floor tiles. Service can be cool and downright rude, so come with a dose of patience and stamina.

U.S. Connection: French Country Living, 10130 Calvin Run Road, Great Falls, Virginia 22066. Tel: (703) 759-2245.

JEAN-PIERRE DE
CASTRO
17 Rue des Francs-
Bourgeois, Paris 4.
Tel: 42.72.04.00.
Métro: Saint-Paul.
Open 10:30 A.M. to 7 P.M.
Tuesday through
Sunday, 2 to 7 P.M.
Monday.
Credit card: V.

A great shop for silver-lovers, where antique silver knives, forks, spoons—you name it—are sold by weight. Selecting from a stack of wicker baskets, you can put together your own place settings. There's an abundant selection, and pieces are generally reasonable. Also silver candlesticks, teapots, and so on.

COEURS D'ALSACE
33 Quai de Bourbon,
Paris 4.
Tel: 46.33.14.03.
Métro: Pont-Marie.
Open 10:30 A.M. to 1 P.M.
and 2:30 to 7 P.M. Closed
Sunday, Monday, and
August.
Credit cards: AE, V.

L ike a trip to the old world, this colorful shop has *anis* cookie stamps, pottery, heart-shaped earthenware cake molds, painted furniture, and cookbooks, all direct from the Alsace region in eastern France.

DEJEUNER SUR L'HERBE
6 Rue Ferdinand Duval,
Paris 4.
Tel: 42.72.30.18.
Métro: Saint-Paul.
Open 2 to 7 P.M. Closed
Monday and three weeks
in August.
Credit cards: AE, V.
Will ship internationally.

E ve Mylonas has filled her tiny Marais shop with country-style artisanal faïence from Provence, Alsatian table linens from Beauville, and brightly printed picnic blankets fit for an Impressionist-style picnic at Giverny. True to its Impressionist name, Déjeuner sur l'Herbe stocks the Giverny model of porcelain, in addition to painted enamel hooks.

D.O.T.
47 Rue de Saintonge,
   Paris 4.
Tel: 40.29.90.34.
Métro: Filles du Calvaire.
Open: 9 A.M. to 6 P.M.
   Closed weekends and
   three weeks in August.
No credit cards.

This charming, old-fashioned–looking shop hidden away in the back of the Marais seems like a casual, bargain version of Au Bain Marie, one of the city's most attractive (and expensive) tableware shops. In fact, the resemblance doesn't end there because D.O.T. manufactures some of Au Bain Marie's original brand label products, and stocks an eclectic array of bric-a-brac and antiques. You won't find rare antique silver and porcelain here: Rather, the windows boast cozier items, including an enormous collection of *café au lait* bowls, bone marrow spoons, asparagus tongs, egg cups, and pots for making hot chocolate, as well as knick-knacks such as whiskey flasks and antique picnic sets. While in the neighborhood, stop by Onfroy Boulangerie for a perfect *pain de seigle* (see Bakeries).

The makings of a dream kitchen.

ERIC DUBOIS
9 Rue Saint-Paul, Paris 4.
Tel: 42.74.05.29.
Métro: Sully-Morland.
Open 11 A.M. to 7 P.M.
  Closed first two weeks
  of August.
Credit cards: AE, DC, V.

A charming antique shop filled with a lovely collection of folkloric antiques and curiosities: You'll find old pottery jugs from the southwest, antique cheese draining cups from the Loire, old handheld metal scales, and copper cooking utensils. You can also rent stock from this shop for use in photographs.

LESCENE-DURA
63 Rue de la Verrerie,
  Paris 4.
Tel: 42.72.08.74.
Fax: 42.76.09.69.
Métro: Hôtel-de-Ville.
Open 9:30 A.M. to 1 P.M.
  and 2 to 7 P.M. Tuesday
  through Saturday. Closed
  Sunday, Monday, and
  two weeks in August.
Credit card: V.

If it is winter, warm your hands at the old wood-burning stove that may well have been in this shop since it was founded in 1875, then peruse the supply of absolutely everything for the winemaker and wine drinker—bottles and corks, small grape presses, beautiful preprinted wine labels as well as those to inscribe yourself for your own house vintage. There are brass-bound wooden measuring containers, casks for aging wine (or making vinegar), along with a variety of corkscrews, tasting cups, and other table accessories.

The shop offers a large selection of glassware, from a special French wine-tasting glass (ask for the one approved by I.N.A.O.) to small Riesling glasses with deep green stems. You can also find *express* coffee machines and pocketknives of every price and description.

AU PAS PERDU
4 Rue du Pas-de-la-Mule,
  Paris 3.
Métro: Chemin-Vert.
Tel: 42.71.87.83.
Open 11 A.M. to 7 P.M.
  Closed Sunday and
  Monday.
Credit card: V.

A tiny shop dedicated to *les arts de la table*, or the fine arts of the table, of yesterday. The perfect shop to know about when searching for unusual antique gifts, including silver napkin rings, lovely old oyster forks, fish knives and forks, silver and glass utensils for serving caviar, little *pots de crème* pots, and even a silver *"pelle,"* or shovel, for serving your best French fries! Prices are reasonable.

AU PUCERON CHINEUR
23 Rue Saint-Paul, Paris 4.
Tel: 42.72.88.20.
Métro: Saint-Paul.
Open 11 A.M. to 7 P.M.
  Closed Tuesday and
  Wednesday.
Credit card: V.

The Rue Saint-Paul is filled with lovely antique shops for browsing, buying, dreaming, and Au Puceron Chineur offers a great selection of colored glass objects in many colors, carafes, decanters, silver, and china.

QUIMPER FAIENCE
84 Rue Saint-Martin,
Paris 4.
Tel: 42.71.93.03.
Métro: Hôtel-de-Ville.
Open 11 A.M. to 7 P.M.
Closed Sunday.
Credit cards: MC, V.
Will ship internationally.

This pretty folkloric shop features the popular, ultra-expensive, brilliantly colored pottery from Brittany known as Quimper Faïence. There's a good selection, and whether you're picking up a teacup or an entire place setting, they'll be happy to ship the pottery home for you. It's the next best thing to a trip to Brittany!

**LAURENCE ROQUE—
LE COMPTOIR DES
OUVRAGES**
69 Rue Saint-Martin,
Paris 4.
Tel: 42.72.22.12.
Métro: Hôtel-de-Ville or
Châtelet–Les Halles.
Open 11 A.M. to 7 P.M.
Closed Sunday and
Monday morning.
Credit card: V.

A charming shop for do-it-yourself decorators: beautiful embroidery and needlepoint patterns, tablecloths and napkins, lace, jaunty-patterned fabrics for edging kitchen shelves, upholstery patterns, and fabrics.

LATIN QUARTER, SAINT-GERMAIN, SEVRES-BABYLONE

5th, 6th, and 7th arrondissements

ATELIER DE SEGRIES
31 Rue de Tournon,
Paris 6.
Tel: 46.34.62.56.
Métro: Odéon.
Open 11 A.M. to 7 P.M.
Closed Sunday, Monday,
and July 20 to
August 20.
Credit cards: AE, V.

The Provençal village of Moustiers—population 580—is rightly famed for its milky-white glazed hand-painted *faïence*, or pottery, made there since 1679. The best (and most expensive) comes from the Atelier de Ségriès, which offers a wide choice of patterns, including those embellished with delicate Provençal wildflowers. This shop is their home in Paris.

MARIE-PIERRE BOITARD
Galerie de l'Assemblée,
9 Place du Palais
Bourbon, Paris 7.
Tel: 47.05.13.30.
Open 10 A.M. to 7 P.M.
Closed Sunday.
Credit cards: AE, V.

This shop would be a good source for decorating the dining room of a *château*. Parisian socialites and old-guard matrons come here to buy wedding presents or to find that extra knickknack for their *hôtel particulier*. Owner Marie-Pierre Boitard displays one-of-a-kind antiques (an 18th century silver *bonbonnière* with leaves that unfold like a tulip), as well as an extensive selection of limited-series porcelain patterns, hand-painted crystal, and silk brocade table linens. Her specialty is thick, stained-glass-like colored Bohemian crystal goblets, as well as crystal edged in gold-leaf. Boitard, who is also a porcelain designer for Havilland, designs many of the items here. Lower-priced, but equally appealing gifts include chic *passementerie* key chains and reproductions of 19th-century potpourri diffusers. The prices are as opulent as the merchandise, and service here can be snooty indeed.

LE CEDRE ROUGE
5 Rue de Médicis, Paris 6.
Tel: 42.33.71.05.
Fax: 43.26.28.22.
Métro: Odéon or
  RER Luxembourg.
Open 10:30 A.M. to 7:30 P.M.
  Closed Monday.
Credit cards: AE, DC, V.

S ee listing, 1st *arrondissement.*

TIANY CHAMBARD
32 Rue Jacob, Paris 6.
Tel: 43.29.73.15.
Métro: Saint-Germain-
  des-Prés.
Open 2 to 7 P.M. Closed
  Sunday, Monday, and
  mid-July through the
  third week in August.
No credit cards.

A tiny shop with tiny things like old, colorful, beautifully designed fruit and liqueur labels from obsolete canneries and distilleries, perfect for framing and hanging in the kitchen or by the bar.

CONTES DE THE
60 Rue du Cherche Midi,
  Paris 6.
Tel: 45.49.45.96.
Métro: Sèvres-Babylone.
Open 10:30 A.M. to 7 P.M.
  Closed Sunday and
  Monday.
Credit cards: AE, V.

T his tiny shop stocks an eclectic and eccentric selection of teapots—up to 300 at Christmastime. Christine Dattner has collected teapots from the world over: Lermontov porcelain from Saint Petersburg in folkloric Russian motifs, hand-painted reproductions of antique Meissen and Milton teapot designs, modern transparent glass models, enamel-lined cast iron teapots from Japan, not to mention the original animal and house-shaped teapots. Perhaps the most unusual item is a Chinese wicker tea picnic basket: Lined in floral silk, it encases an enamel painted teapot and cups—the most perfect way to enjoy tea for two wherever you may be. Contes de Thé (a pun on the French term *contes de fée*—fairy tales) also sells fifty or so varieties of tea from Mariage Frères and Dammans, as well as tea cozies to warm the pot.

GALERIE LA CORNUE
18 Rue Mabillon, Paris 6.
Tel: 46.33.84.74.
Métro: Mabillon.
Open 10 A.M. to 6:30 P.M.
  Closed Sunday.
Credit cards: AE, V.

Another shop for dreaming, not for filling your suitcase. But if you love beautiful, sturdy, last-a-lifetime stoves, then take a look at the restaurant-style collection displayed here. Each and every one is individually made to order, using thick metal, quality enamels, bronze, copper, and cast iron. They're available in both gas and electric. The shop also stocks a small, fine selection of cookware and cooking utensils. U.S. connection: Purcell-Murray Co., 113 Park Lane, Brisbane, CA 94005. Tel: 800-892-4040. Fax:(415) 468-0667.

REGIS DHO BOUTIQUE
92 Boulevard Raspail,
  Paris 6.
Tel: 45.44.00.13.
Fax: 42.84.25.04.
Métro: Notre-Dame-des-
  Champs.
Open 10 A.M. to 7 P.M.
  Closed weekends.
Credit cards: AE, V.

A tiny boutique owned by a young and trendy Parisian artist who designs china and tableware for some of the country's best chefs, including Michel Rostang, Alain Ducasse, and the New York restaurant, Le Cirque. I prefer Regis Dho's simpler, homey items, such as the "fantasy" *escargot* (snail) holders of thick, bright lemon yellow and chocolate brown porcelain. Also nice sets of colorful bowls for your morning *café au lait* and lovely table linens.

DINERS EN VILLE
27 Rue de Varenne, Paris 7.
Tel: 42.22.78.33.
Fax: 45.44.87.25.
Métro: Rue du Bac.
Open 11 A.M. to 7 P.M.
  Closed Sunday and
  Monday morning.
Credit cards: MC, V.

An elegant shop that specializes in both useful and frivolous accessories and objects for home and table, stocking a wide variety of 19th- and 20th-century silver, sets of dishes, coffeepots, teapots and cups, serving dishes, and some fabrics.

BURNED AT THE STEAK!

In the Middle Ages, there was a fixed price on all market items, particularly perishables such as meat pies. If the pies were sold for less, it was assumed that they contained contaminated or tainted meat. The cheap pies were bought by the poor or by children, who often became ill. To discourage such practices, merchants caught selling such discount-priced perishables were forced to burn the offending meat pies in front of their shops.

POUR LA CUISINE MODERNE

Offering the usual and unusual for the kitchen and the table, these shops mix modern and traditional tableware at reasonable prices and have become favorites among young French women—and men. At Culinarion, you'll find *madeleine* tins, *financier* molds, a small roaster for home-roasted coffee beans, egg-shaped timers, and colorful cast-iron cookware. Habitat—a candy store for anyone setting up house—designs state-of-the-art kitchenware but also stocks traditional crockery, marble cheese boards, and picnic baskets. Quatre Saisons and Geneviève Lethu have more of a country style, with a huge selection of handmade baskets, bright striped cotton and cotton/linen blend fabric for making tea towels, Alsatian cookie stamps, white porcelain *chocolatières*, painted pottery dishes, and pretty wicker shopping carts to take to the market.

CULINARION
99 Rue de Rennes, Paris 6.
Tel: 45.48.94.76.
Métro: Rennes or Saint-Sulpice.
Open 10:15 A.M. to 7 P.M. Tuesday through
    Saturday; 11:15 A.M. to 7 P.M. Monday. Closed
    Monday in August, and Sunday.
Will ship internationally. Credit cards: AE, V.

83 bis Rue de Courcelles, Paris 17.
Tel: 42.27.63.32.
Métro: Courcelles.
Open 11:15 A.M. to 7 P.M. Tuesday through
    Saturday. Closed in August.
Will ship internationally.

GENEVIEVE LETHU
1 Rue Pierre Lescot, Forum des Halles, Paris 1.
Tel: 40.39.95.94.
Métro: Châtelet-Les Halles.
Open 10 A.M. to 7 P.M. Tuesday through Saturday;
    Monday 2 to 7 P.M. Closed Monday morning and
    Sunday.
Credit cards: MC, V.

91 Rue de Rivoli, Paris 1.
Tel: 42.60.14.90.
Métro: Louvre-Rivoli.

95 Rue de Rennes, Paris 6.
Tel: 45.44.40.35.
Métro: Rennes.

25 Avenue du Général Leclerc, Paris 14.
Tel: 45.38.71.30.
Métro: Denfert-Rochereau.

1 Avenue Niel, Paris 17.
Tel: 45.72.03.47.
Métro: Ternes.

HABITAT
202 Porte de Rambuteau, Forum des Halles, Paris 1.
Tel: 40.39.91.06.
Métro: Châtelet-Les Halles.
Open 10 A.M. to 7 P.M. Closed Sunday.
Credit card: V.

45 Rue de Rennes, Paris 6.
Tel: 45.44.68.74.
Métro: Saint-Germain-des-Prés.

17 Rue de l'Arrivée, Tour Montparnasse, Paris 15.
Tel: 45.38.69.90.
Métro: Montparnasse-Bienvenue.

35 Avenue de Wagram, Paris 17.
Tel: 47.66.25.52.
Métro: Charles de Gaulle-Etoile or Ternes.

QUATRE SAISONS
203 Porte de Rambuteau, Forum des Halles
Tel: 40.39.98.21.
Métro: Châtelet-Les Halles
Open 10:30 A.M. to 7 P.M. Tuesday through
    Saturday. Closed Monday morning and Sunday.
Credit card: V.

88 Avenue du Maine, Paris 14.
Tel: 43.21.28.99.
Métro: Gaîté.

20 Boulevard de Grenelle, Paris 15.
Tel: 45.77.46.39.
Métro: Bir-Hakeim.

BOUTIQUE LE FLORE
26 Rue Saint-Benoit,
Paris 6.
Tel: 45.44.33.40.
Métro: Saint-Germain-
des-Prés.
Open 10 A.M. to 7 P.M. in
Winter; 10 A.M. to 1 P.M.
and 2 to 7:30 P.M. in
summer. Closed Sunday.
Credit cards: AE, DC, V.

If you've ever been tempted to steal the pretty silver coffee pitchers or trays from a café, this boutique could be a dream come true. Boutique Le Flore sells the table service and café accoutrements from the famous Café Flore next door: white porcelain coffee cups, floor-length waiters' aprons, and café memorabilia that will—for a price—put Saint-Germain-des-Prés on your table long after you return home.

JARDINS IMAGINAIRES
9 Rue d'Assas, Paris 6.
Tel: 42.22.90.03.
Métro: Sèvres-Babylone
or Rennes.
Open:10:30 A.M. to 1 P.M.
and 2 to 6:30 P.M. Closed
Monday morning and
Sunday.
Credit cards: AE, V.

I think that if someone locked me inside this shop, I could easily while away hours studying all the objects within. As the name suggests, it is a bit like an imaginary garden, filled with objects old and new: wicker baskets and planters, but also antique floral paintings, dried flowers, flowered plates, and all sorts of wonderful things for the home, inside and out. I dare you to leave without buying at least a trinket.

_E. Dehillerin, filled to
overflowing with professional
cookware (see entry, page 345)._

FLORENCE ROUSSEAU
9 Rue de Luynes, Paris 7.
Tel: 45.48.04.71.
Métro: Rue du Bac.
Open 2 to 6:30 P.M. Closed
 Sunday, Monday, and
 August.
No credit cards.

A limited but very high quality selection of tabletop furnishings, including *barbotines*—artichoke, oyster, and asparagus plates and serving dishes—turn-of-the-century vases with grandiose patterns, unusual serving platters, silver sugar tongs and spoons. The door of this small shop is often locked, so be sure to knock to be let in.

**GALERIE MICHEL
SONKIN**
10 Rue de Beaune, Paris 7.
Tel: 42.61.27.87.
Métro: Rue du Bac.
Open 2:30 to 7 P.M. Closed
 Sunday and August.
Credit cards: AE, DC, V.

A s much cozy museum as antique shop, Galerie Michel Sonkin is filled with lovingly restored folk objects, most of them in golden, gleaming wood. Monsieur and Madame Sonkin have searched throughout Europe to find their treasures and are particularly proud of their intricately carved, initialed bread stamps, dating from the days when villagers depended on communal ovens for baking. Each loaf was stamped with the family seal or initials, so the baker could tell the loaves apart. Also wooden butter molds, milk filters and carved spoons, porcelain cheese molds, some solid antique chests, and pieces of furniture.

LA TUILE A LOUP
35 Rue Daubenton, Paris 5.
Tel: 47.07.28.90.
Fax: 43.36.40.95.
Métro: Censier-Daubenton.
Open 10:30 A.M. to 1 P.M.
 and 3 to 7:30 P.M.
Closed Sunday afternoon
 and Monday.
Credit cards: AE, V.

A rustic little shop specializing in French regional arts and crafts, pottery dishes in rich green and blue glazes, beautiful handmade wooden bowls, baskets, and candles, and a wide selection of books on the folklore and customs of regional France.

MADELEINE, ARC DE TRIOMPHE, NOTRE-DAME DE LORETTE

8th and 9th arrondissements

AU BAIN MARIE
10 Rue Boissy d'Anglas,
 Paris 8.
Tel: 42.66.59.74.
Fax: 42.66.45.08.
Métro: Concorde.
Open 10 A.M. to 7 P.M.
 Closed Sunday.
Credit cards: AE, DC,
 MC, V.

T hanks to the good taste and energy of Aude Clément, Au Bain Marie is the city's most beautiful, most eclectic shop for the kitchen and table. A mouthwatering selection of antique and modern silver, porcelain, and china, including a large and lovely selection of antique *barbotines* (asparagus, artichoke, and oyster plates). There's a fine assortment of silver, porcelain, exquisite crystal carafes, expensive but incredibly outfitted wicker picnic baskets, plus amusing knife rests, asparagus tongs, posters, caviar chillers, and odd and enviable food-related collector's items. Walk upstairs to find a fine selection of elegant hand-made table and bed linens in silk, cotton, and pure linen.

LA CARPE
14 Rue Tronchet, Paris 8.
Tel: 47.42.73.25.
Fax: 47.42.57.37.
Métro: Havre-Caumartin.
Open 9:30 A.M. to 6:45 P.M.
   Closed Sunday, Monday morning, and August.
Credit cards: MC, V.

Located just off the Place de la Madeleine, this is the place to find items you didn't know you needed: different kinds of oyster knives, cherry and peach pitters, an espresso machine that works off a car battery, and much more. The staff is very friendly and helpful. A catalog is available. Also stop by La Petite Carpe, around the corner at 13 Rue Vignon.

COUTELLERIE CHASTEL
190 Boulevard Haussmann, Paris 8.
Tel: 45.63.20.59.
Métro: Courcelles or Saint-Philippe-du-Roule.
Open 9:45 A.M. to 12:30 P.M. and 1:30 to 6:45 P.M.
   Closed Saturday and Monday afternoon, Sunday, and August.
Credit card: V.

Should you purchase knives in need of a new coat of silver or new blades, stop in to see Alain Chastel, who works out of a tiny boutique on the corner of Rue des Courcelles and Boulevard Haussmann. He's been my "knife doctor" for years, adding new old-fashioned stainless-steel blades to favorite antique knives (which also makes them dishwasher proof), and re-silvering beat-up silverplate cutlery with which I hate to part. Although it takes three weeks for re-silvering, and two weeks for new blades, Monsieur Chastel will be happy to arrange international delivery.

LA JARDINIERE
40 Rue Maubeuge, Paris 9.
Tel: 42.82.02.20.
Métro: Notre-Dame de Lorette.
Open 9 A.M. to 6 P.M.
Credit card: V.

Anyone who loves grilling indoors or out should make a beeline for this shop, where they sell a sturdy, black cast-iron grilling system, which can be purchased in component parts and includes includes a marvelous vertical grill that easily doubles as a radiator on chilly days, a handy horizontal grill, and an electric rotisserie. Not something to slip inside your carry-on luggage, but transportable nonetheless.

PETER CREATIONS
191 Rue du Faubourg
Saint-Honoré, Paris 8.
Tel: 45.63.88.00.
Métro: Saint-Philippe-
de-Roule.
Open 10 A.M. to 1 P.M. and
2 to 6:30 P.M. Closed
Monday morning,
Sunday, and the first
three weeks in August.
Credit card: V.

Peter the silversmith specializes in traditional, handcrafted silverware, in particular, knives with elegant, molded handles made of ebony, lapis, horn, or serpentine. His trademark sterling and solid silver creations and knives of every description cannot be found elsewhere; otherwise, the tableware here is unexceptional.

PUIFORCAT ORFEVRE
22 Rue François 1er, Paris 8.
Tel: 47.20.74.27.
Fax: 47.20.01.62.
Métro: Franklin-D.-
Roosevelt
Open 9:30 A.M. to 1 P.M. and
2 to 6:30 P.M. Tuesday
through Saturday.
Closed Sunday, Monday,
and two weeks in
August.
Credit cards: AE, DC, V.

My favorite Paris shop for superbly designed silver cups—*timbales* (monogrammed, they make perfect baby gifts, ready for use much later in life as brandy or Cognac snifters), elegant silver wine and Champagne buckets, fine reproductions of antique china, and exquisite Puiforcat silver patterns from the 1920s and 1930s.

TERRITOIRE
30 Rue Boissy d'Anglas,
Paris 8.
Tel: 42.66.22.13.
Fax: 40.07.05.27.
Métro: Concorde.
Open 10:30 A.M. to 7 P.M.
Closed Sunday.
Credit cards: AE, DC, V.
Will ship internationally.

A really wonderful idea for a shop: celebrating *les fêtes et les vacances!* Would that we could spend our lives making use of all the goodies found within. There are objects for picnics (great Thermos-style jugs, picnic hampers, you name it) as well as all sorts of paraphernalia for parties, including menu cards, invitations, fireworks, and a great assortment of fantasy birthday candles.

MONTPARNASSE

14th and 15th arrondissements

KITCHEN BAZAAR
11 Avenue du Maine,
Paris 15.
Tel: 42.22.91.17.
Métro: Montparnasse-
Bienvenue.
Open 10 A.M. to 7 P.M.
Closed Sunday.
Credit card: MC, V.

Everything for the kitchen, from timers on strings to Italian-designed balancing scales, tiny chocolate molds, and citrus-fruit peelers, zesters, curlers, all of good quality. Some baking dishes and a small collection of cookbooks.

**KITCHEN BAZAAR
AUTREMENT**
6 Avenue du Maine,
   Paris 15.
Tel: 45.48.89.00.
Métro: Montparnasse-
   Bienvenue.
Open 10 A.M. to 7 P.M.
   Closed Sunday.
Credit card: MC, V.

An annex of Kitchen Bazaar featuring a range of beautiful kitchen objects, including modern designs from Japan and Portugal, Spain and France. A dream of a spot for gifts for friends—or yourself.

A wonderful but difficult choice.

PRESENT TIME
204 Avenue du Maine,
Paris 14.
Tel: 45.42.38.59.
Métro: Alésia.
Open 10:30 A.M. to 1:30 P.M.
and 2:30 to 7:30 P.M.
Closed Monday.

Present Time seems like a contemporary art gallery for the table. Their motto is *"beau et fonctionnel"*, and everything in the thoroughly modern shop fits this description. Each item is beautifully designed and functional, although sometimes you have to look long and hard to figure out just what its function is. You'll find modern designs from all over Europe, especially northern Europe and Italy, as well as handcrafted French pocket knives. Come here for out-of-the-ordinary corkscrews, egg cups, glassware, and cutlery.

PASSY, TERNES
16th and 17th arrondissements

COUTELLERIE DE PASSY
17 Rue de l'Annonciation,
Paris 16.
Tel: 42.24.77.46.
Métro: La Muette or Passy.
Open 10 A.M. to 12:30 P.M.
and 1:30 to 6:30 P.M.
Closed Sunday, Monday,
and August.
Credit cards: AE, V.

This cute mom-and-pop shop on the cobblestoned Rue de l'Annonciation feels as though it's out of another era. As the name suggests, the shop repairs knives, but this seems like an afterthought in comparison to its encyclopedic collection of pocket knives. This is pocket knife heaven with at least thirty different styles of handmade knives from all over France and Europe, from producers such as Laguiole and Nortrons, as well as unusual, colorful, painted Corsican knives.

DINER DE GALA
8 Villa Laugier, Paris 17.
Tel: 42.67.73.14.
Fax: 44.15.97.55.
Métro: Ternes or RER
Péreire-Levallois.
Open 9 A.M. to 6 P.M. and by
appointment. Closed
weekends and August.
Call ahead to make sure
the shop is open.
Credit card: V.

In a shop hidden away in a pretty, private lane, Chantal Mirabeaud paints porcelain by hand, either from her own designs or to order. She also creates hand-painted lamp shades and garden accessories.

LA MAISON IVRE
34 Avenue Niel, Paris 17.
Tel: 47.66.05.72.
Métro: Ternes.
Open 10:30 A.M. to 7 P.M.
Closed Sunday, Monday,
   and three weeks in
   August.
Credit card: V.

Young, friendly Sophie Nobécourt has filled her shop with bright, hand-painted faïence that, as she puts it, "makes you want to have a party." Her collection of artisanal pottery and hand-blown glass comes from all over France, as well as England, Germany, and Portugal. Come here to find traditional floral-design faïence from Provence, including particularly lovely *café au lait* cups, in addition to one-of-a-kind modern designs. Unusual items here include plant-shaped ceramic knife rests, ceramic platters and salad bowls in abstract designs, and wicker cups lined with resin— great for a picnic. She also stocks hand-painted plant sticks with animal-shaped handles; although intended as ornaments, they're perfect for warding away unwanted birds from your herb garden.

The Food Lover's Snack Bible

It's 8 A.M., it's noon or it's midnight. You're lost or you're in an unfamiliar neighborhood, or you're hungry. Or all three. Here's an S.O.S. list, Métro stop by Métro stop, of one hundred invitations to a dependable snack or *casse-croûte*. Contemporary Paris is a snacker's paradise, where rustic sandwiches filled with goat cheese, bagels and brownies, a baker's latest creation, a warming cup of tea or hot chocolate will cure what ails.

ABBESSES
Café Le Sancerre
35 Rue des Abbesses,
  Paris 18.
Tel: 42.58.08.20.
A Poilâne *croque-monsieur*,
  a glass of Sancerre

ALMA-MARCEAU
Bar des Théâtres
6 Avenue Montaigne,
  Paris 8.
Tel: 47.23.34.63.
Actors, singers, models,
  croque-monsieur and
  salade niçoise

**ASSEMBLEE-
  NATIONALE**
Pâtisserie-Salon de Thé
  Pradier
6 and 32 Rue de
  Bourgogne, Paris 7.
Tel: 45.51.78.36 and
  45.51.72.37.
Pastry, tea, and a trip to
  vieille France

BASTILLE
Pâtisserie Paul Bugat
5 Boulevard Beaumarchais,
  Paris 4.
Tel: 48.87.89.88.
Savory tarts, sandwiches,
  fantastic *crème brûlée*

BIR-HAKEIM
Boulangerie Lionel Poilâne
49 Boulevard de Grenelle,
  Paris 15.
Tel: 45.79.11.49.
The city's best bread,
  irresistible apple tarts

BOISSIERE
Produits Régionaux: Au
  Coeur des Landes
33 Rue Boissière, Paris 16.
Tel: 45.53.78.52.
Serrano ham sandwiches,
  foie gras, sheep's milk
  cheese

BOURSE
La Côte Bar à Vins
77 Rue de Richelieu,
  Paris 2.
Tel: 42.97.40.68.
Racing waiters, Loire valley
  wines, homey *plats du
  jour*

CARDINAL LEMOINE
Damman's
20 Rue du Cardinal-
  Lemoine, Paris 5.
Tel: 46.33.61.30.
Ice cream festival: bitter
  mandarin, yogurt,
  chocolate

CENSIER-DAUBENTON
Comptoir du Saumon
49 Rue Censier, Paris 5.
Tel: 43.36.49.05.
A trip to Sweden: Smoked
  salmon and aquavit

CHARONNE
Jacques Melac
42 Rue Léon-Frot, Paris 11.
Tel: 43.70.59.27.
Good times and copious
  food assured

**CHARLES DE GAULLE-
  ETOILE**
Foc Hour
22 Avenue MacMahon,
  Paris 17.
Tel: 46.22.46.45.
Vietnamese spring rolls
  and delicate shrimp
  raviolis

CHATELET
Boulangerie André Cleret
4 Rue des Lavandières-
  Sainte-Opportune,
  Paris 1.
Tel: 42.33.82.68.
Fabulous carry-out
  sandwiches, fantasy
  fougasses

CHEMIN-VERT
Café des Musées
49 Rue de Turenne, Paris 3.
Tel: 42.72.96.17.
Classic café fare near the
    Picasso Museum

LA CITE
Le Valençay Bistrot à Vins
11 Boulevard du Palais,
    Paris 4.
Tel: 43.54.64.67.
Hearty salads, hearty *plats
    du jour,* wines by the
    glass

CONCORDE
Café Flottes
2 Rue Cambon, Paris 8.
Tel: 42.60.80.89
Copious salads and
    sandwiches at the back
    door of W.H. Smith

**CHAMBRE-DES-
    DEPUTES**
Chocolat Richart
258 Boulevard Saint-
    Germain, Paris 7.
Tel: 45.55.66.00.
Chocolates with Sicilian
    pistachios, ginger, or
    saffron

COURCELLES
Fromagerie Alain Dubois
79 Rue de Courcelles,
    Paris 17.
Tel: 43.80.36.42.
Press your nose against the
    window and inhale

DAUMESNIL
Au Métro
8 Place Félix-Eboué,
    Paris 12.
Tel: 43.43.84.01.
A fish café: grilled
    sardines, mussels,
    salmon *rillettes*

DENFERT-ROCHEREAU
Le Rallye Bistro à Vin
6 Rue Daguerre, Paris 14.
Tel: 43.22.57.05.
A glass of Saint-Véran,
    goat cheese, and
    country hams

DUROC
Boulangerie G. Abot
70 Rue de Sèvres, Paris 7.
Tel: 47.34.65.00.
For great olive bread, *petits
    pains* topped with
    cheese

ECOLE MILITAIRE
Café de Mars
11 Rue Augereau, Paris 7.
Tel: 47.05.05.91.
Brownies, cheesecake, and
    Sunday brunch

ETIENNE MARCEL
Lina's
50 Rue Etienne Marcel,
    Paris 1.
Tel: 42.21.16.14.
Pastrami sandwich and
    pecan pie

FAIDHERBE-CHALIGNY
Café Caoua
207 Rue du Faubourg
    Saint-Antoine, Paris 11.
Tel: 43.48.60.97.
A frothy *café crème,* a
    bittersweet brownie

FILLES DU CALVAIRE
Clown Bar
114 Rue Amelot, Paris 11.
Tel: 43.55.87.35.
Put on a happy face: wine,
    plats du jour, circus
    decor

**FRANKLIN-D.-
    ROOSEVELT**
Lina's
8 Rue Marbeuf, Paris 8.
Tel: 47.23.92.33.
A bacon and turkey
    sandwich, and brownies

GAITE
L'Echanson Bistrot à Vin
89 Rue Daguerre, Paris 14.
Tel: 43.22.20.00.
A glass of Saint-Nicholas-
    de-Bourgueil, a copious
    lunch

GARE DE L'EST:
L'Enchotte Bistrot à Vin
11 Rue de Chabrol,
    Paris 10.
Tel: 48.00.05.25
Small-village ambience,
    Alsatian wines, a *plat
    du jour*

GARE DE LYON
Le Train Bleu (in the Gare
    de Lyon)
20 Boulevard Diderot,
    Paris 12.
Tel: 43.43.09.06.
An historic monument, a
    farewell café or a
    welcome repast

GARE DU NORD
Taverne de la Bière
15 Rue de Dunkerque,
    Paris 10.
Tel: 42.85.12.93.
Time for a beer: Alsatian,
    Belgian, Spanish, or
    British

GEORGE-V
Café Fouquet's
99 Avenue des Champs-
    Elysées, Paris 8.
Tel: 47.23.70.60.
For the newly planted
    greenery along the
    Champs-Elysées

LES HALLES
Le Cochon à L'Oreille
15 Rue Montmartre,
    Paris 1.
Tel: 42.36.07.56.
A workingman's bar:
    peanuts at the bar, wine
    by the glass

HOTEL DE VILLE
Au Petit Fer à Cheval
30 Rue Vieille du Temple,
Paris 4.
Tel: 42.72.47.47.
Atmospheric 1900s
neighborhood café,
great horseshoe bar

JULES JOFFRIN
Fromagerie de Montmatre
9 Rue du Poteau, Paris 18.
Tel: 46.06.26.03.
For starters, forty different
varieties of goat cheese

JUSSIEU
Institut du Monde Arabe
1 Rue des Fossés Saint-
Bernard, Paris 5.
Tel: 46.34.15.20.
A rooftop Paris view, great
cafeteria, Lebanese fare

KLEBER
Café Le Copernic
54 Avenue Kléber, Paris 16.
Tel: 47.27.87.65.
Buttery, homemade
croissants and the
morning news

**LAMARCK-
CAULAINCOURT**
Aux Négociants
27 Rue Lambert, Paris 18.
(Across from 48 Rue
Custine.)
Tel: 46.06.15.11.
Ambience, wine by the
glass, a cheery *plat
du jour*

LA TOUR-MAUBOURG
Boulangerie-Pâtisserie
Duchesne
112 Rue Saint-Dominique,
Paris 7.
Tel: 45.51.31.01.
A heavenly *galette de
pommes de terre,* and
more

LEDRU-ROLLIN
Le Passage Bistrot à Vin
18 Passage de la Bonne-
Graine, Paris 11.
Tel: 47.00.73.30.
Steak tartare, *pots de crème,*
great wines by the glass

LIEGE
Androuët
41 Rue d'Amsterdam,
Paris 8.
Tel: 48.74.26.90.
A do-it-yourself
bread/cheese snack,
a Paris institution

LOUVRE-RIVOLI
Verlet
256 Rue Saint-Honoré,
Paris 1.
Tel: 42.60.67.39.
Some of the city's best
coffee, great fresh
pastries

LUXEMBOURG
La Gueuze
19 Rue Sufflot, Paris 5.
Tel: 43.54.63.00
Heady Belgian beer, fries,
and steamed mussels

MABILLON
La Palette
43 Rue de Seine, Paris 6.
Tel: 43.26.68.15.
A Left Bank artist's
landmark with
atmosphere plus

MADELEINE
La Ferme Saint-Hubert
21 Rue Vignon, Paris 8.
Tel: 47.42.79.20.
A cheese tasting
extravaganza, a glass of
Sancerre

**MARCADET-
POISSONNIERS**
Boulangerie au Pain
d'Antan
2 Rue Eugène Sue, Paris 18.
Tel: 42.64.71.78.
Fouace aveyronnaise,
butter-rich *brioche* of
central France

**MAIRIE DE SAINT-
OUEN**
Chez Serge
7 Boulevard Jean-Jaurès,
93400 Saint-Ouen.
Tel: 40.11.06.42.
A great wine bar lunch at
the end of the world

MAUBERT-MUTUALITE
Les Pipos Bar à Vins
2 Rue de l'Ecole
Polytechnique, Paris 5.
Tel: 43.54.11.40.
78-records, Beaume-de-
Venise, copious *plats
du jour*

MIROMESNIL
Ma Bourgogne
133 Boulevard Haussmann,
Paris 8.
Tel: 45.63.50.61.
A businessman's wine bar,
elbow-to-elbow

**MONTPARNASSE-
BIENVENUE**
Boulangerie Saibron
4 Place Constantin
Brancusi, Paris 14.
Tel: 43.21.76.18.
Whole-wheat *baguettes,*
mini-triangles of
raisin rye

MOUTON-DUVERNET
Les Comestibles (lunch
only)
10 Rue Sablière, Paris 14.
Tel: 45.45.47.12.
A copious *plat du jour,* a
price that's right

LA MUETTE
Pâtisserie-Salon de Thé
 Coquelin Aîné
67 Rue de Passy, Paris 16.
Tel: 45.24.44.00.
Join the chic, sugar-loving
 crowd at a high-class
 hangout

NATION
Brasserie l'Espérance
253 Boulevard Voltaire,
 Paris 11.
Tel: 43.73.62.54.
Peanuts at the bar, a cheese
 and salad lunch

**NOTRE-DAME-DES-
 CHAMPS**
La Chocolatière
5 Rue Stanislas, Paris 6.
Tel: 45.49.13.06.
A cup of hot chocolate, a
 chocolate tart, *a tarte
 Tatin*

ODEON
Cosi
54 Rue de Seine, Paris 6.
Tel: 46.33.35.36.
A great Paris snack, pizzas
 in a pocket

OPERA
Marks & Spencer
35 Boulevard Haussman,
 Paris 8.
Tel: 47.42.42.91.
BLT sandwiches, salmon,
 cottage cheese, English
 apples

PALAIS-ROYAL
Juveniles Bistrot à Vins
47 Rue de Richelieu,
 Paris 1.
Tel: 42.97.46.49.
Tapas and one of city's best
 selections of wines by
 the glass

PASTEUR
Pâtisserie Hellegouarch
185 Rue de Vaugirard,
 Paris 15.
Tel: 47.83.29.72.
Award-winning *croissants,*
 great *pain au chocolat*

PELLEPORT
Boulangerie Ganachaud
150 Rue Ménilmontant,
 Paris 20.
Tel: 46.36.13.82.
For thirty different breads,
 and more

PERE-LACHAISE
Café Le Saint-Amour
2 Avenue Gambetta/
 32 Boulevard
 Ménilmontant, Paris 20.
Tel: 47.97.20.15.
Before or after a Père
 Lachaise tour, a meal or
 a snack

PERNETY
Café l'Entrepot
7–9 Rue Francis de
 Pressensé, Paris 14.
Tel: 45.40.78.38.
For film buffs: Poilâne
 croques and *raclette*

PLAISANCE
Boulangerie Le Moulin de
 la Vierge
105 Rue Vercingétorix,
 Paris 14.
Tel: 45.43.09.84.
Bread heaven, rich *sablées,*
 perfect *fougasse*

PLACE DE CLICHY
Pâtisserie Fayeux
56 Rue de Clichy, Paris 9.
Tel: 48.74.37.64.
Financiers, chocolate chip
 brioche, great apple
 fritters

PLACE MONGE
Café Mouffetard
116 Rue Mouffetard,
 Paris 5.
Tel: 43.31.42.50.
Homemade sandwiches
 and *croissants "maison"*

POMPE
Pâtisserie Les Délices de
 Longchamp
150 Avenue Victor Hugo,
 Paris 16.
Tel: 47.27.99.52.
For starters, an herb-filled
 tarte provençale

PONT DE L'ALMA
Boulangerie Bernard
 Desgrippes
16 Avenue Rapp, Paris 7.
Tel: 45.51.66.39.
Great sandwiches to go,
 superb prune-filled
 pastry

PONT-MARIE
Le Flore en l'Ile
42 Quai d'Orléans, Paris 4.
Tel: 43.29.88.27.
A warming cup of tea, a
 sandwich, a view of
 Notre-Dame

PONT-NEUF
Taverne Henri IV
13 Place du Pont-Neuf,
 Paris 1.
Tel: 43.54.27.90.
Hefty Poilâne *tartines,*
 wines by the glass

PORT ROYAL
La Closerie des Lilas
171 Boulevard du
 Montparnasse, Paris 14.
Tel: 43.26.70.50.
Café fare: Hemingway is
 gone, but the memory
 lives on

PORTE-MAILLOT
Cosi
53 Avenue des Ternes,
Paris 17.
Tel: 43.80.86.70.
A wood-fired oven and
goat-cheese-filled pizza
pockets

PORTE D'ORLEANS
Fromagerie Fil o' Fromage
4 Rue Poirier-de-Narçay,
Paris 14.
Tel: 40.44.86.75.
A snack of bread, cheese, a
bottle of wine

PORTE DE VANVES
Boulangerie Max Poilâne
87 Rue Brancion, Paris 15.
Tel: 48.28.45.90.
A stage-set bakery,
miniature sweets, and
tangy bread

PYRAMIDES
Flo Prestige
42 Place du Marché-Saint-
Honoré, Paris 1.
Tel: 42.61.45.46.
The sandwich of your
dreams, a slice of *foie
gras*

PYRENEES
Bistro-Cave des Envierges
11 Rue des Envierges,
Paris 20.
Tel: 46.36.47.84.
Wine, cheese, and fresh
baguettes

RAMBUTEAU
Espace Gourmand
27 Rue des Archives,
Paris 4.
Tel: 42.72.93.94.
Thyme-flecked *fougasse,*
topped with tomatoes
and herbs

RICHELIEU-DROUOT
Micro-Brasserie
106 Rue de Richelieu,
Paris 2.
Tel: 42.96.55.31.
A beer lover's heaven

REUILLY DIDEROT
Boulangerie Bazin
85 bis Rue de Charenton,
Paris 12.
Tel: 43.07.75.21.
Tiny breads filled with
cheese or apples, breads
galore

RENNES
Au Plasir des Pains
62 Rue de Vaugirard,
Paris 6.
Tel: 45.48.40.45.
Copious tomato-mozzarella
sandwiches to eat in or
carry out

REPUBLIQUE
Le Petit Château d'Eau
34 Rue du Château-d'Eau,
Paris 10.
Tel: 42.08.72.81.
A workingman's hangout
with great half moon bar

ROME
Boulangerie Belem
47 Rue Boursault, Paris 17.
Tel: 45.22.38.95.
For Portuguese pastries
filled with vanilla
custard

RUE DU BAC
Café Basile
34 Rue de Grenelle, Paris 7.
Tel: 42.22.59.46.
Left Bank students'
hangout with great *pain
Basile*

SAINT-LAZARE
Pâtisserie Lenôtre
3–5 Rue du Havre, Paris 8.
Tel: 45.22.22.29.
Before or after a train trip,
a perfect snack stop

SAINT-GEORGES
Café à la Place Saint-
Georges
60 Rue Saint-Georges,
Paris 9.
Tel: 42.80.39.32.
Croque-monsieur heaven,
salade aux noix, Saint-
Pourçain

**SAINT-GERMAIN-DES-
PRES**
Café de Flore
172 Boulevard Saint-
Germain, Paris 6.
Tel: 45.48.55.26.
It's Paris-Paris: People
watching and hard-
boiled eggs

SAINT-MICHEL
Miramar
17 Rue Saint-Jacques,
Paris 5.
Tel: 43.54.71.77.
Fragrant Chinese soups,
superb steamed fish

SAINT-PAUL
La Tartine
24 Rue de Rivoli, Paris 4.
Tel: 42.72.76.85.
Open-face sandwiches,
great goat cheese, a
glass of wine

**SAINT-PHILIPPE DU
ROULE**
La Boutique à Sandwiches
12 Rue du Colisée, Paris 8.
Tel: 43.59.56.69.
Great sandwiches or
raclette

SAINT-PLACIDE
Le Nemrod
51 Rue du Cherche-Midi,
Paris 6.
Tel: 45.48.17.05.
A sip of Morgon, Poilâne
bread, copious salads

SEVRES-BABYLONE
Au Sauvignon
80 Rue des Saint-Pères,
   Paris 7.
Tel: 45.48.49.02.
Poilâne *tartines,* wines by
   the glass, people
   watching

SAINT-SULPICE
Bar de la Croix Rouge
2 Carrefour de la Croix
   Rouge, Paris 6.
Tel: 45.48.06.45.
A great coffee, Poilâne
   tartines, raw milk
   cheeses

SENTIER
Café du Croisssant
146 Rue Montmartre,
   Paris 2.
Tel: 42.33.35.04.
In memory of statesman
   Jean-Jaurès: *vin* and
   plats du jour

SOLFERINO
Café des Lettres
53 Rue de Verneuil, Paris 7.
Tel: 42.22.52.17.
A cobbled terrace,
   Scandinavian salads,
   Italian coffee

SULLY-MORLAND
Enoteca
25 Rue Charles V, Paris 4.
Tel: 42.78.91.44.
Antipasti, 100 Italian
   wines, a voyage to Italy

TERNES
Le Stubli Delikatessen
10 Rue Poncelet, Paris 17.
Tel: 42.27.81.86.
Coulibiac, carry-out salads,
   and strudel

TROCADERO
Salon de Thé Carette
4 Place du Trocadéro,
   Paris 16.
Tel: 48.88.98.07.
Yeasty *pain au chocolat* and
   smoky Chinese tea

TUILERIES
Salon de Thé Angelina
226 Rue de Rivoli, Paris 1.
Tel: 42.60.82.00.
Time to go into sugar
   overdrive

VANEAU
Pâtisserie Peltier
66 Rue de Sèvres, Paris 7.
Tel: 47.34.06.62.
Some of Paris's best
   croissants, remarkable
   pastry

VAVIN
Le Dôme
108 Boulevard du
   Montparnasse, Paris 14.
Tel: 43.35.34.82.
White wine, fresh oysters,
   a slice of Montparnasse
   history

VICTOR-HUGO
Cafe Le Victor Hugo
4 Place Victor-Hugo,
   Paris 16.
Tel: 45.00.87.55.
People-watching heaven in
   the "deep 16th"

VILLIERS
Le Dôme de Villiers
4 Avenue de Villiers,
   Paris 17.
Tel: 43.87.28.68.
A stroll through Parc
   Monceau, a *croque-*
   monsieur

VOLONTAIRES
Au Roi du Café
59 Rue Lecourbe, Paris 15.
Tel: 47.34.48.50.
A cheery café for that
   sunny day in May

VOLTAIRE
Café La Palette Bastille
116 Avenue Ledru-Rollin,
   Paris 12.
Tel: 47.00.34.39.
An Art-Nouveau decor,
   Poilâne *croques,*
   Berthillon ice cream

French/English
FOOD GLOSSARY

Ask for your perfect peach in perfect French.

Even for the French, the local restaurant menu can be confusing. For instance, the average Frenchman would be very hard pressed to tell you exactly what goes into a sauce Albuféra (it's a béchamel with sweet peppers) or how a *canard de Barbarie* differs from a *canard de Nantes* (the latter duck is smaller and more delicate).

The following is a brief glossary of common menu terms—words, phrases, and preparations that you are likely to find on a French menu. In all cases, I have tried to offer brief explanations, limiting entries to those that diners are most likely to need when dining in Paris.

A

A.A.A.A.A.: the Association Amicale des Authentiques Amateurs d'Andouillettes gives this label only to the best *andouillettes*, or chitterling sausages.
A point: medium rare.
Abats: organ meats.

Abricot: apricot.
Acidulé: acidic.
Addition: bill.
Affiné(e): aged or refined.
Agneau (de lait): lamb (young, milk fed).
Agrumes: citrus fruits.
Aiglefin, églefin: haddock.
Aigre: sour.
Aigre-doux: sweet and sour.
Aigrelette (sauce): a sour or

tart sauce.
Aiguillettes: thin slivers, usually of duck breast.
Ail: garlic.
Aile: wing of poultry or game bird.
Aile et cuisse: used to describe white breast meat (aile) and dark thigh meat (cuisse), usually of chicken.
Aileron: wing tip.

Aïoli: garlicky blend of eggs and olive oil.

Airelles: wild cranberries.

Albuféra: béchamel sauce with sweet peppers.

Algues: edible seaweed.

Aligot: mashed potatoes with fresh Cantal cheese and garlic.

Allumettes: puff pastry strips; also fried matchstick potatoes.

Alose: shad.

Alouette: lark.

Aloyau: loin area of beef.

Alsacienne (à l'): Alsace style; often including sauerkraut, sausage, or foie gras.

Amande: almond.

Amande de mer: smooth-shelled shellfish, like a small clam, with a sweet, almost hazelnut flavor.

Amer(ère): bitter, as in unsweetened chocolate.

Amertume: bitterness.

Amourettes: spinal bone marrow of calf or ox.

Amuse-bouche (-gueule): literally, amuse the mouth; appetizer..

Ananas: pineapple.

Anchoïade: purée of anchovies, olive oil, and vinegar.

Anchois: anchovy.

Ancienne (à l'): in the old style.

Andouille: cold smoked chitterling (tripe) sausage.

Andouillette: smaller chitterling (tripe) sausage, usually served grilled.

Aneth: dill.

Anis: aniseed.

Apéritif: a before-dinner drink that stimulates the appetite; usually sweet or mildly bitter.

Arachide (huile d'): peanut (oil).

Araignée de mer: spider crab.

Ardennaise (à l'): Ardennes style; often with juniper berries.

Ardoise: literally, slate; usually refers to the day's specialties.

Arêtes: fish bones.

Argenteuil: usually asparagus-flavored soup, named for the Paris suburb that once was the asparagus capital.

Aromates: spices and herbs.

Artichaut (violet): artichoke (small purple).

Asperge: asparagus.

Assiette: plate.

Assiette du pêcheur: assorted fish platter.

Assorti(e): assorted.

Aubergine: eggplant.

Aumônière: literally, beggar's purse; thin *crêpe*, filled, and wrapped like a bundle.

Aurore: béchamel or cream sauce with tomatoes.

Automne: autumn.

Auvergnat(e): Auvergne style; often with cabbage, sausage, and bacon.

Avocat: avocado.

B

Baba au rhum: sponge cake with rum-flavored syrup.

Baguette: classic long, thin loaf of bread.

Baies: berries.

Baies roses: pink peppercorns.

Baigné: bathed.

Ballottine: usually poultry, boned, stuffed, and rolled.

Banane: banana.

Bar: Mediterranean fish,

also known as *loup,* similar to striped bass.

Barbarie (canard de): Barbary breed of duck (see *Canard de Barbarie*).

Barbue: brill, a Mediterranean flatfish related to turbot.

Baron: hindquarters and legs of lamb.

Baron de lapereau: baron (hindquarters and legs) of young rabbit.

Barquette: small pastry shaped like a boat.

Basilic: basil.

Basquaise: Basque style; usually with ham or tomatoes or red peppers.

Bavaroise: cold dessert; a rich custard made with cream and gelatin.

Bavette: skirt steak.

Béarnaise: tarragon-flavored sauce of egg yolks, butter, shallots, white wine, vinegar, and other herbs.

Béatilles: dish combining various organ meats.

Bécasse: woodchuck.

Béchamel: white sauce made with butter, flour and milk, usually flavored with onion, bay leaf, pepper, and nutmeg.

Beignet: fritter or doughnut.

Belon: prized flat-shelled *plate* oyster.

Bercy: fish-stock-based sauce thickened with flour and butter and flavored with white wine and shallots.

Berrichonne: garnish of braised cabbage, glazed baby onions, chestnuts, and lean bacon.

Betterave: beet.

Beurre: butter.

Beurre blanc: reduced sauce of vinegar, white

wine, shallots, and butter.

Beurre noir: sauce of browned butter, lemon juice or vinegar, parsley, and sometimes capers.

Beurre noisette: lightly browned butter.

Biche: female deer.

Bien cuit(e): well done.

Bifteck: steak.

Bigarade: orange sauce.

Bigarreau: red, firm-fleshed variety of cherry.

Bigorneaux: periwinkles, tiny sea snails.

Billy Bi, Billy By: cream of mussel soup.

Biscuits à la cuillère: ladyfingers.

Bisque: substantial soup, usually shellfish.

Blanc (de poireau): white portion (of leek).

Blanc (de volaille): usually breast of chicken.

Blanquette: veal, lamb, chicken, or seafood stew with egg and cream-enriched white sauce.

Blette: Swiss chard.

Bleu: blood rare, usually for steak.

Blinis: small, thick pancakes.

Boeuf à la mode: beef marinated and braised in red wine, served with carrots, mushrooms, onions, and turnips.

Boeuf au gros sel: boiled beef, served with vegetables and coarse salt.

Boissons (non) comprises: drinks (not) included.

Bombe: molded, layered ice cream dessert.

Bonne femme (cuisine): home-style (cooking); also a meat garnish of bacon, potatoes, mush-rooms, and onions; a fish

garnish of shallots, par-sley, mushrooms, and potatoes; or a white wine sauce with shallots, mush-rooms, and lemon juice.

Bordelaise: Bordeaux style; also refers to a brown sauce of shallots, red wine, and bone marrow.

Bouchée: a tiny mouthful; may refer to a bite-size pastry or to a *vol-au-vent.*

Boudin: technically a meat sausage, but generically any sausage-shaped mixture.

Boudin blanc: white sausage, of veal, chicken, or pork.

Boudin noir: pork blood sausage.

Bouillabaisse: Mediterranean fish soup.

Bouillon: a light soup or broth.

Boulette: meatball or fishball.

Bouquet: large reddish shrimp (see also *Crevette rose).*

Bourdaloue: hot poached fruit, sometimes wrapped in pastry.

Bourguignonne: Burgundy style; often with red wine, onions, mushrooms, and bacon.

Bouribut: spicy, red wine duck stew.

Bourride: egg-based Mediterranean fish and shellfish soup served with aïoli.

Braise: live coals.

Braiser: to braise; to cook meat by browning in fat, then simmering in covered dish with small amount of liquid.

Brandade (de morue): warm garlicky purée of salt cod, milk or cream or oil, and sometimes mashed potatoes.

Brebis (fromage de): sheep (sheep's-milk cheese).

Bretonne: in the style of Brittany; a dish served with white beans; or may refer to a white wine sauce with carrots, leeks, and celery.

Brioche: buttery, egg-enriched yeast bread.

Broche (à la): spit-roasted.

Brochet: pike.

Brochette: cubes of meat or fish and vegetables on a skewer.

Brouillé(es): scrambled, usually eggs.

Brûlé: literally, burned; usually refers to dark caramelization.

Brunoise: tiny diced vegetables.

Buccin: (see *Bulot).*

Buffet froid: variety of dishes, served cold, sometimes from a buffet.

Bugnes: sweet fried doughnuts or fritters, originally from Lyons.

Buisson: literally, a bush; generally, a dish including vegetables arranged like a bush; classically, a crayfish presentation.

Bulot: large sea snail, also called *buccin.*

C

Cabécou: small round goat cheese.

Cabillaud: fresh cod.

Caen (à la mode de): named after the Nor-mandy town; usually a dish cooked in Calvados and white wine and/or cider.

Café: coffee, as well as a type of eating place where coffee is served.

Café au lait: coffee with milk.

Café crème: coffee with milk.

Café déca: decaffeinated coffee.

Café liégeois: iced coffee served with ice cream (optional) and whipped cream.

Café noir: black coffee.

Cagouille: small *petit-gris* land snail, found in the Saintonge province of western France.

Caille: quail.

Calmar: small squid, similar to *encornet,* with interior cartilage instead of a bone.

Campagne (à la): country-style.

Canapé: triangular pieces of toasted bread, usually served with game; also, an appetizer with a bread base, garnished with a variety of savory mixtures.

Canard: duck.

Canard à la presse: roast duck served with sauce of juices obtained from pressing the carcass, combined with red wine and Cognac.

Canard de Barbarie: Barbary breed of duck raised in southwest France, with strong-flavored flesh; generally used for braising.

Canard de Nantes: also called *canard de Challans*; very delicate-flavored small duck.

Canard de Rouen: cross between domestic and wild duck; classically, Rouen ducks are smothered and not bled, giving a special taste to the meat.

Canard sauvage: wild duck.

Caneton: young male duck.

Canette: young female duck.

Cannelle: cinnamon.

Caprice: literally, a whim; usually a dessert.

Carafe d'eau: pitcher of tap water.

Carbonnade: a braised beef stew prepared with beer and onions; also refers to a cut of beef.

Cardon: cardoon; large celerylike vegetable in the artichoke family.

Carré d'agneau: rack (ribs) or loin of lamb.

Carré de porc: rack (ribs) or loin of pork.

Carré de veau: rack (ribs) or loin of veal.

Carrelet: summer flounder or plaice.

Carte: menu.

Carvi: caraway seeds.

Casse-croûte: literally, breaking bread; slang for snack.

Casse-pierre: edible seaweed.

Cassis: black currant; also black currant liqueur.

Cassolette: usually a dish presented in a small casserole.

Cassoulet: a casserole of white beans, including various combinations of sausages, duck, pork, lamb, mutton, and goose.

Caviar d'aubergine: cold eggplant purée.

Céleri: celery.

Céleri-rave: celeriac.

Cèpe: large, meaty wild boletus mushroom.

Cerfeuil: chervil.

Cerise: cherry.

Cerise noire: black cherry.

Cerneau: walnut meat; also refers to unripe walnut.

Cervelas: garlicky pork sausage; also refers to

fish and seafood sausage.

Cervelles: brains, of calf or lamb.

Chair: the fleshy portion of either poultry or meat.

Champêtre: rustic, describes a simple presentation of a variety of ingredients.

Champignon: mushroom.
de bois: wild mushroom, from the woods.
de Paris: cultivated mushroom.
sauvage: wild mushroom.

Champignons à la grecque: tiny cultivated mushrooms cooked in water, lemon juice, olive oil, and spices, served as a cold appetizer.

Chanterelle: pale, curly-capped wild mushroom.

Chantilly: sweetened whipped cream.

Chapon: capon, or castrated chicken.

Chapon de mer: Mediterranean fish, in the *rascasse,* or scorpion fish, family.

Charcuterie: cold cuts, sausages, terrines, pâtés; also, shop selling such products.

Chariot (de desserts): rolling cart, usually carrying varied desserts.

Charlotte: molded dessert with lady-fingers and custard filling, served cold; or fruit compote baked with buttered white bread, served hot.

Charolais: light-colored cow that produces high-quality beef.

Chartreuse: a dish of braised partridge and cabbage; also herb-and-spice-based liqueur made by the Chartreux monks.

Chasse: the hunt.

Chasseur: hunter, also sauce with white wine, mushrooms, shallots, tomatoes, and herbs.

Châtaigne: chestnut, smaller than *marron,* with multiple nut meats.

Châteaubriand: thick filet steak, traditionaly served with sautéed potatoes and a sauce of white wine, dark beef stock, butter, shallots, and herbs, or with a *béarnaise* sauce.

Chaud(e): hot or warm.

Chaud-froid: cooked poultry dish served cold, usually covered with a sauce, then with aspic.

Chaudrée: fish stew, sometimes with potatoes.

Chausson: a filled pastry turnover, sweet or savory.

Chemise (en): wrapped; with pastry.

Chèvre (fromage de): goat cheese.

Chevreau: young goat.

Chevreuil: young roe deer.

Chicorée: curly endive.

Chiffonnade: shredded herbs and vegetables, usually green.

Chinchard: saurel; ocean fish with bonelike cartilaginous plates along its backbone, generally used for soups.

Chipiron: Basque name for small squid or *encornet.*

Chocolat: chocolate.

Chocolat amer: bittersweet chocolate, with very little sugar.

Chocolat au lait: milk chocolate.

Chocolat mi-amer: bittersweet chocolate, with more sugar than *chocolat amer.*

Chocolat noir: used interchangeably with *chocolat amer.*

Choix (au): a choice; usually meaning one may choose freely from several offerings.

Choron (sauce): *béarnaise* sauce with tomatoes.

Chou: cabbage.

Chou-fleur: cauliflower.

Chou frisé: kale.

Chou rouge: red cabbage.

Chou vert: curly green Savoy cabbage.

Choucroute: sauerkraut; also main dish of sauerkraut, various sausages, bacon, and pork, served with potatoes.

Choux (pâte à): cream puff (pastry).

Choux de Bruxelles: brussels sprouts.

Ciboulette: chive.

Cidre: cider, either apple or pear.

Citron: lemon.

Citron vert: lime.

Citronelle: lemon grass, an oriental herb.

Citrouille: pumpkin, gourd.

Civelles: spaghettilike baby eels, also called *pibales.*

Civet: a stew of game thickened with blood.

Civet de lièvre: jugged hare.

Clafoutis: traditional tart from the Limousin, made with a kind of *crêpe* batter and fruit, usually black cherries.

Claires: oysters; also a designation given to certain oysters to indicate that they have been put in *claires,* or oyster beds in salt marshes, where they are fattened up for several months before going to market.

Clamart: Paris suburb once famous for its green peas; today a garnish of peas.

Clémentine: small tangerine, from Morocco or Spain.

Clouté: studded with.

Cochon (de lait): pig (suckling).

Cochonnailles: pork products; usually an assortment of sausages and/or pâtés served as a first course.

Cocotte: casserole or cooking pot.

Coeur: heart.

Coeur de filet: thickest (and best) part of beef filet, usually cut into chateaubriand steaks.

Coffret: literally, small box; usually presentation in a small rectangular pastry case.

Coing: quince.

Colin: hake.

Colvert: wild ("green collared") duck.

Compote: stewed fresh or dried fruit.

Concassé: coarsely chopped.

Concombre: cucumber.

Confit: duck, goose, or pork cooked and preserved in its own fat; also fruit or vegetables preserved in sugar, alcohol, or vinegar.

Confiture: jam.

Confiture de vieux garçon: varied fresh fruits macerated in alcohol.

Congeler: to freeze.

Congre: conger eel; a large ocean fish resembling an eel, often used in fish stews.

Consommé: clear soup.

Contre-filet: cut of sirloin taken above the loin on either side of the backbone, tied for roasting or braising (can also be cut for grilling).

Convives (la totalité des): (all) those gathered at a single table.

Copeaux: literally, shavings, such as from chocolate or vegetables.

Coq (au vin): mature rooster (stewed in wine sauce).

Coque: tiny, mild-flavored, clamlike shellfish.

Coque (à la): soft-cooked egg, or anything served in a shell.

Coquelet: young male chicken.

Coquillages: shellfish.

Coquille: shell.

Coquille Saint-Jacques: sea scallop.

Corail: coral-colored egg sac, found in scallops, spiny lobster, or crayfish.

Corbeille (de fruits): basket (of fruit).

Coriandre: coriander, either the fresh herb or dried seeds.

Cornichon: tiny tart pickle.

Côte d'agneau: lamb chop.

Côte de boeuf: beef blade or rib steak.

Côte de veau: veal chop.

Côtelette: thin chop or cutlet.

Cotriade: fish stew from Brittany, which can include sardines, mackerel, and porgy, cooked with butter, potatoes, onions, and herbs.

Cou d'oie (de canard) farci: neck skin of goose (sometimes also duck), stuffed with meat and spices, much like a sausage.

Coulibiac: a hot Russian pâté, usually filled with salmon and covered with *brioche.*

Coulis: purée of raw or cooked vegetables or fruit.

Coupe: cup; refers to dessert served in a goblet.

Courge: squash or gourd.

Courgette: zucchini.

Couronne: ring or circle, usually of bread.

Court-bouillon: broth, or aromatic poaching liquid.

Couscous: granules of semolina, or hard wheat flour; also refers to a complete Moroccan dish that includes the steamed grain, broth, vegetables, meats, hot sauce, and sometimes chick-peas and raisins.

Couteau: knife.

Couvert: a place setting, including dishes, silver, glassware, and linen.

Crabe: crab.

Crapaudine: preparation of grilled poultry or game bird with backbone removed.

Crécy: a carrot garnish or carrot-based dish.

Crème: cream.

Crème anglaise: custard sauce.

Crème brûlée: rich custard dessert with a top of caramelized sugar.

Crème chantilly: sweetened whipped cream.

Crème fouettée: whipped cream.

Crème fraîche: thick, sour, heavy cream.

Crème pâtissière: custard filling for pastries and cakes,

Crème plombières: custard filled with fresh fruits and egg whites.

Crêpe: thin pancake.

Crêpes Suzette: hot *crêpe* dessert flavored with orange butter.

Crépine: caul fat.

Crépinette: small sausage patty wrapped in caul fat.

Cresson(ade): watercress (watercress sauce).

Crête (de coq): cock's comb.

Creuse: elongated, crinkle-shelled oyster.

Crevette grise: tiny soft-fleshed shrimp that remains gray when cooked.

Crevette rose: small firm-fleshed shrimp that turns red when cooked; when large, called *bouquet.*

Criste-marine: edible algae.

Croquant(e): crispy.

Croque-madame: toasted ham and cheese sandwich topped with an egg.

Croque-monsieur: toasted ham and cheese sandwich.

Croquette: ground meat, fish, fowl, or vegetables bound with eggs or sauce, shaped into various forms, usually coated in bread crumbs and deep fried.

Crottin (de Chavignol): firm goat cheese (from Chavignol).

Croustade: usually small, pastry-wrapped dish; also regional southwestern pastry filled with prunes and/or apples.

Croûte (en): in pastry.

Croûte de sel (en): in a salt crust.

Croûtons: small cubes, rounds, or slices of toasted or fried bread.

Cru: raw.

Crudités: raw vegetables.

Crustacés: crustaceans.

Cuillère (à la): to be eaten with a spoon.

Cuisse de poulet: chicken drumstick.
Cuisson: cooking.
Cuissot: haunch, of veal, venison, or wild boar.
Cuit(e): cooked.
Cul: haunch or rear, usually of red meat.
Culotte: rump (usually of beef).
Cure-dent: toothpick.

D

Dariole: usually a garnish in a cylindrical mold.
Darne: a slice or steak from fish, often salmon.
Dattes: dates.
Daube: stew, usually meat.
Daurade: dorade or sea bream, similar to porgy.
Décaféiné: decaffeinated.
Décortiqué(e): shelled or peeled.
Dégustation: tasting or sampling.
Déjeuner: lunch.
Délice: delight, usually used to describe a dessert.
Demi: half; also refers to a 1-cup (25-cl) glass of beer.
Demi-deuil: literally, in half mourning; poached (usually chicken) with truffles inserted under the skin; also, sweetbreads with a truffled white sauce.
Demi-glace: concentrated beef-base sauce lightened with consommé or a lighter brown sauce.
Désossé: boned.
Diable: method of preparing poultry, served with a peppery sauce, often mustard-based.
Dieppoise: Dieppe style; usually white wine, mussels, shrimp,

mushrooms, and cream.
Dijonnaise: Dijon style; usually with mustard.
Dinde: turkey ham.
Dindon(neau): turkey, in general (young turkey).
Dîner: dinner; to dine.
Discrétion (à la): on menu usually refers to wine, which may be consumed —without limit—at the customer's discretion.
Dodine: cold, boned stuffed duck.
Dos: back; also refers to the meatiest portion of the fish.
Dos et ventre: literally, back and front; both sides (usually fish).
Douceurs: sweets or desserts.
Doux, douce: sweet.
Dugléré: white flour-based sauce with shallots, white wine, tomatoes, and parsley.
Duxelles: chopped mushrooms and shallots sautéed in butter, mixed with cream.

E

Eau du robinet: tap water.
Ecailler: to scale fish, also refers to an oyster opener, or seller.
Echalotes: shallots.
Echine: spare ribs.
Echiquier: checkered.
Ecrevisse: freshwater crayfish.
Effiloché: frayed, thinly sliced.
Eglefin, aiglefin: haddock.
Emincé: thin slice; usually of meat.
Encornet: small squid, in Basque region called *chipron.*
Endive: chicory or Belgian endive.

Entrecôte: beef rib steak.
Entrecôte maître d'hôtel: beef rib steak with herb butter.
Entrecôte marchand de vin: beef rib steak with sauce of red wine and shallots.
Entrée: first course.
Entremets: sweets.
Epaule: shoulder, of veal, lamb, mutton, or pork.
Eperlan: smelt or whitebait, usually fried.
Epi de maïs: ear of sweet corn.
Epices: spices.
Epinard: spinach.
Escabèche: a Provençal preparation of sardines or *rouget,* in which the fish are browned in oil, then marinated in vinegar and herbs and served very cold; also raw fish marinated in lemon or lime juice and herbs.
Escalope: thinly sliced meat or fish, usually cut at an angle.
Escargot: land snail.
Escargot de Bourgogne: land snail prepared with butter, garlic, and parsley.
Escargot petit-gris: small land snail.
Espadon: swordfish.
Estofinado: fish stew from Auvergne, made with dried Atlantic cod, and cooked in walnut oil with eggs, garlic, and cream.
Estouffade: stew of beef, pork, onions, mushrooms, orange zest, and red wine.
Estragon: tarragon.
Eté: summer.
Etrille: small crab.
Etuvé(e): cooked in ingredient's own juice; braised.

Eventail (en): fan-shaped; usually refers to shape in which vegetables or fish are cut.

F

Façon (à ma): (my) way of preparing a dish.
Faisan(e): pheasant.
Farandole: rolling cart, usually of desserts or cheese.
Farci(e): stuffed.
Farine: flour.
Faux-filet: sirloin steak.
Fenouil: fennel.
Féra: salmonlike lake fish.
Ferme (fermier): farm-fresh (farmer).
Fermé: closed.
Feu de bois (au): cooked over a wood fire.
Feuille de chêne: oak-leaf lettuce.
Feuille de vigne: vine leaf.
Feuilletage (en): (in) puff pastry.
Fèves: broad beans.
Ficelle (à la): tied with a string; also small, thin *baguette*.
Figue: fig.
Financière: Madeira sauce with truffle juice.
Fines de claire: elongated, crinkle-shelled oysters that stay in fattening beds (*claires*) up to two months.
Fines herbes: mixture of herbs; usually parsley, chives, and tarragon.
Flageolets: small, pale green kidney-shaped beans.
Flagnarde, flaugnarde: hot fruit-filled batter cake made with eggs, flour, milk, and butter, and sprinkled with sugar before serving.
Flamande (à la): Flemish style; usually with stuffed cabbage leaves, carrots, turnips, potatoes, and bacon.
Flambé: flamed.
Flamiche: savory tart with rich bread-dough crust.
Flan: sweet or savory tart; sometimes refers to a crustless custard pie.
Flanchet (de veau): flank (of veal).
Flétan: halibut.
Fleur: flower.
Fleurons: puff pastry crescents.
Florentine: with spinach.
Foie: liver.
Foie de veau: calf's liver.
Foie gras d'oie (de canard): liver of fattened goose (duck).
Foies blonds de volaille: chicken livers; also sometimes a chicken liver mousse.
Foin (dans le): cooked in hay.
Fond: cooking juices from meat, used to make sauces; also, bottom.
Fond d'artichaut: heart and base of an arti-choke.
Fondant: literally, melting; refers to cooked, worked sugar that is flavored, then used for icing cakes.
Fondu(e): melted.
Forestiére: garnish of wild mushrooms, bacon, and potatoes.
Four (au): baked in oven.
Fourchette: fork.
Fourré: stuffed or filled.
Frais, fraîche: fresh or chilled.
Fraise: strawberry.
Fraise des bois: wild strawberry.
Framboise: raspberry.
Frangipane: almond custard filling.

Frappé: usually refers to a drink served very cold or with ice.
Frémis: quivering; often refers to barely cooked oysters.
Friandises: sweets, *petits fours.*
Fricadelles: fried minced meat patties.
Fricandeau: thinly sliced veal or a rump roast, braised with vegetables and white wine.
Fricassée: classically, ingredients braised in wine sauce or butter with cream added; currently denotes any mixture of ingredients— fish or meat—stewed or sautéed.
Frisé(e): curly, usually curly endive.
Frit(es): French fries.
Fritons: coarse pork *rillettes,* or minced spread that includes organ meats.
Fritot: small organ meat fritter, where meat is partially cooked, than marinated in oil, lemon juice, and herbs, dipped in batter, and fried just before serving; also can refer to any small fried piece of meat or fish.
Friture: frying; also refers to preparation of small fried fish, usually white-bait or smelt.
Froid(e): cold.
Fromage: cheese.
Fromage blanc: a smooth low-fat cheese similar to cottage cheese.
Fromage de tête: head-cheese, usually pork.
Fromage maigre: low-fat cheese.
Fruit de la passion: passion fruit.
Fruits confits: preserved

fruits; generally refers to candied fruits.

Fruits de mer: seafood.

Fumé: smoked.

Fumet: fish stock.

G

Galantine: boned poultry or meat that is stuffed, rolled, cooked, glazed with gelatin, and served cold.

Galette: round, flat pastry, pancake, or cake; can also refer to pancake-like savory preparations.

Gambas: large prawns.

Garbure: generally, a hearty soup of cabbage, beans, and preserved pork, goose, duck, or turkey.

Garni(e): garnished.

Garniture: garnish.

Gâteau: cake.

Gaufre: waffle.

Gayettes: small sausage patties made with pork liver and bacon and wrapped in caul fat and bacon.

Gelée: aspic.

Genièvre: juniper berry.

Génoise: sponge cake.

Germiny: garnish of sorrel; sorrel and cream soup.

Gésier: gizzard.

Gibelotte: fricassee of rabbit in red or white wine.

Gibier: game.

Gigot: usually leg of lamb.

Gigot de mer: a preparation, usually of large pieces of monkfish (*lotte*), oven-roasted like a leg of lamb.

Gigue (de): haunch (of) certain game meats.

Gingembre: ginger.

Girofle: cloves.

Girolle: delicate, pale, orange wild mushroom.

Glace: ice cream.

Glacé: iced, crystallized, or glazed.

Gougére: cheese-flavored *chou* pastry.

Goujonnettes: generally used to describe small slices of fish, such as sole, usually fried.

Goujons: small catfish; also often applied to any small fish; also a preparation in which the central part of a larger fish is coated with bread crumbs, then deep fried.

Gourmandises: sweetmeats.

Gousse (d'ail): clove (of garlic).

Graine de moutarde: mustard seed.

Graisse: fat.

Graisserons: crisply fried pieces of duck or goose skin; cracklings.

Grand veneur: usually a brown sauce for game, with red currant jelly.

Granité: water ice.

Gras: fatty.

Gras-double: tripe baked with onions and white wine.

Gratin: crusty-topped dish; also refers to a casserole.

Gratin dauphinois: baked casserole of sliced potatoes, usually with cream, milk, and sometimes cheese.

Gratin savoyard: baked casserole of sliced potatoes, usually with bouillon, cheese, and butter.

Gratiné(e): having a crusty, browned top; also onion soup.

Grattons: crisply fried pieces of pork, goose, or duck skin; cracklings.

Gratuit: free.

Grecque (à la): cold vegetables, usually mushrooms, cooked in seasoned mixture with oil, lemon juice, and water.

Grelot: small white bulb onion.

Grenade: pomegranate.

Grenadin: small veal scallop.

Grenouille (cuisses de): frog legs.

Gribiche (sauce): mayonnaise with capers, *cornichons*, and herbs.

Grillade: grilled meat.

Grillé(e): grilled.

Griotte: shiny, slightly acidic, reddish black cherry.

Grive: thrush.

Grondin: gurnard or gurnet—spiked-head, bony ocean fish, used in fish stews such as *bouillabaisse*.

Gros sel: coarse salt.

Groseille: red currant.

Gruyère: hard, mild cheese.

H

Hachis: minced or chopped meat or fish preparation.

Hareng: herring.

Haricot: bean.

Haricot blanc: white bean, usually dried.

Haricot de mouton: stew of mutton and white beans.

Haricot rouge: red kidney bean; also, preparation of red beans in red wine.

Haricot vert: green bean, usually fresh.

Hiver: winter.

Hochepot: thick stew, usually of oxtail.

Hollandaise: sauce of butter, egg yolks, and

lemon juice.

Homard: lobster.

Hongroise (à la): Hungarian style; usually with paprika and cream.

Hors-d'oeuvre: appetizer; can also refer to a first course.

Huile: oil.

Huile d'arachide: peanut oil.

Huile de pépins de raisins: grapeseed oil.

Huître: oyster.

Hure de porc: head of pig or boar; usually refers to headcheese perparation.

Hure de saumon: a salmon "headcheese," or pâté, prepared with salmon meat, not actually the head.

I

Ile flottante: literally, floating island; most commonly used interchangeably with *oeufs à la neige*, poached meringue floating in *crème anglaise*; classically, a layered cake covered with whipped cream and served with custard sauce.

Impératrice (à l'): usually rice pudding dessert with candied fruit.

Indienne (à l'): East Indian style, usually with curry powder.

Infusion: herb tea.

J

Jambon: ham; also refers to thigh or shoulder of meat, usually pork.

Jambon cru: usually salt-cured or smoked ham that has been aged but not cooked.

Jambon de Bayonne: raw, dried, salt-cured ham.

Jambon de Paris: lightly salted, cooked ham, very pale in color.

Jambon de York: smoked, English-style ham, usually poached.

Jambon d'oie (or *de canard*): breast of fattened goose (or duck), smoked, or salted, or sugar-cured, and resembling ham in flavor.

Jambonneau: pork knuckle.

Jambonnette: boned and stuffed knuckle of ham or poultry.

Jardinière: garnish of fresh cooked vegetables.

Jarret de veau: stew of veal shin.

Jerez: refers to sherry.

Jésus de Morteau: smoked pork sausage from the Franche-Comté.

Jeaune: young.

Joue: cheek.

Julienne: slivered vegatables (sometimes meat).

Jus: juice.

K

Kir: an apéritif made with *crème de Cassis* and most commonly white wine, but sometimes red wine.

Kir royal: a *kir* made with Champagne.

Kougelhopf, kougelhof, kouglof, kugelhopf: sweet, crown-shaped, Alsatian breadlike yeast cake, with almonds and raisins.

L

Lait: milk.

Laitance: soft roe (often of herring), or eggs.

Laitue: lettuce.

Lamelle: very thin slice.

Lamproie: lamprey, eel-shaped fish, either fresh- or saltwater.

Langouste: clawless spiny lobster; sometimes called crawfish or crayfish.

Langoustine: clawed crustacean, smaller than either *homard* or spiny lobster, with very delicate meat.

Languedocienne: garnish, usually of tomatoes, eggplant, and wild *cèpe* mushrooms.

Lapereau: young rabbit.

Lapin: rabbit.

Lapin de garenne: wild rabbit.

Lard: bacon.

Lardon: cube of bacon.

Larme: literally, a teardrop; a very small portion of liquid.

Lèche: thin slice of bread or meat.

Léger(légère): light.

Légume: vegetable.

Lieu (jaune): pollack, a prized small (yellow) saltwater fish.

Lièvre: hare.

Limande: solelike ocean fish, not as firm as sole.

Limande sole: lemon sole.

Lisette: small mackerel.

Lit: bed.

Lotte: monkfish or angler fish, a large, firm-fleshed ocean fish.

Lou magret: breast of fattened duck.

Loup (de mer): Mediterranean fish, also known as *bar*, similar to striped bass.

Lyonnaise (à la): in the style of Lyons, often garnished with onions.

M

Macédoine: diced mixed fruit or vegetables.

Macérer: to steep, pickle, or soak.

Mâche: lamb's lettuce, a tiny, dark green lettuce.

Madeleines: small tea caked.

Madère: Madeira.

Magret de canard (d'oie): breast of fattened duck (goose).

Maigre: thin, non-fatty.

Maïs: corn.

Maison (de la): of the house, or restaurant.

Maître d'hôtel: head waiter; also compound butter, a mixture of butter, parsley and lemon juice.

Maltaise: orange-flavored hollandaise sauce.

Mandarine: tangerine.

Mange-tout: literally, eat it all; a podless green runner bean; a snow pea; a type of apple.

Mangue: mango.

Manière (de): in the style of.

Maquereau: mackerel.

Maraîchère (à la): market-garden style, usually referring to a dish, or salad, that includes various greens.

Marbré(e): marbled.

Marc: distilled residue of grape skins or other fruits after they have been pressed.

Marcassin: young wild boar.

Marchand de vin: wine merchant; also a sauce made with red wine, meat stock, and chopped shallots.

Marché: market.

Marée (la): literally, the tide; usually used to indicate that seafood is fresh.

Marennes: flat-shelled, green-tinged *plate* oysters; also French coastal village where flat-shelled oysters are raised.

Mareyeur: wholesale fish merchant.

Mariné: marinated.

Marinière (moules): method of cooking mussels in white wine with onions, shallots, butter, and herbs.

Marjolaine: marjoram; also, multilayered chocolate and nut cake.

Marmite: small covered pot; also a dish cooked in a small casserole.

Marquise (au chocolat): mousselike (chocolate) cake.

Marron: large chestnut.

Matelote (d'anguilles): freshwater fish stew (or of eels).

Mauviette: wild meadowlark or skylark.

Médaillon: round piece or slice.

Mélange: mixture or blend.

Méli-mélo: an assortment of fish and/or seafood, usually served in a salad.

Melon de Cavaillon: small canteloupelike melon from Cavaillon, a town in Provence known for its wholesale produce market.

Ménagère (à la): literally, in the style of a housewife; usually a simple preparation including onions, potatoes, and carrots.

Menthe: mint.

Menthe poivrée: peppermint.

Mer: sea.

Merguez: small spicy sausage.

Merlan: whiting.

Merle: blackbird.

Merveille: hot sugared doughnuts.

Mesclun, mesclum: mixture of at least seven varieties of multi-shaded salad greens.

Mets: dish or preparation.

Mets selon la saison: seasonal preparation; according to the season.

Meunière (à la): literally, in the style of a miller's wife; refers to a fish that is seasoned, rolled in flour, fried in butter, and served with lemon, parsley, and hot melted butter.

Meurette: in, or with, a red wine sauce; also a Burgundian fish stew.

Miel: honey.

Mignardises: synonym for *petits fours.*

Mignonette: small cubes, usually of beef; also refers to coarsely ground black or white peppercorns.

Mijoté(e) (plat): simmered (dish or preparation).

Mille-feuille: refers to puff pastry with many thin layers; usually a cream-filled rectangle of puff pastry, or a Napoleon.

Mimosa: garnish of chopped hard-cooked egg yolks.

Minute (à la): prepared at the last minute.

Mirabeau: garnish of anchovies, pitted olives, tarragon, and anchovy butter.

Mirabelle: yellow plum.

Mirepoix: cubes of carrots and onions or mixed vegetables, usually used in braising to boost the flavor of a meat dish.

*Miroton (de):*slices (of); also stew of meats flavored with onions.

Mitonnée: a simmered souplike dish.

Mode (à la): in the style of.

Moelle: beef bone marrow.

Moka: refers to coffee, or coffee-flavored dish.

Montagne (de): from the mountains.

Montmorency: garnished with cherries.

Morceau: piece or small portion.

Morille: wild morel mushroom, dark brown and conical-shaped.

Mornay: thickened, milk-based sauce including flour, butter, and egg yolks, with cheese added.

Morue: salted or dried and salted codfish.

Mouclade: creamy mussel stew, sometimes flavored with curry.

Moule: mussel.

Moule de bouchot: small, highly prized cultivated mussel, raised on stakes driven into the sediment of shallow coastal beds.

Moule de Parques: Dutch cultivated mussel, usually raised in fattening beds, or diverted ponds.

Moule d'Espagne: large sharp-shelled mussel, often served raw as part of a seafood platter.

Moules marinière: mussels cooked in white wine with onions, shallots, butter, and herbs.

Mousse: light, airy mixture usually containing eggs and cream, either sweet or savory.

Mousseline: refers to ingredients that are usually lightened with whipped cream or egg whites, as in sauces, or with butter, as in *brioche mousseline.*

Mousseron: tiny, delicate, wild mushroom.

Mouarde (à l'ancienne en graines): mustard (coarse-grained).

Mouton: mutton.

Mulet: mullet, a rustic-flavored ocean fish.

Mûre: blackberry.

Muscade: nutmeg.

Museau de porc (de boeuf): vinegared pork (beef) muzzle.

Myrtille: bilberry (bluish black European blueberry).

Mystère: cone-shaped ice cream dessert; also dessert of cooked meringue with ice cream and chocolate sauce.

N

Nage (à la): aromatic poaching liquid (served in).

Nantua: sauce of crayfish, butter, cream, and truffles; also garnish of crayfish.

Nappé: covered, as with a sauce.

Nature: refers to simple, unadorned preparations.

Navarin: lamb or mutton.

Navet: turnip.

Newburg: lobster preparation with Madeira, egg yolks, and cream.

Nid: nest.

Nivernaise: in the style of Nevers; with carrots and onions.

Noisette: hazelnut; also refers to a small round piece (such as from a potato), generally the size of a hazelnut, lightly browned in butter; also, center cut of lamb chop; also, hazelnut flavor.

Noix: walnut; nut; nut-size.

Normande: in the style of Normandy; sauce of seafood, cream, and mushrooms; also refers to fish or meat cooked with apple cider or Calvados; or dessert with apples, usually served with cream.

Nouilles: noodles.

Nouveau (nouvelle): new or young.

Nouveauté: a new offering.

Noyau: stone or pit.

O

Oeuf à la coque: soft-cooked egg.

Oeuf brouillé: scrambled egg.

Oeuf dur: hard-cooked egg.

Oeuf en meurette: poached egg in red wine sauce.

Oeuf mollet: egg simmered in water for 6 minutes.

Oeuf poché: poached egg.

Oeuf sauté à la poêle, oeuf sur le plat: fried egg.

Oeufs à la neige: literally, eggs in the snow; sweetened whipped egg whites poached in milk and served with vanilla custard sauce.

Offert: offered, free or given.

Oie: goose.

Oignon: onion.

Omble chevalier: freshwater char, a member of the trout family, with firm, flaky flesh varying from white to deep red.

Onglet: cut similar to beef flank steak; also cut of

beef sold as *biftek* and *entrecôte*; technically a tough cut, but better than flank steak.

Oreilles (de porc): ears (of pig).

Orties: nettles.

Ortolan: tiny wild bird from southern France, Italy, Greece, and Spain, formerly very popular in French cuisine, now forbidden due to diminished supply.

Os: bone.

Oseille: sorrel.

Oursin: sea urchin.

Ouvert: open.

P

Paillard (de veau): thick slice (of veal).

Pailles (pommes): fried straw potatoes (finely shredded).

Paillettes: cheese straws, usually made with puff pastry and Parmesan cheese.

Pain: bread.

Paleron: shoulder of beef.

Paletot: literally, coat; the skin, bone, and meat portion of a fattened duck or goose once the liver is removed.

Palmier: palm-leaf-shaped cookie made of sugared pufff pastry

Palmier (coeurs de): palm hearts.

Palombe: wood or wild pigeon.

Palourde: prized medium-size clam.

Pamplemousse: grapefruit.

Panaché: mixed; now liberally used menu term to denote any mixture.

Panade: panada, a thick mixture used to bind forcemeats and *quenelles,*

usually flour and butter based, but can also contain fresh or toasted bread crumbs, rice, or potatoes; also refers to soup of bread, milk, and sometimes cheese.

Panais: parsnip.

Pané(e): breaded.

Panier: basket.

Pannequet: rolled crépe filled with either sweet or savory mixture.

Papillote (en): cooked in parchment paper or foil wrapping.

Paquets (en): (in) packages or parcels.

Parfait: a dessert mousse; also mousselike mixture of chicken, duck, or goose liver.

Parfum: flavor.

Parisienne (à la): varied vegetable garnish that always includes potato balls that have been fried and tossed in a meat glaze.

Parmentier: dish with potatoes.

Partager: to share.

Passe-pierre: edible seaweed.

Pastèque: watermelon.

Pastis: anise liqueur.

Pâte: pastry dough.

Pâte à choux: cream puff pastry.

Pâte brisée: pie pastry.

Pâte sablée: sweeter, richer dough than *pâte sucrée,* sometimes leavened.

Pâte sucrée: sweet pie pastry

Pâté: molded, spiced, minced meat, baked and served hot or cold.

Pâté en croûte: pâté baked in a pastry crust.

Pâtes (fraîches): pasta (fresh).

Pâtisserie: pastry.

Pâtissier: pastry chef.

Patte: paw, foot, or leg of bird or animal.

Patte blanche: small crayfish no larger than 2 to 2½ ounces (60 to 75g).

Patte rouge: large crayfish.

Paupiette: thin slice of meat, usually beef or fish, filled, rolled, then wrapped.

Pavé: literally, paving stone; usually a thick slice of boned beef or of calf's liver, also, a kind of pastry.

Paysan(ne) (à la): country style; also, garnish of carrots, turnips, onions, celery, and bacon.

Peau: skin.

Pêche: peach.

Pêche Melba: poached peach with vanilla ice cream and raspberry sauce.

Pêcheur: literally, fisherman; usually refers to fish preparations.

Pelure: peelings, such as from truffles, often used for flavoring.

Perce-pierre: samphire, edible seaweed.

Perche: perch.

Perdreau: young partridge.

Perdrix: partridge.

Périgourdine (à la): sauce, usually with truffles and foie gras.

Persil: parsley.

Persillade: chopped parsley and garlic.

Petit déjeuner: breakfast.

Petits-gris: small land snail.

Petit-pois: small green peas.

Petits fours: tiny cakes and pastries.

Pétoncle: tiny scallop, similar to American bay scallop.

Pets de nonne: small, dainty fried pastry.

Pibale: small eel, also called *civelle.*

Pièce: portion or piece.

Pied de mouton: meaty, cream-colored wild mushroom; also, sheep's foot.

Pied de porc: pig's foot.

Pigeonneau: young pigeon or squab.

Pignons: pine nuts, or pignoli.

Pilau, pilaf: rice cooked with onions and broth.

Piment (poivre) de Jamaïque: allspice.

Piment doux: sweet pepper.

Pince: claw; also, tongs used when eating snails or seafood.

Pintade: guinea fowl.

Pintadeau: young guinea fowl.

Pipérade: Basque dish of pepper, onions, tomatoes, and often scrambled eggs and ham.

Piquant(e): sharp or spicy tasting.

Piqué: larded; studded.

Pissaladière: a flat open-face tart like a pizza garnished with onions, olives, and anchovies.

Pissenlit: dandelion (leaves).

Pistache: pistachio nuts.

Pistil de safran: thread of saffron.

Pistou: sauce of basil, garlic, and olive oil; also a rich vegetable soup.

Pithiviers: classic puff pastry dessert filled with almond cream.

Plat: a dish.

Plat principal: main dish.

Plate: flat-shelled oyster.

Plates côtes: part of beef ribs usually used in *pot-au-feu.*

Plateau: platter.

Plateau de fruits de mer: seafood platter

combining raw and cooked shellfish; usually includes oysters, clams, mussels, *langoustines,* periwinkles, crabs.

Pleurote: oyster mushroom, very soft-fleshed, feather-edged wild mushroom.

Plie franche: flounder; flat ocean fish; also known as *carrelet* (plaice).

Plombières: dessert of vanilla ice cream, candied fruit, kirsch, and sweetened whipped cream.

Pluches: leaves of herbs or plants, generally used for garnish.

Poché: poached.

Pochouse: freshwater fish stew prepared with white or red wine.

Poêlé: pan-fried.

Pointe (d'asperge): tip (of asparagus).

Poire: pear.

Poireau: leek.

Poires Belle Hélène: poached pears served on vanilla ice cream with hot chocolate sauce.

Pois: pea.

Poisson: fish.

Poitrine: breast (of meat or poultry).

Poitrine demi-sel: unsmoked slab bacon.

Poitrine fumée: smoked slab bacon.

Poivrade: a peppery brown sauce made with wine, vinegar, and cooked vegetables that is strained before serving.

Poivre: pepper.

Poivre frais de Madagascar: green peppercorns.

Poivre noir: black peppercorns.

Poivre rose: pink peppercorns.

Poivre vert: green peppercorns.

Poivron (doux): sweet bell pepper.

Polenta: cooked dish of cornmeal and water, usually with added butter and cheese; also refers to cornmeal.

Pommade (en): usually refers to a thick, smooth paste.

Pomme: apple.
  en l'air: caramelized apple slices, usually served with *boudin noir* (blood sausage).

Pommes (de terre): potatoes.
  à l'anglaise: boiled.
  allumettes: very thin fries, cut in ¼ × 2½-inch (½ × 6½-cm) slices.
  boulangère: potatoes cooked with the meat they accompany; also, a potato gratin of sliced potatoes with onions and sometimes bacon and tomatoes.
  dauphine: mashed potatoes mixed with *chou* pastry, shaped into small balls and fried.
  dauphinoise: baked dish of sliced potatoes, milk, garlic, and cheese.
  duchesse: mashed potatoes with butter, egg yolks, and nutmeg, used for garnish.
  en robe des champs: potatoes cooked with skins on.
  frites: French fries.
  gratinées: baked dish of potatoes, browned often with cheese.
  lyonnaise: sautéed potatoes, with onions.
  paille: potatoes cut into julienne strips, then fried.
Pont-Neuf: classic fries, cut into ½ × 2½-inch

(1 × 6½-cm) slices.

soufflées: small, thin slices of potato fried twice, causing them to inflate, so they look like little pillows.

vapeur: steamed or boiled potatoes.

Porc (carré de): pork (loin).

Porc (côte de): pork (chop).

Porcelet: young suckling pig.

Porto (au): (with) port.

Portugaises: elongated, crinkle-shell oysters.

Potage: soup.

Pot-au-feu: boiled beef prepared with vegetables, often served in two or more courses.

Pot-de-crème: individual custard or mousselike dessert, often chocolate.

Potée: hearty soup of pork and vegetables, generally cabbage and potatoes.

Poularde: fatted hen.

Poule d'Inde: turkey hen.

Poule faisane: female pheasant.

Poulet (rôti): chicken (roast).

Poulet basquaise: Basque-style chicken, with tomatoes and sweet peppers.

Poulet de Bresse: high-quality, free-running, corn-fed chicken.

Poulet de grain: corn-fed chicken.

Poulet fermier: free-range chicken.

Poulpe: octopus.

Pousse-pierre: edible seaweed.

Poussin: baby chicken.

Praire: small clam.

Pralin: ground caramelized almonds.

Praline: caramelized almonds.

Primeur: refers to early fresh fruits and vegetables.

Printanière: garnish of a variety of spring vegetables; or vegetables cut into dice or balls.

Prix fixe: fixed-price menu.

Prix net: service included.

Profiterole: chou pastry dessert, usually filled with ice cream and topped with chocolate sauce.

Provençal(e): in the style of Provence; usually includes garlic, tomatoes, and/or olive oil.

Prune: fresh plum.

Pruneau: prune.

Q

Quenelle: dumpling; usually of veal, fish, or poultry.

Quetsch: small purple Damson plum.

Queue (de boeuf): tail (oxtail).

R

Râble de lièvre (lapin): saddle of hare (rabbit).

Raclette: rustic Swiss dish of melted cheese served with boiled potatoes, *cornichons* and pickled onions; also the cheese used in this dish.

Radis: small red radish.

Radis noir: large black radish, often served with cream, as a salad.

Ragoût: stew, usually of meat.

Raie: skate (fish) or sting ray.

Raifort: horseradish.

Raisin: grape.

Ramequin: small individual casserole; also

a small tart.

Râpé: grated or shredded.

Rascasse: scorpion fish.

Ratatouille: cooked dish of eggplant, zucchini, onions, tomatoes, peppers, garlic, and olive oil.

Rave: category of root vegetables, including celery, turnip, radish.

Ravigote: thick vinaigrette sauce with vinegar, white wine, shallots, herbs; also cold mayonnaise with capers, onions, and herbs.

Réchauffer: to reheat.

Reine-claude: greengage plum.

Reinette (reine de): fall and winter variety of apple.

Rémoulade: sauce of mayonnaise, capers, mushrooms, herbs, anchovies and gherkins.

Rillettes (d'oie): minced spread of pork (goose); also can be made with duck, fish, or rabbit.

Rillons: usually pork belly, cut up and cooked until crisp, then drained of fat; can also be made of duck, goose, or rabbit.

Rince doigt: finger bowl.

Ris d'agneau: lamb sweetbreads.

Ris de veau: veal sweetbreads.

Rivière: river.

Riz: rice.

Riz à l'impératrice: cold rice pudding with candied fruit.

Riz complet: brown rice.

Riz sauvage: wild rice.

Rognonnade: veal loin with kidneys attached.

Rognons: kidneys.

Romarin: rosemary.

Rondelle: round slice.

Rosé: rare (meat).

Rosette (de porc): dried sausage (of pork), usually

from Beaujolais.

Rôti: roast.

Rouelle (de): slice of meat or vegetable cut at an angle.

Rouget (rouget barbet): sweet, red-skinned fish commonly called red mullet; the smallest are most prized.

Rouille: thick, spicy, rust-colored sauce, with olive oil, peppers, tomatoes, and garlic; usually served with fish soups.

Roulade: roll, often stuffed.

Roulé(e): rolled.

Roux: sauce base or thickening made from flour and butter.

S

Sabayon: light sweet sauce of egg yolks, sugar, wine, and flavoring, which is whipped while being cooked in a water bath.

Sablé: shortbreadlike cookie; also, sweet pastry dough.

Safran: saffron.

Saignant(e): very rare (for cooking meat).

Saint-Germain: with peas.

Saint-Hubert: sauce poivrade with chestnuts and bacon added.

Saint-Jacques (coquille): sea scallop.

Saint-Pierre: mild, flat, white ocean fish; John Dory.

Saison (suivant la): according to the season.

Salade folle: mixed salad, usually including green beans and foie gras.

Salade panachée: mixed salad.

Salade verte: green salad.

Salé: salted.

Salicorne: edible algae, often pickled and eaten as a condiment.

Salmis: stewlike preparation of game birds or poultry, with sauce made from the pressed carcass.

Salpicon: diced vegetables, meat, and/or fish in a sauce.

Salsifis: salsify, or oyster plant.

Sandre: perchlike freshwater fish.

Sang: blood.

Sanglier: wild boar.

Sarriette: summer savory; also called *poivre d'âne.*

Saucisse: small fresh sausage.

Saucisson: large dried sausage.

Saucisson de Lyon: air-dried pork sausage, seasoned with garlic and pepper, and studded with chunks of pork fat; also sometimes seasoned with truffles or with pistachio nuts.

Sauge: sage.

Saumon (sauvage): salmon (literally, wild; a noncultivated salmon).

Saumon d'Ecosse: Scottish salmon.

Saumon fumé: smoked salmon.

Saupiquet: classic aromatic wine sauce thickened with bread crumbs.

Sauté: browned in fat.

Sauvage: wild.

Savarin: yeast-leavened cake shaped like a ring, soaked in sweet syrup.

Savoyarde: usually, flavored with Gruyère cheese.

Scarole: escarole.

Seiche: large squid or cuttlefish.

Sel: salt.

Selle: saddle (of meat).

Serpolet: wild thyme.

Service (non) compris: service (not) included.

Serviette: napkin.

Smitane: sauce of cream, onions, white wine, and lemon juice.

Soissons: dried or fresh white beans.

Sorbet: sherbet.

Soubise: onion sauce.

Soufflé: light sweet or savory mixture served either hot or cold, the bulk of whose volume is egg whites.

Steack: beef steak.

Stockfish: salted and air-dried codfish.

Succès au pralin: meringue cake flavored with caramelized almonds and layered with butter cream.

Sucre: sugar.

Suprême: a veal- or chicken-based white sauce thickened with flour and cream; a boneless breast of poultry or a fillet of fish.

T

Tablier de sapeur: tripe that is marinated, breaded, and grilled.

Tagine: spicy North African stew of veal, lamb, chicken, or pigeon with vegetables.

Tanche: tench, a freshwater fish with mild, delicate flavor; often an ingredient in *matelote,* freshwater fish stew.

Tapenade: blend of black olives, anchovies, capers, olive oil, and lemon juice.

Tarama: mullet roe, often made into a spread of the same name.

Tartare: chopped raw beef, seasoned and garnished with raw egg, capers, chopped onion, and parsley.

Tarte: tart; open-face pie or *flan*, usually sweet.

Tarte Tatin: caramelized upside-down apple pie.

Tartine: open-face sandwich; buttered bread.

Tendre: tender.

Tendrons: cartilaginous meat cut from beef or veal ribs.

Terrine: earthenware container used for cooking meat, game, fish, or vegetable mixtures; also the mixture cooked in such a container.

Tête de veau (porc): head of veal (pork), usually used in headcheese.

Thé: tea.

Thon: tuna fish.

Thym: thyme.

Tian: earthenware gratin dish; also vegetable mixture cooked in such a dish.

Tiède: lukewarm.

Tilleul: lime or linden blossom herb tea.

Timbale: round mold with straight or sloping sides; also, a mixture prepared in such a mold.

Topinambour: Jerusalem artichoke.

Tortue: turtle.

Toulousaine: Toulouse style; usually with truffles, or sweetbreads, cock's combs, mushrooms, or *quenelles*.

Tournedos: center portion of beef filet, usually grilled or sautéed.

Tournedos Rossini: sautéed *tournedos* garnished with foie gras and truffles.

Tourteau: large crab.

Tourtière: shallow cooking vessel; also southwestern pastry dish filled with apples and/or prunes and sprinkled with Armagnac.

Tranche: slice.

Travers de porc: spare ribs.

Tripes à la mode de Caen: beef tripe, carrots, onions, leeks, and spices cooked in water, cider, and Calvados (apple brandy).

Tripoux: mutton tripe.

Trompettes des mort: dark brown "horn of plenty" wild mushrooms.

Tronçon: cut of meat or fish resulting in a piece that is wide; generally refers to slices from the largest part of a fish.

Truffe (truffé): truffle (with truffles).

Truite: trout.

Truite saumonée: salmon trout.

Tuile: literally, tile; delicate almond-flavored cookie.

Turban: usually mixture or combination of ingredients cooked in a ring mold.

Turbot(in): turbot (small turbot).

V, X, Y, Z

Vacherin: dessert of baked meringue, with ice cream and cream; also, strong supple winter cheese; the best is Mont-d'Or.

Vallée d'Ange: region of Normandy; also, garnish of cooked apples and cream.

Vanille: vanilla.

Vapeur (à la): steamed.

Veau: veal.

Velouté: veal- or chicken-based sauce thickened with flour.

Venaison: venison.

Ventre: belly or stomach.

Vénus: American clam.

Verjus: juice from unripe grapes, once used in sauces instead of vinegar.

Vernis: large, fleshy clam with varnishlike shell.

Vert-pré: a watercress garnish, sometimes includes potatoes.

Verveine: lemon verbena (herb tea).

Vessie (en): cooked in a pig's bladder (usually a chicken).

Viande: meat.

Vichy: with glazed carrots; also a brand of mineral water.

Vichyssoise: cold, creamy leek and potato soup.

Vierge (beurre): whipped butter sauce with salt, pepper, and lemon juice.

Vierge (huile d'olive): virgin olive oil.

Vieux (vieille): old.

Vigneron: wine grower.

Vinaigre (vieux): vinegar (aged).

Vinaigre de xérès: sherry vinegar.

Vinaigrette: oil and vinegar dressing.

Vivant(e): living.

Vivier: fish tank.

Volaille: poultry.

Vol-au-vent: puff pastry shell.

Xérès (vinaigre de): sherry (vinegar)

Yaourt: yogurt.

Zeste: citrus peel, with white pith removed.

Food Lover's Ready Reference

L'Ami Louis, Paris 3

L'Assiette, Paris 14

Astier, Paris 11

Baracane-Bistrot de l'Oulette, Paris 4

Benoit, Paris 4

Le Boeuf sur le Toit, Paris 8.

Brissemoret, Paris 2

La Butte Chaillot, Paris 16

La Cagouille, Paris 14

Le Caméléon, Paris 6

Campagne et Provence, Paris 6

Cartet, Paris 11

Chardenoux, Paris 11

Aux Charpentiers, Paris 6

La Cigale, Paris 7

Au Cochon d'Or des Halles, Paris 1

Contre-Allée, Paris 14

Le Bistrot d'à Côté-Flaubert, Paris 17

A la Courtille, Paris 20

Aux Crus de Bourgogne, Paris 2

Bistrot du Dôme, Paris 14

Auberge Etchegorry, Paris 13

Bistrot de l'Etoile-Lauriston, Paris 16

La Fontaine de Mars, Paris 5

Les Fontaines, Paris 5

Chez Fred, Paris 17

Gaya, Paris 1

Chez Georges, Paris 2

Au Gigot Fin, Paris 10

Les Gourmets des Ternes, Paris 8

Le Grizzli, Paris 4

Le Bistrot d'Henri, Paris 6

Le Machon d'Henri, Paris 6

L'Impasse, Paris 4

Chez Janou, Paris 3

Lescure, Paris 1

Louis XIV, Paris 1

Chez Louisette, Saint-Ouen

Aux Lyonnais, Paris 2

Le Mâconnais, Paris 7

Chez Mâitre Paul, Paris 6

Manufacture, Issy-les Moulineaux

Le Bistrot de Marius, Paris 8

Moissonnier, Paris 5

Moulin à Vent, Chez Henry, Paris 5

La Niçoise, Paris 17

L'Oeillade, Paris 7

Chez Paul, Paris 11

Perraudin, Paris 5

Chez Philippe, Paris 11

Le Relais du Parc, Parc 16

Chez René, Paris 5

Le Roi du Pot-au-Feu, Paris 9

La Rôtisserie d'en Face, Paris 6

Royal Madeleine, Paris 8

Le Scheffer, Paris 16

A Sousceyrac, Paris 11

La Timonerie, Paris 5

La Tour de Montlhéry, Paris 1

Le Trumilou, Paris 4

Chez la Vieille, Paris 1

Le Vieux Bistro, Paris 4

Le Villaret, Paris 11

Vivario, Paris 5

Les Zygomates, Paris 12

RESTAURANTS: BRASSERIES

Le Boeuf sur le Toit, Paris 8

La Coupole, Paris 14

Le Dôme, Paris 14

Brasserie Flo, Paris 10

Brasserie de l'Isle Saint Louis, Paris 4

Chez Jenny, Paris 3

Julien, Paris 10

Brasserie Lipp, Paris 6

Marty, Paris 5

Au Pied de Cochon, Paris 1

Brasserie Stella, Paris 16

Terminus Nord, Paris 10

Le Train Bleu, Paris 12

Vaudeville, Paris 2

RESTAURANTS COSTING 200 FRANCS OR LESS
(NOT INCLUDING WINE)

Note that many restaurants offer reduced price menus at lunchtime.

Ambassade d'Auvergne, Paris 3

Astier, Paris 11

Baracane-Bistrot de l'Oulette, Paris 4

Le Boeuf sur le Toit, Paris 8

Brissemoret, Paris 2

La Butte Chaillot, Paris 16

La Cagouille, Paris 14 (lunch)

Le Caméléon, Paris 6

Campagne et Provence, Paris 6

Chardenoux, Paris 11

Aux Charpentiers, Paris 6

La Cigale, Paris 7

Le Clos Morillons, Paris 15 (lunch)

La Coupole, Paris 14

A la Courtille, Paris 20

Le Bistrot d'à Côté-Flaubert, Paris 17

Les Délices d'Aphrodite, Paris 5

Bistrot du Dôme, Paris 14

Auberge Etchegorry, Paris 13

Fermette Marbeuf 1900, Paris 8

Brasserie Flo, Paris 10

La Fontaine de Mars, Paris 7

Les Fontaines, Paris 5

Chez Fred, Paris 17

Au Gigot Fin, Paris 10

Les Gourmets des Ternes, Paris 8

Le Grizzli, Paris 4

Le Bistrot d'Henri, Paris 6

Le Machon d'Henri, Paris 6

Brasserie de l'Isle Saint Louis, Paris 4

L'Impasse, Paris 4

Chez Jenny, Paris 3

Julien, Paris 10

Kim-Anh, Paris 15

Lao-Siam, Paris 19

Lao-Thai, Paris 20

Lescure, Paris 1

Chez Louisette, Saint-Ouen

Aux Lyonnais, Paris 2

Le Mâconnais, Paris 7

La Maison du Valais, Paris 8

Chez Maître Paul, Paris 6

Marty, Paris 5

Le Bistrot de Marius, Paris 8

La Niçoise, Paris 17

L'Oeillade, Paris 7

L'Oulette, Paris 12

Chez Paul, Paris 11

Perraudin, Paris 5

Le Petit Marguery, Paris 13 (lunch)

Au Pied de Cochon, Paris 1

Port Alma, Paris 16 (lunch)

Chez René, Paris 5

Le Roi du Pot-au-Feu, Paris 9

La Rôtisserie d'en Face, Paris 6

Royal Madeleine, Paris 8

Le Scheffer, Paris 16

A Sousceyrac, Paris 11 (lunch)

Brasserie Stella, Paris 16

La Table de Fès, Paris 6

Terminus Nord, Paris 10

Timgad, Paris 17

La Timonerie, Paris 5 (lunch)

La Tour de Montlhéry, Paris 1

Le Train Bleu, Paris 12 (lunch)

Au Trou Gascon, Paris 12 (lunch)

Le Trumilou, Paris 4

Vaudeville, Paris 2

Le Villaret, Paris 11

Vivario, Paris 5

Les Zygomates, Paris 12

RESTAURANTS ACCEPTING DINNER RESERVATIONS AT 7 P.M.

Baracane-Bistrot de l'Oulette, Paris 4

Le Boeuf sur le Toit, Paris 8.

La Butte Chaillot, Paris 16

Caviar Kaspia, Paris 8

La Coquille, Paris 17

Aux Charpentiers, Paris 6

Le Bistrot d'à Côté-Flaubert, Paris 17

La Coupole, Paris 14

Les Délices d'Aphrodite, Paris 5

Le Dôme, Paris 14

Erawan, Paris 15

Brasserie Flo, Paris 10

Gaya, Paris 1

Chez Georges, Paris 2

Au Gigot Fin, Paris 10

Goumard-Prunier, Paris 1

Le Machon d'Henri, Paris 6

Issé, Paris 2

Chez Jenny, Paris 3

Julien, Paris 10

Kim-Anh, Paris 15

Lao-Siam, Paris 19

Lao-Thai, Paris 20

Brasserie Lipp, Paris 6

Aux Lyonnais, Paris 2

Chez Maître Paul, Paris 6

Marty, Paris 5

Moissonnier, Paris 5

Chez Pauline, Paris 1

Chez Philippe, Paris 11

Au Pied de Cochon, Paris 1

Pierre au Palais Royal, Paris 1

La Rôtisserie d'en Face, Paris 6

Royal Madeleine, Paris 8

Terminus Nord, Paris 10

La Tour de Montlhéry, Paris 1

Le Train Bleu, Paris 12

Le Trumilou, Paris 4

Vaudeville, Paris 2

Vivario, Paris 5

RESTAURANTS ACCEPTING RESERVATIONS AFTER 11 P.M.

Le Boeuf sur le Toit, Paris 8.

Brissemoret, Paris 2

La Butte Chaillot, Paris 16

Campagne et Provence, Paris 6 (Friday and Saturday)

Caviar Kaspia, Paris 8

Contre-Allée, Paris 14

Les Délices d'Aphrodite, Paris 5

Le Dôme, Paris 14

Le Bistro de l'Etoile-Lauriston, Paris 16

Brasserie Flo, Paris 10

Le Machon d'Henri, Paris 6

Chez Jenny, Paris 3

Julien, Pais 10

Kim-Anh, Paris 15

Brasserie Lipp, Paris 6

Aux Lyonnais, Paris 2

Chez Paul, Paris 11

Au Pied de Cochon, Paris 1

La Table de Fès, Paris 6

Terminus Nord, Paris 10

Le Villaret, Paris 11

RESTAURANTS OPEN ON SATURDAY

Ambassade d'Auvergne, Paris 3

L'Ambroisie, Paris 4

L'Ami Louis, Paris 3

Androuët, Paris 8

L'Assiette, Paris 14

Baracane-Bistrot de l'Oulette, Paris 4 (dinner only)

Le Boeuf sur le Toit, Paris 8

La Butte Chaillot, Paris 16

La Cagouille, Paris 14

Le Caméléon, Paris 6

Campagne et Provence, Paris 6

Carré des Feuillants, Paris 1 (dinner only)

Caviar Kaspia, Paris 8

Aux Charpentiers, Paris 6

Le Clos Morillons, Paris 15 (dinner only)

Au Cochon d'Or des Halles, Paris 1 (dinner only)

Contre-Allée, Paris 14

La Coquille, Paris 17

Le Bistrot d'à Côté-Flaubert, Paris 17

La Coupole, Paris 14

A la Courtille, Paris 20

Les Délices d'Aphrodite, Paris 5

Dodin Bouffant, Paris 5

Le Dôme, Paris 14

Bistrot du Dôme, Paris 14

L'Ecaille de P.C.B., Paris 6 (dinner only)

Erawan, Paris 15

Auberge Etchegorry, Paris 13

Bistro de l'Etoile-Lauiston, Paris 16 (dinner only)

Fermette Marbeuf 1900, Paris 8

Brasserie Flo, Paris 10

La Fontaine de Mars, Paris 7

Les Fontaines, Paris 5

Chez Fred, Paris 17

Gaya, Paris 1

Chez Georges, Paris 2

Au Gigot Fin, Paris 10 (dinner only)

Goumard-Prunier, Paris 1

Le Grizzli, Paris 4

Le Bistrot d'Henri, Paris 6

Le Machon d'Henri, Paris 6

Brasserie de l'Isle Saint Louis, Paris 4

L'Impasse, Paris 4 (dinner only)

Issé, Paris 2 (dinner only)

Chez Jenny, Paris 3

Julien, Paris 10

Kim-Anh, Paris 15

Lao-Siam, Paris 19

Lao-Thai, Paris 20

Lescure, Paris 1 (lunch only)

Brasserie Lipp, Paris 6

Chez Louisette, Saint-Ouen

Aux Lyonnais, Paris 2

Le Mâconnais, Paris 7 (dinner only)

La Maison du Valais, Paris 8

Chez Maître Paul, Paris 6 (dinner only)

Manufacture, Issy-les-Moulineaux (dinner only)

Le Bistrot de Marius, Paris 8

Marty, Paris 5

Miravile, Paris 4 (dinner only)

Moissonnier, Paris 5

Moulin à Vent, Chez Henry, Paris 5

La Niçoise, Paris 17 (dinner only)

L'Oeillade, Paris 7 (dinner only)

L'Oulette, Paris 12 (dinner only)

Chez Paul, Paris 11

Perraudin, Paris 5 (dinner only)

Le Petit Marguery, Paris 13

Pharamond, Paris 1

Au Pied de Cochon, Paris 1

Port Alma, Paris 16

Le Relais du Parc, Paris 16

Le Roi du Pot-au-Feu, Paris 9

La Rôtisserie d'en Face, Paris 6 (dinner only)

Royal Madeleine, Paris 8

Guy Savoy, Paris 17 (dinner only)

Le Scheffer, Paris 16

A Sousceyrac, Paris 11 (dinner only)

Brasserie Stella, Paris 16

La Table de Fès, Paris 6 (dinner only)

Tan Dinh, Paris 7

Terminus Nord, Paris 10

Le Timgad, Paris 17

La Timonerie, Paris 5

La Tour de Montlhéry, Paris 1

Le Train Bleu, Paris 12

Le Trumilou, Paris 4

Vaudeville, Paris 2

Jules Verne, Paris 7

Le Vieux Bistro, Paris 4

Le Villaret, Paris 11

Vivario, Paris 5 (dinner only)

Les Zygomates, Paris 12 (dinner only)

RESTAURANTS OPEN ON SUNDAY

Ambassade d'Auvergne, Paris 3

L'Ami Louis, Paris 3

Arpège, Paris 7 (dinner only)

L'Assiette, Paris 14

Le Boeuf sur le Toit, Paris 8

La Butte Chaillot, Paris 16

La Cagouille, Paris 14

Contre-Allée, Paris 14

La Coquille, Paris 17

Le Bistrot d'à Côté-Flaubert, Paris 17

La Coupole, Paris 14

A la Courtille, Paris 20

Les Délices d'Aphrodite, Paris 5

Le Dôme, Paris 14

Bistrot du Dôme, Paris 14

Fermette Marveuf 1900, Paris 8

Brasserie Flo, Paris 10

Le Machon d'Henri, Paris 6 (dinner only)

Brasserie de l'Isle Saint Louis, Paris 4

Chez Jenny, Paris 3

Julien, Paris 10

Kim-Anh, Paris 15

Lao-Siam, Paris 19

Lao-Thai, Paris 20

Brasserie Lipp, Paris 6

Chez Louisette, Saint-Ouen

Le Bistrot de Marius, Paris 8

Marty, Paris 5

La Niçoise, Paris 17 (dinner only)

Chez Paul, Paris 11

Chez Pauline, Paris 1 (dinner only)

Au Pied de Cochon, Paris 1

Brasserie Stella, Paris 16

Terminus Nord, Paris 10

Timgad, Paris 17

La Tour de Montlhéry, Paris 1

Le Train Bleu, Paris 12

Le Trumilou, Paris 4

Vaudeville, Paris 2

Jules Verne, Paris 7

Le Vieux Bistro, Paris 4

RESTAURANTS OPEN IN AUGUST

Ambassade d'Auvergne, Paris 3

Androuët, Paris 8

Arpège, Paris 7

Baracane-Bistro de l'Oulette, Paris 4

Le Boeuf sur le Toit, Paris 8

Brissemoret, Paris 2

La Butte Chaillot, Paris 16

Le Caméléon, Paris 6

Campagne et Provence, Paris 6

Caviar Kaspia, Paris 8

Aux Charpentiers, Paris 6

Au Cochon d'Or des Halles, Paris 1

Contre-Allée, Paris 14

Le Bistrot d'à Côté-Flaubert, Paris 17

La Coupole, Paris 14

A la Courtille, Paris 20

Les Délices d'Aphrodite, Paris 5

Le Dôme , Paris 14

Bistrot du Dôme, Paris 14

Le Duc, Paris 14

L'Ecaille de P.C.B., Paris 6

Auberge Etchegorry, Paris 13

Le Bistro de l'Etoile-Lauriston, Paris 16

Fermette Marbeuf 1900, Paris 8

Brasserie Flo, Paris 10

La Fontaine de Mars, Paris 7

Gaya, Paris 1

Chez Georges, Paris 2

Au Gigot Fin, Paris 10

Goumard-Prunier, Paris 1

Le Grizzli, Paris 4

Le Bistrot d'Henri, Paris 6

Le Machon d'Henri, Paris 6

Jamin, Paris 16

Chez Jenny, Paris 3

Julien, Paris 10

Kim-Anh, Paris 15

Lao-Siam, Paris 19

Brasserie Lipp, Paris 6

Chez Louisette, Saint-Ouen

Chez Maître Paul, Paris 6

Le Bistrot de Marius, Paris 8

Marty, Paris 5

Miravile, Paris 4

La Niçoise, Paris 17

L'Oulette, Paris 12

Chez Paul, Paris 11

Pharamond, Paris 1

Au Pied de Cochon, Paris 1

Le Relais du Parc, Paris 16

Chez René, Paris 5

Le Roi du Pot-au-Feu, Paris 9

La Rôtisserie d'en Face, Paris 6

Royal Madeleine, Paris 8

Guy Savoy, Paris 17

Le Scheffer, Paris 16

Terminus Nord, Paris 10

Le Timgad, Paris 17

La Timonerie, Paris 5

La Tour de Montlhéry, Paris 1

Le Train Bleu, Paris 12

Trumilou, Paris 4

Vaudeville, Paris 2

Jules Verne, Paris 7

Le Vieux Bistro, Paris 4

RESTAURANTS WITH SIDEWALK TABLES OR OPEN TERRACE

La Butte Chaillot, Paris 16

La Cagouille, Paris 14

Aux Charpentiers, Paris 6

La Cigale, Paris 7

Contre-Allée, Paris 14

Le Bistrot d'à Côté-Flaubert, Paris 17

A la Courtille, Paris 20

Aux Crus de Bourgogne, Paris 2

Les Délices d'Aphrodite, Paris 5

Bistrot du Dôme, Paris 14

Auberge Etchegorry, Paris 13

Fermette Marbeuf 1900, Paris 8

La Fontaine de Mars, Paris 7

Chez Fred, Paris 17

Les Gourmets des Ternes, Paris 8

Le Grizzli, Paris 4

Brasserie de l'Isle Saint Louis, Paris 4

L'Impasse, Paris 4

Chez Janou, Paris 4

Chez Jenny, Paris 3

Lescure, Paris 1

Louis XIV, Paris 1

La Maison du Valais, Paris 8

Manufacture, Issy-les-Moulineaux

Le Bistrot de Marius, Paris 8

Marty, Paris 5

Miravile, Paris 4

Moulin à Vent, Chez Henry, Paris 5

L'Oulette, Paris 12

Chez Paul, Paris 11

Perraudin, Paris 5

Pharamond, Paris 1

Au Pied de Cochon, Paris 1

Le Relais du Parc, Paris 16

Chez René, Paris 5

Royal Madeleine, Paris 8

Le Scheffer, Paris 16

Brasserie Stella, Paris 16

Terminus Nord, Paris 10

Le Trumilou, Paris 4

Vaudeville, Paris 2

Vivario, Paris 5

AIR-CONDITIONED RESTAURANTS

Ambassade d'Auvergne, Paris 3

L'Ambroisie, Paris 4

Androuët, Paris 8

Apicius, Paris 17

Arpège, Paris 7

Astier, Paris 11

Benoit, Paris 4

Le Boeuf sur le Toit, Paris 8

La Butte Chaillot, Paris 16

Le Caméléon, Paris 6

Campagne et Provence, Paris 6

Carré des Feuillants, Paris 1

Caviar Kaspia, Paris 8

Chiberta, Paris 8

La Cigale, Paris 7

Contre Allée, Paris 14

La Coquille, Paris 17

Le Bistrot d'à Côté-Flaubert, Paris 17

La Coupole, Paris 14

Les Délices d'Aphrodite, Paris 5

Dodin Bouffant, Paris 5

Le Dôme, Paris 14

Bistrot du Dôme, Paris 14

L'Ecaille de P.C.B., Paris 6

Erawan, Paris 15

Auberge Etchegorry, Paris 13

Le Bistro de l'Etoile-Lauriston, Paris 16

Fermette Marbeuf 1900, Paris 8

Brasserie Flo, Paris 10

Gaya, Paris 1

Chez Georges, Paris 2

Goumard-Prunier, Paris 1

Les Gourmets des Ternes, Paris 8

Le Grand Véfour, Paris 1

Issé, Paris 2

Jamin, Paris 16

Julien, Paris 10

Kim-Anh, Paris 15

Lao-Siam, Paris 19

Lao-Thai, Paris 20

Lescure, Paris 1

Brasserie Lipp, Paris 6

La Maison du Valais, Paris 8

Manufacture, Issy-les-Moulineaux

Le Bistrot de Marius, Paris 8

Marty, Paris 5

Miravile, Paris 4

La Niçoise, Paris 17

L'Oeillade, Paris 7

L'Oulette, Paris 12

Chez Pauline, Paris 1

Pharamond, Paris 1

Chez Philippe, Paris 11

Au Pied de Cochon, Paris 1

Pile ou Face, Paris 2

Port Alma, Paris 16

Le Relais du Parc, Paris 16

La Rotisserie d'en Face, Paris 6

Guy Savoy, Paris 17

A Sousceyrac, Paris 11

Taillevent, Paris 8

Timgad, Paris 17

La Timonerie, Paris 5

Au Trou Gascon, Paris 12

Jules Verne, Paris 7

Vivarois, Paris 16

RESTAURANTS WITH PRIVATE DINING ROOMS OR DINING AREAS

Ambassade d'Auvergne, Paris 3 (10 to 35)

Androuët, Paris 8 (25)

Arpège, Paris 7 (12)

Benoit, Paris 4 (12 to 18)

Le Boeuf sur le Toit, Paris 8 (30 to 40)

La Butte Chaillot, Paris 16 (20)

La Cagouille, Paris 14 (6 to 20)

Carré des Feuillants, Paris 1 (30)

Chiberta, Paris 8 (20 to 35)

Contre-Allée, Paris 14 (25)

La Coupole, Paris 14 (180)

Aux Crus de Bourgogne, Paris 2 (12 to 20)

Le Dôme, Paris 14 (10)

L'Ecaille de P.C.B., Paris 6 (12)

Auberge Etchegorry, Paris 13 (20)

La Fontaine de Mars, Paris 7 (10 to 18)

Gaya, Paris 1 (10 to 60)

Au Gigot Fin, Paris 10 (20 to 25)

Goumard-Prunier, Paris 1 (4 to 30)

Le Grand Véfour, Paris 1 (8 to 20)

Jamin, Paris 16 (14)

Chez Jenny, Paris 3 (10 to 150)

Lao-Thai, Paris 20 (40)

Louis XIV, Paris 1 (10)

Aux Lyonnais, Paris 2 (12 to 30)

La Maison du Valais, Paris 8 (15 to 26)

Chez Maître Paul, Paris 6 (20)

Marty, Paris 5 (10 to 50)

Miravile, Paris 4 (50)

Chez Paul, Paris 11 (12)

Chez Pauline, Paris 11 (16)

Le Petit Marguery, Paris 13 (16)

Pharamond, Paris 1 (4 to 18)

Au Pied de Cochon, Paris 1 (20 to 40)

Pile ou Face, Paris 2 (8 to 20)

Port Alma, Paris 16 (15)

Royal Madeleine, Paris 8 (20 to 30)

Guy Savoy, Paris 17 (10 to 30)

A Sousceyrac, Paris 11 (20)

La Table de Fès, Paris 6 (30)

Taillevent, Paris 8 (6 to 32)

Tan Dinh, Paris 7 (30)

Terminus Nord, Paris 10 (10)

Timgad, Paris 17 (30)

Le Train Bleu, Paris 12 (30)

La Tour de Montlhéry, Paris 1 (8 to 10)

Le Trumilou, Paris 4 (20 to 55)

Le Vieux Bistro, Paris 4 (30)

Vivario, Paris 5 (12 to 40)

Index

(Following French style, any articles such as *au, la,* or *le* and the words *bar, bistro, boulangerie, brasserie, café, cave, charcuterie, chez, fromagerie,* or *pâtisserie* appearing before the proper name of the establishment are ignored in the alphabetizing. For example Au Pied de Cochon is listed as "Pied de Cochon, Au" and Chez Pauline is listed as "Pauline, Chez," both under the letter *P.* Likewise, when the name of an establishment is also the full name of a person, such as Guy Savoy, the entry appears under the last name (Savoy).

Q, R

Recipe Index